The Responsible Reader

The Responsible Reader

Edited by
Linda Ziff
The Johns Hopkins University

St. Martin's Press   New York

Senior Editor: Nancy Perry
Project Editor: Emily Berleth
Production Supervisor: Julie Toth
Text Design: Caliber Design Planning, Inc.
Cover Design: Darby Downey
Cover Art: *Rhythm/Color: The Concord Cotillion* by Michael James
Cover Photo: David Caras

For information, write St. Martin's Press, Inc.
175 Fifth Avenue
New York, NY 10010

ISBN: 0-312-00262-9
Instructor's Edition ISBN: 0-312-01309-4

ACKNOWLEDGMENTS

Acknowledgments and copyrights are continued at the back of the book on pages 462ff, which constitute an extension of the copyright page.

Abigail Adams, "Letter to Her Sister," from NEW LETTERS OF ABIGAIL ADAMS edited by Stewart Mitchell. Copyright 1947 by the American Antiquarian Society. Copyright ©renewed 1974 by American Antiquarian Society. Reprinted by permission of Houghton Mifflin Company.

Russell Baker, "Amo, Amas, Amat," from GROWING UP by Russell Baker. Copyright ©1982 by Russell Baker. Reprinted by permission of Congdon & Weed, Inc.

James Baldwin, excerpt from NOTES OF A NATIVE SON by James Baldwin, copyright ©1955, renewed 1983 by James Baldwin. Reprinted by permission of the author and Beacon Press.

Toni Cade Bambara, "What It Is I Think I'm Doing Anyhow," by Toni Cade Bambara is reprinted from THE WRITER ON HER WORK, edited by Janet Sternberg, by permission of W. W. Norton & Company, Inc. Copyright ©1980 by Janet Sternberg.

Jacob Bronowski, "The Reach of the Imagination," the Evangeline Wilbour Blashfield Foundation Address, delivered at the joint Ceremonial of the American Academy of Arts and Letters and the National Institute of Arts and Letters on May 25, 1966. First published in the PROCEEDINGS OF THE AMERICAN ACADEMY OF ARTS AND LETTERS AND THE NATIONAL INSTITUTE OF ARTS AND LETTERS, Second Series, No. 17. Copyright 1967. Reprinted with permission of the author and The MIT Press.

Norman Cousins, "An Anatomy of Illness as Perceived by the Patient," reprinted from AN ANATOMY OF ILLNESS by Norman Cousins, by permission of W. W. Norton & Company. Copyright ©1979 by W. W. Norton & Company, Inc.

Preface

This book was written for instructors who believe, as I do, that involved readers bring to a text as much as they take from it. *The Responsible Reader* is the result of many years' teaching composition students the possibilities of reading and writing, observing those students, and learning from them. I concluded that student writers can learn to involve themselves in a text both willingly—with the sense that they *can* contribute something to its meaning—and responsibly—with the conviction that they *should* do so. To contribute to a text's meaning is to read. To read is to write, albeit without ink, because contributing to a text entails making the same kinds of decisions an author makes. And to write without ink is to learn. In its selection of essays and the questions for use following the essays, *The Responsible Reader* was designed on the guiding principle that composition classes are places where learning begins.

The essays, chosen from those written in the first person, invite a collaborative reading. They were selected not for their autobiographical features but because the "I" of the writers immediately includes the "I-ness" of the readers, thus forming a bond between author and audience. The essays are written on a number of topics—informative, argumentative, reflective, and emotive—and for a number of purposes, to give students maximum opportunity for varied response. That the essays have been written by a number of different writers contributes to diverse response as well.

Because this book's ultimate aim is to teach students to write as well as to read, following each essay appropriate questions elicit individual reaction to the essay's features. "Words" calls students' attention to specific words in the essay, how they function and resonate, and what effect they have on the determination of meaning. "Thinking" asks students to examine the content and style of the essay and, in so doing, to consider the author's intention, their own interpretations, and how intention and interpretation combine to create meaning. "Writing" topics, some generated by an idea in the text, others drawing attention to style or strategies, provide students with opportunities to produce their own texts. The *Instructor's Manual* offers comments on each essay and on each question following the essays.

I wish to thank several people who helped make this book: the reviewers, Kathryn A. Bellman (University of Nebraska), Murray T. Callaway (University of Maine—Orono), David Espey (University of Pennsylvania), Gail Lynn Goldberg (Goucher College), Robert E. Hosmer, Jr. (Westfield State College), Catherine E. Metcalf (California State University—Fullerton), George Miller (University of Delaware), and Karen B. Quinn (University of Illinois—Chicago), for their responsible reading of the manuscript; at St. Martin's Press, Laura Starrett for many helpful suggestions, Emily Berleth for her caring production, and Nancy Perry for her faith, good will, and persistence; at Johns Hopkins, the staff of the Practical Composition Program for always asking such good questions of themselves, of their students, and of me; in California, Oliver Ziff and the Bay Area Writing Project, Ellen Ziff, and Sara Ziff; in New York, Joshua Ziff; in Texas, Abby Ziff; in London, Joel Ziff, all of whom shared ideas and suggestions. And I especially wish to thank Larzer Ziff for laughing at the right places and for learning how to cook.

Linda Ziff

Contents

"If we planned our operation with the precision of an exquisitely plotted guerrilla raid, we could even arrive home with our booty still hot."

"It is unfortunate for the children who will not remember or will never know the taste of real food."

8   **Explaining   311**

"I have been assured by a very knowing American of my acquaintance in London, that a young healthy child well nursed is at a year old a most delicious, nourishing, and wholesome food, whether stewed, roasted, baked, or boiled. . . ."

"Even I find it difficult to love, in my special human way, as many bats as I saw in Carlsbad."

Thematic
Guide to the
Contents

Innocence and Experience

Family and Friends

Dilemmas and Confrontations

Convictions

Women

Creativity

Politics and Governments

Racism and Nationalism

Education

Science and Technology

Coercion and Victimization

Other Places and Other People

The Responsible
Reader

Introduction

All writers write for an audience. They write, that is, expecting to be read. Moreover, they understand that a piece of writing depends for its total effect on what the reader as well as the writer brings to it. But although writers create the initial text, you complete that text as you read by interpreting it in the light of your knowledge and experience, and so discover what it says to you. To read this way is to create the text for yourself. Responsible reading is like writing without ink.

All the selections in this book are intended to encourage such reading. The pieces were chosen because they demonstrate in a range of lively ways the connection between reader and writer that experienced writers seek. Whether informative, argumentative, reflective, or emotive, they address the imagination as well as the intellect. There are essays about food and eating, ranging from a fantasy about collecting courses for a Chinese meal to some serious considerations about the effect of food on the moral disposition.

1

There are essays about illness, about dying, and about the strange relation between the mind and the body. There are essays in which writers reminisce about youth or childhood, remembering moments that have shaped their adult lives. There are confessional essays in which the writers recall with shame some past experience that may have taught them about life but that never ceases to be shameful. There are essays in which reflection upon other people's behavior leads writers to realize something about their own lives. There are essays in which writers offer painfully earned wisdom so that others need not repeat the mistakes that led to its acquisition. Then there are essays about the aspects of writing itself; for example, the appeal of dialogue in a story. And there are essays about the less explicable processes of imaginative thinking, such as the way memory affects creativity. Finally, there are essays addressing crucial issues of belief and practice, among them the existence of God, the purpose of education, and women's rights. Although the selections can be read in any order, this wide range of topics is presented in a progression moving from the physical through the moral, speculative, and creative to the intellectual.

As you can see, a variety of subjects is to be found in the following pages. Of equal importance, these topics are treated by many different kinds of writers. When you read a text, you are responding to the writer's style as much as to the topic. What is said is inseparable from the way it is said. And the way something is said is determined by who is saying it. Writing implies the writer. To respond to a number of different writers — even on the same topic — is to recognize, as experienced writers in this book illustrate, the dependence of your response upon the way you express it. Response is like writing, and your response implies you.

Each selection is followed by three types of exercises.

The first draws attention to the interdependence of words and context. After reading a list of familiar words from the selection, you are asked to consider the way in which familiar words acquire surprising force through skillful placement in context. For example, in "On a Hill Far Away" Annie Dillard uses the word *loaded*. Think about the word in conventional phrases such as: a loaded gun, a loaded car, a comment loaded with meaning, or loaded dice. In all cases the word means filled or weighted. Now read it in Dillard's context:

> It was sunset by the time I crossed Tinker Creek by hopping from stone to stone and inching up a fallen tree trunk to the bank. On the far side of the creek I followed a barbed-wire fence through steers' pasture and up to a high grassy hill. I'd never been there before. From the hill the distant creek looked still and loaded with sky.
>
> On the hilltop, just across the barbed-wire fence, were three outbuildings.

Dillard does not give another meaning to the word, yet the way in which she uses it lifts it out of the familiar and makes it new, as if she had invented it for her specific effect. Of course, you look up new words in the dictionary. But the words that are noted after each selection are not new in this way. Rather they are familiar words that have been made new through the writer's craft.

Like Dillard, the other writers in this book amplify the meanings of ordinary words by setting them in unconventional contexts. When you respond as asked to the words listed after each selection, you are making decisions about diction from the writer's viewpoint. Looking at the writing from this viewpoint makes you a more critical reader which, in turn, makes you a more perceptive writer.

Following the question on words, you will find the second type of exercise, questions for discussion. These are concerned with tasks such as identifying specific authorial strategies, explaining why you feel or think as you do about particular events or ideas, and offering alternatives to the views held or the actions taken by the author. The aim of these tasks is to lead you to see the writer's work as a series of decisions and thus to see how you too make a series of decisions when you recreate the text in your response. Although these questions are designed for classroom discussion, if read in advance of the text, they will serve to bring to your reading a sense of what others see as significant issues in a text.

The third type of exercise suggests topics for your own essays. Since these topics come from ideas in the reading that precedes them, some suggestions ask you to discuss that reading. But more generally, the topics for writing do not return to the reading. Rather, they ask that you now offer in specific ways your experience and observations on matters similar to those in the essay.

The controlling principle of *The Responsible Reader* as has been shown is that responsible reading is like writing without ink. From this it follows that when you are asked to write with ink, you do so with the perceptions you gained from reading responsibly.

1

Thinking
about Food

The writers in this chapter regard eating as more than a way to
survive and commentary on it as more than nutritional information.
They write about food as an expression of culture. A society's
culture is grounded in its pattern of response to living everyday life.
The way food is procured, prepared, and presented, what precisely
counts as food, how it is judged, and how it is consumed are,
therefore, matters of basic cultural importance. High culture, that
is, the production, judgment, and consumption of art, of literature,
of architecture, and of music, comes later. To understand a total
culture requires recognition of both basic and high cultures.

The writers here direct readers' attention to part of basic
culture through offering observations about food: for example, that
there are concepts of the good in food; that today ideas of efficient
marketing are more important than the immediacy of fresh food;
that too much food robs the imagination; that eating is the result
of the body's hunger and the mind's habit, curiosity, and pleasure;

and that preparing food can be a social occasion like the bestowing of a gift.

In search of the good in food, Calvin Trillin imagines dining with the late Chinese Chairman Mao and recalls a dream of eating the perfect Chinese meal. He assembles this perfection in the fantasy, one course at a time from various Chinese restaurants, the best each has to offer. In the next two selections, the writers turn their attention to values. Alice Waters sees packaging food in the name of efficiency as a barrier between us and what we eat. She urges us instead to get in touch, literally, with food and to trust our instincts when we cook and eat. Henry David Thoreau declares his need to feed the imagination whenever he eats, not with rich food but with only the plainest fare. That way, he claims, the imagination has something on which to feed. When M. F. K. Fisher stops for a meal at a French country restaurant, she finds herself in a nightmarish but delicious lunch, battling an unseen chef who plies her with dish after dish long after she is full. She is also battling herself, eating far too much, for the food is perfect and she cannot risk offending the chef. Finally, Peter Feibleman puts food preparation in a social context as he describes how to make the famous Spanish dish *paella*. His instructions include what should happen to the cook during the preparation and to the guests waiting to eat. He includes the recipe for *paella* in case we wish to experience for ourselves what happens.

Calvin Trillin

Calvin Trillin (b. 1935) was born in Kansas City, Missouri, and educated at Yale University. He began his writing career as a reporter for *Time* magazine and later became a staff writer for *The New Yorker*. Although he has written novels, Trillin is perhaps best known for his commentaries on American eating habits. He sees what we eat, where we eat, and how we eat as a kind of American cultural history. His books about eating include *America Fried* and *Third Helpings*. The selection here is from *Alice, Let's Eat: Further Adventures of a Happy Eater* and is based on a fantasy in which Trillin has been asked to take the late Chinese leader Mao Tse-tung to dinner.

Mao and Me

For years, I have had the recurring fantasy that Mao Tse-tung makes an official visit to the United States and I am asked by the State Department to take him eating for a week in New York. The fantasy was not altered in the least by the news of Mao's death. For a while, I did consider changing to the new leaders, but that possibility melted away within a few weeks of their ascension. They simply didn't strike me as either hearty eaters or cheerful dining companions; they reminded me of the dour Kremlin crowd that took over from Krushchev and then bad-mouthed him for "phrasemongering" and other qualities I admired. I decided that for the purposes of my fantasy I would not recognize Mao's death. That sort of thing is permitted in fantasies; Abigail and Sarah do it all the time.

Even before Mao died, I had one sticking point in my fantasy. Why would the State Department choose me instead of one of the people Alice persists in calling "grown up food writers?" I have no influence in the State Department. Just about everyone I have ever known who entered the Foreign Service seems to have been sent immediately to Ouagadougou, Upper Volta, which, as I understand it, is not where Foreign Service officers want to be sent. Why wouldn't the wise heads at State ask, say, Craig Claiborne or Mimi Sheraton to show the Chairman around? Claiborne has co-authored a cookbook of Chinese recipes, so he might even be able to speak a couple of words of Mandarin to Chairman Mao—at least if the couple of words the Chairman wanted to hear happened to be words like "bamboo shoots" or "black mushrooms" or "hot and spicy."

Finally, after staring out of a lot of airplane windows with Mao on my mind, I invented a satisfactory reason for my receiving the assignment—an invention that permitted me to continue to what might be called the meat of the fantasy. I was specifically requested by the political officer of the Chinese delegation to the United Nations. He found me ideologically appealing. After some research, he had been able to ascertain that I was an enthusiast rather than as expert— "glutton" is a word that has occasionally been used by the unkind— and therefore a fine choice for anyone wanting to avoid the crimes of elitism or careerism or professionalism. The Chinese Cultural Revolution happens to be raging during my fantasy, and what, after all, would one call a teenage Red Guard who took over the directorship of a medical school during that period except an enthusiast rather than an expert? Asking someone like Mimi Sheraton to be the guide merely because she may know something about the subject would have made no more sense than having the former director of the medical school perform an operation merely because he happened to be a surgeon. The political officer asks the State Department for me, by name and address, adding, in slightly inexact English, "The Chairman sees with pleasure toward meeting that folk type which people in your Medium Western states are sometimes saying as a Big Hungry Boy."

Alice is, of course, appalled. The power of a fantasizer to control the fantasy may extend to reincarnating the Chairman of the Central Committee of the Communist Party of the People's Republic of China, but it falls short of being able to alter Alice's inevitable reaction to my plans for some serious eating. In my fantasy Alice had, just before

the word from State came through, prevailed upon me to start a diet
for which I have sworn unswerving allegiance to a peck of carrots.   *

"But you promised to lose ten pounds," she says, when I inform
her that I've received the call.

"I wish I could keep that promise, but my country comes before
any personal considerations," I say. "Think of all those people who
have gone off to Ouagadougou with hardly a murmur of complaint."

"I'm afraid you're going to start looking more and more like the
Chairman yourself."

"A man must do what he must do," I say.

Alice pauses for a while. "You know that Mao is the one who
started calling your friend Khrushchev a phrasemonger," she finally
says. This, I realize, is what the marriage counselors mean by "playing
dirty." I am silent. "It was Mao who said Khrushchev was in a
'revisionist quagmire,' " Alice continues.

"The people from State asked me not to talk politics," I say.

My Chairman Mao fantasy has to do not just with tossing aside a
diet but with an old dream I have had about being able to eat a favorite
dish in one restaurant and then dash off (by limousine with diplomatic
license plates, if at all possible) for another favorite dish in another
restaurant. It is a dining method I have always been embarrassed to
employ without having the excuse of shepherding around a visiting
head of state who has to sample many American dishes in the short
time his busy schedule allots him. I did engage in a sort of trial run
once, on a very small scale. While some friends were visiting us one
day, it was decided that a friend I'll call Jones and I should pick up
some food in Chinatown and bring it back to the assembled eaters.
I no longer remember why we all didn't just go to Chinatown for
dinner; perhaps the city was locked in a bagel-bakers' strike, making
it impossible for Sarah to enter a Chinese restaurant.

On the way to Chinatown it occurred to me that there was no
reason to get everything at the same restaurant. We could park the
car in a strategic spot, then separate and hit two or three restaurants
apiece, picking up a favorite dish in each place. In my heart of hearts,
of course, I have always believed that what may actually be my favorite
dish in a number of Chinatown restaurants is something I have never
even had the opportunity to taste, simply because of my inability to

read the wall signs that announce some house specialties in Chinese. Some time ago—many years, I would say, before such intimate family disclosures became the rage—I revealed publicly that Alice and I   *
had been through a family disagreement concerning the signs, Alice having arbitrarily dismissed a reasonable and politely worded request that she assign some Chinese immigrant students in a class she was teaching at City College to translate the signs as a way of polishing up their English. Even without the secret dishes, though, Jones and I faced an opportunity to snatch up a spectacular variety of food within easy running distance of where we parked the car. If we planned our operation with the precision of an exquisitely plotted guerrilla raid,   *
we could even arrive home with our booty still hot. "I don't think the flounder Fukienese style from Foo Joy will travel, so I'll grab the cold spiced kidney from Chef Ma's while you're getting the eggplant with garlic from Szechuan Cuisine," I told Jones. I hated to give up the flounder—some texture specialists of my acquaintance have rated it "eighty percent crunch"—but in these sorts of operations losses have to be cut ruthlessly and decisions made with no hesitation. If someone paused to bemoan the fact that green fish from Say Eng Look or pork dumplings from one of the *dim sum* houses might not make it from Chinatown to the Village in good order, he could ruin the entire operation. Ten minutes after Jones and I had fanned out—if two people can be said to have fanned—we were back in the car, loaded with specialties. We had taken no losses except for a slight bruise I   *
had acquired when I knocked over an elderly lady while escaping from Phoenix Garden with the Pepper and Salty Shrimp. The operation was, in other words, a remarkable success. I think it would have gone even better if Jones had not, for reasons I can't imagine, declined to make a map of the strike zone and synchronize our watches.

Thinking about Writing

Words

    Powerful words both depend on and help shape their context. In what way does each word in the list below depend on its context for

strength? What does each contribute to its context? Can you think of any other word the author might have used in its place? How does the word strike you, and how do you respond to the sentence or passage because of the word?

allegiance
disclosures
exquisitely
losses

Thinking

1. How does Trillin's comment about enthusiasts versus experts during the Chinese Cultural Revolution reinforce his view of himself as an enthusiast rather than an expert about food?
2. Do you agree with Trillin when he says an enthusiast is safer than an expert? Who decides whether someone is an enthusiast or an expert? Can we decide for ourselves whether we are one or the other?
3. Why do you think Trillin compares a food enthusiast to a teenage medical-school director when he is talking about danger? How could this comparison be taken as a sly dig at the Cultural Revolution?
4. Do you think that Trillin's tone is disrespectful toward the Chinese or is the fantasy all in good fun? What do you think keeps the fantasy from appearing as an attack on Chinese ideology?

Writing

1. Trillin and his friend once bought several dishes from various Chinese restaurants, preferring one dish from one place, another from another. Write about your ideal meal that comes from several sources, combining the best of several restaurants as did Trillin's old dream "about being able to eat a favorite dish in one restaurant and then dash off for another favorite dish in another restaurant."
2. Write an essay in which you examine the way Trillin has used a military metaphor to describe his search for a Chinese dinner. He says the search was like "an exquisitely plotted guerrilla raid." You

might wish to describe the way a metaphor works and why talking about one concept or experience in terms of another clarifies, rather than obscures, the writing. Do you find Trillin's metaphor appropriate or is there another you might have used?

Alice Waters

Alice Waters was raised in Chatham, New Jersey, and educated at the University of California at Berkeley where she studied French language and history. After graduation, she traveled in Europe. It was in France that she first became interested in cooking and the fine art of dining, fascinated by her friends hotly debating what they should eat that night and searching for just the right restaurant. Waters thus discovered that this preoccupation with food was not to be taken lightly. Back in America, Waters returned to Berkeley where she began to try out some of the recipes she had noted in France, applying methods she had observed abroad on the wealth of fresh foods and local wines she found in California. The results were stunning. In 1971, Waters opened the now famous restaurant, Chez Panisse, in Berkeley. Today, the restaurant thrives and Waters is considered one of America's great chefs. She still holds with her ideas of fresh foods. She also believes that many cooks and diners tend to separate themselves from food, retreating behind a wall of plastic wrap and slick packaging. The result is a form of alienation, a dehumanizing of what, after all, is a glorious act. In the selection here, which comes from her *Chez Panisse Menu Cookbook*, Waters deplores our detachment from real foods and suggests we take a closer look at—and touch—what's cooking.

What I Believe about Cooking

My approach to cooking is not radical or unconventional. It may seem so simply because we as a nation are so removed from any real involvement with the food we buy, cook, and consume. We

13

have become alienated by the frozen and hygienically sealed foods. I want to stand in the supermarket aisles and implore the shoppers, their carts piled high with mass-produced artificiality, "Please. . .look at what you are buying!" Food should be experienced through the senses, and I am sad for those who cannot see a lovely, unblemished apple just picked from the tree as voluptuous, or a beautifully perfect pear as sensuous, or see that a brown-spotted two-foot-high lettuce, its edges curling and wilted, is ugly and offensive. It is a fundamental fact that no cook, however creative and capable, can produce a dish of a quality any higher than that of the raw ingredients.

It is unfortunate for the children who will not remember or will never know the taste of real food. They will believe that the mass-produced imitation, the phony, is the real and the genuine, and I worry that they will be deprived of so much pure pleasure. Communication around the dinner table and the sense of family which comes with it are largely missing in our society. One of my goals at Chez Panisse is to re-establish the gastronomic excitement that inspires and encourages conversation and conviviality. Depersonalized, assembly-line fast food may be "convenient" and "time-saving," but it deprives the senses and denies true nourishment.

Much of the alienation we suffer at the hands of the fast-food giants comes from the distance they create and emphasize between the food and the diners. The high plastic containers, disposable dishes, and emphasis on a minimum of contact between the foods and human hands—to ensure "cleanliness and hygiene"—also ensure distance and estrangement between the diners and those who prepare the food, to say nothing of the distance between the "cooks" and the food itself. I am reminded of a small neighborhood restaurant where I have eaten for years. It is run by an Indian man and his Mexican wife who do everything themselves: they prepare the food and serve it. The restaurant continues to support itself and thrive modestly against the prevailing winds of faster and faster food purveyors. Seated at one of their tables, I am always captivated as I watch them prepare our order in their tiny kitchen. If I should look out the window, I find my gaze captured by the scene in the doughnut shop across the street: the customers, totally isolated from one another and the food itself by the gleaming white sterility of the plastic counters, tables, and walls, are all facing in different directions. The result can be nothing but alienation from one another, as well as from the food and those who cook and serve it. It is doubly sad to me because they *could* simply have walked across the street to reap the humane benefits of this little restaurant for virtually the same price!

As I have watched the transformation of a stressed and rather uninterested diner at Chez Panisse into an involved, excited, and participatory member of his party, I have more clearly understood the necessity and importance of feedback from the kitchen to the dining room and back again. It all has to do with the opening up of the senses on the part of the diners, and I do believe that such things as flowers, food on display, lovely linens, and appealing china can greatly enhance the experience and aid in bringing about the metamorphosis of that hurried and harried diner into the relaxed patron who has submerged himself in the very pleasurable act of $*$ eating. But basically it is the genuine involvement with food that fosters this sensory receptiveness.

Flexibility is an essential component of good cooking. You should never feel locked in to a recipe or a menu unless it involves a basic principle regarding procedure or technique such as those involved in breadmaking and pastry. I don't ever want to write anything in this book that is so precise that the reader must invoke great powers of concentration on every last detail in order to ensure the success of a recipe or a dinner; ingredients are simply too variable. I want to *suggest* the expected taste; I want to *suggest* the appearance of the completed dish; I want to *suggest* the combination of ingredients; and I want to *suggest* the overall harmony and balance of the meal. Then it will be up to you to determine the correct balance and $*$ composition. Perhaps the garlic is sharp and strong and you will use it sparingly in a particular presentation, or you may find the garlic to be sweet and fresh and you will want to use twice as much!

We all cook differently. On many occasions I have tasted the same dish prepared by different cooks using the same recipe; the results were similar, but they were *not* identical! My pinch of salt may be larger than your pinch of salt; or I may prefer a slightly saltier taste, while you may, quite justifiably and correctly, fancy a more lightly salted flavor. If your ingrained philosophy tells you that an ingredient or an amount called for in a particular recipe wouldn't be right, eliminate the component or change it to one which falls into the same categories of flavor, texture, and aroma; you should alter the amount of any element you think needs change. And it is vitally important that you continually taste and retaste your ingredients, raw and cooked.

Learn to trust your own instincts. A good cook needs only to have positive feelings about food in general, and about the pleasures of eating and cooking. I have known some cooks who did not seem to discover pleasure and gratification in things culinary. At the restaurant, I look for employees who are interested in working in the kitchen for reasons above and beyond those of simply needing a job, any job. This applies equally to the home cook: a cook who dislikes food is a bad cook. Period. Even an ambivalent cook is a bad cook. Yet a person who responds to the cooking processes and the mound of fresh ingredients with a genuine glow of delight is likely to be, or become, a very good cook indeed. Technical skills can be acquired and perfected along the way, but dislike or ambivalence toward food cannot always be overcome.

In the early stages of my culinary pursuits, I cooked as I had seen cooking done in France. I copied some of the more traditional cooks, and I stayed within the bounds they had laid out so carefully because I didn't trust my own instincts yet. Having imitated their styles, I found that with time and experience, their fundamental principles had become a part of my nature and I began to understand why they had done certain things in a particular way. Then I could begin to develop a different and more personal style based on the ingredients available to me here in California.

Cooking, preparing food, involves far more than just creating a meal for family or friends: it has to do with keeping yourself intact.   *
Because most people cook and eat three meals a day, this process becomes an integral part of one's daily routine. These eating and cooking habits can either be sensually nourishing, even on an unconscious level, or they can rapidly become redundant. There is a marvelous scene in a film by Les Blank of the morning-coffee ritual of an old Southern lady. We watch her reach into her store of coffee beans for

a handful, which she puts in a pan on the stove to roast. When she is satisfied with the degree and depth of roast, she shakes the fragrant beans into a hand-cranked coffee grinder and proceeds to pulverize them into a cloth napkin filter. Then she boils the water and pours it through the coffee-filled filter to produce a cup of coffee for herself—one you know must be wonderful. She sits and drinks her coffee in a totally intimate and relaxed manner, and eventually rises to wash out the napkin and hang it out to dry. This ritual is important because she is making a celebration out of the act of making coffee for herself. *
For others, this coffee habit can be as alienating as a Styrofoam cup of coffee from a vending machine.

So many people believe that by using a myriad of machines and equipment in their cooking, they're simplifying it and making the whole process easier. Somehow, we have been indoctrinated into believing that by making food preparation easier and less time-consuming, we're gaining valuable free time. No mention is ever made of what we lose by this whittling away at our direct contact with our food or what better thing we might do with the time thus gained. I strongly believe that much of what has gone wrong with American food has been the result of mechanization and the alienation that comes with it. The quality of the home food prepared in France has deteriorated, too. It is no longer a simple matter to find hand-kneaded and -shaped bread and homemade aïoli. The harsh sounds of the machine have replaced the rhythmic chop of the knife.

I simply don't believe that all the "gourmet" equipment and utensils are vital. To begin with, the terms "gourmet" or "gourmet cooking" have all the wrong associations for me: they somehow seem to imply that one is more interested in the gleaming copper pans and the flashy chrome and plastic of the food processors than in what one is cooking, and certainly more impressed with them than with the food itself. It is far easier to cook with good sharp knives, but you *can* cook without them. Perversely, some of the very best times to cook are those occasions when you are faced with virtually nothing in terms of equipment—you must make do, improvise, and focus primarily on the food itself. So you may gather rosemary branches from the yard and use them to skewer the meat before you put it on the charcoal grill.

If you do, you will have learned something fundamental about food, unrestricted and unhampered by equipment. You need to learn to cook first, and then you learn what equipment is genuinely important to you.

When you use a machine, you never really touch the food, a fact that deprives you of much of the sensual pleasure and sensory experience so important in developing good cooking habits. When learning to make pesto, you *need* to rub the olive oil into the pounded garlic and the basil with your pestle in hand. You *need* to be able to stick your finger into the mixture to feel the transformation of the ingredients. Otherwise the information just does not come through all your senses. The senses of smell, touch, and hearing, in addition to sight and taste, must work together to enable you to judge what is happening to the ingredients. Machines have a place, but only after you have reached a point in your cooking at which you *know* what you are sacrificing in sensory stimulation for the questionable exchange of a slight saving in time and effort.

Every time we make pesto at the restaurant, it's different. If it isn't garlic with a hotter taste or the basil with a bitterness from too much sun, it's the cook pounding it differently—or it may be that the customer who loved it last time isn't in the mood this time. Maybe every six months the waiters are in the right mood, the cooks cook it right, the customers feel like eating that particular dinner, and I feel satisfied with the results; when that happens, I know that it has been worth the effort.

Thinking about Writing

Words

Powerful words both depend on and help shape their context. In what way does each word in the list below depend on its context for strength? What does each contribute to its context? Can you think of any other word the author might have used in its place? How does the word strike you, and how do you respond to the sentence or passage because of the word?

submerged
correct
intact
celebration

Thinking

1. Waters talks about alienation and about how people now seem to be removed from any real involvement with food, remarking then on the people she has observed in the doughnut shop across from the Indian-Mexican restaurant where she eats happily. Have you ever experienced alienation in either a restaurant or a supermarket? In what way does prepackaging of meats and produce keep us at a "safe" distance from the unpleasant aspects of food acquisition? Do you think we would either buy differently or eat differently if we saw what the food looks like before it is packaged?

2. Do you agree with Waters when she says that machines may save "valuable free time" but in so doing they rob us of direct contact with food? What machines can you think of that either present or prepare food, while distancing us from the food?

3. Explain whether you think table manners are a form of distancing us not only from the food we are eating but from our dining companions as well. Why, for example, should we have our own plates at dinner when we dip from a common bowl at a party? Why do we spear our food with a fork and slash it with a knife when it could be presented to us in small bits that could be picked up with the fingers?

Writing

1. Write about being alienated from food in either a restaurant or a supermarket, trying to discover the reasons for the feeling: not knowing the farmer or seeing the land, the field or tree, the pen or roost; being surrounded by plastic-wrapped food, by boxes and

bottles with pictures of what you are supposed to be buying and pictures of your pleasure at consuming what's inside; not seeing bread made, not smelling it being baked, or touching the raw dough. You will think of many such intrusions: write about them and what "connects" you to food.

2. "My pinch of salt may be larger than your pinch of salt," says Waters as she discusses different cooks. How might this concept be applied to other occupations than cooking? Write about learning to do something—such as playing a musical instrument or cooking or building something—where you learned the fundamental "correct" way but where your own style and instinct made the outcome better than the ordinary. What led you to follow your instincts? Do you think we must go through the early stages of learning something "correctly" in order to depart from the structured norm as we follow our instincts?

3. Waters says elsewhere that she always eats salads with her fingers, not with a fork. Does this habit surprise you? Disgust you? Do you have any eating "foibles" like Waters's salad-eating? Do you like to eat with your hands? Do you touch the food you are cooking? Write an essay exploring your own views about food contact, considering restraints imposed in the name of hygiene or manners. Where do you draw the line?

Henry David Thoreau

Henry David Thoreau (1817–62) was born in Concord and educated at Harvard University. A writer, a poet, and a philosopher, Thoreau joined Ralph Waldo Emerson's circle of thinkers called the Transcendentalists, a group who concentrated on ideas and principles, avoiding attachment to property and transcending the material side of life. Thoreau is perhaps best known for his essay "Civil Disobedience," in which he tells why he could not pay taxes to a state (Massachusetts) that was sympathetic to pro-slavery states, and for *Walden, Or Life in the Woods*, an account of the two years he spent living simply beside Walden Pond, close to nature and as removed as possible from material possessions. In the selection here, which comes from *Walden*, Thoreau describes feeding the imagination when he sits down to a meal. Not surprisingly, he says the plainest food feeds the imagination much better than rich dishes do because simple fare gives his imagination something to think about.

Feeding the Imagination

I have found repeatedly, of late years, that I cannot fish without falling a little in self-respect. I have tried it again and again. I have skill at it, and, like many of my fellows, a certain instinct for it, which revives from time to time, but always when I have done I feel that it would have been better if I had not fished. I think that I do not mistake. It is a faint intimation, yet so are the first streaks of morning. There is unquestionably this instinct in me which belongs to the lower orders of creation; yet with every year I am less a fisherman, though without more humanity or even wisdom; at present I am no fisherman at all. But I see that if I were to live in a wilderness, I should again be tempted to become a fisher and hunter in earnest. Beside, there is something essentially unclean about this diet and all flesh, and I began to see where housework commences, and whence the endeavor, which costs so much, to wear a tidy and respectable appearance each day, to keep the house sweet and free from all ill odors and sights. Having been my own butcher and scullion and cook, as well as the gentleman for whom the dishes were served up, I can speak from an unusually complete experience. The practical objection to animal food in my case was its uncleanness; and besides, when I had caught and cleaned and cooked and eaten my fish, they seemed not to have fed me essentially. It was insignificant and unnecessary, and cost more * than it came to. A little bread or a few potatoes would have done as well, with less trouble and filth. Like many of my contemporaries, I had rarely for so many years used animal food, or tea, or coffee, etc.; not so much because of any ill effects which I had traced to them, as because they were not agreeable to my imagination. The repugnance to animal food is not the effect of experience, but is an instinct. It appeared more beautiful to live low and fare hard in many respects; and though I never did so, I went far enough to please my imagination. I believe that every man who has ever been earnest to preserve his higher or poetic faculties in the best condition has been particularly * inclined to abstain from animal food, and from much food of any kind. It is a significant fact, stated by entomologists, —I find it in Kirby and Spence, —that "some insects in their perfect state, though furnished with organs of feeding, make no use of them;" and they lay it down as "a general rule, that almost all insects in this state eat much less than in that of larvae. The voracious caterpillar when transformed into a butterfly . . . and the gluttonous maggot when become a fly" content themselves with a drop or two of honey or some other sweet liquid. The abdomen under the wings of the butterfly still represents the larva. This is the tidbit which tempts his insectivorous fate. The gross feeder is a man in the larva state; and there are whole nations in that condition, nations without fancy or imagination, whose vast abdomens betray them.

It is hard to provide and cook so simple and clean a diet as will not offend the imagination; but this, I think, is to be fed when we feed the body; they should both sit down at the same table. Yet perhaps this may be done. The fruits eaten temperately need not make us ashamed of our appetites, nor interrupt the worthiest pursuits. But put an extra condiment into your dish, and it will poison you. It is not worth the while to live by rich cookery. Most men would feel shame if caught preparing with their own hands precisely such a dinner, whether of animal or vegetable food, as is every day prepared for them by others. Yet till this is otherwise we are not civilized, and, if gentlemen and ladies, are not true men and women. This certainly suggests what change is to be made. It may be vain to ask why the imagination will not be reconciled to flesh and fat. I am satisfied that it is not. Is it not a reproach that man is a carnivorous *
animal? True, he can and does live, in a great measure, by preying on other animals; but this is a miserable way, —as any one who will go to snaring rabbits, or slaughtering lambs, may learn, —and he will be regarded as a benefactor of his race who shall teach man to confine himself to a more innocent and wholesome diet. Whatever my own practice may be, I have no doubt that it is a part of the destiny of the human race, in its gradual improvement, to leave off eating animals, as surely as the savage tribes have left off eating each other when they came in contact with the more civilized.

Yet, for my part, I was never unusually squeamish; I could sometimes eat a fried rat with a good relish, if it were necessary. I am glad to have drunk water so long, for the same reason that I prefer the natural sky to an opium-eater's heaven. I would fain keep sober always; and there are infinite degrees of drunkenness. I believe that water is the only drink for a wise man; wine is not so noble a liquor; and think of dashing the hopes of a morning with a cup of *
warm coffee, or of an evening with a dish of tea! Ah, how low I fall when I am tempted by them! Even music may be intoxicating. Such apparently slight causes destroyed Greece and Rome, and will destroy England and America. Of all ebriosity, who does not prefer to be intoxicated by the air he breathes? I have found it to be the most serious objection to coarse labors long continued, that they compelled me to eat and drink coarsely also. But to tell the truth, I find myself at

present somewhat less particular in these respects. I carry less religion to the table, ask no blessing; not because I am wiser than I was, but, I am obliged to confess, because, however much it is to be regretted, with years I have grown more coarse and indifferent. Perhaps these questions are entertained only in youth, as most believe of poetry. My practice is "nowhere," my opinion is here.

Thinking about Writing

Words

Powerful words both depend on and help shape their context. In what way does each word in the list below depend on its context for strength? What does each contribute to its context? Can you think of any other word the author might have used in its place? How does the word strike you, and how do you respond to the sentence or passage because of the word?

essentially
poetic
reproach
dashing

Thinking

1. One of the best times to go fishing is during the "first streaks of morning." Yet, Thoreau sees fishing and these first signs of dawn as portending something. What do you gather from the writing that he sees wrong with fishing? How does he connect fishing with other qualities he dislikes? Once you understand his thinking, you might suggest something else in place of fishing that would function as well: what else could he have said besides fishing, to get his point across? In other words, if he dislikes fishing because of his philosophy of life, what else might he dislike for the same reason?
2. Does Thoreau's concern with the effects of food on the imagination, rather than "ill effects," make sense to you? In what way

do we feed the imagination today concerning food? Do you agree that nations without fancy or imagination with regard to food have "vast abdomens"? What do you think Thoreau would say about restaurants, master chefs, food magazines, prime beef, diet pills, and supermarkets?

3. What effect has food on your imagination? In what way is Thoreau's desire to feed his imagination more challenging than a twelve-course dinner?

4. In what way is Thoreau's attitude toward food not a denial of pleasure for him? Would it be a denial for you? Or is his theory also yours: the simpler the better?

Writing

1. Write an essay about some of the pleasures you get from food. You might consider shopping, dining in a restaurant or at home, preparing food for others to eat, or other situations involving food.

2. Thoreau seems to say that people who lack imagination get fat. America has now both poverty and poor diet along with immense amounts of food. The next time you are in the supermarket, look around you at the bulging carts and the people pushing them. Notice the tabloids that are sold at the checkout stands: how many offer advertisements for sensational, quick diets. In what ways does our national concern with food and diets result from a lack of "fancy or imagination"?

   Write an essay which explores the eating and dieting habits of Americans as you see them.

M. F. K. Fisher

M. F. K. Fisher (b. 1908) was born Mary Frances Kennedy in Albion, Michigan, and educated at UCLA and in France at The University of Dijon. Since then, Fisher has divided her adult life between the south of France and California. She writes about the culture of both places, always including talk about food, wine, and personal encounters. In this selection, from a book of her essays called *As They Were*, she finds herself in a near-nightmare lunch, where every course is followed by another. She feels herself battling the unseen chef, Monsieur Paul, who is working feverishly in the kitchen. As soon as she has gained ground and polished off one course, there is another on its way. It is the kind of meal on which dreams are made. But there is a problem. She is full. Fisher is caught in a net; the food is excellent, and besides one must not offend the chef.

I Was Really Very Hungry

I

Once I met a young servant in northern Burgundy who was almost frighteningly fanatical about food, like a medieval woman possessed by a devil. Her obsession engulfed even my appreciation of the dishes she served, until I grew uncomfortable.

It was the off season at the old mill which a Parisian chef had bought and turned into one of France's most famous restaurants, and my mad waitress was the only servant. In spite of that she was neatly uniformed, and showed no surprise at my unannounced arrival and my hot dusty walking clothes. I looked at her stocky young body, and her butter-colored hair, and noticed her odd pale voluptuous mouth before I said, "Mademoiselle, I shall drink an apéritif. Have you by any chance—"

"Let me suggest," she interrupted firmly, "our special dry sherry. *
It is chosen in Spain for Monsieur Paul."

And before I could agree she was gone, discreet and smooth.

She's a funny one, I thought, and waited in a pleasant warm tiredness for the wine.

It was good. I smiled approval at her, and she lowered her eyes, and then looked searchingly at me again. I realized suddenly that in this land of trained nonchalant waiters I was to be served by a small waitress who took her duties seriously. I felt much amused, and matched her solemn searching gaze.

"Today, Madame, you may eat shoulder of lamb in the English style, with baked potatoes, green beans, and a sweet."

My heart sank. I felt dismal, hot and weary, and still grateful for the sherry.

But she was almost grinning at me, her lips curved triumphantly, *
and her eyes less palely blue.

"Oh, in *that* case," she remarked as if I had spoken, "in *that* case a trout, of course—a *truite au bleu* as only Monsieur Paul can prepare it!"

She glanced hurriedly at my face, and hastened on. "With the trout, one or two young potatoes—oh, very delicately boiled," she added before I could protest, "very light."

I felt better. I agreed. "Perhaps a leaf or two of salad after the fish," I suggested. She almost snapped at me. "Of course, of course! And naturally our hors d'oeuvres to commence." She started away.

"No!" I called, feeling that I must assert myself now or be forever lost. "No!"

She turned back, and spoke to me very gently. "But Madame *
has never tasted our hors d'oeuvres. I am sure that Madame will be pleased. They are our specialty, made by Monsieur Paul himself. I am sure," and she looked reproachfully at me, her mouth sad, "I am sure that Madame would be very much pleased."

I smiled weakly at her, and she left. A little cloud of hurt *
gentleness seemed to hang in the air where she had last stood.

I comforted myself with the sherry, feeling increasing irritation with my own feeble self. Hell! I loathed hors d'oeuvres! I conjured * disgusting visions of square glass plates of oily fish, of soggy vegetables glued together with cheap mayonnaise, of rank radishes and tasteless butter. No, Monsieur Paul or not, sad young pale-faced waitress or not, I hated hors d'oeuvres.

I glanced victoriously across the room at the cat, whose eyes seemed closed.

II

Several minutes passed. I was really very hungry.

The door banged open, and my girl came in again, less discreet this time. She hurried toward me.

"Madame, the wine! Before Monsieur Paul can go on—" Her eyes watched my face, which I perversely kept rather glum.

"I think," I said ponderously, daring her to interrupt me, "I think that today, since I am in Burgundy and about to eat a trout," and here I hoped she noticed that I did not mention hors d'oeuvres, "I think I shall drink a bottle of Chablis 1929."

For a second her whole face blazed with joy, and then subsided into a trained mask. I knew that I had chosen well, had somehow satisfied her in a secret and incomprehensible way. She nodded politely and scuttled off, only for another second glancing impatiently at me as I called after her, "Well cooled, please, but not iced."

I'm a fool, I thought, to order a whole bottle. I'm a fool, here all alone and with more miles to walk before I reach Avallon and my fresh clothes and a bed. Then I smiled at myself and leaned back in my solid wide-seated chair, looking obliquely at the prints of Gibson girls, English tavern scenes, and hideous contrysides that hung on the papered walls. The room was warm; I could hear my companion cat purring under the ferns.

The girl rushed in, with flat baking dishes piled up her arms like the plates of a Japanese juggler. She slid them off neatly in two rows onto the table, where they lay steaming up at me, darkly and infinitely appetizing.

"*Mon Dieu!* All for me?" I peered at her. She nodded, her discretion quite gone now and a look of ecstatic worry on her pale face and eyes and lips.

There were at least eight dishes. I felt almost embarrassed, and *
sat for a minute looking weakly at the fork and spoon in my hand.

"Perhaps Madame would care to start with the pickled herring?
It is not like any other. Monsieur Paul prepares it himself, in his own
vinegar and wines. It is very good."

I dug out two or three brown filets from the dish, and tasted.
They were truly unlike any others, truly the best I had ever eaten,
mild, pungent, meaty as fresh nuts.

I realized the maid had stopped breathing, and looked up at her.
She was watching me, or rather a gastronomic X ray of the herring
inside me, with a hypnotized glaze in her eyes.

"Madame is pleased?" she whispered softly.

I said I was. She sighed, and pushed a sizzling plate of broiled
endive toward me, and disappeared.

I had put a few dull green lentils on my plate, lentils scattered
with minced fresh herbs and probably marinated in tarragon vinegar
and walnut oil, when she came into the dining room again with the
bottle of Chablis in a wine basket.

"Madame should be eating the little baked onions while they
are hot," she remarked over her shoulder as she held the bottle in a
napkin and uncorked it. I obeyed meekly, and while I watched her I *
ate several more than I had meant to. They were delicious, simmered
first in strong meat broth, I think, and then drained and broiled with
olive oil and new-ground pepper.

I was fascinated by her method of uncorking a vintage wine.
Instead of the Burgundian procedure of infinite and often exaggerated
precautions against touching or tipping or jarring the bottle, she
handled it quite nonchalantly, and seemed to be careful only to keep
her hands from the cool bottle itself, holding it sometimes by the
basket and sometimes in a napkin. The cork was very tight, and I
thought for a minute that she would break it. So did she: her face
grew tight, and did not loosen until she had slowly worked out the
cork and wiped the lip. Then she poured an inch of wine in a glass,
turned her back to me like a priest taking Communion, and drank it
down. Finally some was poured for me, and she stood with the bottle
in her hand and her full lips dropping until I nodded a satisfied yes.
Then she pushed another of the plates toward me, and almost rushed
from the room.

I ate slowly, knowing that I should not be as hungry as I ought to be for the trout, but knowing too that I had never tasted such delicate savory morsels. Some were hot, some cold. The wine was light and cool. The room, warm and agreeably empty under the rushing sound of the stream, became smaller as I grew used to it.

My girl hurried in again, with another row of plates up one arm, and a large bucket dragging at the other. She slid the plates deftly onto the table, and drew a deep breath as she let the bucket down against the table leg.

"Your trout, Madame," she said excitedly. I looked down at the gleam of the fish curving through its limited water. "But first a good slice of Monsieur Paul's pâté. Oh yes, oh yes, you will be very sorry if you miss this. It is rich, but appetizing, and not at all too heavy. Just this one morsel!"

And willy-nilly I accepted the large gouge she dug from a terrine. I prayed for ten normal appetites and thought with amused nostalgia of my usual lunch of cold milk and fruit as I broke off a crust of bread and patted it smooth with the paste. Then I forgot everything but the exciting faint decadent flavor in my mouth.   *

I beamed up at the girl. She nodded, but from habit asked if I was satisfied. I beamed again, and asked, simply to please her, "Is there not a faint hint of marc, or perhaps cognac?"

"Marc, Madame!" And she awarded me the proud look of a teacher whose pupil has showed unexpected intelligence. "Monsieur Paul, after he has taken equal parts of goose breast and the finest pork, and broken a certain number of egg yolks into them, and ground them very, very fine, cooks all with seasoning for some three hours. But," she pushed her face nearer, and looked with ferocious gloating at the pâté inside me, her eyes like X rays, "he never stops stirring it! Figure to yourself the work of it—stir, stir, never stopping!

"Then he grinds in a suspicion of nutmeg, and then adds, very thoroughly, a glass of marc for each hundred grams of pâté. And is Madame not pleased?"

Again I agreed, rather timidly, that Madame was much pleased, that Madame had never, indeed, tasted such an unctuous and exciting pâté. The girl wet her lips delicately, and then started as if she had been pin-stuck.

"But the trout! My God, the trout!" She grabbed the bucket, and her voice grew higher and more rushed.

"Here is the trout, Madame. You are to eat it *au bleu*, and you should never do so if you had not seen it alive. For if the trout were dead when it was plunged into the *court bouillon* it would not turn blue. So, naturally, it must be living."

I knew all this, more or less, but I was fascinated by her absorption in the momentary problem. I felt quite ignorant, and asked her with sincerity, "What about the trout? Do you take out its guts before or after?"

"Oh, the trout!" She sounded scornful. "Any trout is glad, truly glad, to be prepared by Monsieur Paul. His little gills are pinched, with one flash of the knife he is empty, and then he curls in agony in the *bouillon* and all is over. And it is the curl you must judge, Madame. A false *truite au bleu* cannot curl."

She panted triumph at me, and hurried out with the bucket.

III

She *is* a funny one, I thought, and for not more than two or three minutes I drank wine and mused over her. Then she darted in, with the trout correctly blue and agonizingly curled on a platter, and on her crooked arm a plate of tiny boiled potatoes and a bowl.

When I had been served and had cut off her anxious breathings with an assurance that the fish was the best I had ever tasted, she peered again at me and at the sauce in the bowl. I obediently put some of it on the potatoes: no fool I, to ruin *truite au bleu* with a hot concoction! There was more silence.

"Ah!" she sighed at last. "I knew Madame would feel thus! Is it not the most beautiful sauce in the world with the flesh of a trout?"

I nodded incredulous agreement.

"Would you like to know how it is done?"

I remembered all the legends of chefs who guarded favorite recipes with their very lives, and murmured yes.

She wore the exalted look of a believer describing a miracle at Lourdes as she told me, in a rush, how Monsieur Paul threw chopped chives into hot sweet butter and then poured the butter off, how he added another nut of butter and a tablespoonful of thick cream for each person, stirred the mixture for a few minutes over a slow fire, and then rushed it to the table.

"So simple?" I asked softly, watching her lighted eyes and the tender lustful lines of her strange mouth.

"So simple, Madame! But," she shrugged, "you know, with a master—"

I was relieved to see her go: such avid interest in my eating wore on me. I felt released when the door closed behind her, free for a minute or so from her victimization. What would she have done, I wondered, if I had been ignorant or unconscious of any fine flavors?

She was right, though, about Monsieur Paul. Only a master could live in this isolated mill and preserve his gastronomic dignity through loneliness and the sure financial loss of unused butter and addled eggs. Of course there was the stream for his fish, and I knew his *pâtés* would grow even more edible with age; but how could he manage to have a thing like roasted lamb ready for any chance patron? Was the consuming interest of his one maid enough fuel for his flame?

I tasted the last sweet nugget of trout, the one nearest the blued tail, and poked somnolently at the minute white billiard balls that had been eyes. Fate could not harm me, I remembered winily, for I had indeed dined today, and dined well. Now for a leaf of crisp salad, and I'd be on my way.

The girl slid into the room. She asked me again, in a respectful but gossipy manner, how I had liked this and that and the other things, and then talked on as she mixed dressing for the endive.

"And now," she announced, after I had eaten one green sprig and dutifully pronounced it excellent, "now Madame is going to taste Monsieur Paul's special terrine, one that is not even on the summer menu, when a hundred covers are laid here daily and we have a headwaiter and a wine waiter, and cabinet ministers telegraph for tables! Madame will be pleased."

And heedless of my low moans of the walk still before me, of my appreciation and my unhappily human and limited capacity, she cut a thick heady slice from the terrine of meat and stood over me while I ate it, telling me with almost hysterical pleasure of the wild ducks, the spices, the wines that went into it. Even surfeit could not make me deny that it was a rare dish. I ate it all, knowing my luck, and wishing only that I had red wine to drink with it.

I was beginning, though, to feel almost frightened, realizing myself an accidental victim of these stranded gourmets, Monsieur Paul and his handmaiden. I began to feel that they were using me for a safety valve, much as a thwarted woman relieves herself with tantrums or a fit of weeping. I was serving a purpose, and perhaps a noble one, but I resented it in a way approaching panic.

I protested only to myself when one of Monsieur Paul's special cheeses was cut for me, and ate it doggedly, like a slave. When the girl said that Monsieur Paul himself was preparing a special filter of coffee for me, I smiled servile acceptance: wine and the weight of food and my own character could not force me to argue with maniacs. When, before the coffee came, Monsieur Paul presented me, through his idolater, with the most beautiful apple tart I had ever seen, I allowed it to be cut and served to me. Not a wince or a murmur showed the waitress my distressed fearfulness. With a stuffed careful smile on my face, and a clear nightmare in my head of trussed wanderers prepared for his altar by this hermit-priest of gastronomy, I listened to the girl's passionate plea for fresh pastry dough.

"You cannot, you *cannot*, Madame, serve old pastry!" She seemed ready to beat her breast as she leaned across the table. "Look at that delicate crust! You may feel that you have eaten too much." (I nodded idiotic agreement.) "But this pastry is like feathers—it is like snow. It is in fact good for you, a digestive! And why?" She glared sternly at me. "Because Monsieur Paul did not even open the flour bin until he saw you coming! He could not, he *could* not have baked you one of his special apple tarts with old dough!"

She laughed, tossing back her head and curling her mouth voluptuously.

IV

Somehow I managed to refuse a second slice, but I trembled under her surmise that I was ready for my special filter.

The wine and its fortitude had fled me, and I drank the hot coffee as a suffering man gulps ether, deeply and gratefully.

I remember, then, chatting with surprising glibness, and sending to Monsieur Paul flowery compliments, all of them sincere and well won, and I remember feeling only amusement when a vast glass of *marc* appeared before me and then gradually disappeared, like the light in the warm room full of water-sounds. I felt surprise to be alive still, and suddenly very grateful to the wild-lipped waitress, as if her *
presence had sustained me through duress. We discussed food and wine. I wondered bemusedly why I had been frightened.

The *marc* was gone. I went into the crowded bedroom for my jacket. She met me in the darkening hall when I came out, and I paid my bill, a large one. I started to thank her, but she took my hand, drew me into the dining room, and without words poured more spirits into my glass. I drank to Monsieur Paul while she watched me intently, her pale eyes bulging in the dimness and her lips pressed inward as if she too tasted the hot, aged *marc*.

The cat rose from his ferny bed, and walked contemptuously out of the room.

Suddenly the girl began to laugh, in a soft shy breathless way, and came close to me.

"Permit me!" she said, and I thought she was going to kiss me. But instead she pinned a tiny bunch of snowdrops and dark bruised cyclamens against my stiff jacket, very quickly and deftly, and then ran from the room with her head down.

I waited for a minute. No sounds came from anywhere in the old mill, but the endless rushing of the full stream seemed to strengthen, like the timed blare of an orchestra under a falling curtain.

She's a *funny* one, I thought. I touched the cool blossoms on my coat and went out, like a ghost from ruins, across the courtyard toward the dim road to Avallon.

Thinking about Writing

Words

Powerful words both depend on and help shape their context. In what way does each word in the list below depend on its context for

strength? What does each contribute to its context? Can you think of any other word the author might have used in its place? How does the word strike you, and how do you respond to the sentence or passage because of the word?

firmly
triumphantly
gently
hurt
feeble
embarrassed
meekly
decadent
grateful

Thinking

1. At what point does the meal become almost a war of wills? How does the author convey this tension between herself and the waitress? What do you think about Fisher continuing to eat and never refusing anything? Does she strike you as a victim (she uses this word)? Are you surprised when, at the end of the selection, she talks about being frightened? Who or what do you think frightened her?

2. Did you remain curious throughout Fisher's account of her experience? Did you want to find out what would finally happen? If you felt curious about the outcome, how did Fisher make you feel curious?

3. In what ways is this account more than a simple description of a meal Fisher once had? How does Fisher draw us into the dining room, using visual images as well as her other senses?

4. Notice how Fisher concentrates on the waitress's mouth as a source of reaction, coercion, and power outside Fisher, instead of, for example, the waitress's hands. In what way is this concentration appropriate?

5. Do you think there really is a Monsieur Paul, a chef, in the kitchen? In what way does the waitress create Monsieur Paul and then use him in her confrontation with Fisher?

Writing

1. Have you ever been caught up in a situation that got out of
hand — a party that became a brawl, a visit that became an argument or a war of wills, a reunion that stirred up old animosities —
but a situation from which you, for whatever reasons, could not
withdraw? Did you anticipate a pleasant experience only to find
yourself in a devilish involvement? How did your experience end?
Write about the situation, and, as you write, try to think about
how you can make your account both nightmarish, as it was for
you, and compelling for your readers.
2. This selection is more than an account of a large meal. How has
Fisher's writing escaped the limitations of the cookbook style, of
mere food description? How has she created the atmosphere of
personalities that makes the writing almost a piece of fiction?

   Write an essay that examines Fisher's techniques for rounding
out and enriching what is, after all, just a report of a rather big
lunch. Quote from Fisher's writing to support your observations.
You may want to compare Peter Feibleman's account of preparing
paella with Fisher's writing, as he too enriches his prose.

Peter Feibleman

Peter Feibleman (b. 1930) was born in New York City and educated at the Carnegie Institute, where he studied drama. When he was a child, Feibleman was an actor who appeared on the radio in this country and in numerous films abroad. Today, he is a novelist, a screenwriter, and a cook. His long friendship with the late writer Lillian Hellman resulted in their collaborating on a cookbook, *Cooking Together*, from which this selection comes. More than a simple recipe, this account talks affectionately about the famous Spanish dish *paella* and about anyone who wishes to cook this recipe. The resulting essay both sets the scene and whets the appetite, for it confirms the fact that eating is a social act. Preparing food is similarly social and, like writing, its creator bestows a kind of gift on others, hoping it will bring satisfaction and even happiness. (The recipe has been tested. Try it.)

Paella

Of all the dishes in Spain, the most famous and the most messed * with is something called *paella*. Lillian used to wince at the sight of *paella* till I made it for her outdoors at a picnic one day, and then she got so interested in the cooking that she forgot what she was eating and wound up liking it.

If fifty recipes for *gazpacho*[1] are easy to come by, multiply that by ten for *paella* and you'll be missing some, since all it has to contain is rice, saffron and whatever looks cheap and fresh at the market. The dish is named after the *paellera*, the pan in which it's made, but an

[1]*gazpacho*: a cold tomato soup, also Spanish. —Ed.

iron skillet will do just as well. If you like, cooking outdoors, a *paella* can turn a picnic into a party.

The original dish came from a freshwater lagoon known as La Albufera, close to the city of Valencia on Spain's Levantine coast; it contained eels, green beans and snails and was eaten with small whole onions instead of bread. The dish you see on restaurant menus all over the world listed as *Paella Valenciana* is probably a concoction,   * and certainly a misnomer. Among the vast spectrum of *paellas*, the Valencian one is not high on the scale, for Valencians, culinarily speaking, are a tightassed lot, given to rigid inhibitions about the mixing of meat and fish, fish and shellfish and meat with certain other meat. The polychromatic, dramatic-looking dish most people think of as *paella* is to be found around Alicante, and is worth the trouble you have to go through to find it.

The reason *paella* is easier to cook outdoors than indoors has to do with heat control: the pan is large and the flame on a stovetop is usually too limited in area. An electric stove can sometimes do the job if you like electric stoves (I don't) or if you're stuck with one, as Lillian is on the Vineyard. If you're cooking indoors and worst comes to worst, which it often does, you can always put the *paella* into the oven when you're ready to cook the rice.

What you want to do first is prepare things so that you can reach for them when you need them. Take some mussels, clams, shrimp and whitefish (or any combination thereof), and boil all of it in water for the required time—then remove it, save the water and peel the shrimp. Put the shrimp shells back into the same water and boil them for at least 30 minutes or longer. Then take the shells out, discard them and set that water aside.

Let's assume you're outdoors. If you have a barbecue handy, use it. If you don't, use three stones to hold the pan up, then make a fire of wood sticks around them. The sticks should all point inward like spokes, up toward a central point where the fire will be hottest. Light it and wait. When it gets going, place the pan on top and splash a   * little olive oil into it.

As soon as the oil starts to smoke, add some chicken parts, giblets, pieces of pork and slices of sausage (exact amounts are given below). By now the fire ought to be licking at the entire surface of the bottom of the pan. When the meat is browned on all sides, lift it out, set it aside and replace it with thinly sliced onion. When the onion looks as if it had started to rust, add mashed garlic, tomatoes and (optionally) coarse salt.

What you now have is called a *sofrito*. Mush it all up together with a wooden spoon, take the pan off the flame for long enough to add some paprika, stir it again and put the pan back on. Add some crushed saffron, stir once more and put the meats back into the *sofrito*.

Stir all hell out of that.

About now you ought to check the fire. If it's low, push the partly burned sticks toward the center till the flames are high again.

Then add the rice.

At this point, if people don't gravitate toward the pan, attracted by the smell, you're doing something wrong. The odor should be aromatic, a combination of sea- and land-food, zesty and sharp, the kind of smell that has an immediate effect on the salivary glands and (from time to time) the gonads. Do not answer questions about what you're doing. Let people stand around, and keep doing it. See that somebody gives them a drink while you go on stirring for a couple of minutes until the rice has browned in the *sofrito*.

Now add the water you saved from the seafood and shrimp shells. It should be whitish, and you want twice as much water as rice. Fresh garden peas, squid rings and small artichokes can go in now if you happen to have any hanging around. One last stir, then kill the flames ∗ by pulling the last of the wood sticks out of the spoke formation—away from the pan—so that the pan sits on the hot embers. (If you're on a barbecue grill, mash the coals into one flat layer and lower the pan. If you're indoors, good luck.)

The rice is cooked, they say in Alicante, when the rice is cooked. What they mean is, look at it and taste it. Depending on what kind of rice you're using, after about 18 minutes it should be dark yellow and it should have risen almost to the top and sides of the pan. Chew a couple of grains. It shouldn't be too hard or too soft. When it's done, slide the last of the coals out from under the pan with a stick.

This is the time to insert the cooked clams, shrimp, mussels and whitefish—plus any other shellfish you've boiled, lobster or crawfish. You may garnish the finished *paella* with pimiento strips crisscrossed over the top, and you are now finished cooking. Wash your hands.

If you want to eat the *paella* the way they do at an Alicante outdoor family picnic, you and your friends will all be eating out of the pan you cooked in. It goes like this:

First, let people look at it. Seat them in a circle around the pan and give them each a spoon and a fork. Small wooden spoons are best, but any spoons will do. For every couple of people, set out a dish to be used as a sewer for shells and bones.   *

Next, take a small white plate and place it, upside down, in the very center of the *paella*, on top of the rice.

Now listen carefully. On top of that plate, place another plate, right side up. The second plate should contain a salad composed of lettuce, tomato and onions, with a plain oil and vinegar dressing.

Tell people to use their spoons and tell them to eat the *paella* up to the plate, stopping to pick up their forks and spear a piece of tomato or onion when they want from the salad at the center. By the time the salad is finished, the *paella* around it should be gone too.

Then lift both plates off and expose the final center portion, still warm, for anybody who wants seconds.

You should have a good time at your picnic. If you do, as Lillian says, do not thank me. Pay me.

FOOD FOR A FRIENDLY PICNIC
Paella Ingredients
Serves 6
1 2-pound lobster
6 shrimps, shell on
6 littleneck clams
6 mussels
3 links chorizo
1 small chicken, cut into 12 pieces
2 teaspoons salt
1 teaspoon black pepper
1/2 cup olive oil
2 ounces pork, cut into 1/4-inch cubes
1/2 cup onions, minced
1 teaspoon garlic, minced
1 red or green pepper, julienned

1 tomato, peeled, seeded and chopped
3 cups long-grain rice, uncooked
1/4 teaspoon saffron threads, pulverized
6 cups boiling water
1/2 cup green peas
2 lemons, cut into 6 wedges

Thinking about Writing

Words

Powerful words both depend on and help shape their context. In what way does each word in the list below depend on its context for strength? What does each contribute to its context? Can you think of any other word the author might have used in its place? How does the word strike you, and how do you respond to the sentence or passage because of the word?

messed with
concoction
splash
hanging around
sewer

Thinking

1. Feibleman approaches this recipe by talking about the food in a casual way that appears at first to be almost a short narrative. Does this highly descriptive approach to a recipe appeal to your sense of order, or does it seem too imprecise a way for a recipe to be written?
2. In what ways is Feibleman using unconventional and perhaps surprising techniques to present his recipe? Discuss some of his turns of phrase. What is the effect for you of his style?
3. Refer to another cookbook's recipe for *paella*. Compare the language in the other cookbook with Feibleman's. Which do you

prefer? Could you make *paella* following Feibleman's recipe? Is
there anything not clear?

Writing

1. Find a recipe in any traditional cookbook, choosing something
   that is fairly complicated with several steps. Following Feibleman's
   style, write about the making and serving of your chosen dish.
   (Since this account may be imaginary, you may embroider the
   narrative as much as you want as long as you remain faithful to the
   ingredients.) Make your account as descriptive and social as you
   care to, finally including the recipe itself. Exchange recipes with a
   classmate: could you make your classmate's dish if you wanted to?
   Is your recipe clear to your classmate?
2. Write a short paper in which you compare the Feibleman approach
   with a traditional recipe. (See Thinking question 3 for prewriting
   ideas.) How does the language used in Feibleman's approach differ
   from that in a traditional recipe? What is the tone of each? The
   style? The overall effect? Which do you prefer, and why do you
   prefer it? Be sure to consider the drawbacks and virtues of both
   approaches.
3. Although eating, in our culture, is a social act, preparation of food
   may not be. For some, cooking may be almost a secret activity that
   tolerates few interruptions. (Have you ever been chased out of the
   kitchen by someone "working on" dinner?) For others, cooking
   is a convivial event, where everyone gathers in the kitchen, each
   contributing to the meal. For them, making the meal is as festive
   as consuming it. Which type are you? Write an essay in which
   you explore the social or the antisocial aspects of food preparation,
   including your reaction to Feibleman's advice: "Do not answer
   questions about what you're doing."

2

Minding
the Body

Although this chapter is concerned with illness, the writers here are more interested in the mental aspects of illness than in the physical. They are concerned with the way the mind responds to the body being ill. It is the mind that first notices something is amiss, and it is through the minds of patient and physician that illness is identified, qualified, and treated. The hard facts of pulse rates and body temperatures are meaningless until they are interpreted.

It is the mind that regards death fearfully and that must be calmed before that finality. Emma Goldman, working in a women's prison hospital, finds this so. Watching one of her charges approaching death with great anxiety, Goldman sends for a priest. Death is frightening, even at the end of a painful life.

It is the mind that announces the body's recovery from illness, M. F. K. Fisher finds. Although well enough to travel after an illness, she is not yet convinced of her recovery. Then, she observes a stressful situation which acts as a focus for her mind. When the tension subsides, Fisher knows she is well again.

It is the mind that refuses to stop creating even when illness has robbed the body's vitality. Although she is gravely ill, Katherine Mansfield continues to write, creating scenes and imagining conversations beyond her sickroom. Her mind carries on. It even informs her of her malady's progress.

It is the mind of a small child, full of fear, which prompts her to hide an illness first from her parents and then from the doctor. William Carlos Williams is the physician who finds himself battling this terrified creature in order to discover the truth.

It is the mind in a willing state that can trigger mechanisms of recovery in a body, Norman Cousins finds. It is the strong will that makes rapid recovery possible, and the mind when fooled that allows placebos, dummy drugs, to work.

It is the mind that tells the body to behave in certain ways during illness or indisposition. Lewis Thomas finds that the unconscious is responsible for much that happens to the body. For example, the way warts go away is best explained in terms of the unconscious.

Emma Goldman

Emma Goldman (1869–1940) was born in Russia. She came to America when she was seventeen, landing in New York where she searched for work, any kind of work, to keep alive. She found a job in a sweatshop—a workplace where laborers were crammed together at benches or tables, laboring for hours, for pennies. As welcome as her meager wages were, the life was appalling, dangerous, and humiliating. Goldman was outraged. And so she complained. At first, she just made enough noise to be heard; later, she developed her speaking talents as she realized that she could hold crowds with her words. Thus, Goldman began a life dedicated to erasing what she saw as inequities in the life of the poor, lecturing and writing about her radical views. But she shocked people, for she was an alien, an anarchist, an agitator, a spellbinding speaker, a feminist, and a pacifist. She was jailed for her dangerous words. In the selection here, from her autobiography entitled *Living My Life*, Goldman recalls an incident in jail where she is serving a sentence and working as a nurse. A dying prisoner asks for a priest and Goldman, although an atheist, doesn't hesitate. She complies, for she has compassion and knows that dying is not easy, even when life has been harsh.

Calling
for a Priest

In March 1894 we received a large influx of women prisoners. They were nearly all prostitutes rounded up during recent raids. The city had been blessed by a new vice crusade. The Lexow Committee, * with the Reverend Dr. Parkhurst at its head, wielded the broom which was to sweep New York clean of the fearful scourge. The men found in the public houses were allowed to go free, but the women were arrested and sentenced to Blackwell's Island.

Most of the unfortunates came in a deplorable condition. They were suddenly cut off from the narcotics which almost all of them had been habitually using. The sight of their suffering was heart-breaking. With the strength of giants the frail creatures would shake the iron bars, curse, and scream for dope and cigarettes. Then they would fall exhausted to the ground, pitifully moaning through the night.

The misery of the poor creatures brought back my own hard struggle to do without the soothing effect of cigarettes. Except for the ten weeks of my illness in Rochester, I had smoked for years, sometimes as many as forty cigarettes a day. When we were very hard pressed for money, and it was a toss-up between bread and cigarettes, we would generally decide to buy the latter. We simply could not go for very long without smoking. Being cut off from the satisfaction of the habit when I came to the penitentiary, I found the torture almost beyond endurance. The nights in the cell became doubly hideous. The only way to get tobacco in prison was by means of bribery. I knew that if any of the inmates were caught bringing me cigarettes, they would be punished. I could not expose them to the risk. Snuff tobacco was allowed, but I could never take to it. There was nothing to be done but to get used to the deprivation. I had resisting power and I could forget my craving in reading.

Not so the new arrivals. When they learned that I was in charge of the medicine chest, they pursued me with offers of money; worse still, with pitiful appeals to my humanity. "Just a whiff of dope, for the love of Christ!" I rebelled against the Christian hypocrisy which allowed the men to go free and sent the poor women to prison for having ministered to the sexual demands of those men. Suddenly cutting off the victims from the narcotics they had used for years seemed ruthless. I would have gladly given the addicts what they craved so terribly. It was not fear of punishment which kept me from bringing them relief; it was Dr. White's faith in me. He had trusted me with the medicines, he had been kind and generous—I could not fail him. The screams of the women would unnerve me for days, but I stuck to my responsibility.

One day a young Irish girl was brought to the hospital for an operation. In view of the seriousness of the case Dr. White called in two trained nurses. The operation lasted until late in the evening, and then the patient was left in my charge. She was very ill from the effect of the ether, vomited violently, and burst the stitches of her wound, which resulted in a severe hemorrhage. I sent a hurry call to the Charity Hospital. It seemed hours before the doctor and his staff arrived. There were no nurses this time and I had to take their place.

All night I watched her struggle for life. In the morning I sent for the priest. Everyone was surprised at my action, particularly the head matron. How could I, an atheist, do such a thing, she wondered, and choose a priest, at that! I had declined to see the missionaries as well as the rabbi. She had noticed how friendly I had become with the two Catholic sisters who often visited us on Sunday. I had even made coffee for them. Didn't I think that the Catholic Church had always been the enemy of progress and that it had persecuted and tortured the Jews? How could I be so inconsistent? Of course, I thought so, I assured her. I was just as opposed to the Catholic as to the other Churches. I considered them all alike, enemies of the people. They preached submission, and their God was the God of the rich and the mighty. I hated their God and would never make peace with him. But if I could believe in any religion at all, I should prefer the Catholic Church. "It is less hypocritical," I said to her; "it makes allowance for human frailties and it has a sense of beauty." The Catholic sisters and the priest had not tried to preach to me like the missionaries, the minister, and the vulgar rabbi. They left my soul to its own fate; they talked to me about human things, especially the priest, who was a cultured man. My poor patient had reached the end of a life that had been too hard for her. The priest might give her a few moments of peace and kindness; why should I not have sent for him? But the * matron was too dull to follow my argument or understand my motives. * I remained a "queer one," in her estimation.

Before my patient died, she begged me to lay her out. I had been kinder to her, she said, than her own mother. She wanted to know that it would be my hand that would get her ready for the last journey. I would make her beautiful; she wanted to look beautiful to meet Mother Mary and the Lord Jesus. It required little effort to make her as lovely in death as she had been in life. Her black curls made her alabaster face more delicate than the artificial methods she had used to enhance her looks. Her luminous eyes were closed now; I had closed them with my own hands. But her chiselled eyebrows and long, black lashes were remindful of the radiance that had been hers. How she must have fascinated men! And they destroyed her. Now she was beyond their reach. Death had smoothed her suffering. She looked serene in her marble whiteness now.

Thinking about Writing

Words

Powerful words both depend on and help shape their context. In what way does each word in the list below depend on its context for strength? What does each contribute to its context? Can you think of any other word the author might have used in its place? How does the word strike you, and how do you respond to the sentence or passage because of the word?

blessed
peace
dull

Thinking

1. How does Goldman use the technique of always tying herself into the narrative? From this writing, do you know more about her or about others? If we see the others through Goldman's eyes, point out any information here that "rings false" for you, that you feel is exaggerated or slanted because of Goldman's feelings. Where does Goldman place herself in relation to the others, and how does the writing place her for you? If you believe her account and opinions, what in the writing makes them credible?
2. According to Goldman, during the clean sweep of the vice crusade, women prostitutes were sent to prison while the men found in the

raids were allowed to go free. What do you think was the reasoning behind such actions? What double standards can you think of that exist today? Do you defend any double standards? If so, what are your arguments?

3. Goldman had several reasons for not sending for a priest: she was a Jew by birth; she had become an anarchist and, through this political persuasion, an atheist; she was in prison and the authorities would certainly refuse to send a priest (they did refuse). Still, she persisted. Why do you think she felt moved to call for a priest, in spite of all the motives against her doing so?

Writing

1. Write an essay in which you consider double standards for expected behavior as you have either witnessed them or experienced them yourself, in school (even when you were very young), in college, in social situations, or on the job.

2. Do you think it is possible for someone to believe in some creed or code and not apply those beliefs to every situation and to everyone? What do you think are the limits of tolerance? Where does compassion begin? Write a defense of either Emma Goldman's act or some other apparently contradictory act of faith.

M. F. K. Fisher

M. F. K. Fisher (b. 1908) was born in Michigan, but she has divided her adult life between the south of France and California. She finds both these areas rich in food, wine, and personal encounters, and she writes often about all three. In the selection here, which comes from a collection of her essays, *As They Were*, Fisher tells how she traveled to the famous divorce city, Reno, Nevada, in order to shed her tiresome "companion," an illness. Once in Reno, she uses a racial incident which she observes as an external focus for the illness, finding that as the air clears and the tension subsides, her ailment is completely gone. Her account suggests that, although her body had finished with the illness, her mind needed some kind of focus so that she would know she had indeed recovered.

The Changeover

I went up to Reno from San Francisco after a long illness, to break a pattern of convalescence. Most people go there for amorous or marital or financial reasons, but I went to get a divorce from myself, the sick or malingering self. It was early spring, and I felt like a refugee from the clinics and the test tubes.

On the train, which I took in Oakland, across the Bay, I looked with deliberate interest from my window as the land and water slid by. I liked the movement of heading into something unknown, although the cars crowded with people already stripping themselves and stretching out for the long sit-up ride to Kansas City were not attractive.

I staggered through the cluttered aisles to the club car, and after a martini I went on to the diner. I ate simply and well, and everything tasted mildly exhilarating, the way it should when a person stops being ill and suddenly is not too afraid to be well and vertical again. Reno came along fairly soon after I had walked back through the tilting, lurching cars, over all the legs, to my assigned seat. I pulled my coat and makeup box off the rack, and we slowed down.

Out in the cold grey station, it was complicated to get two suitcases that had been checked into the baggage car in Oakland. A polite sleepy porter turned up finally and managed it for me, in spite of locked doors and dark rooms and a general air of disuse about the place. He and I seemed to be the only people who still believed this silent building was a railroad station. He carried my things out to the empty street and put them beside a lamppost. "You be all right here," he said gently. "I call for a cab. Take some time but be along."

I was not thinking one way or another, about Time or anything else, but a cab did come, although I never saw the sleepy porter again. On the way to the hotel at which I had made a reservation, suddenly there was a flash of almost audible light, and, sure enough, I had   * not forgotten the street of neon and thick gaudy signs with the arch blazing over it. I was in Reno, symbol of sin, of quick divorce and quicker marriage, of unlicensed license, and the hotel lobby seemed a normal projection of the flash-by of the street from that earlier train window—a glitter and glow under the low ceiling, with hundreds of slot machines crashing and flickering and ringing bells, and chaotic decorations twirling in the air to say that even if Time meant nothing, Easter and daffodils and bunnies were next on the calendar.

There were rows of tables for roulette and whatever other games are played on tables, and the people around them were mute—an   * old Ernst Lubitsch movie of Monte Carlo. It was the slot machines that seemed alive—certainly more alive than the unsmiling men and women who stood woodenly in front of them, not even blinking or twitching when lights flashed for a jackpot. Plump little cash girls packed into white satin shirts and black slacks moved through the voiceless crowds, changing bills into dollars, dollars into nickels. Very loud mariachi music blanketed us raggedly.

In one corner, hidden, was the hotel desk. A trim young man in tight frontier pants and high-heeled boots carried my bags there, and then, when I had registered, he crowded me into a minuscule elevator   * and we shot past a few floors smoothly. In the room, he did a kind of precision dance of turning on lights, flicking his eyes here and there over ashtrays and such, showing me how to adjust the heat, taking the tip. At the door, he smiled warmly and drawled, "Y'all have fun, now."

The room was from a hyped-up motel, somewhat elegant. I sniffed it like a cat, and was there. In the bathroom were packets of aspirin and a hangover remedy, and courtesy samples of hand lotion, and free shoe polishers. The drinking glasses and the toilet seat and even the telephone by the bed were marked *Sterilized for your protection*, and there was a little package of buttons and threaded needles on the television set. One wall of the room was glass, and, below the balcony outside, the Truckee River rushed backward and ducks fought the high water and clutched at the banks in the colored, shifting lights from the lobby, a few floors beneath me.

I began to feel more like a person. I flicked the TV on and off, and then the radio on and off. I read through all the folders on the desk about what was at my fingertips—my beck and call—and what I could eat in the various dining places and when, and mostly what I could drink. For an odd sum like $7.84, or perhaps $14.23, I could have almost instantly a hospitality kit containing fifths each of vodka, scotch, bourbon, rye, gin, ice, and my choice of setups, brought to my room by a smiling cowboy.

It seemed ridiculous to me to pass up the one chance of my life to take a long cool look at the ground floor of this place. I felt that my vision was ready, cleared by illness. I would never again, if I lived here a thousand nights instead of one, be able to see it as I would this night. I called for room service.

The same bellboy who had shown me to my room came, almost as if he had been outside the door. He was neatly strong, and short in spite of his heels, and as impersonal as a geranium in a pot. "Y'all want me?" His smile was a really nice one.

I asked him if he thought it would be all right if I went downstairs by myself, to look around.

He figured me financially, logistically, alcoholically, sexually, in one quick look. I passed. "Y'all's safer here than in your own home," he said. "Once you get accustomed, this place is real fun, and no harm done. They keep an eye on things downstairs. Go right ahead."

I said, like a docile child. "Thank you very much. I really didn't want anything else."

He beamed kindly at me and said, "Just go right on down," and closed the door on a silhouette of slim solid hips and tiny gleaming boots.

Back in the incredible lobby, I felt stiff and shy. I wandered from one aisle of slot machines to the next, trying not to stare too much, not to goggle as the automatic people pulled at the handles and   * fed in coins and then did or did not scoop up more coins and feed them back again. I told myself that I was invisible, but very soon I knew that I was not. I was being watched covertly by the small plump girls wearing sailor caps marked *cash*, and by the tellers on their raised platforms, and by the nonchalant plainclothesmen chatting here and there. Probably the cowboy had told them that I was loose in the place—not because I was going to drink too much or even play too much or pick up a man or a girl but because I was a strange one, not yet identifiable. I was not dressed like the rest, basically. I was alone. I might perhaps be a suicide? I had no perceptible rendezvous arranged, in or out of the hotel, so if I was a go-between, between what and what? The eyes were on me.

I decided to go right on drifting, and gradually I knew where the restrooms were (they were large and comfortable, and a woman in Levi's and a shabby catskin coat was writing postcards in German script), and where the coffee shop kept open twenty-four hours a day, and where a boy in a high white bonnet made hot roast-beef sandwiches twenty-four hours a day for the gamblers, who forgot whether it was time for what—breakfastlunchdinner. There were people eating orange-juice-coffee-poached-eggs-on-toast, with the preoccupied shaving-lotion look of suburban commuters at 7:22 A.M. At the bar, to which the main aisle through the slot machines led, people were meeting for a cocktail, the women looking very wives-of-suburban-commuters in short brocade sheaths and pearls and mink scarves, and it was long after midnight instead of 7:22 A.M.

Behind the bar was a small stage, somewhat above the bottles, and first there was the blasty mariachi band I had heard when I came into the hotel and then, with a special blink and blare, there was a small jazz combo of four men, with a girl singer. They were Navajo Indians, with an impervious disdain behind their show-biz smiles but dressed snappily and playing fairly well.

Feeling weary, I sat down at one of the small tables between the active part of the lobby and the bar. Around me were several other single men and women, but there did not seem to be any open interest in pickups. I ordered a double Gibson from the motherly waitress. I felt curious about how a drink which I considered an apéritif would taste at that incongruous hour, in that unbelievable place, with no meal to follow. It was good, and I enjoyed it slowly.

The m.c. of the Navajo band was clumsy about being Indian, and angry. He made one too many jokes about it, and told one too many long stories, and gradually I realized that in the aisle leading to the bar two groups of six or eight young men had gathered, not one-arming but just standing there. They were blond and sharply dressed,   *
and they were getting ready to make trouble with the increasingly racist man at the mike—prearranged trouble. The men in the combo were watching, as they beat and tootled, and the girl, who was perhaps more Mexican than Indian, and almost white-skinned, was watching, too, from behind her trite, sexy singing. All the eyes that I had felt on me before were fastened now on the two groups of boys gathered closer and closer to the bar, the bottles, the stage.

The m.c. told another barely funny story of how the Indian would be here to live on his land again after the atomic bomb had taken care of the white man, and the boys slid on in—and with them, as gently as the flanges of an oyster or the spreading hood of a cobra,   *
the security men in their well-tailored business suits moved in, and the boys, tense with racial hatred and envy and whatever else it may have been, moved on out and away.

The music kept on, but the young sweating m.c. mopped his face and let the girl singer take over and handle the act, and disappeared. The people at the bar and the little tables kept on drinking. I ordered a single Gibson, and felt that I had just taken the last step to safety from a plank stretched across boiling oil. The mariachi players came grinning onstage, and a fat *castrado* yelped and whimpered through "Guadalajara." It was time for me to go.

Upstairs, I was painfully hungry. The discreet meal on the train was a century behind me. The folded cards and menus on the Formica desk said I could order almost any dish at almost any time, and by now I knew that downstairs day and night did not mean what I had always thought. Why should I not call room service and ask for scrambled eggs and a glass of milk, a bottle of beer, a split of champagne, or perhaps a hospitality kit? Far below the balcony, the Truckee still flowed backward, uphill. There were no ducks now, clutching at the banks against the swift water.

I adjusted the heat, turned the TV and the radio on and then off, and decided that I did not want to see the smiling cowboy again, ever, even bringing me nourishment with his good smile. The sun would be along soon, and meanwhile I knew that I was not ill anymore. The divorce had been granted. I had complete custody of myself.

Thinking about Writing

Words

Powerful words both depend on and help shape their context. In what way does each word in the list below depend on its context for strength? What does each contribute to its context? Can you think of any other words the author might have used in its place? How does the word strike you, and how do you respond to the sentence or passage because of the word?

audible
mute
crowded
automatic
blond
hood

Thinking

1. Why does Fisher write so much about the time before she knew she was cured and so little of the time afterward? If, as she says in the beginning of this selection, she came to Reno to get "divorced" from illness, how do you know she was "divorced" and could return home?

2. Why do you think Fisher feels she is being watched in the casino? When she says she is not "yet" identifiable, what feeling does she convey? Why does she baffle the casino managers and employees? What does she tell us she does that confuses people?
3. How does Fisher use the incident with the band as a focus to show a turning point in her illness?

Writing

1. Most people know the signs of illness coming on but are less attuned to the signs of recovery, except that the fever goes away, the pain is less oppressive, and the physician reports a normal blood count. What signs have you had of recovery beginning? Write about rediscovering yourself after an illness and becoming aware of being "well and vertical again."
2. Fisher uses the racist incident with the band as a powerful focus on her way back to health. Although the whole trip to Reno is a meaningful setting for her recovery, it is the tense moment with the band that seems to act as a catalyst for recovery, almost as if she is then totally free from her former illness. Have you ever experienced such a turning point when you may have only observed some incident, but the incident was so powerful that you could use it as a focus for your turning point?

    Write about your changeover, describing the moment of clarity after which you knew you were a changed person. Your change may have been a step in growing up, a powerful shift in a love affair, or an intense moment in a job. Try to consider why the observed moment, because it was actually outside you as part of your objective experience, was so powerful a focus. Why, in fact, does such a moment seem to be useful only when it happens outside our subjective experience? Do we feel "safe" being merely the observer and, in our safety, endow the moment with all the energy we need to recover from an illness, grow up, change a relation, or attain a different status in a job? Consider these points when you write your paper.

Katherine Mansfield

Katherine Mansfield (1880–1923) was born in Wellington, New Zealand. She moved to England when she decided, as a young woman, to pursue a writing career. She wrote short stories, poetry, and criticism, achieving some fame for the stories. Although she often set her stories in New Zealand, she spent the better part of her short life in England and France, where she died after a life she found difficult. One reason for her discomfort was that she suffered from tuberculosis, well named in those days "consumption," an illness that left her restless and burning, even when she was exhausted. And so she wrote constantly, even when she lay ill in bed, listening to street noises beneath her room, watching the sky out the window, and remembering absent people. Perhaps she felt time running out, for she died young, leaving these intense, restless lines. These selections come from the *Journal of Katherine Mansfield*, which was edited and published after her death by her husband, John Middleton Murry, who was also a writer.

Illness

I am in bed; I feel very sick. Queer altogether—decomposing a bit. It's a pale silent day: I would like to be walking in a wood, far away.

Health seems to me now more remote than anything—unattainable. Best to stay in bed and be horrid from there. This sky in waves of blue and cream and grey is like the sky overhanging a dead calm sea, when you hear someone rowing, far far away; and then the voices from the boat and the rattle of the chain and the barking of the ship's dog all sound loud. There is as usual a smell of onions and chop bones in the house.

May 19. 6 P.M. I wish I had some idea of how old this note book is. The writing is very faint and far away. Now it is May 1919. Six o'clock. I am sitting in my own room thinking of Mother: I want to cry. But my thoughts are beautiful and full of gaiety. I think of *our* house, *our* garden, *us* children—the lawn, the gate, and Mother coming in. "Children! Children!" I really only ask for time to write it all—time to write my books. Then I don't mind dying. I live to write. The lovely world (God, how lovely the external world is!) is there and I bathe in it and am refreshed. But I feel as though I had   *
a DUTY, someone has set me a task which I am bound to finish. Let me finish it: let me finish it without hurrying—leaving all as fair as I can . . . .

My little Mother, my star, my courage, my *own*. I seem to dwell in her now. We live in *the same world*. Not quite this world, not quite another. I do not care for people: and the idea of fame, of being a success,—that's nothing, less than nothing. I love my family and a few others dearly, and I love, in the old—in the ancient way, through and through, my husband.

Not a soul knows where she is. She goes slowly, thinking it all   *
over, wondering how she can express it *as she wants to*—asking for time and for peace.

A bad day. I feel ill, in an obscure way—horrible pains and so on, and weakness. I could do nothing. The weakness was not only physical. I *must heal my Self* before I will be well.

Yes, that is the important thing. No attention is needed here.   *
This must be done alone and at once. It is at the root of my not getting better. My mind is not *controlled*. I idle, I give away, I sink into despair.

One must write a story about a doctor's waiting room. The glass doors with the sun from outside shining through; the autumn trees pale and fine; the cyclamen, like wax. Now a cart shakes by.

Think of the strange places that illness carries one into; the strange people among whom one passes from hand to hand; the succession of black-coated gentlemen to whom she'd whispered 99, 44, 1 — 2 — 3.[1] The last waiting-room. All before had been so cheerful.

"Then you don't think my case is hopeless?"

"The disease is of long standing, but certainly *not* hopeless."

This one, however, leaned back and said: "You really want to know?"

"Yes, of course. Oh, you can be quite frank with me."

"Then, I DO!"

The carriage came and drove her away, her head buried in her collar.

. . . When one is little and ill and far away in a remote bedroom all that happens *beyond* is marvelous . . . . Alors, I am always in that remote bedroom. Is that why I seem to see, this time in London — nothing but what is marvellous — marvellous — and incredibly beautiful?

The tide is full in the Redcliffe Road. One by one the doors have   *
opened, have slammed shut. Now, in their blind way, the houses are fed. That poor little violin goes on, tearing up note after note — there is a strange dazzling white cloud over the houses and a pool of blue.

On these summer evenings the sound of the steps along the street is quite different. They knock-knock-knock along, but lightly and easily, as though they belonged to people who were walking home at their ease, after a procession or a picnic or a day at the sea.

The sky is pale and clear: the silly piano is overcome and reels out waltzes — old waltzes, spinning, drunk with sentiment — gorged   *
with memory.

This is the hour when the poor underfed dog appears, at a run, nosing the dry gutter. He is so thin that his body is like a cage on four wooden pegs . . . . His lean triangle of a head is down, his long straight tail is out, and up and down, up and down he goes, silent and fearfully eager. The street watches him from its creeper-covered

[1]99, 44, 1 — 2 — 3: numbers like these were among the sounds that patients with respiratory ailments were asked to repeat so that the physician could hear the tones in the chest. Mansfield suffered from tuberculosis. — Ed.

balconies, from its open windows—but the fat lady on the ground floor who is no better than she should be comes out—down the steps to the gate, with a bone. His tail as he waits for her to give it to him, bangs against the gate post, like a broomhandle—and the street says she's a fool to go feeding strange dogs. Now she'll never be rid of him.

Thinking about Writing

Words

Powerful words both depend on and help shape their context. In what way does each word in the list below depend on its context for strength? What does each contribute to its context? Can you think of any other word the author might have used in its place? How does the word strike you, and how do you respond to the sentence or passage because of the word?

bathe
She
attention
tide
drunk with sentiment—gorged

Thinking

1. How does Mansfield, writing these entries while she was ill, give us a good picture of her moods and her thinking? How can you tell from her comments and expressions how she felt about herself? Consider, for example, her saying she is "decomposing a bit" and that she is being "horrid." What does this language tell you about Mansfield's view of herself?
2. To what extent can we trust the comments of sick people? How may people who are ill be in better touch with their feelings than those of us who are walking around and putting on a good face?
3. People confined to bed are particularly sensitive to sounds; they are also, for better or worse, prey to the imagination. In the

absence of radio or television, Mansfield gave free rein to her fancy, employing both immediate sounds and past memories in her thoughts. What kinds of stories and scenes did she compose as she lay in bed? How can you tell, or guess, which comments are true and which are fiction? How do you reach your conclusions from Mansfield's words?

Writing

1. Find some place from which you can listen to the world for a few minutes, imagining whatever you like from the sounds outside. Then write an episode to fit the sounds. Do this several times, keeping the episodes brief and crisp. You may create any situation to fit the sounds.

2. Mansfield, toying with the idea of writing a story about a doctor's waiting room, begins to imagine the place, finally adding a conversation between physician and patient. Write a description of a doctor's or dentist's waiting room, including the furniture and other objects, the other patients, the receptionist or nurse, the noises and smells. If you like, include a short conversation, imagined, between you and the doctor or dentist. You may feel that you will write more freely if you refer to yourself as *he* or *she*.

3. Mansfield's world is divided in many ways, most obviously, of course, between sickness and health. You can discover many other divisions by reading again the entries. Write an essay in which you describe Mansfield's divided world, quoting from the author to support your observations.

William Carlos Williams

William Carlos Williams (1883–1963) was born in New Jersey and educated in medicine at the University of Pennsylvania and the University of Leipzig in Germany. Williams was a physician, a poet, a playwright, and a novelist. As a doctor, he practiced in the poor urban sections of northern New Jersey. From the people there, he drew much of his inspiration, touched as he often was by their ignorance and their misery. Winner of the National Book Award for poetry and the Bollingen Award for his work, Williams wrote about the lives of these people, listening to their speech and observing their habits. In the selection here, which comes from a collection called *The Doctor Stories*, he recalls matching wits with a sick child, loving her for her fighting spirit while hating her for being so ferocious and stubborn, *almost* as much as he is.

The Use of Force

They were new patients to me, all I had was the name, Olson. Please come down as soon as you can, my daughter is very sick.

When I arrived I was met by the mother, a big startled looking woman, very clean and apologetic who merely said, Is this the doctor? and let me in. In the back, she added. You must excuse us, doctor, we have her in the kitchen where it is warm. It is very damp here sometimes.

The child was fully dressed and sitting on her father's lap near the kitchen table. He tried to get up, but I motioned for him not to bother, took off my overcoat and started to look things over. I could see that they were all very nervous, eyeing me up and down distrustfully. As often, in such cases, they weren't telling me more than they had to, it was up to me to tell them; that's why they were spending three dollars on me.

The child was fairly eating me up with her cold, steady eyes, and no expression to her face whatever. She did not move and seemed, inwardly, quiet; an unusually attractive little thing, and as strong as a heifer in appearance. But her face was flushed, she was breathing rapidly, and I realized that she had a high fever. She had magnificent blonde hair, in profusion. One of those picture children often reproduced in advertising leaflets and the photogravure sections of the Sunday papers.

She's had a fever for three days, began the father and we don't know where it comes from. My wife has given her things, you know, like people do, but it don't do no good. And there's been a lot of sickness around. So we tho't you'd better look her over and tell us what is the matter.

As doctors often do I took a trial shot at it as a point of departure. Has she had a sore throat?

Both parents answered me together, No . . . No, she says her throat don't hurt her.

Does your throat hurt you? added the mother to the child. But the little girl's expression didn't change nor did she move her eyes from my face.

Have you looked?

I tried to, said the mother, but I couldn't see.

As it happens we have been having a number of cases of diphtheria in the school to which this child went during that month and we were all, quite apparently, thinking of that, though no one had as yet spoken of the thing.

Well, I said, suppose we take a look at the throat first. I smiled in my best professional manner and asking for the child's first name I said, come on, Mathilda, open your mouth and let's take a look at your throat.

Nothing doing.

Aw, come on, I coaxed, just open your mouth wide and let me take a look. Look, I said opening both hands wide, I haven't anything in my hands. Just open up, and let me see.

Such a nice man, put in the mother. Look how kind he is to you. Come on, do what he tells you to. He won't hurt you.

At that I ground my teeth in disgust. If only they wouldn't use the word "hurt" I might be able to get somewhere. But I did not allow myself to be hurried or disturbed but speaking quietly and slowly I approached the child again.

As I moved my chair a little nearer suddenly with one catlike movement both her hands clawed instinctively for my eyes and she *
almost reached them too. In fact she knocked my glasses flying and they fell, though unbroken, several feet away from me on the kitchen floor.

Both the mother and father almost turned themselves inside out in embarrassment and apology. You bad girl, said the mother, taking her and shaking her by one arm. Look what you've done. The nice man . . .

For heaven's sake, I broke in. Don't call me a nice man to her. I'm here to look at her throat on the chance that she might have diphtheria and possibly die of it. But that's nothing to her. Look here, I said to the child, we're going to look at your throat. You're old enough to understand what I'm saying. Will you open it now by yourself or shall we have to open it for you?

Not a move. Even her expression hadn't changed. Her breaths however were coming faster and faster. Then the battle began. I had to do it. I had to have a throat culture for her own protection. But first I told the parents that it was entirely up to them. I explained the danger but said that I would not insist on a throat examination so long as they would take the responsibility.

If you don't do what the doctor says you'll have to go to the hospital, the mother admonished her severely.

Oh yeah? I had to smile to myself. After all, I had already fallen in love with the savage brat, the parents were contemptible to me. In the ensuing struggle they grew more and more abject, crushed, exhausted while she surely rose to magnificent heights of insane fury of effort bred of her terror of me.

The father tried his best, and he was a big man but the fact that she was his daughter, his shame at her behavior and his dread of hurting her made him release her just at the critical moment several times when I had almost achieved success, till I wanted to kill him. But his dread also that she might have diphtheria made him tell me to go on, go on though he himself was almost fainting, while the mother moved back and forth behind us raising and lowering her hands in an agony of apprehension.

Put her in front of you on your lap, I ordered, and hold both her wrists.

But as soon as he did the child let out a scream. Don't, you're hurting me. Let go of my hands. Let them go I tell you. Then she shrieked terrifyingly, hysterically. Stop it! Stop it! You're killing me!

Do you think she can stand it, doctor! said the mother.

You get out, said the husband to his wife. Do you want her to die of diphtheria?

Come on now, hold her, I said.

Then I grasped the child's head with my left hand and tried to get the wooden tongue depressor between her teeth. She fought, with clenched teeth, desperately! But now I also had grown furious—at a child. I tried to hold myself down but I couldn't. I know how to expose a throat for inspection. And I did my best. When finally I got the wooden spatula behind the last teeth and just the point of it into the mouth cavity, she opened up for an instant but before I could see anything she came down again and gripping the wooden blade between her molars she reduced it to splinters before I could get it out again.

Aren't you ashamed, the mother yelled at her. Aren't you ashamed to act like that in front of the doctor?

Get me a smooth-handled spoon of some sort, I told the mother. We're going through with this. The child's mouth was already bleeding. Her tongue was cut and she was screaming in wild hysterical shrieks. Perhaps I should have desisted and come back in an hour or more. No doubt it would have been better. But I have seen at least two children lying dead in bed of neglect in such cases, and feeling that I must get a diagnosis now or never I went at it again. But the worst of it was that I too had got beyond reason. I could have torn *
the child apart in my own fury and enjoyed it. It was a pleasure to attack her. My face was burning with it.

The damned little brat must be protected against her own idiocy, one says to one's self at such times. Others must be protected against her. It is social necessity. And all these things are true. But a blind

fury, a feeling of adult shame, bred of a longing for muscular release
are the operatives. One goes on to the end.

In a final unreasoning assault I overpowered the child's neck and   *
jaws. I forced the heavy silver spoon back of her teeth and down her
throat till she gagged. And there it was—both tonsils covered with
membrane. She had fought valiantly to keep me from knowing her   *
secret. She had been hiding that sore throat for three days at least
and lying to her parents in order to escape just such an outcome as
this.

Now truly she *was* furious. She had been on the defensive before
but now she attacked. Tried to get off her father's lap and fly at me
while tears of defeat blinded her eyes.

Thinking about Words

Words

Powerful words both depend on and help shape their context. In
what way does each word in the list below depend on its context for
strength? What does each contribute to its context? Can you think of
any other word the author might have used in its place? How does the
word strike you, and how do you respond to the sentence or passage
because of the word?

instinctively
reason
unreasoning
valiantly

Thinking

1. Why do you suppose Williams says he had "already fallen in love
   with the savage brat," while "the parents were contemptible to
   me"? As you read this account, for which of the people involved
   do you feel sympathy? How do you feel when the husband says,

"You get out," to his wife? How do you feel toward the child? The father? The mother? The doctor?

2. "I could have torn the child apart in my own fury and enjoyed it." How do you react to this frank admission from a doctor? If you accept Williams's admission without faulting him for it, why do you? Have you ever thought of your doctor as a human being with feelings, not all of them noble? Why do you think we expect a physician always to show a calm, unruffled exterior?

3. Why do you think the child doesn't want her parents, and then the doctor, to know about her sore throat? What might her reasons be—a fear of the consequences, a feeling of guilt for being sick, for somehow failing to be in good health, or some other motive?

Writing

1. Have you ever, because of some outside cause, behaved shamefully while you were doing a job properly? Did you realize you were behaving badly? What kept you going? Were you afraid to lose ground or lose face? Was yours a case of being right and wrong at the same time? Write about the experience.

2. Williams makes no effort to present himself as the perfectly composed physician paying a house call on a sick child. How does his picture of himself as furious strike you as you read? Which do you feel is the stronger emotion, his anger or the child's?

   Write an essay in which you consider the humanizing force that Williams's admission of fury, as well as his love, lends this account. In addition to Williams, you may wish to consider either George Orwell as he presents his flawed self in "Shooting an Elephant" in chapter 4 or Richard Selzer (another physician) as he presents himself in "Letter to a Young Surgeon III" in chapter 6.

Norman Cousins

Norman Cousins (b. 1915) was born in New Jersey and educated at Teachers College of Columbia University. Editor for many years of *The Saturday Review*, Cousins has written and traveled widely, devoting himself to humanitarian issues of democracy, nuclear power, and personal freedom. His own brush with death from a serious illness prompted him to consider a patient's freedom—or lack of freedom—given what he saw as inadequacies of modern medical care. When his doctor had given him slim chance to live, Cousins took matters into his own hands and designed a course of recuperation for himself. He was determined to live, if only to see if his system was effective. He survived and later wrote about his experience. In both *Anatomy of an Illness* and *The Healing Heart*, Cousins writes of the patient's fear, depression, and helplessness when faced with illness. He firmly believes that a patient's mental outlook influences the prognosis of an illness. In the selection here, from *Anatomy of an Illness*, Cousins explores the mystery of the placebo, the "dummy drug," which often will cure, although it is nothing but powder, because people believe it will.

Dummy Drugs

The word placebo comes from the Latin verb meaning "I shall please." A placebo in the classical sense, then, is an imitation medicine—generally an innocuous milk-sugar tablet dressed up like an authentic pill—given more for the purpose of placating a patient than for meeting a clearly diagnosed organic need. The placebo's most frequent use in recent years, however, has been in the testing of new drugs. Effects achieved by the preparation being tested are measured against those that follow the administration of a "dummy drug" or placebo.

While the way the placebo works inside the body is still not completely understood, some placebo researchers theorize that it activates the cerebral cortex, which in turn switches on the endocrine system in general and the adrenal glands in particular. Whatever the precise pathways through the mind and body, enough evidence already exists to indicate that placebos can be as potent as—and sometimes more potent than—the active drugs they replace.

It is doubtful whether the placebo—or any drug, for that matter—would get very far without a patient's robust will to live. For the will to live is a window on the future. It opens the individual to such help as the outside world has to offer, and it connects that help to the body's own capability for fighting disease. It enables the human body to make the most of itself. The placebo has a role to play in transforming the will to live from a poetical conception to a physical reality and a governing force.

Some years ago, I had an opportunity to observe African witch-doctor medicine at first hand in the Gabon jungle country. At the dinner table of the Schweitzer Hospital at Lambarene, I had ventured the remark that the local people were lucky to have access to the Schweitzer clinic instead of having to depend on witch-doctor supernaturalism. Dr. Schweitzer asked me how much I knew about witch doctors. I was trapped by my ignorance—and we both knew it. The next day *le grand docteur*[1] took me to a nearby jungle clearing, where he introduced me to *un de mes collègues*,[2] an elderly witch doctor. After a respectful exchange of greetings, Dr. Schweitzer suggested that his American friend be allowed to observe African medicine.

For the next two hours, we stood off to one side and watched the witch doctor at work. With some patients, the witch doctor merely put herbs in a brown paper bag and instructed the ill person in their use. With other patients, he gave no herbs but filled the air with incantations. A third category of patients he merely spoke to in a subsided voice and pointed to Dr. Schweitzer.

[1] *le grand docteur*: the great doctor.— Ed.
[2] *un de mes collègues*: one of my (Dr. Schweitzer's) colleagues.—Ed.

On our way back to the clinic, Dr. Schweitzer explained what had happened. The people who had assorted complaints that the witch doctor was able to diagnose readily were given special herbs to make into brews. Dr. Schweitzer guessed that most of those patients would improve very rapidly since they had only functional, rather than organic, disturbances. Therefore, the "medications" were not really a major factor. The second group had psychogenic ailments that were being treated with African psychotherapy. The third group had more   *
substantial physical problems, such as massive hernias or extrauterine pregnancies or dislocated shoulders or tumorous conditions. Many of these problems required surgery, and the witch doctor was redirecting the patients to Dr. Schweitzer himself.

"Some of my steadiest customers are referred to me by witch   *
doctors," Dr. Schweitzer said with only the slightest trace of a smile. "Don't expect me to be too critical of them."

When I asked Dr. Schweitzer how he accounted for the fact that anyone could possibly expect to become well after having been treated by a witch doctor, he said that I was asking him to divulge a secret that doctors have carried around inside them ever since Hippocrates. [3]

"But I'll tell you anyway," he said, his face still illuminated by that half-smile. "The witch doctor succeeds for the same reason all the rest of us succeed. Each patient carries his own doctor inside him. They come to us not knowing that truth. We are at our best when we give the doctor who resides within each patient a chance to go to work."

The placebo is the doctor who resides within.

Thinking about Writing

Words

Powerful words both depend on and help shape their context. In what way does each word in the list below depend on its context for

---

[3]Hippocrates: Greek physician during the fifth century B.C. who is called the father of medicine. Doctors swear to abide by the Hippocratic oath when they qualify as physicians. — Ed.

strength? What does each contribute to its context? Can you think of any other word the author might have used in its place? How does the word strike you, and how do you respond to the sentence or passage because of the word?

psychotherapy
customers

Thinking

1. Cousins offers a scientific explanation for how a placebo might work: that is, the placebo activates the cerebral cortex which sets in motion the recovery system. Why do you think Cousins also refers to the "robust will to live," which is spiritual rather than scientific? What does this tell us about the way Cousins views recovery?

2. What can a witch doctor who effects cures for patients have in common with a sophisticated and trained physician—the kind of doctor we consult?

3. Cousins reports observing a witch doctor at work on a visit to Albert Schweitzer's hospital in Africa. How do we know, from Cousins's prose, his impression of the witch doctor? What does Schweitzer think of witch doctors?

Writing

1. Do you think we are a "drug-happy" or "pill-happy" culture? Are we conditioned by advertising to reach for a pill whenever anything bothers either our minds or our bodies? When you are watching television or reading magazines, notice the number of products we are encouraged to buy in order to "doctor" ourselves. (Especially note how many advertisements first *tell* us we are not well and then tell us what is wrong so that we can buy the product to fit the ailment.) Walk through the aisles of a drugstore or the drug section of the supermarket, noting the products there and the illnesses or discomforts these products are supposed to alleviate (if not exactly cure).

   Then, write an essay based on your observations about common ailments and their treatments for which we can buy "over the counter" medications, without a prescription from a physician, in order to cure ourselves.

2. Write an explanation of placebos, adding some information from the library. If you can, talk to a research chemist, a physician, or a psychologist in order to get information about how a placebo is used as a control mechanism in testing new drugs.

3. Write an essay on the term *witch doctor*, including its source and something of its history. Be sure to explain in your report just how the term was first used and, if you can find out, whose terminology it was. For example, did witch doctors call themselves this, or was the term applied by European observers?

Lewis Thomas

Lewis Thomas (b. 1913) was born in New York and educated at Princeton University and Harvard Medical School. A member of the National Academy of Sciences, and President Emeritus of Memorial Sloan-Kettering Cancer Center, Thomas has had a long career of writing about science. A contributor to numerous scientific and medical journals such as the *New England Journal of Medicine*, Thomas has written many books, among them *The Lives of a Cell: Notes of a Biology Watcher*, for which he won the National Book Award, and *The Medusa and the Snail: More Notes of a Biology Watcher*, from which the essay here comes. In this selection, Thomas wonders about the peculiar personality of the common wart, which can be ordered away by the host's unconscious. What Thomas really wonders about, as the reader will discover, is the unconscious itself. Thomas uses the wart as a lure to which we go happily, for he writes the kind of scientific language nonspecialists can understand.

On Warts

Warts are wonderful structures. They can appear overnight on any part of the skin, like mushrooms on a damp lawn, full grown and splendid in the complexity of their architecture. Viewed in stained sections under a microscope, they are the most specialized of cellular arrangements, constructed as though for a purpose. They sit there like turreted mounds of dense, impenetrable horn, impregnable, designed for defense against the world outside.

In a certain sense, warts are both useful and essential, but not for us. As it turns out, the exuberant cells of a wart are the elaborate reproductive apparatus of a virus.

73

You might have thought from the looks of it that the cells infected by the wart virus were using this response as a ponderous way of defending themselves against the virus, maybe even a way of becoming more distasteful, but it is not so. The wart is what the virus truly wants; it can flourish only in cells undergoing precisely this   *
kind of overgrowth. It is not a defense at all; it is an overwhelming welcome, an enthusiastic accommodation meeting the needs of more and more virus.

The strangest thing about warts is that they tend to go away. Fully grown, nothing in the body has so much the look of toughness and permanence as a wart, and yet, inexplicably and often very abruptly, they come to the end of their lives and vanish without a trace.

And they can be made to go away by something that can only be called thinking, or something like thinking. This is a special property of warts which is absolutely astonishing, more of a surprise than cloning or recombinant DNA or endorphin or acupuncture or anything else currently attracting attention in the press. It is one of the great mystifications of science: warts can be ordered off by the skin by hypnotic suggestion.

Not everyone believes this, but the evidence goes back a long way and is persuasive. Generations of internists and dermatologists, and their grandmothers for that matter, have been convinced of the phenomenon. I was once told by a distinguished old professor of medicine, one of Sir William Osler's original bright young men, that it was his practice to paint gentian violet over a wart and then assure the patient firmly that it would be gone in a week, and he never saw it fail. There have been several meticulous studies by good clinical investigators, with proper controls. In one of these, fourteen patients with seemingly intractable generalized warts on both sides of the body were hypnotized, and the suggestion was made that all the warts on one side of the body would begin to go away. Within several weeks the results were indisputably positive; in nine patients, all or nearly all of the warts on the suggested side had vanished, while the control side had just as many as ever.

It is interesting that most of the warts vanished precisely as they were instructed, but it is even more fascinating that mistakes were made. Just as you might expect in other affairs requiring a clear understanding of which is the right and which the left side, one of the subjects got mixed up and destroyed the warts on the wrong side. In a later study by a group at the Massachusetts General Hospital, the warts on both sides were rejected even though the instructions were to pay attention to just one side.

I have been trying to figure out the nature of the instructions used by the unconscious mind, whatever that is, under hypnosis. It seems to me hardly enough for the mind to say, simply, get off, eliminate yourselves, without providing something in the way of specifications as to how to go about it.

I used to believe, thinking about this experiment when it was just published, that the instructions might be quite simple. Perhaps nothing more detailed than a command to shut down the flow through all the precapillary arterioles in and around the warts to the point of strangulation. Exactly how the mind would accomplish this with precision, cutting off the blood supply to one wart while leaving others intact, I couldn't figure out, but I was satisfied to leave it there anyhow. And I was glad to think that my unconscious mind would have to take the responsibility for this, for if I had been one of the subjects I would never have been able to do it myself.

But now the problem seems much more complicated by the information concerning the vital etiology of warts, and even more so by the currently plausible notion that immunologic mechanisms are very likely implicated in the rejection of warts.

If my unconscious can figure out how to manipulate the mechanisms needed for getting around that virus, and for deploying all the various cells in the correct order for tissue rejection, then all I have to say is that my unconscious is a lot further along than I am. I wish I had a wart right now, just to see if I am that talented.

There ought to be a better word than "Unconscious," even capitalized, for what I have, so to speak, in mind. I was brought up to regard this aspect of thinking as a sort of private sanitarium, walled off somewhere in a suburb of my brain, capable only of producing such garbled information as to keep my mind, my proper Mind, always a little off balance.

But any mental apparatus that can reject a wart is something else again. This is not the sort of confused, disordered process you'd expect at the hands of the kind of Unconscious you read about in books, out at the edge of things making up dreams or getting mixed up on words or having hysterics. Whatever, or whoever, is responsible for this has the accuracy and precision of a surgeon. There almost has to be a Person in charge, running matters of meticulous detail beyond anyone's comprehension, a skilled engineer and manager, a chief executive officer, the head of the whole place. I never thought before that I possessed such a tenant. Or perhaps more accurately, such a landlord, since I would be, if this is in fact the situation, nothing more than a lodger.

Among other accomplishments, he must be a cell biologist of world class, capable of sorting through the various classes of one's lymphocytes, all with quite different functions which I do not understand, in order to mobilize the right ones and exclude the wrong ones for the task of tissue rejection. If it were left to me, and I were somehow empowered to call up lymphocytes and direct them to the vicinity of my wart (assuming that I could learn to do such a thing), mine would come tumbling in all unsorted, B cells and T cells, suppressor cells and killer cells, and no doubt other cells whose names I have not learned, incapable of getting anything useful done.

Even if immunology is not involved, and all that needs doing is to shut off the blood supply locally, I haven't the faintest notion how to set that up. I assume that the selective turning off of arterioles can be done by one or another chemical mediator, and I know the names of some of them, but I wouldn't dare let things like these loose even if I knew how to do it.

Well, then, who does supervise this kind of operation? Someone's got to, you know. You can't sit there under hypnosis, taking suggestions in and having them acted on with such accuracy and precision, without assuming the existence of something very like a controller. It wouldn't do to fob off the whole intricate business on lower centers without sending along a quite detailed set of specifications, way over my head.

Some intelligence or other knows how to get rid of warts, and   *
this is a disquieting thought.

It is also a wonderful problem, in need of solving. Just think what we would know, if we had anything like a clear understanding of what goes on when a wart is hypnotized away. We would know the identity of the cellular and chemical participants in tissue rejection, conceivably with some added information about the ways that viruses create foreignness in cells. We would know how the traffic of these reactants is directed, and perhaps then be able to understand the nature of certain diseases in which the traffic is being conducted in wrong directions, aimed at the wrong cells. Best of all, we would be finding out about a kind of superintelligence that exists in each of us, infinitely smarter and possessed of technical know-how far beyond our present understanding. It would be a War on Warts, a Conquest of Warts, a National Institute of Warts and All.

Thinking about Writing

Words

Powerful words both depend on and help shape their context. In what way does each word in the list below depend on its context for strength? What does each contribute to its context? Can you think of any other word the author might have used in its place? How does the word strike you, and how do you respond to the sentence or passage because of the word?

wants
whatever that is
disquieting

Thinking

1. Have you ever had a wart just disappear, as Thomas says they do? If so, what, if anything, did you do to get the wart to go? "Generations of internists and dermatologists, and their grandmothers" believe warts can be ordered off. Why would you agree or disagree that grandmothers belong in this group of believers? What home remedies does your family have that may seem odd to the outside world but that succeed all the same in effecting cures? How might this concept of ordering warts off be connected

with Cousins's thoughts about placebos in "Dummy Drugs"? Do you think Cousins's "robust will to live" is the same as Thomas's Unconscious? Explain your answer, based on what these writers say.

2. Thomas says that the ordering off of warts is more astonishing than cloning, recombinant DNA, endorphin, or acupuncture. Why do you agree or disagree? Why do you suppose Thomas is so impressed with the Unconscious? Why do you think he says, "There almost has to be a Person in charge"? How do you explain his using both a capital U and a capital P?

3. Although warts are unattractive in the sense that they lack what our culture thinks of as beauty, they still fascinate and puzzle us. Consider why this is so. Why are we interested in something we cannot understand or control? Why do you suppose Thomas invites us to consider the Unconscious mind, "whatever it is," as "a Person in charge"? Why do we tend to personify what we don't understand? Why do you think Thomas, after telling us about our inability to understand warts, shifts the focus to the Unconscious (which we also fail to understand)?

Writing

1. If you have ever had firsthand experience with an unexplained cure, or have observed one in somebody else, write about the remedy. Try to offer some kind of explanation: we are, after all, supposed to be reasonable human beings living in a somewhat rational world. Your explanation need not be scientific if you cannot think of any reasons why the cure is effective, but let it be imaginative.

2. Using this piece of writing as a starting point, write a short essay which explores our desire to come to terms with certain things we do not understand by naming them, then by attributing human characteristics to them. We call hurricanes by name and talk about the "eye"; Thomas calls the unconscious the "Unconscious" first and then a "Person in charge." The ancient Greeks and Romans had gods and goddesses for war, love, the hearth, and other aspects of life.

Think about the desire to rationalize, to make reasonable, areas where there is little or no understanding. Then write about this desire, using any examples you can from your reading or experience. You might begin by looking at old wives' tales or adages, proverbs, and superstitions to see just how much sense they actually make.

3

Remembering

The readings in this chapter are all accounts of past experiences. Each writer has used the memory of a past event to explain a discovery about life. All these experiences center on chance discoveries made while the writer was occupied with some physical activity such as playing a game, fishing and boating, packing for a trip, digging a ditch, or rummaging in a bureau drawer. Being older and wiser doesn't lessen the impact of these remembered moments. Rather, the experienced adult can look back at these moments and see them as formative and decisive, something not possible to do at the time the experiences take place.

Vladimir Nabokov recalls his bold cousin Yuri, sophisticated, even a little world weary in adolescence, as he himself was not, and daring beyond young Nabokov's wildest dreams. Remembering Yuri, Nabokov remembers himself, and concludes that people who lack judgment may be wonderful fun but they run the risk of dying young.

E. B. White recalls returning to the lake where he spent boyhood summers, being reminded there of the passing of time and with it approaching death. He takes his young son along and sometimes imagines the boy is himself as a child while he is his own father.

When Margaret Mead makes her first field trip, she recalls, she is so poorly prepared that only innocence and curiosity can outweigh the need for such material possessions as decent clothes and a good reading lamp. Later, the mature Mead remembers this moment and understands that her innocence and curiosity were what made her field work possible.

The summer job that Richard Rodriguez remembers teaches him a truth about himself, that although he would like to pretend he is a Mexican fieldhand, he is really an American middle-class college man. Once he knows this, he can literally accept his own skin.

And the child Eudora Welty, curious about where babies come from, accidentally discovers the death of a baby brother and the near-death of her mother. That her mother can talk more easily about death than about life becomes meaningful to the child who, even then, notices life as a writer does.

Vladimir Nabokov

Vladimir Nabokov (1899–1977) was born in St. Petersburg—now Leningrad—to an aristocratic family of landowners. He was educated in England at Cambridge University, where he studied Romance languages. Forced to abandon his homeland after the Russian Revolution in 1917, Nabokov lived in Berlin and then Paris before coming to the United States. He spent several years here teaching Russian literature and creative writing at various universities. A lepidopterist as well as novelist, he has had several species of butterflies and moths named for him, and he was once a Fellow of Harvard's Museum of Comparative Zoology. He has written many novels in English, which he learned as a child, as well as an autobiography, *Speak, Memory*, from which the selection here comes. In this piece, we find out about his fabulous cousin Yuri. We also learn about young Vladimir.

Cousin Yuri

We shall now meet my cousin Yuri, a thin, sallow-faced boy with a round cropped head and luminous gray eyes. The son of divorced parents, with no tutor to look after him, a town boy with no country home, he was in many respects different from me. He spent his winters in Warsaw, with his father, Baron Evgeniy Rausch von Traubenberg, its military governor, and his summers at Batovo or Vyra, unless taken abroad by his mother, my eccentric Aunt Nina, to dull Central European spas, where she went for long solitary walks leaving him to the care of messenger boys and chambermaids. In the country, Yuri got up late, and I did not see him before my return to lunch, after four or five hours of butterfly hunting. From his earliest boyhood, he was absolutely fearless, but was squeamish and wary of "natural history,"

83

could not make himself touch wriggly things, could not endure the
amusing emprisoned tickle of a small frog groping about in one's fist
like a person, or the discreet, pleasantly cool, rhythmically undulating   *
caress of a caterpillar ascending one's bare shin. He collected little   *
soldiers of painted lead—these meant nothing to me but he knew
their uniforms as well as I did different butterflies. He did not play
any ball games, was incapable of pitching a stone properly, and could
not swim, but had never told me he could not, and one day, as we
were trying to cross the river by walking over a jam of pine logs afloat
near a sawmill, he nearly got drowned when a particularly slippery
bole started to plop and revolve under his feet.   *

   We had first become aware of each other around Christmas 1904
(I was five and a half, he seven), in Wiesbaden: I remember him
coming out of a souvenir shop and running toward me with a breloque,
an inch-long little pistol of silver, which he was anxious to show
me—and suddenly sprawling on the sidewalk but not crying when he
picked himself up, unmindful of a bleeding knee and still clutching his
minuscule weapon. In the summer of 1909 or 1910, he enthusiastically
initiated me into the dramatic possibilities of the Mayne Reid books.
He had read them in Russian (being in everything save surname much
more Russian than I) and, when looking for a playable plot, was prone
to combine them with Fenimore Cooper and his own fiery inventions.
I viewed our games with greater detachment and tried to keep to the
script. The staging took place generally in the park of Batovo, where
the trails were even more tortuous and trappy than those of Vyra.
For our mutual manhunts we used spring pistols that ejected, with
considerable force, pencil-long sticks (from the brass tips of which we
had manfully twisted off the protective rubber suction cups). Later
came airguns of various types, which shot wax pellets or small tufted
darts, with nonlethal, but often quite painful consequences. In 1912,
the impressive mother-of-pearl plated revolver he arrived with was
calmly taken away and locked up by my tutor Lenski, but not before   *
we had blown to pieces a shoebox lid (in prelude to the real thing,
an ace), which we had been holding up by turns at a gentlemanly
distance in a green avenue where a duel was rumored to have been
fought many dim years ago. The following summer he was away in
Switzerland with his mother—and soon after his death (in 1919),

upon revisiting the same hotel and getting the same rooms they had occupied that July, she thrust her hand into the recesses of an armchair in quest of a fallen hairpin and brought up a tiny cuirassier, unhorsed but with bandy legs still compressing an invisible charger.

When he arrived for a week's visit in June 1914 (now sixteen and a half to my fifteen, and the interval was beginning to tell), the first thing he did, as soon as we found ourselves alone in the garden, was to take out casually an "ambered" cigarette from a smart silver *
case on the gilt inside of which he bade me observe the formula 3 × 4 = 12 engraved in memory of the three nights he had spent, at last, with Countess G. He was now in love with an old general's young wife in Helsingfors and a captain's daughter in Gatchina. I witnessed with a kind of despair every new revelation of his man-of-the-world style. "Where can I make some rather private calls?" he *
asked. So I led him past the five poplars and the old dry well (out of which we had been rope-hauled by three frightened gardeners only a couple of years before) to a passage in the servants' wing where the cooing of pigeons came from an inviting windowsill and where there hung on the sun-stamped wall the remotest and oldest of our countryhouse telephones, a bulky boxlike contraption which had to be clangorously cranked up to educe a small-voiced operator. Yuri was now even more relaxed and sociable than the mustanger of former *
years. Sitting on a deal table against the wall and dangling his long legs, he chatted with the servants (something I was not supposed to do, and did not know how to do)—with an aged footman with sideburns whom I had never seen grin before or with a kitchen flirt, of whose bare neck and bold eyes I became aware only then. After Yuri had concluded his third long-distance conversation (I noticed with a blend of relief and dismay how awful his French was), we walked down to the village grocery which otherwise I never dreamed of visiting, let alone buying there a pound of black-and-white sunflower seeds. Throughout our return stroll, among the late afternoon butterflies that were preparing to roost, we munched and spat, he showing me how to perform it conveyer-wise: split the seed open between the right-side back teeth, ease out the kernel with the tongue, spit out the husk halves, move the smooth kernel to the leftside molars, and munch there, while the next seed which in the meantime has already

been cracked on the right, is being processed in its turn. Speaking of right, he admitted he was a staunch "monarchist" (of a romantic rather than political nature) and went on to deplore my alleged (and perfectly abstract) "democratism." He recited samples of his fluent album poetry and proudly remarked that he had been complimented by Dilanov-Tomski, a fashionable poet (who favored Italian epigraphs and sectional titles, such as "Songs of Lost Love," "Nocturnal Urns," and so on), for the striking "long" rhyme *"vnemlyu múze ya"* ("I hearken to the Muse") and *"lyubvi kontúziya"* ("love's contusion"), which I countered with my best (and still unused) find: *"zápoved"'* (commandment) and *"posápivat"'* (to sniffle). He was boiling with anger over Tolstoy's dismissal of the art of war and burning with admiration for Prince Andrey Bolkonski—for he had just discovered *War and Peace* which I had read for the first time when I was eleven (in Berlin, on a Turkish sofa, in our somberly rococo Privatstrasse flat giving on a dark, damp back garden with larches and gnomes that have remained in that book, like an old postcard, forever).

I suddenly see myself in the uniform of an officers' training school: we are strolling again villageward, in 1916, and (like Maurice Gerald and doomed Henry Pointdexter) have exchanged clothes— Yuri is wearing my white flannels and striped tie. During the short week he stayed that year we devised a singular entertainment which I have not seen described anywhere. There was a swing in the center of a small circular playground surrounded by jasmins, at the bottom of our garden. We adjusted the ropes in such a way as to have the green swingboard pass just a couple of inches above one's forehead and nose if one lay supine on the sand beneath. One of us would start the fun by standing on the board and swinging with increasing momentum; the other would lie down with the back of his head on a marked spot, and from what seemed an enormous height the swinger's board would swish swiftly above the supine one's face. And three years later, as   * a cavalry officer in Denikin's army, he was killed fighting the Reds in northern Crimea. I saw him dead in Yalta, the whole front of his skull pushed back by the impact of several bullets, which had hit him like the iron board of a monstrous swing, when having outstripped his detachment he was in the act of recklessly attacking alone a Red machine-gun nest. Thus was quenched his lifelong thirst for intrepid

conduct in battle, for that ultimate gallant gallop with drawn pistol *
or unsheathed sword. Had I been competent to write his epitaph, I
might have summed up matters by saying—in richer words than I can
muster here—that all emotions, all thoughts, were governed in Yuri
by one gift: a sense of honor equivalent, morally, to absolute pitch.

Thinking about Writing

Words

Powerful words both depend on and help shape their context. In
what way does each word in the list below depend on its context for
strength? What does each contribute to its context? Can you think of
any other word the author might have used in its place? How does the
word strike you, and how do you respond to the sentence or passage
because of the word?

dull
discreet
caress
plop
calmly
casually
rather private
mustanger
swish swiftly
gallant gallop

Thinking

1. Nabokov tells us that Yuri was "in many respects different from
   me," and then, by describing Yuri, he also describes himself. For
   example, when little Yuri falls down he doesn't cry, so we may
   assume that under the same circumstances little Vladimir would
   most likely have burst into tears. What else do we know about
   Nabokov by reading his description of Yuri? What do you think

Nabokov is telling us about himself when he says of Yuri's sense of honor that it was "equivalent, morally, to absolute pitch"?

2. Why is comparing himself to, and contrasting himself with Yuri not, finally, enough to make a compelling piece of writing? What conclusion has Nabokov drawn, after he has shown the similarities and differences between the two boys?

3. The author tells us that Yuri was fearless yet squeamish. How does he illustrate this statement? What do you think is the difference between fearlessness and lack of squeamishness? How can one person be both fearless and squeamish?

4. Why was the author so relieved at Yuri's bad French? What can you assume about the author's French?

Writing

1. Write about someone with whom you grew up, someone who was roughly your age but different from you in many ways. What circumstances put you two together? How could you have spent time together if, in fact, you were so unlike? Was it a case of mutual tolerance, or were your basic similarities stronger than your apparent differences? How were you similar? Did you finally drift apart or do you still see each other?

2. Yuri was fearless, yet squeamish. Write about some anomaly in your own character or in that of someone you know which may surprisingly contrast with another trait. What do you think accounts for each trait? In what ways can you illustrate each trait?

3. What was your favorite creative game when you were a child? What was its inspiration? Write about how your game evolved. What were its limitations or rules? Was it a game that had to be won, or was it a "situation" game that gave pleasure without needing a winner? Did it depend on the weather? Did you exclude anyone? What do you think playing taught you about your friends? About yourself?

    Write about your game. You might want to begin your essay by discussing the value of children's games, generally, and what we gain from pretending.

4. Young Vladimir was happy about Yuri's bad French. Have you ever found—with relief—one "redeeming fault" in someone you knew who otherwise would have been unbearably perfect? Write about this person and the effect on you of discovering a fault among many virtues. In what way did the fault help make the person more human?

E. B. White

E. B. White (1899–1985) was born in Mount Ver-
non, New York, and educated at Cornell University.
He served in the army during World War I and immediately after the war began his writing career. Today,
White is remembered for three notable achievements: one
is his long association as contributing editor with *The
New Yorker* magazine; another is his revision of William
Strunk's *Elements of Style*; and the third is his remarkable talent for writing children's stories—*Charlotte's Web*,
Stuart Little, and *The Trumpet of the Swan*. In the selection here, from *Essays of E. B. White*, he contemplates
mortality. Slipping into the persona of his father, White
for the moment sees his own son as the child White himself was once. This deliberate shifting of roles becomes a
reminder of time and, of course, death.

Once More
to the Lake

One summer, along about 1904, my father rented a camp on
a lake in Maine and took us all there for the month of August. We
all got ringworm from some kittens and had to rub Pond's Extract on
our arms and legs night and morning, and my father rolled over in
a canoe with all his clothes on; but outside of that the vacation was
a success and from then on none of us ever thought there was any
place in the world like that lake in Maine. We returned summer after
summer—always on August 1 for one month. I have since become
a salt-water man, but sometimes in summer there are days when the
restlessness of the tides and the fearful cold of the sea water and the
incessant wind that blows across the afternoon and into the evening

make me wish for the placidity of a lake in the woods. A few weeks ago this feeling got so strong I bought myself a couple of bass hooks and a spinner and returned to the lake where we used to go, for a week's fishing and to revisit old haunts.

I took along my son, who had never had any fresh water up his nose and who had seen lily pads only from train windows. On the journey over to the lake I began to wonder what it would be like. I wondered how time would have marred this unique, this holy spot—the coves and streams, the hills that the sun set behind, the camps and the paths behind the camps. I was sure that the tarred road would have found it out, and I wondered in what other ways it would be desolated. It is strange how much you can remember about   *
places like that once you allow your mind to return into the grooves that lead back. You remember one thing, and that suddenly reminds you of another thing. I guess I remembered clearest of all the early mornings, when the lake was cool and motionless, remembered how the bedroom smelled of the lumber it was made of and of the wet woods whose scent entered through the screen. The partitions in the camp were thin and did not extend clear to the top of the rooms, and as I was always the first up I would dress softly so as not to wake the others, and sneak out into the sweet outdoors and start out in the canoe, keeping close along the shore in the long shadows of the pines. I remembered being very careful never to rub my paddle against the gunwale for fear of disturbing the stillness of the cathedral.   *

The lake had never been what you would call a wild lake. There were cottages sprinkled around the shores, and it was in farming country although the shores of the lake were quite heavily wooded. Some of the cottages were owned by nearby farmers, and you would live at the shore and eat your meals at the farmhouse. That's what our family did. But although it wasn't wild, it was a fairly large and undisturbed lake and there were places in it that, to a child at least, seemed infinitely remote and primeval.

I was right about the tar: it led to within half a mile of the shore. But when I got back there, with my boy, and we settled into a camp near a farmhouse and into the kind of summertime I had known, I could tell that it was going to be pretty much the same as it had been before—I knew it, lying in bed the first morning smelling the bedroom and hearing the boy sneak quietly out and go off along the shore in a boat. I began to sustain the illusion that he was I, and therefore, by simple transposition, that I was my father. This sensation persistently kept cropping up all the time we were there. It was not an entirely new feeling, but in this setting it grew much stronger. I seemed to be living a dual existence. I would be in the middle of some simple act, I would be picking up a bait box or laying down a table fork, or I would be saying something and suddenly it would be not I but my father who was saying the words or making the gesture. It gave me a creepy sensation.

We went fishing the first morning. I felt the same damp moss covering the worms in the bait can, and saw the dragonfly alight on * the tip of my rod as it hovered a few inches from the surface of the water. It was the arrival of this fly that convinced me beyond any doubt that everything was as it always had been, that the years were a mirage and that there had been no years. The small waves were the same, chucking the rowboat under the chin as we fished at anchor, and the boat was the same boat, the same color green and the ribs broken in the same places, and under the floorboards the same fresh water leavings and debris—the dead helgramite, the wisps of moss, the rusty discarded fishhook, the dried blood from yesterday's catch. We stared silently at the tips of our rods, at the dragonflies that came and went. I lowered the tip of mine into the water, tentatively, pensively dislodging the fly, which darted two feet away, poised, darted two feet back, and came to rest again a little farther up the rod. There had been no years between the ducking of this dragonfly and the other one—the one that was part of memory. I looked at the boy, who was silently watching his fly, and it was my hands that held his rod, my eyes watching. I felt dizzy and didn't know which rod I was at the end of.

We caught two bass, hauling them in briskly as though they were mackerel, pulling them over the side of the boat in a businesslike manner without any landing net, and stunning them with a blow on the back of the head. When we got back for a swim before lunch, the lake was exactly where we had left it, the same number of inches from the dock, and there was only the merest suggestion of a breeze. This seemed an utterly enchanted sea, this lake you could leave to its own devices for a few hours and come back to, and find that it

had not stirred, this constant and trustworthy body of water. In the shallows, the dark, water-soaked sticks and twigs, smooth and old, were undulating in clusters on the bottom against the clean ribbed sand, and the track of the mussel was plain. A school of minnows swam by, each minnow with its small individual shadow, doubling the attendance, so clear and sharp in the sunlight. Some of the other campers were in swimming, along the shore, one of them with a cake of soap, and the water felt thin and clear and unsubstantial. Over the years there had been this person with the cake of soap, this cultist,   *
and here he was. There had been no years.

Up to the farmhouse to dinner through the teeming dusty field, the road under our sneakers was only a two-track road. The middle track was missing, the one with the marks of the hooves and the splotches of dried, flaky manure. There had always been three tracks to choose from in choosing which track to walk in; now the choice was narrowed down to two. For a moment I missed terribly the middle alternative. But the way led past the tennis court, and something about the way it lay there in the sun reassured me; the tape had loosened along the backline, the alleys were green with plantains and other weeds, and the net (installed in June and removed in September) sagged in the dry noon, and the whole place steamed with midday heat and hunger and emptiness. There was a choice of pie for dessert, and one was blueberry and one was apple, and the waitresses were the same country girls, there having been no passage of time, only the illusion of it as in a dropped curtain—the waitresses were still fifteen; their hair had been washed, that was the only difference— they had been to the movies and seen the pretty girls with the clean hair.

Summertime, oh, summertime, pattern of life indelible with fade-proof lake, the wood unshatterable, the pasture with the sweet-   *
fern and the juniper forever and ever, summer without end; this was the background, and the life along the shore was the design, the cottages with their innocent and tranquil design, their tiny docks with the flagpole and the American flag floating against the white clouds in the blue sky, the little paths over the roots of the trees leading from camp to camp and the paths leading back to the outhouses and the can of lime for sprinkling, and at the souvenir counters at the

store the miniature birch-bark canoes and the postcards that showed things looking a little better than they looked. This was the American family at play, escaping the city heat, wondering whether the newcomers in the camp at the head of the cove were "common" or "nice," wondering whether it was true that the people who drove up for Sunday dinner at the farmhouse were turned away because there wasn't enough chicken.

It seemed to me, as I kept remembering all this, that those times and those summers had been infinitely precious and worth saving. There had been jollity and peace and goodness. The arriving (at the beginning of August) had been so big a business in itself, at the railway station the farm wagon drawn up, the first smell of the pine-laden air, the first glimpse of the smiling farmer, and the great importance of the trunks and your father's enormous authority in such matters, and the feel of the   *
wagon under you for the long ten-mile haul, and at the top of the last long hill catching the first view of the lake after eleven months of not seeing this cherished body of water. The shouts and cries of the other campers when they saw you, and the trunks to be unpacked, to give up their rich burden. (Arriving was less exciting nowadays, when you sneaked up in your car and parked it under a tree near the camp and took out the bags and in five minutes it was all over, no fuss, no loud wonderful fuss about trunks.)

Peace and goodness and jollity. The only thing that was wrong now, really, was the sound of the place, an unfamiliar nervous sound of the outboard motors. This was the note that jarred, the one thing that would sometimes break the illusion and set the years moving. In those other summertimes all motors were inboard; and when they were at a little distance, the noise they made was a sedative, an ingredient of summer sleep. They were one-cylinder and two-cylinder engines, and some were make-and-break and some were jump-spark, but they all made a sleepy sound across the lake. The one-lungers throbbed and fluttered, and the twin-cylinder ones purred and purred, and that was a quiet sound, too. But now the campers all had outboards. In the daytime, in the hot mornings, these motors made a petulant, irritable sound; at night in the still evening when the afterglow lit the water, they whined about one's ears like mosquitoes. My boy loved our rented outboard, and his great desire was to achieve single-handed mastery over it, and authority, and he soon learned the trick of choking it a little (but not too much), and the adjustment of the needle valve. Watching him I would remember the things you could do with the old one-cylinder engine with the heavy flywheel, how you could have it eating out of your hand if you got really close to it spiritually. Motorboats in those days didn't have clutches, and you would make a landing by shutting off the motor at the proper time and coasting in with a dead rudder. But there was a way of reversing them, if you learned the trick, by cutting the switch and putting it on again exactly on the final dying revolution of the flywheel, so that it would kick back against compression and begin reversing. Approaching a dock in a strong following breeze, it was difficult to slow up sufficiently by the ordinary coasting method, and if a boy felt he had complete mastery over his motor, he was tempted to keep it running beyond its time and then reverse it a few feet from the dock. It took a cool nerve, because if you threw the switch a twentieth of a second too soon you would catch the flywheel when it still had speed enough to go up past center, and the boat would leap ahead, charging bull-fashion at the dock.

We had a good week at the camp. The bass were biting well and the sun shone endlessly, day after day. We would be tired at night and lie down in the accumulated heat of the little bedrooms after the long hot day and the breeze would stir almost imperceptibly outside and the smell of the swamp drift in through the rusty screens. Sleep would come easily and in the morning the red squirrel would be on the roof, tapping out his gay routine. I kept remembering everything, lying in bed in the mornings—the small steamboat that had a long rounded stern like the lip of a Ubangi, and how quietly she ran on the moonlight sails, when the older boys played their mandolins and the girls sang and we ate doughnuts dipped in sugar, and how sweet the music was on the water in the shining night, and what it had felt like to think about girls then. After breakfast we would go up to the store and the things were in the same place—the minnows in a bottle, the plugs and spinners disarranged and pawed over by the youngsters from the boys' camp, the Fig Newtons and the Beeman's gum. Outside, the road was tarred and cars stood in front of the store. Inside, all was just as it had always been, except there was more Coca-Cola and not so much Moxie and root beer and birch beer and sarsaparilla. We would walk out with the bottle of pop apiece and sometimes the pop would backfire up our noses and hurt. We explored the streams, quietly, where the turtles slid off the sunny logs and dug their way into the soft bottom; and we lay on the town wharf and fed worms to the tame bass. Everywhere we went I had trouble making out which was I, the one walking at my side, the one walking in my pants.

One afternoon while we were at that lake a thunderstorm came up. It was like the revival of an old melodrama that I had seen long ago with childish awe. The second-act climax of the drama of the electrical disturbance over a lake in America had not changed in any important respect. This was the big scene, still the big scene. The whole thing was so familiar, the first feeling of oppression and heat and a general air around camp of not wanting to go very far away. In midafternoon (it was all the same) a curious darkening of the sky, and a lull in everything that had made life tick; and then the way the boats suddenly swung the other way at their moorings with the coming of a breeze out of the new quarter, and the premonitory rumble. Then the kettle drum, then the snare, then the bass drum and cymbals, then crackling light against the dark, and the gods grinning and licking their chops in the hills. Afterward the calm, the rain steadily rustling in the calm lake, the return of light and hope and spirits, and the campers running out in joy and relief to go swimming in the rain, their bright cries perpetuating the deathless joke about how they were   *
getting simply drenched, and the children screaming with delight at the new sensation of bathing in the rain, and the joke about getting drenched linking the generations in a strong indestructible chain. And the comedian who waded in carrying an umbrella.

When the others went swimming my son said he was going in, too. He pulled his dripping trunks from the line where they had hung all through the shower and wrung them out. Languidly, and with no thought of going in, I watched him, his hard little body, skinny and bare, saw him wince slightly as he pulled up around his vitals the small, soggy, icy garment. As he buckled the swollen belt, suddenly my groin felt the chill of death.

Thinking about Writing

Words

Powerful words both depend on and help shape their context. In what way does each word in the list below depend on its context for strength? What does each contribute to its context? Can you think of any other word the author might have used in its place? How does the word strike you, and how do you respond to the sentence or passage because of the word?

desolated
cathedral
the dragonfly
cultist
fade-proof
your
deathless

Thinking

1. Why do you imagine White returned to the lake with his son rather than taking a friend along or even going alone? How do you think he would have reacted if he had been instead with a friend or alone? What purpose does his son's presence serve?
2. Some things had changed for White, while others had remained the same. Which do you think made more impression on White, and why do you say this? When you see a place again after an absence, which impresses you more, the sameness or the change?
3. Much of this account is centered on physical activities such as fishing and paddling a canoe. White has completely ignored conversations, specific people, even his son's name and age. Why do you think he has done this? Would you have liked to know what the boy was called or how he looked? As you were reading, did you "see" the boy? What did your picture of the boy look like?
4. After describing the arrival by farm wagon, why does White use the wording "when you sneaked up in your car" to describe the

arrival now? What do you learn about White, from these words, and from his saying, "it was all over, no fuss, no loud wonderful fuss"?

Writing

1. Write a paper about returning to a place like this lake, but imagine that the account is told by someone returning to the place alone. How could you convey the sense of time elapsing without the father-son relation? (See Orwell's account of his return to a changed city in the essay "Barcelona," in chapter 7, for another treatment of this theme.)
2. Write an account of a return visit to some old, familiar place. If you wanted to return, why was remembering the place not enough to satisfy your mind? What happened when you actually went back? Did you go back in time and become the person you were before? (See Joan Didion's comments about her former selves in "On Keeping a Notebook" in chapter 8.) Ask yourself if the return has changed you from the person you were just before the return.
3. Have you ever been made aware suddenly of the passing of time, of your being no longer a child or somehow "too old" for something, an article of clothing, an occupation, a piece of music? Did some particular experience trigger your awareness? Write about this realization and how it came to you. Did your recognition involve other people, or did it come to you alone?
4. Write an essay that compares the modern way of doing something with the old way. What are the gains? The losses? (See Alice Waters's comments on efficiency in "What I Believe about Cooking" in chapter 1.) Perhaps you know an older person who clings to some outmoded object or to what you consider an old, inefficient way of performing a task. Try to include some comment on the pleasure that "inefficiency" affords. In what ways does efficiency affect our relationships with our materials and with each other?

Margaret Mead

Margaret Mead (1901–78) was born in Philadelphia and educated at DePauw University, Barnard College, and Columbia University. Mead began studying anthropology when the field was relatively new. Before her time, people had measured another group primarily in terms of its economy, considering the group itself as prehistoric, simple folk who didn't know as much as "civilized" people did. Mead, however, began to define cultural anthropology as the study of the many facets that shape a group's nature, including its language, its economy, its tribal and national character, its ecology, its sexuality, and its competition and cooperation. In the selection here, from her autobiography *Blackberry Winter*, Mead remarks on how poorly prepared but how enthusiastic she was when she set out on her first field trip.

Preparing for the Field

When I sailed for Samoa, I realized only very vaguely what a commitment to field work and writing about field work meant. My decision to become an anthropologist was based in part on my belief that a scientist, even one who had no great and special gift such as a great artist must have, could make a useful contribution to knowledge. I had responded also to the sense of urgency that had been conveyed to me by Professor Boas and Ruth Benedict. Even in remote parts of the world ways of life about which nothing was known were vanishing before the onslaught of modern civilization. The work of recording these unknown ways of life had to be done now—*now*—or they would *

99

be lost forever. Other things could wait, but not this most urgent task. All this came to a head at the Toronto meetings in 1924, where I was the youngest participant and everyone else had talked about "my people" and I had no people to talk about. From that time on I was determined to go to the field, not at some leisurely chosen later date, but immediately—as soon as I had completed the necessary preliminary steps.

But I really did not know much about field work. The course on methods that Professor Boas taught was not about field work. It was about theory—how material could be organized to support or to call in question some theoretical point. Ruth Benedict had spent a summer working with a group of quite acculturated Indians in California, where she had taken her mother along for a vacation, and she had worked in Zuñi. I had read Ruth's descriptions of the landscape, of how the Zuñi looked, of the fierceness of the bedbugs and the difficulties of managing food, but I knew little about how she went about her work. Professor Boas always spoke of the Kwakiutl as "my dear friends," but this was not followed by anything that helped me to know what it was like to live among them.

When I agreed to study the adolescent girl and Professor Boas consented to my doing this field work in Samoa, I had a half hour's instruction in which Professor Boas told me that I must be willing to seem to waste time just sitting about and listening, but that I must not ✳ waste time doing ethnography, that is, studying the culture as a whole. Fortunately, many people—missionaries, jurists, government officials, and old-fashioned ethnographers—had been to Samoa, and so the temptation to "waste time" on ethnography would be less. During the summer he also wrote me a letter in which he once more cautioned me to be careful of my health and discussed the problem he had set me.

For the rest, there was G. Stanley Hall, who had written a huge ✳ book on adolescence in which, equating stages of growth with stages of culture, he had discussed his belief that each growing child recapitulated the history of the human race. There were also the assumptions set forth in textbooks, mainly derived from German theory, about puberty as a period of storm and stress. At that time puberty and adolescence were firmly equated in everyone's thinking. Only much later, students of child development began to say that there was perhaps a "first adolescence" around the age of six and a second crisis at puberty and that adolescence could be prolonged into the twenties and might in some sense reappear in adults in their forties.

My training in psychology had given me ideas about the use of samples, tests, and systematic inventories of behavior. I had also some very slight experience of social case work. My aunt Fanny was working at the Juvenile Protective Association at Hull House, in Chicago, and one summer I had sat on the floor and read their records. This had given me an idea of what the social context of individual behavior was—how one had to look at the household and place the household in the setting of the community.

I knew that I would have to learn the language. But I did not know anyone who was colloquially proficient in the language of the people they studied except missionaries, or the children of missionaries, turned ethnologists.

The expectation that we may at any time be confronted by some as yet unrecorded mode of behavior is the basis on which anthropologists often clash with psychologists, whose theories have developed out of their efforts to be "scientific" and out of their skepticism   * about philosophical constructs. It is also the basis of our clash with economists, political scientists, and sociologists, to the extent that they use the model of our own social arrangements in their studies of other societies.

The tough treatment given us by Professor Boas shook us up, prepared us for the unexpected, and be it said, the extremely difficult. But we did not learn how to organize work on a strange new language to the point at which a grammar could be worked out on the basis of which we could learn to speak the language.

Our training equipped us with a sense of respect for the people we would study. They were full human beings with a way of life that could be compared with our own and with the culture of any other people. No one spoke of the Kwakiutl or the Zuñi—or any other people—as savages or barbarians. They were, it was true, primitive; that is, their culture had developed without script and was maintained without the use of script. That was all the term "primitive" meant to us. We were carefully taught that there was no regular progression from simple "primitive" languages to complex "civilized" languages; that, in fact, many primitive languages were far more complex than some written ones. We were taught also that whereas some art styles had been elaborated from simple designs, other art styles were reduced to simpler forms from originally more elaborate ones.

We had, of course, had lectures on evolution. We knew that it had taken millions of years for the first human-like creatures to develop language, to make tools, to work out forms of social organization that could be taught to the next generation, for all these things, once acquired, had to be taught and learned. But we went to the field not to look for earlier forms of human life, but for forms that were different from those known to us—different because particular groups of primitive people had lived in isolation from the mainstreams of the great civilizations. We did not make the mistake of thinking, as Freud, for example, was misled into thinking, that the primitive peoples living on remote atolls, in desert places, in the depths of jungles, or in the Arctic north were equivalent to our ancestors. True, we might learn from them how long it took to chop down a tree with a stone axe or even how much of the food supply women may have contributed in societies based on male hunting. But these isolated peoples were not in the line of our ancestors. Obviously our ancestors had been located at various crossroads where peoples met and exchanged ideas and traded goods. They had crossed mountains, they had sailed the seas and returned. They had borrowed and copied. They had stimulated and had been stimulated by the discoveries and inventions of other peoples to an extent that was not possible among peoples who lived in much greater isolation.

We knew that in our field work we could expect to find differences—differences far greater than those we would expect to find among the related cultures of the Western world or in the lives of people at different periods in our own history. The record of what we found out about the way of life of each primitive people we studied was to be our principal contribution to the accumulating store of exact knowledge about the world.

As far as anthropology was concerned, this was my intellectual equipment. I had, of course, acquired some knowledge of the techniques in use for categorizing, for example, the uses a people made of their natural resources or the forms of social organizations they had developed. And I had some practice in analyzing the observations that had been made by other fieldworkers.

But nobody really asked what were the young fieldworker's skills and aptitudes—whether he had, for instance, the ability to observe and record accurately or the intellectual discipline to keep at the job, day after day, when there was no one to supervise, no one to compare notes with, to confess delinquencies to, or even to boast to on an especially successful day. No one considered whether we could stand loneliness. No one inquired how we would get along with the colonial or military or Indian Service officials through whom we would have to work; and no one offered us any advice.

. . . Field work is a very difficult thing to do. To do it well, one has to sweep one's mind clear of every presupposition, even those about other cultures in the same part of the world in which one is working. Ideally, even the appearance of a house should come to one as a new, fresh impression. In a sense it should come to one as a surprise that there are houses and that they are square or round or oval, that they do or do not have walls, that they let in the sun or keep out the wind or rain, that people do or do not cook or eat in a dwelling house. In the field one can take nothing for granted. For as soon as one does, one cannot see what is before one's eyes as fresh and distinctive, and when one treats what is new merely as a variant of something already known, this may lead one far astray. Seeing a house as bigger or smaller, grander or meaner, more or less watertight than some other kind of house one already knows about cuts one off from discovering what *this* house is in the minds of those who live in it. Later, when one has come to know the new culture, everything has to be reassimilated into what is already known about other peoples living in that area, into our knowledge about primitive peoples, and into our knowledge about all human beings, *so far*. But the point of * going to the field at all is to extend further what is already known, and so there is little value merely in identifying new versions of the familiar when we might, instead, find something wholly new. But to clear one's mind of presuppositions is a very hard thing to do and, without years of practice, all but impossible when one is working in one's own culture or in another that is very close to it.

. . . All this is important, but it gives no sense of what the day-to-day tasks will be. For there is no way of knowing in advance what the people will be like or even what they will look like. There may be photographs of them, but by the time one arrives they may look different. The summer I worked among the Omaha Indians, the girls were getting their first permanent waves—something I could not have foreseen. One doesn't know what the particular officials, the planters, the police, the missionaries, or the traders will be like. One doesn't know where one will live or what there will be to eat or whether it will turn out to be a good thing to have rubber boots, mosquito boots, sandals that keep one's feet cool, or woolen socks to absorb the sweat. So there is a great tendency—and when fieldworkers were poor there was a greater tendency—to take along as little as possible and to make very few plans.

When I set out for Samoa I had half a dozen cotton dresses (including two very pretty ones) for I had been told that silk rotted in the tropics. But when I arrived, I found that the Navy wives dressed in silk. I had a small strongbox in which to keep my money and papers, a small Kodak, and a portable typewriter. Although I had been married for two years, I had never stayed alone in a hotel and I had made only short journeys by train as far as the Middle West. Living in cities and small towns and in the Pennsylvania countryside, I had known a good many different kinds of Americans, but I had no idea of the kind of men who enlisted in the United States Navy in peacetime, nor did I know anything about the etiquette of naval life on an outstation. I had never been to sea.

At a party in Berkeley, where I stopped briefly on my way out, Professor Kroeber came and sat next to me on the floor and asked in   * a firmly sympathetic voice, "Have you got a good lamp?" I did not have any lamp at all. I had six large fat notebooks, some typing and carbon paper, and a flashlight. But no lamp.

Thinking about Writing

Words

Powerful words both depend on and help shape their context. In what way does each word in the list below depend on its context for strength? What does each contribute to its context? Can you think of

any other word the author might have used in its place? How does the word strike you, and how do you respond to the sentence or passage because of the word?

now — *now*
waste time
huge
"scientific"
so far
floor

Thinking

1. Why do you think Mead's professors sent her into the field so poorly prepared for the realities of life there? What advantages can you think of to going into a new situation with a minimum of prior knowledge? In what circumstances would you tell a friend who was going to experience something you already knew about, "I won't tell you any more," because you wanted the experience to be fresh? For example, would you tell the plot of a new movie? Would you try to describe the experience of wearing certain clothing or eating certain foods? How would you decide what to tell?

2. Although Mead is complaining here about not being prepared adequately for her first field trip, she doesn't seem self-pitying. What does her attitude seem to be? How does she convey her attitude to us?

3. At what point do you think Mead realized that she had been very poorly informed? How do you know that she realized this? Does the text tell you or are you extrapolating?

4. Do you feel a conflict between the idea of sweeping "one's mind clear of every presupposition" and being warned about conditions of life and research? Consider whether one can remain open to new insights if one is told what to expect.

Writing

1. Write about an experience for which you had been given minimal preparation and about which you had scant knowledge, much of

which may have proved to be false. In retrospect, do you wish you had been told nothing at all of what to expect, or do you wish you had been better informed? What was the price of your ignorance? What were the benefits, if any?

2. According to Mead, "Ideally, even the appearance of a house should come to one as a new, fresh impression." Describe a house or a building on campus (perhaps the chapel or the field house), trying to avoid reference to other houses or buildings. Consider its features as if you were a cultural anthropologist studying what the building "is in the minds of those who live in it" or use it. Thus, for example, you might describe the entrance as "a place through which people pass in order to. . ." In the same way, consider a window or an elevator.

Richard Rodriguez

Richard Rodriguez (b. 1944) was born in San Francisco and educated at Stanford University, Columbia University, the University of California, and the Warburg Institute of London University. The son of Mexican immigrants, Rodriguez spoke Spanish when he started school. His teachers urged his parents to make their children speak English so that they might adjust to American life as quickly as possible. Rodriguez's parents complied, and their children learned to speak English, even at home. So important was this new language acquisition to Rodriguez that he has become a vigorous opponent of bilingual education. Still, there is a price to be paid for rapid adjustment to a new life, and this price is some loss of ethnicity. In the selection here, Rodriguez considers the loss of ethnicity as he pretends that he is at heart really a *bracero*, a Mexican laborer, working on a construction site. The selection is part of his autobiography, *Hunger of Memory: The Education of Richard Rodriguez*.

Running in the Sun

I went to college at Stanford, attracted partly by its academic reputation, partly because it was the school rich people went to. I found myself on a campus with golden children of western America's * upper middle class. Many were students both ambitious for academic success *and* accustomed to leisured life in the sun. In the afternoon, they lay spread out, sunbathing in front of the library, reading Swift or Engels or Beckett. Others went by in convertibles, off to play tennis

107

or ride horses or sail. Beach boys dressed in tank-tops and shorts were my classmates in undergraduate seminars. Tall tan girls wearing white strapless dresses sat directly in front of me in lecture rooms. I'd study them, their physical confidence. I was still recognizably kin to the boy I had been. Less tortured perhaps. But still kin. At Stanford, it's true, I began to have something like a conventional sexual life. I don't think, however, that I really believed that the women I knew found me physically appealing. I continued to stay out of the sun. I didn't linger in mirrors. And I was the student at Stanford who remembered to notice the Mexican-American janitors and gardeners working on campus.

It was at Stanford, one day near the end of my senior year, that a friend told me about a summer construction job he knew was available. I was quickly alert. Desire uncoiled within me. My friend *
said that he knew I had been looking for summer employment. He knew I needed some money. Almost apologetically he explained: It was something I probably wouldn't be interested in, but a friend of his, a contractor, needed someone for the summer to do menial jobs. There would be lots of shoveling and raking and sweeping. Nothing too hard. But nothing more interesting either. Still, the pay would be good. Did I want it? Or did I know someone who did?

I did. Yes, I said, surprised to hear myself say it.

In the weeks following, friends cautioned that I had no idea how hard physical labor really is. ("You only *think* you know what it is like to shovel for eight hours straight.") Their objections seemed to me challenges. They resolved the issue. I became happy with my plan. I decided, however, not to tell my parents. I wouldn't tell my mother because I could guess her worried reaction. I would tell my father only after the summer was over, when I could announce that, after all, I did know what "real work" is like.

The day I met the contractor (a Princeton graduate, it turned out), he asked me whether I had done any physical labor before. "In high school, during the summer," I lied. And although he seemed to regard me with skepticism, he decided to give me a try. Several days later, expectant, I arrived at my first construction site. I would take off my shirt to the sun. And at last grasp desired sensation. No longer afraid. At last become like a *bracero.* "We need those tree stumps out of here by tomorrow," the contractor said. I started to work.

I labored with excitement that first morning—and all the days after. The work was harder than I could have expected. But it was never as tedious as my friends had warned me it would be. There was too much physical pleasure in the labor. Especially early in the day, I would be most alert to the sensations of movement and straining. Beginning around seven each morning (when the air was still damp but the scent of weeds and dry earth anticipated the heat of the sun), I would feel my body resist the first thrusts of the shovel. My arms, tightened by sleep, would gradually loosen; after only several minutes, sweat would gather in beads on my forehead and then—a short while later—I would feel my chest silky with sweat in the breeze. I would   *
return to my work. A nervous spark of pain would fly up my arm and settle to burn like an ember in the thick of my shoulder. An hour, two passed. Three. My whole body would assume regular movements; my shoveling would be described by identical, even movements. Even later in the day, my enthusiasm for primitive sensation would survive the heat and the dust and the insects pricking my back. I would strain wildly for sensation as the day came to a close. At three-thirty, quitting time, I would stand upright and slowly let my head fall back, luxuriating in the feeling of tightness relieved.

Some of the men working nearby would watch me and laugh. Two or three of the older men took the trouble to teach me the right way to use a pick, the correct way to shovel. "You're doing it wrong, too fucking hard," one man scolded. Then proceeded to show me— what persons who work with their bodies all their lives quickly learn— the most economical way to use one's body in labor.

"Don't make your back do so much work," he instructed. I stood impatiently listening, half listening, vaguely watching, then noticed his work-thickened fingers clutching the shovel. I was annoyed. I wanted to tell him that I enjoyed shoveling the wrong way. And I didn't want to learn the right way. I wasn't afraid of back pain. I liked the way my body felt sore at the end of the day.

I was about to, but, as it turned out, I didn't say a thing. Rather it was at that moment I realized that I was fooling myself if I expected a few weeks of labor to gain me admission to the world of the laborer. I would not learn in three months what my father had meant by "real work." I was not bound to this job; I could imagine its rapid conclusion. For me the sensations of exertion and fatigue could be savored. For my father or uncle, working at comparable jobs when they were my age, such sensations were to be feared. Fatigue took a different toll on their bodies—and minds.

It was, I know, a simple insight. But it was with this realization that I took my first step that summer toward realizing something even more important about the "worker." In the company of carpenters, electricians, plumbers, and painters at lunch, I would often sit quietly, observant. I was not shy in such company. I felt easy, pleased by the knowledge that I was casually accepted, my presence taken for granted by men (exotics) who worked with their hands. Some days the younger men would talk and talk about sex, and they would howl at women who drove by in cars. Other days the talk at lunchtime was subdued; men gathered in separate groups. It depended on who was around. There were rough, good-natured workers. Others were quiet. The more I remember that summer, the more I realize that there was no single *type* of worker. I am embarrassed to say I had not expected such diversity. I certainly had not expected to meet, for example, a plumber who was an abstract painter in his off hours and admired the work of Mark Rothko. Nor did I expect to meet so many workers with college diplomas. (They were the ones who were not surprised that I intended to enter graduate school in the fall.) I suppose what I really want to say here is painfully obvious, but I must say it nevertheless: The men of that summer were middle-class Americans. They certainly didn't constitute an oppressed society. Carefully completing their work sheets; talking about the fortunes of local football teams; planning Las Vegas vacations; comparing the gas mileage of various makes of campers—they were not *los pobres* my mother had spoken about.

On two occasions, the contractor hired a group of Mexican aliens. They were employed to cut down some trees and haul off debris. In all, there were six men of varying age. The youngest in his late twenties; the oldest (his father?) perhaps sixty years old. They came and they left in a single old truck. Anonymous men. They were never introduced to the other men at the site. Immediately upon their

arrival, they would follow the contractor's directions, start working—
rarely resting—seemingly driven by a fatalistic sense that work which
had to be done was best done as quickly as possible.

I watched them sometimes. Perhaps they watched me. The only
time I saw them pay me much notice was one day at lunchtime when I
was laughing with the other men. The Mexicans sat apart when they
ate, just as they worked by themselves. Quiet. I rarely heard them
say much to each other. All I could hear were their voices calling
out sharply to one another, giving directions. Otherwise, when they
stood briefly resting, they talked among themselves in voices too hard
to overhear.

The contractor knew enough Spanish, and the Mexicans—or at
least the oldest of them, their spokesman—seemed to know enough
English to communicate. But because I was around, the contractor
decided one day to make me his translator. (He assumed I could speak
Spanish.) I did what I was told. Shyly I went over to tell the Mexicans
that the *patrón* wanted them to do something else before they left for
the day. As I started to speak, I was afraid with my old fear that I
would be unable to pronounce the Spanish words. But it was a simple
instruction I had to convey. I could say it in phrases.

The dark sweating faces turned toward me as I spoke. They
stopped their work to hear me. Each nodded in response. I stood there.
I wanted to say something more. But what could I say in Spanish, even
if I could have pronounced the words right? Perhaps I just wanted
to engage them in small talk, to be assured of their confidence, our   *
familiarity. I thought for a moment to ask them where in Mexico they
were from. Something like that. And maybe I wanted to tell them (a
lie, if need be) that my parents were from the same part of Mexico.

I stood there.

Their faces watched me. The eyes of the man directly in front of
me moved slowly over my shoulder, and I turned to follow his glance
toward *el patrón* some distance away. For a moment I felt swept up
by that glance into the Mexicans' company. But then I heard one of
them returning to work. And then the others went back to work. I
left them without saying anything more.

When they had finished, the contractor went over to pay them
in cash. (He later told me that he paid them collectively—"for the

job," though he wouldn't tell me their wages. He said something quickly about the good rate of exchange "in their own country.") I can still hear the loudly confident voice he used with the Mexicans. It was the sound of the *gringo* I had heard as a very young boy. And I can still hear the quiet, indistinct sounds of the Mexican, the oldest, who replied. At hearing that voice I was sad for the Mexicans. Depressed by their vulnerability. Angry at myself. The adventure of the summer seemed suddenly ludicrous. I would not shorten the distance I felt from *los pobres* with a few weeks of physical labor. I would not become like them. They were different from me.

After that summer, a great deal—and not very much really— changed in my life. The curse of physical shame was broken by the sun; I was no longer ashamed of my body. No longer would I deny myself the pleasing sensations of my maleness. During those years when middle-class black Americans began to assert with pride, "Black is beautiful," I was able to regard my complexion without shame. I am today darker than I ever was as a boy. I have taken up the middle-class sport of long-distance running. Nearly every day now I run ten or fifteen miles, barely clothed, my skin exposed to the California winter rain and wind or the summer sun of late afternoon. The torso, the soccer player's calves and thighs, the arms of the twenty-year-old I never was, I possess now in my thirties. I study the youthful parody shape in the mirror: the stomach lipped tight by muscle; the shoulders rounded by chin-ups; the arms veined strong. This man. A man. I meet him. He laughs to see me, what I have become.

The dandy. I wear double-breasted Italian suits and custom-made *
English shoes. I resemble no one so much as my father—the man pictured in those honeymoon photos. At that point in life when he abandoned the dandy's posture, I assume it. At the point when my parents would not consider going on vacation, I register at the Hotel Carlyle in New York and the Plaza Athenée in Paris. I am as taken by the symbols of leisure and wealth as they were. For my parents, however, those symbols became taunts, reminders of all they could not achieve in one lifetime. For me those same symbols are reassuring reminders of public success. I tempt vulgarity to be reassured. I am

filled with the gaudy delight, the monstrous grace of the nouveau riche.

In recent years I have had occasion to lecture in ghetto high schools. There I see students of remarkable style and physical grace. (One can see more dandies in such schools than one ever will find in middle-class high schools.) There is not the look of casual assurance I saw students at Stanford display. Ghetto girls mimic high-fashion models. Their dresses are of bold, forceful color; their figures elegant, long; the stance theatrical. Boys wear shirts that grip at their overde-veloped muscular bodies. (Against a powerless future, they engage images of strength.) Bad nutrition does not yet tell. Great disappoint-ment, fatal to youth, awaits them still. For the moment, movements in school hallways are dancelike, a procession of postures in a sexual masque. Watching them, I feel a kind of envy. I wonder how different my adolescence would have been had I been free. . . . But no, it is my parents I see—their optimism during those years when they were entertained by Italian grand opera.

The registration clerk in London wonders if I have just been to Switzerland. And the man who carries my luggage in New York guesses the Caribbean. My complexion becomes a mark of my leisure. Yet no one would regard my complexion the same way if I entered such hotels through the service entrance. That is only to say that my complexion assumes its significance from the context of my life. My skin, in itself, means nothing. I stress the point because I know there are people who would label me "disadvantaged" because of my color. They make the same mistake I made as a boy, when I thought a disadvantaged life was circumscribed by particular occupations. That summer I worked in the sun may have made me physically indistinguishable from the Mexicans working nearby. (My skin was actually darker because, unlike them, I worked without wearing a shirt. By late August my hands were probably as tough as theirs.) But I was not one of *los pobres*. What made me different from them was an attitude of *mind*, my imagination of myself.

I do not blame my mother for warning me away from the sun when I was young. In a world where her brother had become an old man in his twenties because he was dark, my complexion was something to worry about. "Don't run in the sun," she warns me today. I run. In the end, my father was right—though perhaps he did not know how right or why—to say that I would never know what real work is. I will never know what he felt at his last factory job. If tomorrow I worked at some kind of factory, it would go differently for me. My long education would favor me. I could act as a public person—able to defend my interests, to unionize, to petition, to speak up—to challenge and demand. (I will never know what real work is.) I will never know what the Mexicans knew, gathering their shovels and ladders and saws.

Their silence stays with me now. The wages those Mexicans received for their labor were only a measure of their disadvantaged condition. Their silence is more telling. They lack a public identity. They remain profoundly alien. Persons apart. People lacking a union obviously, people without grounds. They depend upon the relative good will or fairness of their employers each day. For such people, lacking a better alternative, it is not such an unreasonable risk.

Their silence stays with me. I have taken these many words to describe its impact. Only: the quiet. Something uncanny about it. Its compliance. Vulnerability. Pathos. As I heard their truck rumbling away, I shuddered, my face mirrored with sweat. I had finally come face to face with *los pobres*.

Thinking about Writing

Words

Powerful words both depend on and help shape their context. In what way does each word in the list below depend on its context for strength? What does each contribute to its context? Can you think of any other word the author might have used in its place? How does the word strike you, and how do you respond to the sentence or passage because of the word?

golden
uncoiled
silky
our
dandy

Thinking

1. Why do you think Rodriguez entertained the romantic notion of being a *bracero*? Why do you suppose he could only play at doing physical labor? In what ways had his "long education" separated him irreversibly from manual labor?

2. In what way did Rodriguez, knowing the summer would end, have a safety net which allowed him to be content playing at being something he wasn't?

3. Where in the writing does Rodriguez let the reader know how he feels about receiving a "long education"? In what ways does he reveal how he sees both the advantage and the burden of such training?

4. How does Rodriguez describe making choices at the time in his life that he is writing about? Do you think that he is free to make choices or that he is a victim of circumstances and his family's wishes? What in the writing leads you to your views?

5. How does Rodriguez use words to tell the reader what he was *not*? What gives the reader the idea that he has finally found himself? At what moment do you finally feel certain that he knows who he is? What words and phrases tell you this?

6. Why do you think Rodriguez paints such a grim picture of the future for the students in the ghetto school? How do you feel about him when he says, "I wonder how different my adolescence would have been had I been free. . . ."?

Writing

1. Rodriguez has unified his writing by using the concept of color, in his case the desire of his family that he should ultimately succeed in life by having, among other qualities, light skin. (Elsewhere in his account he talks about his family's insistence that he speak English,

also with a view to his getting ahead.) How has Rodriguez used images of light and dark throughout this piece of writing? What is the effect of this language on the reader? What do we know of the author at the time of this episode through his use of such language? Why do you think he has finished the account as he has, in terms of light and dark? What does this tell us about the mature Rodriguez and the lesson he has learned about color?

Write an essay in which you examine the author's use of light and dark words and images, as he recounts coming to terms with himself.

2. After describing the students in the ghetto school, Rodriguez briefly wonders about his own adolescence. "But no," he says, returning to images of his parents, as if they have left their mark and their desires in him. How is Rodriguez ultimately like his parents, according to this account? Write an essay that shows, through the author's words, how the young Rodriguez circled around his parents and their life, moving out to taste something of his fantasy life and returning finally to the family mold as he realized that he was not one of the workers but the son of his parents.

3. We all have fantasies of one sort or another in which we are somehow grander than we are in real life. At the time that he writes about, Rodriguez felt that being a *bracero* was grander than being a middle-class college student. How was this fantasy important for Rodriguez? What does Rodriguez learn from having first entertained, then rejected, his fantasy? Why are such fantasies important to growing up?

Here are two possible ideas for writing about fantasy. First, you might write an essay that discusses the importance of "playing out" a fantasy in order to learn something and then consider how Rodriguez learns from his. Or, if you prefer, you might write an essay about the value of fantasy, recounting one of your own experiences as you learned something about yourself by "playing out" a fantasy.

Eudora Welty

Eudora Welty (b. 1909) was born and has lived most of her life in Jackson, Mississippi. She was educated at Mississippi State College for Women, the University of Wisconsin, and the Columbia School of Advertising. Author of short stories, novels, and novellas, Welty first worked for radio stations and newspapers. With a keen ear and eye for the speech patterns and social situations of people, she writes a visual, idiomatic prose that satisfies a reader's inner eye and ear. She has won numerous prizes for her work: the Pulitzer, the American Book Award, and a Gold Medal from the American Academy and Institute of Arts and Letters. The selection here is part of a longer work, *One Writer's Beginnings*, which originated in lectures Welty delivered at Harvard University. In this piece, she returns to her early childhood when, on the trail of where babies come from, she discovers death.

A Little Life

It was when my mother came out onto the sleeping porch to tell me goodnight that her trial came. The sudden silence in the double bed meant my younger brothers had both keeled over in sleep, and I in the single bed at my end of the porch would be lying electrified, waiting for this to be the night when she'd tell me what she'd promised for so long. Just as she bent to kiss me I grabbed her and asked: "Where do babies come from?"

My poor mother! But something saved her every time. Almost any night I put the baby question to her, suddenly, as if the whole outdoors exploded, Professor Holt would start to sing. The Holts lived next door; he taught penmanship (the Palmer Method), typing, bookkeeping and shorthand at the high school. His excitable voice

117

traveled out of their dining-room windows across the two driveways between our houses, and up to our upstairs sleeping porch. His wife, usually so quiet and gentle, was his uncannily spirited accompanist at the piano. "High-ho! Come to the Fair!" he'd sing, unless he sang "Oho ye oho ye, who's bound for the ferry, the briar's in bud and the sun's going down!"

"Dear, this isn't a very good time for you to hear Mother, is it?"

She couldn't get started. As soon as she'd whisper something, Professor Holt galloped into the chorus, "And 'tis but a penny to Twickenham town!" "Isn't that enough?" she'd ask me. She'd told me that the mother and the father had to both *want* the baby. This couldn't be enough. I knew she was not trying to fib to me, for she never did fib, but also I could not help but know she was not really *telling* me. And more than that, I was afraid of what I was going to hear next. This was partly because she wanted to tell me in the dark. I thought *she* might be afraid. In something like childish hopelessness I thought she probably *couldn't* tell, just as she *couldn't* lie.

On the night we came closest to having it over with, she started to tell me without being asked, and I ruined it by yelling, "Mother, look at the lightning bugs!"

In those days, the dark was dark. And all the dark out there was filled with the soft, near lights of lightning bugs. They were everywhere, flashing on the slow, horizontal move, on the upswings, rising and subsiding in the soundless dark. Lightning bugs signaled and answered back without a stop, from down below all the way to the top of our sycamore tree. My mother just gave me a businesslike kiss and went on back to Daddy in their room at the front of the house. Distracted by lightning bugs, I had missed my chance. The fact is she never did tell me.

I doubt that any child I knew ever was told by her mother any more than I was about babies. In fact, I doubt that her own mother ever told her any more than she told me, though there were five brothers who were born after Mother, one after the other, and she was taking care of babies all her childhood.

Not being able to bring herself to open that door to reveal its secret, one of those days, she opened another door.

In my mother's bottom bureau drawer in her bedroom she kept treasures of hers in boxes, and had given me permission to play with one of them—a switch of her own chestnut-colored hair, kept in a heavy bright braid that coiled around like a snake inside a cardboard box. I hung it from her doorknob and unplaited it; it fell in ripples nearly to the floor, and it satisfied the Rapunzel in me to comb it out. But one day I noticed in the same drawer a small white cardboard box such as her engraved calling cards came in from the printing house. It was tightly closed, but I opened it, to find to my puzzlement and covetousness two polished buffalo nickels, embedded in white cotton. I rushed with this opened box to my mother and asked if I could run out and spend the nickels.

"No!" she exclaimed in a most passionate way. She seized the box into her own hands. I begged her; somehow I started to cry. Then she sat down, drew me to her, and told me that I had had a little brother who had come before I did, and who had died as a baby before I was born. And these two nickels that I'd wanted to claim as my find were his. They had lain on his eyelids, for a purpose untold and unimaginable. "He was a fine little baby, my first baby, and he shouldn't have died. But he did. It was because your mother almost died at the same time," she told me. "In looking after me, they too nearly forgot about the little baby."

She'd told me the wrong secret—not how babies could come but   *
how they could die, how they could be forgotten about.

I wondered in after years: how could my mother have kept those two coins? Yet how could someone like herself have disposed of them in any way at all? She suffered from a morbid streak which in all the life of the family reached out on occasions—the worst occasions—and touched us, clung around us, making it worse for her; her unbearable moments could find nowhere to go.

The future story writer in the child I was must have taken unconscious note and stored it away then: one secret is liable to be revealed in the place of another that is harder to tell, and the substitute secret when nakedly exposed is often the more appalling.

Perhaps telling me what she did was made easier for my mother by the two secrets, told and still not told, being connected in her deepest feeling, more intimately than anyone ever knew, perhaps even herself. So far as I remember now, this is the only time this baby was ever mentioned in my presence. So far as I can remember, and I've tried, he was never mentioned in the presence of my father, for whom he had been named. I am only certain that my father, who could never bear pain very well, would not have been able to bear it.

It was my father (my mother told me at some later date) who saved her own life, after that baby was born. She had in fact been given up by the doctor, as she had long been unable to take any nourishment. (That was the illness when they'd cut her hair, which formed the switch in the same bureau drawer.) What had struck her was septicemia, in those days nearly always fatal. What my father did was to try champagne.

I once wondered where he, who'd come not very long before from an Ohio farm, had ever heard of such a remedy, such a measure. Or perhaps as far as he was concerned he invented it, out of the strength of desperation. It would have been desperation augmented   * because champagne couldn't be bought in Jackson. But somehow he knew what to do about that too. He telephoned to Canton, forty miles north, to an Italian orchard grower, Mr. Trolio, told him the necessity, and asked, begged, that he put a bottle of his wine on Number 3, which was due in a few minutes to stop in Canton to "take on water" (my father knew everything about train schedules). My father would be waiting to meet the train in Jackson. Mr. Trolio did—he sent the bottle in a bucket of ice and my father snatched it off the baggage car. He offered my mother a glass of chilled champagne and she drank it and kept it down. She was to live, after all.

Now, her hair was long again, it would reach in a braid down her back, and now I was her child. She hadn't died. And when I came, I hadn't died either. Would she ever? Would I ever? I couldn't face *ever*. I must have rushed into her lap, demanding her like a baby. And she had to put her first-born aside again, for me.

Thinking about Writing

Words

Powerful words both depend on and help shape their context. In what way does each word in the list below depend on its context for

strength? What does each contribute to its context? Can you think of
any other word the author might have used in its place? How does the
word strike you, and how do you respond to the sentence or passage
because of the word?

electrified
wrong
augmented

Thinking

1. If young Welty really wanted to know about where babies come
   from, why do you think she always waited until dark to ask her
   mother or called attention to the lightning bugs at the crucial
   moment of revelation?
2. How did you feel when Welty discovered the nickels? Why do you
   think she cried when her mother said that she could not spend
   them?
3. How can "the substitute secret when nakedly exposed" be "more
   appalling" than the original? In what ways do you agree or disagree
   with the idea that death is more appalling than life? Why could
   Welty's mother discuss death with such ease while she remained
   embarrassed about life?
4. Welty regards the keeping of the coins as part of a "morbid streak"
   that "clung around" them, yet she makes no critical comment
   about her mother keeping a braid of hair. Why do you think Welty
   discriminates this way between objects her mother treasured?

Writing

1. Our parents and grandparents, having lived before we were born,
   had lives about which we can know very little. Now and then,
   by finding an old photograph or some treasured object, we get a
   glimpse not only into the past but into the lives which now appear
   quite different to us. We may be surprised or amused that these
   people managed to live quite well, happily or sadly, without us.
   Write about some moment when you realized that, for example,
   your grandmother was once a pretty young woman or that the

dashing young man in a photograph is your father the year he married. Read again the passage in Richard Rodriguez's "Running in the Sun" where he refers to an old photograph of his father, calling him a dandy and telling us how he himself took up being the dandy where his father left off. How much of yourself do you find in the relics and mementos of your family's past? How excluded do you feel when you see these objects as if you are an outsider from another age? Write about your discoveries.

2. Welty refers to "The future story writer in the child I was," storing the memory of the episode with the pennies for future consideration. She sees herself as having been a "writer" even then although she was a small child. What is there in Welty's account that would support her contention that the writer-to-be was always present in the small child? How does she support the idea? What behavior of the child could, in fact, contribute to the later writer?

   Write an essay exploring the idea that this little girl was observing, experiencing, and reacting to life around her in a way that she would later find useful in her career as a writer. Quote from Welty's own words whenever possible.

3. Write about the future in the child you were, perhaps as a specific ability that was obviously going to shape your life or as something that was lurking in the shadows of your experience, waiting for you to discover it. This ability need not be a specific career—about which you may not have yet decided—but may be some strong ability, a hobby, or a strength of personality that has always been with you.

4

Confessing

There is an art to confessing. The confessor must be able to tell the worst about some transgression while maintaining distance, dignity, and the respect of readers or listeners. We respect these writers, not for their bald confessions, and certainly not for their unfortunate acts, but because they have already judged themselves and found themselves wanting.

As they confess, these writers do not offer excuses any more than they give us assurance they will never again transgress. In fact, we know that they probably will make mistakes again because they are human. We are asked not to run over familiar territory, to say again that certain behavior is reprehensible, or to judge these confessors on the basis of their faults, but rather to note how each has learned something valuable as the result of regarding objectively some aspect of shameful behavior. It is their learning that makes these confessors acceptable to us.

Confessions before God are different from confessions before people. In the former, the sense of sin is so great that the penitent asks for God's forgiveness. The writers here do not ask for forgiveness. Although they recognize that they have behaved shamefully, they also seem aware of having learned something from the experience. Learning, of course, does not excuse the behavior. But it makes the contemplation of such behavior more tolerable.

Norman Mailer recounts his appearance on a television talk show when he was so sure that he was outshining the two other prominent writers on the show that he even felt charity toward them. Later, when he saw a film of the program and heard various friends' reactions, he knew the truth. He had not shone; in fact, he had been a bit dull. So wounded was he by the truth, he shaved off his beard in an act of self-effacement. Only later did he lick his wounds enough to call the great American television public too ignorant to appreciate his intelligence. What had he learned? Never underestimate mediocrity.

George Orwell describes an experience he had in Burma serving as a member of the British Imperial Police, wielding authority over thousands who hated him. These subjects were powerless as individuals but, as Orwell knew, they could become a dangerous mob should they ever move to act together. Once, finding himself faced with either killing a harmless elephant or running the risk of being killed himself by an angry mob, Orwell shoots the animal. Later he is commended for his action. What had Orwell learned? Never take for granted the dirty work of Empire.

Mark Twain describes an experience in the early days of the Civil War, when he and other raw recruits were gathered and billeted while they awaited action. They lived in a kind of stupor of boredom waiting for the real war to begin, not knowing what they would do when it did, disconnected as they were from the serious business of battle. It was not surprising, then, for this small group of inexperienced soldiers to behave first as if they were on a holiday and then, when they thought they were being threatened by the enemy, to behave as they thought soldiers should. To shoot at the enemy seemed only correct and yet, when they shot and killed a lone man, they felt remorse. For Twain the killing was a shameful act. But he learned a good soldier does not feel shame.

Russell Baker recounts an incident that occurred during his high school years, when he realized that he knew more than either his sister or his mother did. The form this realization took was, sadly, an arrogance toward these women, especially toward the mother whose own education had been minimal but whose spirit of inquiry drove Baker to seek a better education for himself. During a difficult translation from Latin, Baker decided to set a trap for his mother in order to humiliate her and point out the inadequacies of her Latin learning, for she had reached the limits of her knowledge and Baker now knew more than she did. He knew he would have to leave her behind as she faltered with her ridiculous translation. He had learned that to exert himself might require a certain degree of cruelty but in the cruelty he had won his independence.

Charles Dickens's hero Pip tells of the moments just before he left home in search of his own identity, when he longed for another life which waited for him elsewhere. He did not know quite what this new life would be any more than he knew why his present life could no longer satisfy him. The life he was giving up was a decent one and not unhappy; yet, he was ashamed of it and wanted to make another for himself. It was shame that sent him away from home in search of another life. Later he felt guilty for that shame. But he had learned that without experiencing discontent he might never have left his good home.

Norman Mailer

Norman Mailer (b. 1923) was born in Long Branch, New Jersey, and educated at Harvard University. While still an undergraduate, he began writing short stories. Mailer served in the army during World War II, writing a war novel, *The Naked and the Dead*, that brought him recognition. Later, his *Armies of the Night*, an account of anti–Vietnam War activities, won him a Pulitzer Prize. A novelist, a playwright, a journalist, and an editor, Mailer helped found the *Village Voice* and has contributed to numerous periodicals. He is an outspoken critic of the feminist movement. Never reclusive, he has always enjoyed playing the public figure and once ran for mayor of New York City. In the selection here, which comes from a collection of his essays called *Pieces and Pontifications*, Mailer recalls appearing on a television talk show hosted by David Susskind, when two other writers also appeared, the shy Dorothy Parker and the not-so-shy Truman Capote. Here Mailer believes that he has stolen the show to such an extent that he begins to behave charitably toward Capote.

Channel 6

He was not to see Dottie Parker again until this evening they would meet on *Open End* eight years later, and when he arrived at the studio in Newark, and saw her waiting, older, more fragile, close to desperately nervous and certainly not cordial, his feelings were only in a small way hurt that she was not happy to see him again and showed an obvious preference for Truman Capote. He was, by his own measure, not the same writer she had known before. He had met her, after all, in the season after *The Naked and the Dead* when he went out to Hollywood, and much had been made of him. Now, after this early success, he had gone through a number of years in which people spoke of him as a failure. Since he had written two novels, *Barbary Shore* and *The Deer Park*, which he thought had received unfair reviews, he had a view of himself that was at odds with others, and he did not like to be snubbed by people who had been friendly to him ten years ago. All the same, it gave justification to his anger. So her unfriendliness left him in a well-balanced position. If it came to it, he would not have to be too friendly on the show.

David Susskind also gave small welcome. "We met a long time ago," Susskind said.

"I remember."

"I do, too," said Susskind in a chilly voice. It had been at a party on a very hot summer night in 1948, and they had talked on a Manhattan roof. Susskind was then a young agent, and he had wanted to sell *The Naked and the Dead* to the movies. Mailer had made fun of him. "Don't you understand?" he had said to Susskind, "*they* can't make it into a film, and I don't want it made."

Of course, years later, he sold it after all, and *they* had made a very bad film. So he felt at a disadvantage now with Susskind and said, "Maybe I should have listened to you."

Susskind's face showed what he thought of people who were rude years ago and ready to flatter now. Their relations for this night were certainly not off to a good start.

He had only Capote. They had gotten along well on the drive out to Newark, each—they had not met before—intensely curious of the other. Since Mailer's wife accompanied him again, and again was looking her best, he had made a point of having her sit between Truman and himself. Since she was twice Truman's size and had the overpowering sexuality, on occasion—this was such an occasion—of her burgeoning Latin blood, it had been an advantage equal to playing on one's home court.

Truman did much complaining on the trip out. "I didn't want to do this show," he said in a dry little voice that seemed to issue   *
from an unmoistened reed in his nostril. "I told Bennett Cerf it was a mistake, but Bennett thinks television is going to be very important for selling our books. I hope he's wrong," said Truman Capote and laughed.

Once the show began, Norman thought himself splendid. Unlike the night with Mike Wallace, he felt at his best, thoughts came clearly, he was full of energy and the others seemed bewildered. Susskind labored in the early minutes to put Dorothy Parker at ease but he was not able to succeed; she simply would not trust him. She spoke in a pained and quavering voice, hardly able to make herself heard. Truman did not add much, and Mailer, pleased with his powers, began to take over. Soon he and Susskind were doing most of the talking, that is, most of the debating, for it was obvious Susskind was irritated by what he had to say. Whenever Norman would launch on a flight of what he considered well-stated criticism of society, Susskind would make a point of looking at his watch. Whenever he could, Susskind tried to give time to the others, but it did not work. The others seemed apathetic. Once, while executing a panegyric[1] about politicians, Norman Mailer flew so high as to say, "They're all whores."

Dottie Parker interrupted then to say with a little real force, "That's a sweeping remark."

"Well," said Mailer, "it may be sweeping, but it certainly is true."

It put Dorothy Parker back into silence—who was she, after all, to defend politicians?—and it irritated Susskind more. After close to an hour of TV time that felt wholly enjoyable to Mailer, he began to grow irritated at Susskind's efforts to slow him up. Since his host seemed determined to shut off this most interesting part of the show, Norman could see no reason not to allow the host to hang himself, and so he ceased speaking. Susskind began immediately to draw upon Truman Capote, and Capote, having digested a few of the peculiar processes of this odd medium, and measured the possible fit for himself, began at last to speak, and was, Mailer thought, not unamusing. He laughed encouragingly at Truman's remarks; he offered attention. Truman was so tiny that something gallant came to you from the fact of his existence itself. Mailer felt generous indeed. Few moods are as charitable as this sensation of being physically superior to everyone in the room.

[1]panegyric: a praising speech. —Ed.

In such a state, feeling handsome, vital, and more interesting than anyone had a right to be, he got into a discussion with Truman about the merits of Jack Kerouac. Since Mailer was not without his jealousy of the large attention paid Kerouac that year, he gave a defense of *On the Road* that was built on the basis of calling Kerouac, Jack—that is, he was two-thirds for Jack's virtues and one-third against Jack's vices.

Capote detested Kerouac. As Mailer grew benign, Capote grew precise. He rose at last to his own peroration and invoked the difficulties of the literary craft in contrast to Mr. Kerouac's undisciplined methods of work. Finally, in a tone of fearless and absolute severity, Capote said: "It is not writing. It is only typing."

"I agree," said Dorothy Parker in a hoarse voice.

"Well, I don't," said Mailer, only to give a limp defense. He was empty of vast indignation at this dreadful put-down of Kerouac. He even decided it might look good to let Truman have his winning little moment, certainly better than trying to hog the show.   *

Open End came to a finish. As they walked off the set, a few technicians were studying the kinescope of what they had just done. Therefore, Parker, Capote, Susskind, Mailer and Mrs. Mailer stopped to watch a minute of it.

Dorothy Parker did not look good on TV. She took one peek at herself, gasped, and said to Susskind, "No, I really don't want to see another instant of it." Solicitous as St. Peter, Susskind led her away.

In contrast, Norman Mailer had the pleasure of seeing himself as he wanted to look. The kinescope caught him as he was making a point, and his face looked forceful, his language was good, yes, he appeared even better on TV, he thought, than in the mirror. "Didn't I tell you," said Truman, "that you're terrific on this? You're *telegenic!*" It was true. But then, in every intermission, Truman had been telling him how splendidly he was doing.

Truman groaned when the camera shifted to him. There was a medium shot of Truman looking a hint bewildered at the beginning of the show, and he winced as he heard his voice. "I told my publishers I shouldn't go on," he declared with annoyance.

In the limousine on the way back to Manhattan, Truman kept saying, "I shouldn't have done it. I didn't want to, I've never appeared

on television, not once—even though I've had many invitations—
and I certainly oughtn't to have been here tonight. What I can do
is special, it's *very* literary, and I shouldn't attempt to *intrude* my
personality. I'm not good at that like you, Norman. Television is good
for you."

Mailer lay back in the limousine, enjoying a winner's ride, and
his wife said encouragingly to Capote, "You were good, too, Truman.
You really got better as it went on."

"Do you think so?" asked Truman. "Do you really think so?"

Now, both Mr. and Mrs. Mailer assured Truman Capote that
he was better than he thought he had been.

"Well, at least," said Truman, "I was better than poor Dorothy
Parker. When she looked at herself afterward . . . " He shuddered
in sympathy. "Wasn't that *Disasterville?*" They laughed, but not in
pleasure at her woe so much as in wonder at the clear lines of Judgment
itself.

Truman could not quite get out of his bad mood, however.
Before they said goodnight he suggested they have a drink with him
at El Morocco. Before long, they thought to have supper. Despite
all the sandwiches served on *Open End*, they were starved. Truman
insisted on treating. A prince, he seemed to hint, must play the host
after a sorry loss—it is the only way to come close to one's blood
again.

It was late on Sunday night and they had the place to
themselves. Under the solicitousness of the waiters and the captain,
and finally the manager himself, who all came over to assure Capote
of their unremitting attention, under the spell of this wholly superior
service Truman was obviously accustomed to receiving whenever he
went into El Morocco, his spirits not only revived but turned charming, and he began to offer an attention to Adele Mailer that had
her believing in the unique properties of her attractiveness and her
wit; yes, Truman was charming. Mailer saw why he had become the
in-house author of the most important hostesses in New York, and   *
envied him honestly, the way one good athlete will have respect for
another. Just as a pitcher will think, "If I had as much stuff to my
curve, I'd win more games because of my superior ball sense," so did
Mailer think wistfully that if he could get to a few of the select parties

Truman got to, why, boy, he'd have more to say about society. Of course, how could you be a radical yet intimate to the top drawer of the world—that was the iron warp of irony itself.

They had a fine time. They discovered unexpected points of agreement, and lively places to disagree, they had each had such curiosity about the other after all these years—their first novels had come out within a year of one another, both had been celebrated almost instantly. It was a grand evening, and at the end, Truman announced they would be great friends forever, and thanked them for taking him through what would otherwise have been a terribly depressing night—"God, was I awful on that show," he said as they parted, and he made a face to simulate the gargoyle of god-awfulness.

There were not many nights when Norman Mailer went to bed so pleased with his wife, himself, and what they were able to do for each other as on this evening. He woke up early in the morning, enjoyed his breakfast, and could hardly wait for the phone to ring, and the praises of his friends to begin. But when he had heard from his parents (who loved the show) from an aunt and uncle (loved the show) from his sister who liked what he had done ("generally") and was somewhat taken with Truman, "what an interesting personality he has really," she said; and when he had gotten tired of waiting for his friends to ring, and called up one instead, there was a pause at the other end, and then the friend said in sorrow, "Oh, man, did Truman take you!"

He called other friends. They seemed not to have seen the show and left a pall equal to the message of the medium itself. He went out on the street for a walk; since he was living in Greenwich Village, it was not hard to run into a few acquaintances. One stopped, saluted, and said: "It is not writing; it is *only* typing," and gave a long phlegmy laugh as he went on down the street. Another said; "Truman; too much!" A third said, "Could you get me to meet Capote?"

More serious friends were balanced. "In terms of polemical points I think you made the most. Of course, Capote does suggest real authority."

He called Truman a couple of days later.

"Yes," said Capote, "isn't it the *strangest* thing? Everybody has been telling me how marvelous I was. I can't believe it. 'Norman

Mailer is the one who was marvelous,' I say to them, and they reply, 'Truman, you were *wunderbar*. Don't sell yourself short.' 'Honey,' I told this friend, 'I been short all my life,'" Truman guffawed with pleasure even more profound than the night at El Morocco. "It certainly is a mystery," he said with complacency.

Mailer couldn't bear it. He finally called *Open End* and asked to see a kinescope. It became his first introduction to our hypothesis that television is not a technological process that reproduces images of real life by way of electronics, but is rather a machine (more or less cosmically operated) to anticipate the judgments and/or anathema of Limbo; the technicians pitch in with camera angles.

He discovered that the nice close-up he had seen of himself immediately after the show was one of the few close-ups they had chosen to give him. The more he talked, and the more Susskind looked at his watch, why the more they relegated him to medium shots and long shots. There is something pathetic about a man speaking at the bottom of a long shot; he does not sound convinced by himself. He is, after all, at the end of the tunnel.

In contrast, they gave many close-ups to Truman. Capote did not look small on the show but large! His face, in fact, was extraordinary, that young-old face, still pretty and with much promise of oncoming ugliness; that voice, so full of snide rustlings and unforgiving nasalities; it was a voice to knock New York on its ear. The voice had survived; it spoke of horrors seen and passed over; it told of judgments that would be merciless.

Watching the kinescope, Mailer realized at last what an impact Capote had made on the television viewers of New York. They had never seen anyone remotely like him. Once Truman finally opened his mouth, the camera never left his face. The camera would turn to Capote even as Norman was speaking.

His own arguments that sounded so forceful to him a few nights ago now seemed vague, and with his beard, pious. (He shaved off the ＊ beard a week or two later.) Talking about large matters on television with all the passion and all the lack of specific detail these immense theses encouraged, speaking in a voice that came out of the depths of a medium shot proved to be not nearly so exhilarating to a viewer as it had felt for him in the middle of articulating his thoughts. His obvious pride in his ideas now seemed fatuous. His physical superiority

was gone. He was only intense, vague, and a bit out of focus. Whereas *
Capote took his unforgettable personality and added to it, practicality,
common sense, and pride. In so misty a medium, the best gift a guest
could provide was pearls. The certainty of a pearl! Yes, to light upon
a problem and come up with a good one-line answer was to produce a
pearl of the mind. How much interest could viewers have in a point
that took five minutes to make? That was something they could not
do. It spoke of too good a college education. So they preferred people
with a one-line answer, barroom knockouts, one-punch pearls. There
is no man or woman on the street whose mind will not produce a
pearl from time to time. They loved Truman because he had given
them "It is not writing. It is only typing."

From now on, thought Mailer, he would not try to show how
intelligent he was; he would look for pearls. That became his latest
hypothesis: the light from a TV screen was flattering to a pearl.

Of course, he was always miserable without an hypothesis. The
hypothesis could later prove invalid, but it had to be interesting
enough so that he could live with it for a while. That the orgy
would benefit humankind more than the family was one of his early
hypotheses, Bolshevist as hell. That the war in Vietnam was a bad
war because rich boys should not fight poor boys unless there was
equality in the weapons was another, and that offered the best of
conservative principles: the rich had better be terrific. Whether the
particular hypothesis was good or bad, however, he leaned on it.
There was something so rigid in his upbringing that for reference he
had great need of a straight line—a straight line is, after all, the very
first of the hypotheses (and, according to Einstein, wholly incorrect,
since no line can run straight in space given the curly route of a
light wave and the oval field of magnetic force). Mailer sometimes
wondered if he was one of the first to recognize that 186,000 miles a
second was not the true speed of light, but only its calculated progress
along a nonexistent straight line. If you measured the speed of light by
the time it took to wind through the waves, then a beam might travel
up to 1,000,000 miles a second in order to traverse 186,000 miles.
That, doubtless, was one more reason why the sum of a million was
magical to Americans.

Such were a few of Mailer's conclusions after his defeat by
Capote.

The next time they met, Truman had a new assurance to put on top of the old one. In these few weeks, he confessed, there had been numerous invitations, all turned down, to appear on other shows; a difference in Truman's idea of himself had begun to appear. That personality he had presented, with all his early bravado, to a most special part of the world, was, it seemed, going to be accepted by all the world. He obviously felt stronger already. And Mailer, stunned as any confident contender who has been abruptly knocked out, now felt, measure to measure, weaker. It was obvious to him (for no one understands the future reactions of a snob so well as an unsuccessful snob) that never again would Truman spend a night trying to recoup the losses of his ego out of *this* Mr. and Mrs. Mailer.

Thinking about Writing

Words

Powerful words both depend on and help shape their context. In what way does each word in the list below depend on its context for strength? What does each contribute to its context? Can you think of any other word the author might have used in its place? How does the word strike you, and how do you respond to the sentence or passage because of the word?

dry little voice
bewildered
apathetic
so tiny
winning little moment
in-house author
beard, pious
out of focus

Thinking

1. What does the author tell us about himself by choosing a vocabulary of competition and physical size? Why, for example, do

you think he finds it important to tell us that his wife is twice as big as Truman Capote? Look for other instances of this kind of vocabulary. What do these words lend to the picture of Mailer we get as we read?

2. How does Mailer's use of the third person affect you? At what point do you realize that he is talking about himself? Try to substitute the first person for the third in a sentence or two. What is lost? What, if anything, is gained? Which do you feel is more honest? Which do you prefer?

3. In what ways do you agree with Mailer when he says that television anticipates limbo (a place outside heaven where souls are forgotten)? How well can you remember a favorite television show of a year ago? What do you recall—a plot, a joke, or a scene? What were the performers' names? Who were the characters? Are these details in limbo today? If limbo is outside heaven, what could heaven be? In other words, where are souls remembered?

4. Mailer willingly sets himself up for eventual degradation. How does he do this? How do you react to Mailer? Are there any ways in which you ever feel sorry for Mailer? for Capote? for Parker? Why does Mailer exaggerate his confidence?

5. How do you feel about Mailer's downfall? Were you pleased about the degradation? When he says, "There is no man or woman on the street whose mind will not produce a pearl from time to time," how do you think Mailer feels?

Writing

1. Write about some moment in your life when you were at first convinced that you were superb, to the extent that you could even be charitable toward your opponent(s), only to realize later that you had in fact not triumphed at all, but had appeared a bit foolish and second best. If you offered yourself any consolation, be sure to include how you did this.

2. The Bible appears to warn us about flying too high in such words as "How are the mighty fallen" (2 Sam. 1:19) and "Pride goes before destruction, and a haughty spirit before a fall" (Prov. 16:18). Mailer even calls himself an unsuccessful snob, hinting that he was

brought down from his lofty peak by the realities of life. (Whether or not he likes those realities—and he doesn't—is not important.) Write an essay in which you attempt to reconcile the warnings against pride with the desire to be confident and to feel proud of doing well. Ask yourself when feeling a certain pride is not only justified but called for.

3. What does Mailer think of the people around him here? How does his vocabulary reveal his attitude toward them? Why, for example, when Dorothy Parker speaks, does Mailer use the word *interrupted*, adding that she speaks with "a little real force"? Notice his next words about Parker's political perceptions. Since these are Mailer's words, they are Mailer's views, and as such they actually tell the reader more about Mailer than about Parker or any of the others here.

   Write an essay that explores Mailer's views of others and himself, as revealed by his use of particular words and phrases. You might begin shaping your ideas by simply listing the names mentioned in the selection. Under these names begin to flesh out Mailer's views by listing words the author uses as he refers to each. See, as these lists grow, if you can find a tendency toward certain types of words for particular people. Then, begin writing your essay, asking yourself what you think about each person as a result of Mailer's words. For example, if Dorothy Parker has already been introduced as somewhat frail and timid, what are we to do with *interrupted*? Think about each of the words he uses when talking about others.

George Orwell

George Orwell (1903–50) was born Eric Blair in Bengal, India, and educated in England. His first job was with the British Imperial Police Service in Burma. However, a passionate interest in the politics of oppression combined with a desire to write about social coercion turned him to a career in journalism, or as he described it, the life of "a sort of pamphleteer." He chose his pseudonym and began to write essays, social commentary, and novels, among them *Animal Farm* and *Nineteen Eighty-Four*. He sought to make his writing the political voice for oppressed people. In the essay here, which comes from a collection called *Shooting an Elephant and Other Essays*, Orwell tells what happens when a tyrant behaves the way people expect. In this case, Orwell represents the tyrant, Great Britain in Burma, and so he becomes something of a tyrant himself. His heart tells him to do otherwise, but to his shame he cannot.

Shooting an Elephant

In Moulmein, in Lower Burma, I was hated by large numbers of people—the only time in my life that I have been important enough for this to happen to me. I was sub divisional police officer of the town, and in an aimless, petty kind of way anti-European feeling was very bitter. No one had the guts to raise a riot, but if a European woman went through the bazaars alone somebody would probably spit betel juice on her dress. As a police officer I was an obvious target and was baited whenever it seemed safe to do so. When a nimble Burman tripped me up on the football field and the referee (another Burman) looked the other way, the crowed yelled with hideous laughter. This happened more than once. In the end the sneering yellow faces of young men that met me everywhere, the insults hooted after me when I was at a safe distance, got badly on my nerves. The young Buddhist priests were the worst of all. There were several thousands of them in the town and none of them seemed to have anything to do except stand on street corners and jeer at Europeans.

All this was perplexing and upsetting. For at that time I had already made up my mind that imperialism was an evil thing and the sooner I chucked up my job and got out of it the better. Theoretically—and secretly, of course—I was all for the Burmese and all against their oppressors, the British. As for the job I was doing, I hated it more bitterly than I can perhaps make clear. In a job like that you see the dirty work of Empire at close quarters. The wretched prisoners huddling in the stinking cages of the lock-ups, the grey, cowed faces of the long term convicts, the scarred buttocks of the men who had been flogged with bamboo—all these oppressed me with an intolerable sense of guilt. But I could get nothing into perspective. I was young and ill-educated and I had had to think out my problems in the utter silence that is imposed on every Englishman in the East. I did not even know that the British Empire is dying, still less did I know that it is a great deal better than the younger empires that are going to supplant it. All I knew was that I was stuck between my hatred of the empire I served and my rage against the evil-spirited little beasts who tried to make my job impossible. With one part of my mind I thought of the British Raj[1] as an unbreakable tyranny, as something clamped down, in *saecula saeculorum*[2], upon the will of prostrate peoples; with another part I thought that the greatest joy in the world would be to drive a bayonet into a Buddhist priest's guts. Feelings like these are the normal by products of imperialism; ask any Anglo-Indian official, if you can catch him off duty.

One day something happened which in a roundabout way was enlightening. It was a tiny incident in itself, but it gave me a better glimpse than I had had before of the real nature of imperialism—the real motives for which despotic governments act. Early one morning the sub-inspector at a police station the other end of the town rang me

[1]British Raj: British rule in Burma and India.—Ed.
[2]*saecula saeculorum*: for eternity.—Ed.

up on the phone and said that an elephant was ravaging the bazaar. Would I please come and do something about it? I did not know what I could do, but I wanted to see what was happening and I got on to a pony and started out. I took my rifle, an old .44 Winchester and much too small to kill an elephant, but I thought the noise might be useful *in terrorem*. Various Burmans stopped me on the way and told me about the elephant's doings. It was not, of course, a wild elephant, but a tame one which had gone "must." It had been chained up, as tame elephants always are when their attack of "must" is due, but on the previous night it had broken its chain and escaped. Its mahout, the only person who could manage it when it was in that state, had set out in pursuit, but had taken the wrong direction and was now twelve hours' journey away, and in the morning the elephant had suddenly reappeared in the town. The Burmese population had no weapons and were quite helpless against it. It had already destroyed somebody's bamboo hut, killed a cow and raided some fruit stalls and devoured the stock; also it had met the municipal rubbish van and, when the driver jumped out and took to his heels, had turned the van over and inflicted violences upon it.

The Burmese sub-inspector and some Indian constables were waiting for me in the quarter where the elephant had been seen. It was a very poor quarter, a labyrinth of squalid bamboo huts, thatched with palm-leaf, winding all over a steep hillside. I remember that it was a cloudy, stuffy morning at the beginning of the rains. We began questioning the people as to where the elephant had gone and, as usual, failed to get any definite information. That is invariably the case in the East; a story always sounds clear enough at a distance, but the nearer you get to the scene of events the vaguer it becomes. Some of the people said that the elephant had gone in one direction, some said that he had gone in another, some professed not even to have heard of any elephant. I had almost made up my mind that the whole story was a pack of lies, when we heard yells a little distance away. There was a loud, scandalized cry of "Go away, child! Go away this instant!" and an old woman with a switch in her hand came round the corner of a hut, violently shooing away a crowd of naked children. Some more women followed, clicking their tongues and exclaiming; evidently there was something that the children ought not to have seen. I rounded the hut and saw a man's dead body sprawling in the mud. He was an Indian, a black Dravidian coolie, almost naked, and he could not have been dead many minutes. The people said that the elephant had come suddenly upon him round the corner of the hut, caught him with its trunk, put its foot on his back and ground him into the earth. This was the rainy season and the ground was soft, and his face had scored a trench a foot deep and a couple of yards long. He was lying on his belly with arms crucified and head sharply twisted to one side. His face was coated with mud, the eyes wide open, the teeth bared and grinning with an expression of unendurable agony. (Never tell me, by the way, that the dead look peaceful. Most of the corpses I have seen looked devilish.) The friction of the great beast's foot had stripped the skin from his back as neatly as one skins a rabbit. As soon as I saw the dead man I sent an orderly to a friend's house nearby to borrow an elephant rifle. I had already sent back the pony, not wanting it to go mad with fright and throw me if it smelt the elephant.

The orderly came back in a few minutes with a rifle and five cartridges, and meanwhile some Burmans had arrived and told us that the elephant was in the paddy fields below, only a few hundred yards away. As I started forward practically the whole population of the quarter flocked out of the houses and followed me. They had seen the rifle and were all shouting excitedly that I was going to shoot the elephant. They had not shown much interest in the elephant when he was merely ravaging their homes, but it was different now that he was going to be shot. It was a bit of fun to them, as it would be to an English crowd; besides they wanted the meat. It made me vaguely uneasy. I had no intention of shooting the elephant—I had merely sent for the rifle to defend myself if necessary—and it is always unnerving to have a crowd following you. I marched down the hill, looking and feeling a fool, with the rifle over my shoulder and an ever- *
growing army of people jostling at my heels. At the bottom, when you got away from the huts, there was a metalled road and beyond that a miry waste of paddy fields a thousand yards across, not yet ploughed but soggy from the first rains and dotted with coarse grass. The elephant was standing eight yards from the road, his left side towards us. He took not the slightest notice of the crowd's approach. He was tearing up bunches of grass, beating them against his knees to clean them and stuffing them into his mouth.

I had halted on the road. As soon as I saw the elephant I knew with perfect certainty that I ought not to shoot him. It is a serious matter to shoot a working elephant—it is comparable to destroying a huge and costly piece of machinery—and obviously one ought not to do it if it can possibly be avoided. And at that distance, peacefully eating, the elephant looked no more dangerous than a cow. I thought then and I think now that his attack of "must" was already passing off; in which case he would merely wander harmlessly about until the mahout came back and caught him. Moreover, I did not in the least want to shoot him. I decided that I would watch him for a little while to make sure that he did not turn savage again, and then go home.

But at that moment I glanced round at the crowd that had followed me. It was an immense crowd, two thousand at the least and growing every minute. It blocked the road for a long distance on either side. I looked at the sea of yellow faces above the garish clothes—faces all happy and excited over this bit of fun, all certain that the elephant was going to be shot. They were watching me as they would watch a conjurer about to perform a trick. They did not like me, but with the magical rifle in my hands I was momentarily worth watching. And suddenly I realized that I should have to shoot the elephant after all. The people expected it of me and I had got to do it; I could feel their two thousand wills pressing me forward, irresistibly. And it was at this moment, as I stood there with the rifle in my hands, that I first grasped the hollowness, the futility of the white man's dominion in the East. Here was I, the white man with his gun, standing in front of the unarmed native crowd—seemingly the leading actor of the piece; but in reality I was only an absurd puppet pushed to and fro by the will of those yellow faces behind. I perceived in this moment that when the white man turns tyrant it is his own freedom that he destroys. He becomes a sort of hollow, posing dummy, the conventionalized figure of a sahib. For it is the condition of his rule that he shall spend his life in trying to impress the "natives," and so in every crisis he has got to do what the "natives" expect of him. He wears a mask, and his face grows to fit it. I had got to shoot the elephant. I had committed myself to doing it when I sent for the rifle. A sahib has got to act like a sahib; he has got to appear resolute, to know his own mind and do definite things. To come all that way, rifle in hand, with two thousand people marching at my heels, and then to trail feebly away, having done nothing—no, that was impossible. The crowd would laugh at me. And my whole life, every white man's life in the East, was one long struggle not to be laughed at.

But I did not want to shoot the elephant. I watched him beating his bunch of grass against his kness, with that preoccupied grandmotherly air that elephants have. It seemed to me that it would be murder to shoot him. At that age I was not squeamish about killing animals, but I had never shot an elephant and never wanted to. (Somehow it always seems worse to kill a *large* animal.) Besides, there was the beast's owner to be considered. Alive, the elephant was worth at least a hundred pounds, dead, he would be only worth the value of his tusks, five pounds, possible. But I had got to act quickly. I turned to some experienced-looking Burmans who had been there when we arrived, and asked them how the elephant had been behaving. They all said the same thing; he took no notice of you if you left him alone, but he might charge if you went too close to him.

It was perfectly clear to me what I ought to do. I ought to walk up to within, say, twenty-five yards of the elephant and test his behavior. If he charged, I could shoot; if he took no notice of me, it would be safe to leave him until the mahout came back. But also I knew that I was going to do no such thing. I was a poor shot with a rifle and the ground was soft mud into which one would sink at every step. If the elephant charged and I missed him, I should have about as much chance as a toad under a steam-roller. But even then I was not thinking particularly of my own skin, only of the watchful yellow faces behind. For at that moment, with the crowd watching me, I was not afraid in the ordinary sense, as I would have been if I had been alone. A white man mustn't be frightened in front of "natives"; and so, in general, he isn't frightened. The sole thought in my mind was that if anything went wrong those two thousand Burmans would see me pursued, caught, trampled on and reduced to a grinning corpse like that Indian up the hill. And if that happened it was quite probable that some of them would laugh. That would never do. There was only one alternative. I shoved the cartridges into the magazine and lay down on the road to get a better aim.

The crowd grew very still, and a deep, low, happy sign, as of people who see the theatre curtain go up at last, breathed from innumerable throats. They were going to have their bit of fun after all. The rifle was a beautiful German thing with cross hair sights. I did not then know that in shooting an elephant one would shoot to cut an imaginary bar running from ear-hole to ear-hole. I ought, therefore, as the elephant was sideways on, to have aimed straight at his ear hole; actually I aimed several inches in front of this, thinking the brain would be further forward.

When I pulled the trigger I did not hear the bang or feel the kick—one never does when a shot goes home—but I heard the devilish roar of glee that went up from the crowd. In that instant, in too short a time, one would have thought, even for the bullet to get there, a mysterious terrible change had come over the elephant. He neither stirred nor fell, but every line of his body had altered. He looked suddenly stricken, shrunken, immensely old, as though the frightful impact of the bullet had paralyzed him without knocking him down. At last, after what seemed a long time—it might have been five seconds, I dare say—he sagged flabbily to his knees. His mouth slobbered. An enormous senility seemed to have settled upon him. One could have imagined him thousands of years old. I fired again into the same spot. At the second shot he did not collapse but climbed with desperate slowness to his feet and stood weakly upright, with legs sagging and head drooping. I fired a third time. That was the shot that did for him. You could see the agony of it jolt his whole body and knock the last remnant of strength from his legs. But in falling he seemed for a moment to rise, for as his hind legs collapsed beneath him he seemed to tower upward like a huge rock toppling, his trunk reaching skyward like a tree. He trumpeted, for the first and only time. And then down he came, his belly toward me, with a crash that seemed to shake the ground even where I lay.

I got up. The Burmans were already racing past me across the mud. It was obvious that the elephant would never rise again, but he was not dead. He was breathing very rhythmically with long rattling gasps, his great mound of a side painfully rising and falling. His mouth was wide open—I could see far down into caverns of pale pink throat. I waited a long time for him to die, but his breathing did not weaken. Finally I fired my two remaining shots into the spot where I thought

his heart must be. The thick blood welled out of him like red velvet, *
but still he did not die. His body did not even jerk when the shots
hit him, the tortured breathing continued without a pause. He was
dying, very slowly and in great agony, but in some world remote from
me where not even a bullet could damage him further. I felt that I
had got to put an end to that dreadful noise. It seemed dreadful to
see the great beast lying there, powerless to move and yet powerless
to die, and not even to be able to finish him. I sent back for my small
rifle and poured shot after shot into his heart and down his throat.
They seemed to make no impression. The tortured gasps continued as
steadily as the ticking of a clock.

In the end I could not stand it any longer and went away. I heard
later that it took him half an hour to die. Burmans were bringing dahs
and baskets even before I left, and I was told they had stripped his
body almost to the bones by the afternoon.

Afterward, of course, there were endless discussions about the
shooting of the elephant. The owner was furious, but he was only an
Indian and could do nothing. Besides, legally I had done the right
thing, for a mad elephant has to be killed, like a mad dog, if its
owner fails to control it. Among the Europeans opinion was divided.
The older men said I was right, the younger men said it was a damn
shame to shoot an elephant for killing a coolie, because an elephant *
was worth more than any damn Coringhee coolie. And afterwards I
was very glad that the coolie had been killed; it put me legally in the
right and it gave me a sufficient pretext for shooting the elephant. I
often wondered whether any of the others grasped that I had done it
solely to avoid looking a fool.

Thinking about Writing

Words

Powerful words both depend on and help shape their context. In
what way does each word in the list below depend on its context for
strength? What does each contribute to its context? Can you think of
any other word the author might have used in its place? How does the

word strike you, and how do you respond to the sentence or passage
because of the word?

utter silence
beasts
looking and feeling a fool
two thousand
hollowness
theatre
trumpeted
caverns
velvet
coolie

Thinking

1. Although he was British, Orwell deplored the "dirty work of
   Empire," but he also hated the way the Burmese behaved toward
   him. Secretly, he sympathized with the Burmese. Why, then,
   couldn't he simply be friendly toward them, and they to him? Considering what each side expected of the other, and how each side
   thought it should behave, do you think Orwell acted rashly, or was
   he just playing a part? How could he have acted otherwise?
2. Orwell admits he would have liked to "drive a bayonet into a
   Buddhist priest's guts." How do you react to this frankness? How
   does it make you feel about Orwell the man? Orwell the tyrant?
   Can you excuse him and, if so, on what grounds? (Compare this
   admission with Williams's statement in "The Use of Force": "I
   could have torn the child apart in my own fury and enjoyed it.")
3. Orwell refers to "the leading actor" and "an absurd puppet." Who
   is who in this account? What have they in common, and how do
   they differ?
4. What opposing forces were troubling Orwell's thinking? Do you
   believe that two wrongs make a right, or that two wrongs make
   something very wrong? What solution do you offer to the problem
   Orwell encountered?
5. Orwell confesses, "I had done it solely to avoid looking a fool." Do
   you think this comment represents Orwell's later reflection about

the incident, or do you think Orwell knew that he wanted to avoid looking the fool while he was in the process of killing the elephant? At what point in the incident could Orwell have avoided shooting the elephant? What do you think might have happened if he had not carried through with the killing?

Writing

1. Human behavior is sometimes like a chess match: if I do this, you could do that, and so forth. Describe a difficult situation where you weighed all the possibilities and then made a decision—the wrong one, as you later realized. You wished you could go back, but you could not. The deed was done, and you had to live with it. How did you learn to live with it, and what did you learn? Has time helped to smooth your feelings of regret, or are you still haunted by lost possibilities? Write about the experience.

2. Have you ever observed an actor/puppet situation in some power structure? Have you ever supposed yourself to be a leading actor, only to realize you were no such thing, but only a puppet after all? Write about the situation, how it evolved, and what you feel now.

3. We've all done things to keep people from laughing at us, for being laughed at is a form of rejection. Write about one time when you acted in a particular way, in order to avoid being laughed at. How did you feel before, during, and after the episode? Do you regret having behaved as you did?

4. In killing the hapless elephant, Orwell has committed a shameful act. Yet we don't hate him or lose respect for him. In fact, something in his writing makes us admire and even like him. Write an essay in which you examine how Orwell, through his words and phrases, has managed to win our sympathy. With what do we actually sympathize? Why can we admire and like him? We have only his word for what happened, his word and his words. How does he leave the reader feeling? How does he control the tension in this situation? Quote Orwell whenever possible to support your observations.

Mark Twain

Mark Twain (1835–1910) was born Samuel Lang-
horne Clemens in Missouri. He left school at the age of
twelve, when he was apprenticed to a printer. Although
he qualified as a journeyman printer, he later succumbed
to the attraction of the Mississippi River and became a
licensed riverboat pilot. During the Civil War, Twain was
charged with treason and desertion from a military company fighting for the confederacy. To escape prosecution,
he fled west to Nevada, where he began to write for a
newspaper. It was then that he adopted his pseudonym,
Mark Twain, a water-depth measure used by riverboat
pilots. Devoted to the American idiom of speech and
thought, Twain wrote numerous short pieces and novels,
among them *Life on the Mississippi* and *The Adventures of
Huckleberry Finn*. In the section here, part of a longer
essay from *Selected Shorter Writings of Mark Twain*, he tells
what an incompetent soldier he was. Twain and a group of
friends have formed a military company; they are billeted
with a farmer named Mason.

A Campaign
that Failed

We stayed several days at Mason's; and after all these years
the memory of the dullness, and stillness, and lifelessness of that
slumberous farmhouse still oppresses my spirit as with a sense of the
presence of death and mourning. There was nothing to do, nothing
to think about; there was no interest in life. The male part of the
household were away in the fields all day, the women were busy and
out of our sight; there was no sound but the plaintive wailing of a *

spinning-wheel, forever moaning out from some distant room—the most lonesome sound in nature, a sound steeped and sodden with homesickness and the emptiness of life. The family went to bed about dark every night, and as we were not invited to intrude any new customs, we naturally followed theirs. Those nights were a hundred years long to youths accustomed to being up till twelve. We lay awake and miserable till that hour every time, and grew old and decrepit waiting through the still eternities for the clock-strikes. This was no place for town boys. So at last it was with something very like joy that we received news that the enemy were on our track again. With a new birth of the old warrior spirit, we sprang to our places in line of battle and fell back on Camp Ralls.

Captain Lyman had taken a hint from Mason's talk, and he now gave orders that our camp should be guarded against surprise by the posting of pickets. I was ordered to place a picket at the forms of the road in Hyde's prairie. Night shut down black and threatening. I told Sergeant Bowers to go out to that place and stay till midnight; and, just as I was expecting, he said he wouldn't do it. I tried to get others to go, but all refused. Some excused themselves on account of the weather; but the rest were frank enough to say they wouldn't go in any kind of weather. This kind of thing sounds odd now, and impossible, but there was no surprise in it at the time. On the contrary, it seemed a perfectly natural thing to do. There were scores of little camps scattered over Missouri where the same thing was happening. These camps were composed of young men who had been born and reared to a sturdy independence, and who did not know what it meant to be ordered around by Tom, Dick, and Harry, whom they had known familiarly all their lives, in the village or on the farm. It is quite within the probabilities that this same thing was happening all over the South. James Redpath recognized the justice of this assumption, and furnished the following instance in support of it. During a short stay in East Tennessee he was in a citizen colonel's tent one day talking, when a big private appeared at the door, and, without salute or other circumlocution, said to the colonel,—

"Say, Jim, I'm a-goin' home for a few days."

"What for?"

"Well, I hain't b'en there for a right smart while, and I'd like to see how things is comin' on."

"How long are you going to be gone?"

"Bout two weeks."

"Well, don't be gone longer than that; and get back sooner if you can."

That was all, and the citizen officer resumed his conversation where the private had broken it off. This was in the first months of the war, of course. The camps in our part of Missouri were under Brigadier-General Thomas H. Harris. He was a townsman of ours, a first-rate fellow, and well liked; but we had all familiarly known him as the sole and modest-salaried operator in our telegraph office, where he had to send about one dispatch a week in ordinary times, and two when there was a rush of business; consequently, when he appeared in our midst one day, on the wing, and delivered a military command of some sort, in a large military fashion, nobody was surprised at the response which he got from the assembled soldiery, —

"Oh, now, what'll you take to *don't*, Tom Harris!"

It was quite the natural thing. One might justly imagine that we were hopeless material for war. And so we seemed, in our ignorant state; but there were those among us who afterward learned the grim trade; learned to obey like machines; became valuable soldiers; fought   * all through the war, and came out at the end with excellent records. One of the very boys who refused to go out on picket duty that night, and called me an ass for thinking he would expose himself to danger in such a foolhardy way, had become distinguished for intrepidity before he was a year older.

I did secure my picket that night—not by authority, but by diplomacy. I got Bowers to go by agreeing to exchange ranks with him for the time being, and go along and stand the watch with him as his subordinate. We stayed out there a couple of dreary hours in the pitchy darkness and the rain, with nothing to modify the dreariness but Bowers's monotonous growlings at the war and the weather; then we began to nod, and presently found it next to impossible to stay in the saddle; so we gave up the tedious job, and went back to the camp without waiting for the relief guard. We rode into camp without interruption or objection from anybody, and the enemy could have done the same, for there were no sentries. Everybody was asleep; at midnight there was nobody to send out another picket, so none was sent. We never tried to establish a watch at night again, as far as I remember, but we generally kept a picket out in the daytime.

In that camp the whole command slept on the corn in the big corn-crib; and there was usually a general row before morning, for the place was full of rats, and they would scramble over the boys' bodies and faces, annoying and irritating everybody; and now and then they would bite some one's toe, and the person who owned the toe would start up and magnify his English and begin to throw corn in the dark.   *
The ears were half as heavy as bricks, and when they struck they hurt. The persons struck would respond, and inside of five minutes every man would be locked in a death-grip with his neighbor. There was a grievous deal of blood shed in the corn-crib, but this was all that was   *
spilt while I was in the war. No, that is not quite true. But for one circumstance it would have been all. I will come to that now.

Our scares were frequent. Every few days rumors would come that the enemy were approaching. In these cases we always fell back on some other camp of ours; we never stayed where we were. But the rumors always turned out to be false; so at last even we began to grow indifferent to them. One night a negro was sent to our corn-crib with the same old warning: the enemy was hovering in our neighborhood. We all said let him hover. We resolved to stay still and be comfortable. It was a fine warlike resolution, and no doubt we   *
all felt the stir of it in our veins—for a moment. We had been having a very jolly time, that was full of horse-play and school-boy hilarity; but that cooled down now, and presently the fast-waning fire of forced jokes and forced laughs died out altogether, and the company became silent. Silent and nervous. And soon uneasy—worried—apprehensive. We had said we would stay, and we were committed. We could have been persuaded to go, but there was nobody brave enough to suggest it. An almost noiseless movement presently began in the dark, by a general but unvoiced impulse. When the movement was completed, each man knew that he was not the only person who had crept to the front wall and had his eye at a crack between the logs. No, we were all there; all there with our hearts in our throats, and staring out toward the sugar-troughs where the forest footpath came through. It was late, and there was a deep woodsy stillness everywhere. There was a veiled moonlight, which was only just strong enough to enable

us to mark the general shape of objects. Presently a muffled sound
caught our ears, and we recognized it as the hoof-beats of a horse
or horses. And right away a figure appeared in the forest path; it could   *
have been made of smoke, its mass had so little sharpness of outline.
It was a man on horseback, and it seemed to me that there were
others behind him. I got hold of a gun in the dark, and pushed it
through a crack between the logs, hardly knowing what I was doing,
I was so dazed with fright. Somebody said, "Fire!" I pulled the trigger.
I seemed to see a hundred flashes and hear a hundred reports; then   *
I saw the man fall down out of the saddle. My first feeling was of
surprised gratification; my first impulse was an apprentice-sportsman's
impulse to run and pick up his game. Somebody said, hardly audibly,
"Good—we've got him!—wait for the rest." But the rest did not
come. We waited—listened—still no more came. There was not a
sound, not the whisper of a leaf; just perfect stillness; an uncanny
kind of stillness, which was all the more uncanny on account of the
damp, earthy, late-night smells now rising and pervading it. Then,   *
wondering, we crept stealthily out, and approached the man. When
we got to him the moon revealed him distinctly. He was lying on his
back with his arms abroad; his mouth was open and his chest heaving
with long gasps, and his white shirt-front was all splashed with blood.
The thought shot through me that I was a murderer; that I had killed
a man—a man who had never done me any harm. That was the
coldest sensation that ever went through my marrow. I was down by
him in a moment, helplessly stroking his forehead; and I would have
given anything then—my own life freely—to make him again what he
had been five minutes before. And all the boys seemed to be feeling
in the same way; they hung over him, full of pitying interest, and
tried all they could to help him, and said all sorts of regretful things.
They had forgotten all about the enemy; they thought only of this
one forlorn unit of the foe. Once my imagination persuaded me that   *
the dying man gave me a reproachful look out of his shadowy eyes,
and it seemed to me that I could rather he had stabbed me than done
that. He muttered and mumbled like a dreamer in his sleep, about his
wife and his child; and I thought with a new despair, "This thing that
I have done does not end with him; it falls upon *them* too, and they
never did me any harm, any more than he."

In a little while the man was dead. He was killed in war; killed in fair and legitimate war; killed in battle, as you may say; and yet he was as sincerely mourned by the opposing force as if he had been their brother. The boys stood there a half hour sorrowing over him, and recalling the details of the tragedy, and wondering who he might be, and if he were a spy, and saying that if it were to do over again they would not hurt him unless he attacked them first. It soon came out that mine was not the only shot fired; there were five others, — a division of guilt which was a great relief to me, since it in some degree lightened and diminished the burden I was carrying. There were six shots fired at once; but I was not in my right mind at the time, and my heated imagination had magnified my one shot into a volley.

The man was not in uniform, and was not armed. He was a stranger in the country; that was all we ever found out about him. The thought of him got to preying upon me every night; I could not get rid of it. I could not drive it away, the taking of that unoffending life seemed such a wanton thing. And it seemed an epitome of war; that all war must be just that—the killing of strangers against whom you feel no personal animosity; strangers whom, in other circumstances, you would help if you found them in trouble, and who would help you if you needed it. My campaign was spoiled. It seemed to me that I was not rightly equipped for this awful business; that war was intended for men, and I for a child's nurse. I resolved to retire from this avocation of sham soldiership while I could save some remnant of my self-respect. These morbid thoughts clung to me against reason; for at bottom I did not believe I had touched that man. The law of probabilities decreed me guiltless of his blood; for in all my small experience with guns I had never hit anything I had tried to hit, and I knew I had done my best to hit him. Yet there was no solace in the thought. Against a diseased imagination demonstration goes for nothing.

The rest of my war experience was of a piece with what I have already told of it. We kept monotonously falling back upon one camp or another, and eating up the farmers and their families. They ought to have shot us; on the contrary, they were as hospitably kind and courteous to us as if we had deserved it. In one of these camps we found Ab Grimes, an Upper Mississippi pilot, who afterward became

famous as a dare-devil rebel spy, whose career bristled with desperate
adventures. The look and style of his comrades suggested that they
had not come into the war to play, and their deeds made good the
conjecture later. They were fine horsemen and good revolver shots;
but their favorite arm was the lasso. Each had one at his pommel,
and could snatch a man out of the saddle with it every time, on a full
gallop, at any reasonable distance.

In another camp the chief was a fierce and profane old blacksmith of sixty, and he had furnished his twenty recruits with gigan-
tic home-made bowie-knives, to be swung with two hands, like the
machetes of the Isthmus. It was a grisly spectacle to see that earnest
band practising their murderous cuts and slashes under the eye of that
remorseless old fanatic.

The last camp which we fell back upon was in a hollow near
the village of Florida, where I was born — in Monroe County. Here
we were warned one day that a Union colonel was sweeping down on
us with a whole regiment at his heel. This looked decidedly serious.
Our boys went apart and consulted; then we went back and told the
other companies present that the war was a disappointment to us, and
we were going to disband. They were getting ready, themselves, to
fall on some place or other, and were only waiting for General Tom
Harris, who was expected to arrive at any moment; so they tried to
persuade us to wait a little while, but the majority of us said no, we
were accustomed to falling back, and didn't need any of Tom Harris's
help; we could get along perfectly well without him — and save time
too. So about half of our fifteen, including myself, mounted and left
on the instant; the others yielded to persuasion and stayed — stayed
through the war.

An hour later we met General Harris on the road, with two or
three people in his company — his staff, probably, but we could not
tell; none of them were in uniform; uniforms had not come into vogue
among us yet. Harris ordered us back; but we told him there was a
Union colonel coming with a whole regiment in his wake, and it
looked as if there was going to be a disturbance; so we had concluded
to go home. He raged a little, but it was of no use; our minds were
made up. We had done our share, had killed one man, exterminated   *
one army, such as it was; let him go and kill the rest, and that would

end the war. I did not see that brisk young general again until last year; then he was wearing white hair and whiskers.

In time I came to know that Union colonel whose coming frightened me out of the war and crippled the Southern cause to that extent—General Grant. I came within a few hours of seeing him when he was as unknown as I was myself; at a time when anybody could have said, "Grant?—Ulysses S. Grant? I do not remember hearing the name before." It seems difficult to realize that there was once a time when such a remark could be rationally made; but there *was*, and I was within a few miles of the place and the occasion too, though proceeding in the other direction.

The thoughtful will not throw this war-paper of mine lightly aside as being valuless. It has this value: it is a not unfair picture of what went on in many and many a militia camp in the first month of the rebellion, when the green recruits were without discipline, without the steadying and heartening influence of trained leaders; when all their circumstances were new and strange, and charged with exaggerated terrors, and before the invaluable experience of actual collision in the field had turned them from rabbits into soldiers. If this side of the picture of that early day has not before been put into history, then history has been to that degree incomplete, for it had and has its rightful place there. There was more Bull Run material scattered through the early camps of this country than exhibited itself at Bull Run. And yet it learned its trade presently, and helped to fight the great battles later. I could have become a soldier myself, if I had waited. I had got part of it learned; I knew more about retreating than the man that invented retreating.

Thinking about Writing

Words

Powerful words both depend on and help shape their context. In what way does each word in the list below depend on its context for strength? What does each contribute to its context? Can you think of

any other word the author might have used in its place? How does the word strike you, and how do you respond to the sentence or passage because of the word?

wailing
machines
magnify
blood shed
warlike resolution
or horses
a hundred flashes
late-night smells
unit
exterminated

Thinking

1. What does Twain think about the killing? How do we know what he thinks? Point out anything in this piece of writing that gives us an impression of Twain's view of killing, any killing, in war.
2. What do you think bothers Twain more, the lack of strict discipline or the idea of war? Point out anything in the writing that would lead you to believe that today Twain would be a pacifist.
3. One of the most puzzling aspects of war is our having to learn to hate someone, and to learn to define this person as the enemy. After the war, we must unlearn the hate and go back to getting along with those we just finished hating. How do we learn both these ways of behaving?
4. How do you feel when the man is killed? How do you feel toward Twain at this moment? How does Twain, through his writing, separate himself from the others who continue as soldiers?

Writing

1. The killing was terrible because it was, somehow, inappropriate. The context was not strictly warlike, although Twain says, "He was killed in war; killed in fair and legitimate war; killed in battle, as you may say." Nevertheless, the atmosphere was too unprofessional.

Write an essay that examines Twain's use of dialogue and domestic detail to paint a picture of quiet, even boring, country life, against which the killing occurs. Try to include some comment of your own that shows how Twain's placing the killing against such a peaceful background affects your reaction as a reader. Quote from the author's words and expressions to support your views.

2. How do we stir up enthusiasm for killing and destruction, especially when we are raised to "love thy neighbor"? How do advertisements and propaganda convince people to behave in particular ways? Write an essay in which you explore some aspect of influencing people to behave a certain way, either through advertising or propaganda.

3. Write an essay about unlearning after learning, trying to forget, changing our thoughts about people, or, conversely, trying *not* to forget in order to clarify certain positions and occurrences before it is too late. You may want to consider war monuments and memorials, or the market for foreign cars, electronics, and tourism.

Russell Baker

Russell Baker (b. 1925) was born in rural Virginia into a poor, largely uneducated family. In spite of the poverty which struck many families during the Depression, Baker managed to find scholarships to good schools, and he eventually graduated from Johns Hopkins University. He began immediately after graduation to pursue what was to become a long career in journalism. He wrote first for the *Baltimore Sun*, later becoming the *Sun's* bureau chief in London. From there he moved to the *New York Times*, where his column, "The Observer," appears. His witty approach to his subject matter often fails to mask a deep concern for the human condition. In fact, his Pulitzer Prize-winning autobiography, *Growing Up*, is as much a social commentary as it is an account of his own life. In the selection here, which comes from his autobiography, Baker reveals how he declared his independence from his mother.

Swimming Alone

There wasn't much that could be done about my cadaverous physique except avoid all situations that required me to take off my shirt. This meant never going to beaches or swimming pools, which became impossible after I entered high school. I was appalled the first day there to discover it had an Olympic-size pool and required all students to take swimming instruction. I was doubly stricken to learn that everyone was expected to swim buck naked. There was no getting out of it either. The idea that my fellow students--it was an all-boys school—would now see me in all my skinniness and laugh about me behind my back was enough to make me ponder suicide. Instead I chose humiliation. When we were all lined up nude at the edge of the pool, nobody pointed at me and laughed, but I was certain that everyone was busily counting my plainly visible ribs. I spent so much time in swimming class worrying about my boney profile that despite four years of instruction in that pool I never learned to swim a stroke.

To make up for so many shortcomings, I flung myself furiously into the one thing I was good at, which was book learning, and found a little self-respect in the successful chase for high grades. In short order I developed intellectual arrogance. This was encouraged   *
by the special program I was taking in high school, a four-year course for fast learners, which, when completed, would supply me with enough credits to enter college at the second-year level. There was no possibility of my going to college, of course. Not on my mother's meager earnings. When she learned that the program was available, though, she insisted that I apply.

"At least you'll get a year of college learning out of high school," she said. "And who knows, maybe by the time you're through with high school something may come along."

Well, it was another opportunity to help me make something of myself, and she overlooked no possibility, no matter how remote. For me it meant early escape from the junior high school I hated; boys accepted in the program were freed from junior high after eighth grade and sent to do their ninth grade in high school. I leaped at the chance to change schools. If I'd known about the nude swimming I would have resisted. But then my mother would have forced me to apply anyhow. The school catering to us ambitious bookworms was called City College. Despite its name, which dated from the nineteenth century, when it had been a city college, it was merely a high school, though a very good one whose best graduates were equipped to enter the best universities in the country.

The program I entered was in the classical tradition. There was very little science, but by graduation you were expected to have mastered mathematics through elementary calculus. Grammar, rhetoric, and English literature were heavily emphasized, and the course included two years of German, three years of French, and four years of Latin, at the end of which we were expected to have read Caesar, Cicero, Virgil, Ovid, Horace, and Livy.

This was a far world from the rough and tumble of junior high, where you could have your brains beaten out in the schoolyard, and   *

I took to the rarefied scholarly air with gusto. The school was located an hour's trolley ride from West Lombard Street in what seemed by comparison one of Baltimore's snootiest neighborhoods. It was a mammoth gray stone structure topped by a huge gray tower, the whole thing sprawling across the highest hill in Baltimore like some grim Gothic fortress heaved up to shelter civilization from the Vandals. My classmates came from all sections of the city. Most, I discovered, were just as formidable at the books as I was, and many were my betters at the grind. After the first year thinned out our ranks of sluggards who   * couldn't keep the pace, some twenty-five of us survived as a small elite cadre of scholars, and when I realized that I was good enough to keep up with the best I began to view myself with extraordinary respect. I also began to look upon the common masses of humanity with pleasurable disdain.

When Doris asked for help with her arithmetic, I tore up her solutions in disgust while enthusiastically explaining that she would never be able to master the mysteries of trigonometry. Worse, I began to punish my mother. For years she had been my tutor in everything academic, the eternal schoolteacher forcing me to learn to read when reading bored me, watching over my shoulder while I did my home-work, encouraging me when I complained it was too hard. "Just calm down and think it through, Buddy. You can get it if you try." And if I couldn't in spite of trying, she had always sat down beside me and helped me do it.

In the past I had been in awe of her education, her year of college where she had read Shakespeare and learned Latin. In my first year at City, when we were reading Caesar and I was having terrible trouble, she sat beside me long nights at the dining-room table on Lombard Street and helped me solve the puzzles of Latin declensions and conjugations. She was good at Caesar. But now, as I moved on into Cicero and Virgil, I realized that I was leaving her behind. I was like a swimmer in deep ocean waters pulling away from someone too weak to keep up. Nevertheless, she wanted to stay abreast of me, and many nights she still took her seat beside me at the table hoping to be helpful.

"What's the trouble, Buddy?"

"Cicero, I can't get this passage here," I said, showing her the book.

She looked at it silently for a long time, then tried to translate it. I knew her translation was far off the mark. Even my own, which was not very good, was better than hers. At this early stage I didn't yet have it in me to hurt her, and so would nod and say, "Thanks, let me try it that way and see if I can work it out."

Gradually she became glad to let me work out the Latin by myself, and I knew I was outdistancing her. The same progress took place in mathematics, and though she tried to help as she had always helped, her powers failed when we reached quadratic equations, and she left me to swim alone into trigonometry and analytic geometry. One of the oldest links in the chain binding us together had snapped. She was no longer my ultimate schoolteacher.

As my intellectual pride increased I began to take pleasure in the feeling that my education was superior to hers. For years I had heard about her year of college, her Latin classes, her schoolteacher's art, and now I was pleased to realize that despite all that, she could no longer keep up with me. One evening I yielded to an evil impulse to show her how little Latin she knew.

In school we were then reading the *Aeneid*.[1] In class that day we had translated a difficult passage concluding with the line *"forsan et haec meminisse iuvabit."* After great difficulty and with much help from the teacher I had worked this out to mean, "Someday we shall recall these trials with pleasure." While doing my homework that night I called her to the table and showed her the passage, pretending I was having trouble with it. "You're the Latin expert around here," I said. "Can you translate this line for me?"

She sat down, took the book, and studied the passage, then began consulting the Latin dictionary. Knowing from my class that day how tricky the line was to translate, I was filled with inner giggles. Still, she made the effort, laboriously working out a couple of lines and getting them wrong and finally translating the last line to read, "Perhaps and this it will help to remember."

"It doesn't make any sense that way," I said.

She was apologetic. "I never got up to the *Aeneid* when I was in school," she said. I ignored this.

---

[1]The *Aeneid*: an epic by the Latin poet Virgil. —Ed.

"Don't you think that it makes more sense this way?" I asked, and read the entire passage as the teacher had helped translate it earlier, concluding, "Someday, we shall recall these trials with pleasure."

"If you knew it already, why did you bother to ask me?" she said.

"I thought maybe you could improve it," I said.

"Improve it for yourself," she said, and left the table.

Something else that had bound us together parted that night. It had been cruelly done, but I had issued my first declaration of independence from childhood.

Thinking about Writing

Words

Powerful words both depend on and help shape their context. In what way does each word in the list below depend on its context for strength? What does each contribute to its context? Can you think of any other word the author might have used in its place? How does the word strike you and how do you respond to the sentence or passage because of the word?

ponder
arrogance
brains
ranks

Thinking

1. Although Baker was horrified by the swimming sessions in his new school, he nonetheless uses the metaphor of swimmers as he describes outdistancing his mother's limited education. Did you visualize the swimming class? When Baker was telling about himself and his mother during the Latin homework scene, did you visualize mother and son or swimmers, as the metaphor suggests? How is a physical metaphor useful in describing an intellectual situation? What other metaphor could describe such a situation?
2. "It had been cruelly done," says Baker, about severing the bond with his childhood. Explain whether you think he also sev-

ered the bond with his mother. In what way was the episode a "rite of passage," like a ceremony that allowed Baker to proceed in life? From the writing here, what can you tell about the relation between mother and son?

3. Do you ever find yourself rejecting your parents' values in order to strengthen your own ideas, perhaps picturing your family as muddled, weak, or old-fashioned so that you feel efficient, strong, and clear-headed? If so, why do you think you must have an either/or situation, as if the world isn't large enough to hold both views, yours and theirs?

Writing

1. Baker begins this account of declaring independence by describing the frustrations of his swimming class in school. He then continues the swimming concept in the metaphor he uses to describe striving against, gaining on, and eventually pulling away from his mother and her meager education.

   Write an essay in which you tie together the two acts of swimming, the real one in school and the metaphorical one at home. Try to explain how the failure of one is counterbalanced with success in the other. Quote from the essay to support your observations.

2. Have you ever hurt someone's feelings or done something unfair in order to reach a goal that was important to you? Have you ever "yielded to an evil impulse" to tease someone or make someone appear foolish not just for fun but because you could see the—to you at least—noble end?

   Write about what happened, how you found yourself behaving, and what finally resulted. Did you reason with yourself, excusing your actions? If you excused yourself, was it before you acted (yielded) or later, when you took stock of the outcome?

3. How do you justify growing up, either to yourself or your family? Does, or did, the situation create tension? Have you ever rejected people you respect? Do you equate growing up with pulling ahead of your family, as Baker did? (Also see Thinking question 3.) Write an essay about making the break for independence.

Charles Dickens

Charles Dickens (1812–70) was born in Portsea, England, and minimally educated. Poverty left its mark on both the Dickens family and the writer. While Dickens was still a child, his father was sent to debtor's prison, and the boy was sent to work. In spite of this hardship, Dickens turned to writing as a profession, first as a Parliamentary reporter for an uncle's newspaper who scribbled fiction as a sideline. Eventually he became a successful author whose works were greedily consumed by an avid public in America as well as his native England. Many of his novels are concerned with the effects of ambition, success, and downfall within the framework of nineteenth-century society. The selection here, from *Great Expectations*, concerns Pip, now grown, as he recalls his early shame of being only a blacksmith's apprentice and his terrible fantasy that one day the wealthy and beautiful Estella would see him working at the forge.

Ashamed of Home

It is a most miserable thing to feel ashamed of home. There may be a black ingratitude in the thing and the punishment may be retributive and well deserved, but that it is a miserable thing, I can testify.

Home had never been a very pleasant place to me, because of my sister's temper. But Joe had sanctified it, and I believed in it. I had believed in the best parlor as a most elegant saloon; I had believed in the front door as a mysterious portal of the Temple of State whose solemn opening was attended with a sacrifice of roast fowls; I had believed in the kitchen as a chaste though not magnificent apartment; I had believed in the forge as the glowing road to manhood and independence. Within a single year all this was changed. Now, it was all coarse and common, and I would not have had Miss Havisham and Estella see it on any account.

How much of my ungracious conduct of mind may have been   *
my own fault, how much Miss Havisham's, how much my sister's, is now of no moment to me or to any one. The change was made in me; the thing was done. Well or ill done, excusably or inexcusably, it was done.

Once it had seemed to me that when I should at last roll up my shirt-sleeves and go into the forge, Joe's 'prentice, I should be distinguished and happy. Now the reality was in my hold, I had only   *
felt that I was dusty with the dust of the small coal, and that I had a weight upon my daily remembrance to which the anvil was a feather.   *
There have been occasions in my later life (I suppose as in most lives) when I have felt for a time as if a thick curtain had fallen on all its interest and romance, to shut me out from anything save dull endurance any more. Never has that curtain dropped so heavy and blank as when my way in life stretched out straight before me through the newly-entered road of apprenticeship to Joe.

I remember that at a later period of my "time," I used to stand about the churchyard on Sunday evenings, when night was falling, comparing my own perspective with the windy marsh view, and mak-   *
ing out some likeness between them by thinking how flat and low both were, and how on both there came an unknown way and dark mist and then the sea. I was quite as dejected on the first working-day of my apprenticeship as in that after-time; but I am glad to know that I never breathed a murmur to Joe while my indentures lasted. It is about the only thing I *am* glad to know of myself in that connection.

For, though it includes what I proceed to add, all the merit of what I proceed to add was Joe's. It was not because I was faithful, but because Joe was faithful, that I never ran away and went for[1] a soldier or a sailor. It was not because I had a strong sense of the virtue of industry, but because Joe had a strong sense of the virtue of industry, that I worked with tolerable zeal against the grain. It   *
is not possible to know how far the influence of any amiable hon-est-hearted duty-doing man flies out into the world, but it

[1]and went for: and became. —Ed.

is very possible to know how it has touched one's self in going by, and I know right well that any good that intermixed itself with my apprenticeship came of plain contented Joe, and not of restless aspiring discontented me.

What I wanted, who can say? How can *I* say, when I never knew? What I dreaded was that in some unlucky hour I, being at my grimiest and commonest, should lift up my eyes and see Estella looking in at one of the wooden windows of the forge. I was haunted by the fear that she would, sooner or later, find me out, with a black face and hands, doing the coarsest part of my work, and would exult over me and despise me. Often after dark, when I was pulling the bellows for Joe, and we were singing Old Clem, and when the thought how we used to sing it at Miss Havisham's would seem to show me Estella's face in the fire, with her pretty hair fluttering in the wind and her eyes scorning me—often at such a time I would look towards those panels of black night in the wall which the wooden windows then were, and would fancy that I saw her just drawing her face away, and would believe that she had come at last.

After that, when we went in to supper, the place and the meal would have a more homely look than ever, and I would feel more ashamed of home than ever, in my own ungracious breast.

Thinking about Writing

Words

Powerful words both depend on and help shape their context. In what way does each word in the list below depend on its context for strength? What does each contribute to its context? Can you think of any other word the author might have used in its place? How does the word strike you and how do you respond to the sentence or passage because of the word?

ungracious
distinguished
remembrance

perspective
tolerable zeal

Thinking

1. How does the vocabulary Dickens uses to describe Pip's home life when Pip accepted it differ from the vocabulary used for his home life after he rejected it? How does Dickens use particular images in each description in order to express Pip's attitudes?
2. Even if you haven't read *Great Expectations*, the novel from which this selection is taken, you can feel the tensions within the young man's mind as he pulls away from home. How does the author create this tension? What words and expressions does he use to convey Pip's misery?
3. Why do you think Dickens has made Pip only imagine a fantasy, and a highly unlikely one at that, in order to make the break from home? In what way is a fantasy more powerful than a fact?
4. How does a little dissatisfaction with home help us to grow up? How can this same dissatisfaction work as an incentive to forging ahead on new paths?

Writing

1. The misery and discontent that Pip feels in this piece are created by contrasts drawing him two ways. Home life is strong, yet something calls him to the outside world. How has the author used particular words and images to demonstrate Pip's confusion? Write a paper that describes Pip's dilemma, using the author's words to support your observations.
2. Assume that Dickens is reflecting nineteenth-century attitudes toward home and work as he tells the story of Pip. From this piece (you need not consult history books), write an essay describing those attitudes. For example, Dickens sanctifies the home in such a manner that anyone breaking from it would feel "ungracious." You might find it helpful to consult a large dictionary to clarify words like *ungracious*, *indentures*, and *homely* as they are used here.
3. We control our fantasies but we cannot control facts. How may we actually benefit from being able to fantasize about what troubles

or frightens us? Read again the essay "Running in the Sun," in chapter 3, in which Richard Rodriguez tried to become what he dreamed about, a *bracero*. How are both Pip's and Rodriguez's fantasies similar? How are they different?

Write an essay in which you compare and contrast the two young men on the way to independence.

5

Reflecting

The writers in this chapter have learned something about their own behavior by reflecting on those around them. These writers are interested in what others are doing, have done, or might do, not just out of idle curiosity but because they have learned to use the behavior of other people as a point of departure in judging their own lives. They do not emulate those on whom they reflect but rather, because they do not agree with what they see, they can use others' behavior as a contrast to what they themselves wish. Reflecting on others helps them decide about themselves.

For Toni Cade Bambara, being black, female, and a writer living in the second half of twentieth-century America helps to define the way she writes. But when she reflects on other writers, she often finds that their writing inadequately expresses her thinking and so she must devise a style that remains true to herself as a black woman writer. She explains in her essay just why she writes as she does and why she cannot write in any other way and remain true to herself. Primarily by reflecting on other writers.

The speakers in William Shakespeare's sonnets have reflected on others' behavior and so defined something about their own. The speaker in the first sonnet has decided that if that people grow old and forget things, it might be valuable to keep a notebook to consult in later years. The speaker in the second sonnet, reflecting on his absent beloved, realizes that he himself is the designer of the affection he holds for the beloved. And the speaker in the third sonnet, reflecting on the way most people's faces reveal their emotions while his own beloved's face reveals nothing but joy, concludes that he must be the victim of an unfaithful relationship.

Old age gives Malcolm Cowley, now over eighty, an opportunity to reflect on its virtues and vices. He observes old people and their habits and decides that the worst of the vices is giving up. He regards old people who succumb to the continuing struggle not to give up as pathetic. Although he tries to be sympathetic, it is clear that he has little patience, for he himself is so determined not to give up that seeing others doing so bothers him tremendously. By regarding others' behavior, Cowley reaches conclusions about himself.

Annie Dillard writes about a moment in her life when she realizes the enormous difference between solitude, which she had sought deliberately one afternoon, and loneliness, which nobody seeks but which she observes in a little boy playing forlornly by himself. Reflecting on the boy's loneliness, Dillard thanks God for her own happy childhood peopled with sisters and playmates. Listening to the boy's desperate attempts to hold her in conversation for even one more precious minute, Dillard draws conclusions about her own fortunate life.

And Chilean writer Pablo Neruda, reflecting on New Year's Eve celebrations he has observed all over the world, decides that Valparaiso, the capital of Chile, is the best place to be on New Year's Eve. He has heard fireworks, gongs, and bells in Saigon and he has seen old furniture being thrown out of windows in Naples. Then, reflecting on those scenes, he suddenly pictures the twinkling lights of a small ship lying at anchor in the port of Valparaiso one New Year's Eve and he knows that Chile is his favorite place. Once again, a writer demonstrates how reflecting on others' behavior clarifies his own thoughts.

Toni Cade Bambara

Toni Cade Bambara (b. 1939) was born in New York City and educated at Queens College in New York and in Italy at the University of Florence. She also studied mime in France at the École de Mime and dance with the Katherine Dunham Dance Studio in New York. Besides being a writer, an actress, and a dancer, Bambara has taught writing at universities and has contributed to reading books for school children. Her fiction includes *The Salt Eaters* and collections of short stories, *Gorilla, My Love* and *The Seabirds are Still Alive and Other Stories*. In the selection here, which comes from Janet Sternberg's *The Writer on her Work*, a collection of essays in which women writers talk about their creative lives, Bambara defends the way she writes. Deliberately choosing a narrative that remains faithful to the black woman's position, Bambara deplores any other plot choice. For, if she had been false to her position as a black, as a woman, and as a writer, "How would I have explained that to my daughter?"

What It Is I Think I'm Doing Anyhow

Winter 1979. We are now in the fourth year of the last quarter of the twentieth century. And the questions that face the millions of us on the earth are—in whose name will the twenty-first century be claimed? Can the planet be rescued from the psychopaths? Where are the evolved, poised-for-light adepts who will assume the task of administering power in a human interest, of redefining power as being not the privilege or class right to define, deform, and dominate but as the human responsibility to define, transform, and develop?

171

The previous quarter-century, from 1950 to 1975, was an era hallmarked by revolution, a period in which was experienced a radical shift in the political-power configurations of the globe. The current quarter, from 1976 to 2000, is also characterized by revolution, a period in which we are awakening to and experiencing a profound change in the psychic-power configurations of the globe.

There is a war going on and a transformation taking place. That war is not simply the contest between the socialist camp and the capitalist camp over which political/economic/social arrangement will enjoy hegemony in the world, nor is it simply the battle over turf and resources. Truth is one of the issues in this war. The truth, * for example, about inherent human nature, about our potential, our agenda as earth people, our destiny.

Writing is one of the ways I participate in struggle — one of the ways I help to keep vibrant and resilient that vision that has kept the Family going on. Through writing I attempt to celebrate the tradition of resistance, attempt to tap Black potential, and try to join the chorus of voices that argues that exploitation and misery are neither inevitable nor necessary. Writing is one of the ways I participate in the transformation—one of the ways I practice the commitment to explore bodies of knowledge for the usable wisdoms they yield. In writing, I hope to encourage the fusion of those disciplines whose split (material science versus metaphysics versus aesthetics versus politics versus . . .) predisposes us to accept fragmented truths and distortions as the whole. Writing is one of the ways I do my work in the world.

There are no career labels for that work, no facile terms to describe the tasks of it. Suffice to say that I do not take lightly the fact that I am on the earth at this particular time in human history, and am here as a member of a particular soul group and of a particular sex, having this particular adventure as a Pan-Africanist-socialist-feminist in the United States. I figure all that means something—about what I'm here to understand and to do.

. . .The old folks say, "It's not how little we know that hurts so, but that so much of what we know ain't so." As a mother, teacher, writer, community worker, neighbor, I am concerned about accurate information, verifiable facts, sound analyses, responsible research, principled study, and people's assessment of the meaning of their lives. I'm interested in usable truths. Which means rising above my training, thinking better than I've been taught, developing a listening habit, making the self available to intelligence, engaging in demystification, and seeking out teachers at every turn. In many respects the writings are notebooks I'm submitting to those teachers for examination. There have been a host of teachers. Once I thought anyone with enthusiasm about information was a good teacher. Then, anyone with an analysis of this country who could help illuminate the condition, status, and process of the Family, who could help me decide how to put my wrath and my skills to the service of folks who sustain me. Later, anyone who could throw open the path and lead me back to the ancient wisdoms was teacher. In more recent times, any true dialectician (material/spiritual) who could increase my understanding of all, I say all, the forces afoot in the universe was teacher. I'm entering my forties with more simplistic criteria—anyone with a greater capacity for love than I is a valuable teacher. And when I look back on the body of book reviews I've produced in the past fifteen years, for all their socioideolitero brilliant somethinorother, the underlying * standard always seemed to be—Does this author here genuinely love his/her community?

The greatest challenge in writing, then, in the earlier stages was to strike a balance between candor, honesty, integrity, and truth— terms that are fairly synonymous for crossword puzzlers and thesaurus ramblers but hard to equate as living actions. Speaking one's mind, after all, does not necessarily mean one is in touch with the truth or even with the facts. Being honest and frank in terms of my own where—where I'm at at a given point in my political/spiritual/etc. * development—is not necessarily in my/our interest to utter, not nec- essarily in the interest of health, wholesomeness. Certain kinds of poisons, for example—rage, bitterness, revenge—don't need to be in the atmosphere, not to mention in my mouth. I don't, for example, hack up racists and stuff them in metaphorical boxes. I do not wish to lend them energy, for one thing. Though certainly there are "heavies" * that people my stories. But I don't, for example, conjure up characters for the express purpose of despising them, of breaking their humps in public. . . .

I'm not convinced that ugly is *the* truth that can save us, redeem us. The old folks teach that. Be triflin' and ugly and they say, "Deep down, gal, you know that ain't right," appealing to a truth about our deep-down nature. Good enough for me. Besides, I can't get happy writing ugly weird. If I'm not laughing while I work, I conclude that I am not communicating nourishment, since laughter is the most sure-fire healant I know. I don't know all my readers, but I know well for whom I write. And I want for them no less than I want for myself—wholesomeness.

It all sounds so la-di-da and tra-la-la. I can afford to be sunny. *
I'm but one voice in the chorus. The literatures(s) of our time are a collective effort, dependent on so many views, on so many people's productions. I am frequently asked to name my favorite writer, or the one writer who best captures the Black experience, or the one sister who is really doing it. What can I do but crack up and stuff another carrot in the juicer? No way in the world I can swing over to that frame of reference so dominated by solo-voice thinking. Given the range of experiences available to a soul having the human adventure in this time and place, given that we have just begun to tap the limitless reservoir of cultural, societal, global, possibilities. Hell, there aren't even phrases in the languages for half the things happening just on the block where I live, not yet anyhow. Who could possibly be this *one* writer that interviewers and reviewers are always harping about? . . .

Time out to say this—I often read in reviews that my stories are set in the sixties and are nostalgic and reminiscent of days when revolution was believed in. News to me. With the exception of "The Long Night," all the stories in *Seabirds* are in the "right now" time they were drafted. I suppose for too many people the idea that struggle is neither new nor over is hard to grasp, that there is a radical tradition as old as the H.M.S. *Jesus* or whatever that ship was that hauled over the first boatload. Some weeks ago, I read from my new work at a workshop of novels-in-progress. It was an excerpt about an elderly woman recalling the days when she worked for the Sleeping Car Porters and organized Ida B. Wells clubs in Harlem. Two out of three people at the reading assumed that the novel was set in the late sixties and that the woman was talking about the earlier sixties.

Gives a person pause. Amnesia is a hellafying thing. The impulse to pronounce the Movement dead ain't no joke either. . . .

I got a lot of mixed reactions about the story "The Organizer's Wife" in *Seabirds*. Feminist types didn't like the title; some said they refused to read the story because the title was such a putdown. Others liked the fact that Virginia, the lead character, kicked the preacher's ass for more reasons than for turning her husband in but, nonetheless, would have been happier had she left town or died in childbirth, by way of my protesting the system. Some letters and calls said I should have had Graham, the organizer, die some gruesome death in that southern jail to protest, etc. Kill Graham off and have Virginia go batty, or leave, or die in childbirth? What kind of message would that have been? How would I have explained that to my daughter? She's looking forward to growing up as a responsible change agent.   *
I'm well aware that we are under siege, that the system kills, that the terms of race and class war have not altered very much. But death is not a truth that inspires, that pumps up the heart, that mobilizes. It's defeatist to dwell always on the consequences of risks. It's proracist to assume we can't take a chance. I am not interested in collaborating with the program of the forces that systematically underdevelop. So Graham lives and Virginia wakes up.

. . .To drive Virginia nuts or Graham to death is not a message I want to send to my heart, my lungs, my brain. My daughter. My readers. Or, to the Grahams and Virginias. But then I come from a particular tradition. I identify with the championship tradition.

Ali, in his autobiography, *I Am the Greatest*, defines a champion as one who takes the telling blow on the chin and hits the canvas hard, can't possibly rally, arms shot, energy spent, the very weight of the body too heavy a burden for the legs to raise, can't possibly get up. So you do. And you keep getting up. *The Awakening* by Kate Chopin is not my classic. *Their Eyes Were Watching God* by Zora Neale Hurston is. Sylvia Plath and the other obligatory writers on women's studies *
lists—the writers who hawk despair, insanity, alienation, suicide, all in the name of protesting woman's oppression, are not my mentors. I was raised on stories of Harriet Tubman, Ida B. Wells, Paul Robeson, and my grandmother, Annie, whom folks in Atlanta still remember as an early Rosa Parks. So Virginia does not go batty and Graham

does not die. Were I to do them in, my granny would no doubt visit me in the night to batter me gingerly about the head and shoulders with an ancestral bone pulled out of the Ethiopic Ocean called the Atlantic.

. . . When I replay the tapes on file in my head, tapes of speeches I've given at writing conferences over the years, I invariably hear myself saying—"A writer, like any other cultural worker, like any other member of the community, ought to try to put her/his skills in the service of the community." Some years ago when I returned south, my picture in the paper prompted several neighbors to come visit. "You a writer? What all you write?" Before I could begin the catalogue, one old gent interrupted with—"Ya know Miz Mary down the block? She need a writer to help her send off a letter to her grandson overseas." So I began a career as the neighborhood scribe—letters to relatives, snarling letters to the traffic chief about the promised stop sign, nasty letters to the utilities, angry letters to the principal about that confederate flag hanging in front of the school, contracts to transfer a truck from seller to buyer etc. While my efforts have been graciously appreciated in the form of sweet potato dumplings, herb teas, hair braiding, and the like, there is still much room for improvement—"For a writer, honey, you've got a mighty bad hand. Didn't they teach penmanship at that college?" Another example, I guess, of words setting things in motion. What goes around, comes around, as the elders say.

It will be a pleasure to get back to the shorts; they allow me to share. I much prefer to haul around story collections to prisons, schools, senior citizen centers, and rallies and then select from the "menu" something that suits the moment and is all of a piece. But the novel's pull is powerful. And since the breakthrough achieved in the sixties by the Neo-Black Arts Movement, the possibilities are stunning. Characters that have been waiting in the wings for generations, characters that did not fit into the roster of stereotypes, can now be brought down center stage. Now that I/we have located our audience, we are free to explore the limits of language. Now that American history, American literature, the American experience is being redefined by so many communities, the genre too will undergo changes. So I came to the novel with a sense that everything is possible. And I'm attempting to blueprint for myself the merger of these two camps: the political and the spiritual. The possibilities of healing that split are exciting. The implications of actually yoking those energies and of fusing that power quite take my breath away.

Thinking about Writing

Words

Powerful words both depend on and help shape their context. In what way does each word in the list below depend on its context for strength? What does each contribute to its context? Can you think of any other word the author might have used in its place? How does the word strike you, and how do you respond to the sentence or passage because of the word?

turf
somethinorother
where
energy
la-di-da and tra-la-la
H.M.S. *Jesus*
change agent
obligatory

Thinking

1. Bambara refuses to kill off her troubled characters, although her public wants her to get tough with them. Why do you think she refuses? When she says, "But death is not a truth that inspires," how do you react? If death is a fact of everyone's existence, is Bambara avoiding the issue? What does she offer instead of death?
2. Bambara says she submits her writings to teachers who have been changing over the years. Who do you assume these teachers are? Why do you think she calls them teachers? How have her teachers changed over the years? Explain how these changes reflect changes

in Bambara. In what way does she require certain teachers at certain times?

3. Bambara sees herself on a "particular adventure," a member "at this particular time," "of a particular soul group and of a particular sex," "a Pan-Africanist-socialist-feminist in the United States." As such, she feels she has certain obligations. Using her hyphenated adjective style, describe yourself. Who are you and what are your obligations? (This is a question that is designed for either discussion or writing. Try it either way, or talk about it in class and then write.)

4. "It will be a pleasure to get back to the shorts," says Bambara, talking about her short stories which she loves. Which do you prefer generally, short stories or novels? How can you connect Bambara's love of short stories with her refusal to kill off her troubled characters?

Writing

1. In her writing Bambara slips away from certain rules and conventions while still writing vibrant prose. How does she do it? For example, Bambara can talk about driving Virginia "nuts," and we don't object. In fact, "insane" would be an awkward intrusion here while something in us welcomes "nuts" as the perfect word. (You try it and your instructor will howl, as you know.) Further, Bambara writes sentence fragments like "My readers." What's more, we understand her perfectly. She writes perfectly.

Write an essay in which you examine Bambara's use of language. Try to see just how much of traditional grammar and convention she keeps and where she takes off. You may be surprised at just how conventional she is after all. You might begin by looking at every instance of what appears to be slang, casual language, or made up words. She is usually at her most serious then. When you've examined her wonderful, outrageous language, try to tell why you think she deliberately writes this way in moments of deep seriousness. What do you think this practice tells us about Bambara the writer?

2. Why does Bambara, as a matter of personal policy, make fun of "obligatory" writing? What does she tell us accounts for her impatience at being subjected to such depressing writing (as she sees it)? Write an essay that explains, from her writing, what she finds objectionable about the concept, "ugly," quoting her wherever possible.

3. Write an essay about the various teachers (influences) in your life. These needn't be specific people, such as Mr. Brown in biology, but may be ideals of those types of people who have responded best to your needs and have inspired you to go on, those who could "throw open the path." As you describe your various teachers, think about how you are also describing yourself and your needs at particular periods in your life.

4. Read Kate Chopin's *The Awakening* and Zora Neale Hurston's *Their Eyes Were Watching God*, both short novels. With Bambara's comments in mind, compare the outlooks of the two heroines. Then, consider why Bambara says the Chopin story is not her "classic," while the Hurston is. Which do you prefer, and for what reasons? Write an essay on your observations, using Bambara's comments as a starting point for your writing.

William Shakespeare

William Shakespeare (1564–1616) was born in Stratford-on-Avon, England, and educated at the local grammar school. The desire to become an actor took him to London, where he established the Globe Theater, acted, and wrote. In addition to comedies, tragedies, and historical plays, Shakespeare wrote long poems and sonnets like the three selections here. The sonnet form, because it is so short, uses concise imagery that convinces and produces satisfaction at the same time. In the first sonnet here, the speaker recommends writing down ideas the "memory cannot contain" in order to read them later with pleasure. The second sonnet here presents to the reader the feelings of a lovesick insomniac who suddenly realizes he cannot sleep not because of his beloved's affections for him, but because of his own love for his beloved. In the third sonnet here, the speaker claims that while sometimes he can read the truth in other people's faces, he hasn't the remotest idea what's on his beloved's mind, because "thy looks" don't reveal anything, of either affection or deception.

Three Sonnets

Sonnet 77

Thy glass will show thee how thy beauties wear,
Thy dial how thy precious minutes waste;
The vacant leaves thy mind's imprint will bear,   **
And of this book this learning mayst thou taste.   *
The wrinkles which thy glass will truly show   5
Of mouthed graves will give thee memory;   *
Thou by thy dial's shady stealth mayst know
Time's thievish progress to eternity.   *

180

Look, what thy memory cannot contain
Commit to these waste blanks, and thou shalt find   10
Those children nursed, deliver'd from thy brain
To take a new acquaintance of thy mind.
   These offices, so oft as thou wilt look,
   Shall profit thee and much enrich thy book.

Thinking about Writing

Words

     Powerful words both depend on and help shape their context. In what way does each word in the list below depend on its context for strength? What does each contribute to its context? Can you think of any other word the author might have used in its place? How does the word strike you, and how do you respond to the sentence or passage because of the word?

vacant leaves
mind's imprint
taste
memory
thievish progress

Thinking

1. Do you find the poet's metaphor of ideas as children appropriate? If so, why do you? What other metaphor for ideas can you think of?
2. The poet has used the word *waste* in two distinct ways. How do you interpret each of these uses? How does the whole sonnet hinge on the ideas contained in these two uses of one word? Why would the poet, having decided to repeat a word, use it with two disparate meanings, rather than a single meaning?

Writing

1. Joan Didion, in her essay "On Keeping a Notebook" in Explaining, tells why she writes things down. Using lines from Didion, Shakespeare, and yourself, write a convincing argument for writing things down.
2. First, write the sonnet mechanically, line by line, in modern American English. Use slang, jargon, or any language you wish to convey the thoughts here. You might begin by rewriting the first line, "Thy glass will show thee how thy beauties wear," as "When you look in the mirror, you're going to see how old you've become and then you'll realize how time's just slipping by. . . ."

    Then, after you've written the sonnet mechanically, write an essay in which you examine a few of the impressions Shakespeare creates, explaining what each one suggests in modern language and how Shakespeare uses a few well-chosen words to create vivid impressions. For example, the first line creates the image of someone looking into a mirror or contemplating an hour glass and marking changes time brings. The end of the line, "how thy beauties wear," could mean more than just how you are aging. It also implies, "You are beautiful today, but you may not always be so." It even suggests that time affects beauty and there is no prediction how you'll look in age. What's certain is that time will pass, and over that you have no control. Looking back on the first line after reading the second enriches the impression of time passing for the person looking in the glass (the mirror) or watching an hour glass (a clock) or a sundial. After doing this kind of analysis, try to write broadly and fully on each impression you select, in order to demonstrate how concise imagery contains layers of meaning.

    Incidentally, this writing assignment is useful for any of the sonnets here as well as for reading any difficult poem.

Sonnet 61

Is it thy will thy image should keep open
My heavy eyelids to the weary night?   *
Dost thou desire my slumbers should be broken,   *
While shadows like to thee do mock my sight?

Is it thy spirit that thou send'st from thee   5
So far from home into my deeds to pry,   *
To find out shames and idle hours in me,
The scope and tenor of thy jealousy?
O, no! thy love, though much, is not so great:
It is my love that keeps mine eye awake;   10
Mine own true love that doth my rest defeat,   *
To play the watchman ever for thy sake: *
    For thee watch I whilst thou doth wake elsewhere,
    From me far off, with others all too near.   *

Thinking about Writing

Words

Powerful words both depend on and help shape their context. In what way does each word in the list below depend on its context for strength? What does each contribute to its context? Can you think of any other word the author might have used in its place? How does the word strike you, and how do you respond to the sentence or passage because of the word?

weary night
broken
pry
defeat
play the watchman
with others all too near

Thinking

1. What do you feel is the force of the contrast throughout between *thy* and *my* or *thee* and *me*? What do you think about the "others" in the last line? How did *they* get in? Why do you think Shakespeare might have decided to include them and to put them in the last line?
2. As well as being a celebration of love, this sonnet is a lament for being separated from a lover. What can you gather about the

relation between the two people? What words or phrases give you this impression?

3. Why do you think the poet first asks the three questions and then answers them with "O, no!"? In modern, everyday English, what do the three questions say to you? Consider each, then put them together as one question.

Writing

1. We say that beauty is in the eye of the beholder. The poet here seems to be saying something similar about love: that when we love someone, *we* contain the love.

   Write an essay in which you show how Shakespeare presents this sad fact through the speaker in the poem realizing that his love is just that, *his*. Quote the poet's words to support your observations. You might find it helpful to review the first Thinking question.

2. Shakespeare's speaker in this sonnet and Pip in Dickens's "Ashamed of Home" in chapter 4 both discuss the fantasy of being observed by the beloved. Both sad lovers talk in terms of shame.

   Write an essay in which you examine the idea of being ashamed while being observed, even in fantasy, by a loved one, as discussed by these two writers. Quote from both Dickens and Shakespeare whenever you want to support your claims.

Sonnet 93

So shall I live, supposing thou art true,
Like a deceived husband; so love's face
May still seem love to me, though alter'd new;
Thy looks with me, thy heart in other place:
For there can live no hatred in thine eye,   5
Therefore in that I cannot know thy change.
In many's looks the false heart's history
Is writ in moods and frowns and wrinkles strange,
But heaven in thy creation did decree
That in thy face sweet love should ever dwell;   10
Whate'er thy thoughts or thy heart's workings be,
Thy looks should nothing thence but sweetness tell.

How like Eve's apple doth thy beauty grow,
If thy sweet virtue answer not thy show.   ***

Thinking about Writing

Words

Powerful words both depend on and help shape their context. In what way does each word in the list below depend on its context for strength? What does each contribute to its context? Can you think of any other word the author might have used in its place? How does the word strike you, and how do you respond to the sentence or passage because of the word?

If
virtue
show

Thinking

1. The speaker in this sonnet seems to be in a state of ignorance about his lover. What words and ideas expressing doubt or deception can you find?
2. Why do we want to sense the full range of emotional responses when we care about someone? How do you know from the speaker's words that he seeks more than just the look of love? What do you think he actually wants?
3. If the beloved's face could show love or hatred, which face do you think the speaker would assume was the deceptive one? Why? Why do you think the poet refers to Eve's apple?

Writing

1. Consider all three sonnets, looking at their structures, their rhymes, and the number of lines. How does the last word of each line thread the argument together? Is the impact in the same line for each sonnet? Do you feel any connection between opening and closing lines?

Write an essay in which you explore your favorite of the three sonnets, taking into account the flow of the argument, how the sonnet sounds in modern English, and what the sonnet says to you. Quote your favorite words or expressions and explain why these mean something to you.

2. Even on a first reading, you can easily understand that this sonnet is concerned with the doubts a lover feels about his beloved's fidelity. Look at all the words in the sonnet that connote deception or uncertainty. Read the sonnet again and you will see just how fragile is the thread of hope by which the speaker's thoughts hang. Write an essay in which you examine the concept of doubt as expressed in this sonnet. Quote words and phrases to support your observations.

Malcolm Cowley

Malcolm Cowley (b. 1898) was born in Pennsylvania and educated at Harvard University and the University of Montpellier in France. Still at Harvard when World War I began, Cowley interrupted his studies in order to drive an ambulance in France for the American Field Service. After the war, Cowley returned to France to live in Paris, where he became friends with a number of young American writers and artists living there. It was here that he first knew F. Scott Fitzgerald, Ernest Hemingway, John Dos Passos, and William Faulkner. Cowley became more than a friend to these writers; his literary judgment made him their advisor as well. A gifted editor and literary historian, Cowley worked with the *New Republic* and later with Viking Press. His own writing includes poetry, letters, and criticism. In 1981, the American Academy of Arts and Letters awarded him their Gold Medal. In the selection here, from *The View from 80*, Cowley celebrates his arrival at eighty by explaining the behavior of people who reach this advanced age.

The View from 80

Even before he or she is 80, the aging person may undergo another identity crisis like that of adolescence. Perhaps there had also been a middle-aged crisis, the male or the female menopause, but for the rest of adult life he had taken himself for granted, with his capabilities and failings. Now, when he looks in the mirror, he asks himself, "Is this really me?"—or he avoids the mirror out of distress at what it reveals, those bags and wrinkles. In his new makeup he is called upon to play a new role in a play that must be improvised. André Gide, that long-lived man of letters, wrote in his journal,

"My heart has remained so young that I have continual feeling of playing a part, the part of the 70-year-old that I certainly am; and the infirmities and weaknesses that remind me of my age act like a prompter, reminding me of my lines when I tend to stray. Then, like the good actor I want to be, I go back into my role and I pride myself on playing it well."

In his new role the old person will find that he is tempted by new vices, that he receives new compensations (not so widely known), and that he may possibly achieve new virtues. Chief among these is the heroic or merely obstinate refusal to surrender in the face of time. One admires the ships that go down with all flags flying and the captain on the bridge.

Among the vices of age are avarice, untidiness, and vanity, which last takes the form of a craving to be loved or simply admired. Avarice is the worst of those three. Why do so many old persons, men and women alike, insist on hoarding money when they have no prospect of using it and even when they have no heirs? They eat the cheapest food, buy no clothes, and live in a single room when they could afford better lodging. It may be that they regard money as a form of power; there is a comfort in watching it accumulate while other powers are dwindling away. How often we read of an old person found dead in a hovel, on a mattress partly stuffed with bankbooks and stock certificates! The bankbook syndrome, we call it in our family, which has never succumbed.   *

Untidiness we call the Langley Collyer syndrome. To explain, Langley Collyer was a former concert pianist who lived alone with his 70-year-old brother in a brownstone house on upper Fifth Avenue. The once fashionable neighborhood had become part of Harlem. Homer, the brother, had been an admiralty lawyer, but was now blind and partly paralyzed; Langley played for him and fed him on buns and oranges, which he thought would restore Homer's sight. He never threw away a daily paper because Homer, he said, might want to read them all. He saved other things as well and the house became filled with rubbish from roof to basement. The halls were lined on both sides with bundled newspapers, leaving narrow passageways in which Langley had devised booby traps to catch intruders.

On March 21, 1947, some unnamed person telephoned the

police to report that there was a dead body in the Collyer house. The police broke down the front door and found the hall impassable, then they hoisted a ladder to a second-story window. Behind it Homer was lying on the floor in a bathrobe; he had starved to death. Langley had disappeared. After some delay, the police broke into the basement, chopped a hole in the roof, and began throwing junk out of the house, top and bottom. It was 18 days before they found Langley's body, gnawed by rats. Caught in one of his own booby traps, he had died in a hallway just outside Homer's door. By that time the police had collected, and the Department of Sanitation had hauled away, 120 tons of rubbish, including besides the newspapers, 14 grand pianos and the parts of a dismantled Model T Ford.

Why do so many old people accumulate junk, not on the scale of Langley Collyer, but still in a dismaying fashion? Their tables are piled high with it, their bureau drawers are stuffed with it, their closet rods bend with the weight of clothes not worn for years. I suppose that the piling up is partly from lethargy and partly from the feeling that everything once useful, including their own bodies, should be preserved. Others, though not so many, have such a fear of becoming Langley Collyers that they strive to be painfully neat. Every tool they own is in its place, though it will never be used again; every scrap of paper is filed away in alphabetical order. At last their immoderate neatness becomes another vice of age, if a milder one.

The vanity of older people is an easier weakness to explain, and to condone. With less to look forward to, they yearn for recognition of what they have been: the reigning beauty, the athlete, the soldier, the scholar. It is the beauties who have the hardest time. A portrait of themselves at twenty hangs on the wall, and they try to resemble it by making an extravagant use of creams, powders, and dyes. Being young at heart, they think they are merely revealing their essential persons. The athletes find shelves for their silver trophies, which are polished once a year. Perhaps a letter sweater lies wrapped in a bureau drawer. I remember one evening when a no-longer athlete had guests for dinner and tried to find his sweater, "Oh, that old thing," his wife said. "The moths got into it and I threw it away." The athlete sulked and his guests went home early.

Often the yearning to be recognized appears in conversation as an innocent boast. Thus, a distinguished physician, retired at 94, remarks casually that a disease was named after him. A former judge bursts into chuckles as he repeats bright things that he said on the bench. Again scholars complain in letters (or one of them does), "As I approach 70 I'm becoming avid of honors, and such things—medals, honorary degrees, etc.—are only passed around among academics on a *quid pro quo* basis (one hood capping another)." Or they say querulously, "Bill Underwood has ten honorary doctorates and I have only three. Why didn't they elect me to . . . ?" and they mention the name of some learned society. That search for honors is a harmless passion, though it may lead to jealousies and deformations of character, as with Robert Frost in his later years. Still, honors cost little. Why shouldn't the very old have more than their share of them?

To be admired and praised, especially by the young, is an autumnal pleasure enjoyed by the lucky ones (who are not always the most deserving). "What is more charming," Cicero observes in his famous essay *De Senectute*, "than an old age surrounded by the enthusiasm of youth! . . . Attentions which seem trivial and conventional are marks of honor—the morning call, being sought after, precedence, having people rise for you, being escorted to and from the forum. . . . What pleasures of the body can be compared to the prerogatives of influence?" But there are also pleasures of the body, or the mind, that are enjoyed by a greater number of older persons.

Those pleasures include some that younger people find hard to appreciate. One of them is simply sitting still, like a snake on a sun-warmed stone, with a delicious feeling of indolence that was seldom attained in earlier years. A leaf flutters down; a cloud moves by inches across the horizon. At such moments the older person, completely relaxed, has become a part of nature—and a living part, with blood coursing through his veins. The future does not exist for him. He thinks, if he thinks at all, that life for younger persons is still a battle royal of each against each, but that now he has nothing more to win or lose. He is not so much above as outside the battle, as if he had assumed the uniform of some small neutral country, perhaps Liechtenstein or Andorra. From a distance he notes that some of the combatants, men or women, are jostling ahead—but why do they fight so hard when the most they can hope for is a longer obituary? He can watch the scrounging and gouging, he can hear the shouts of exultation, the moans of the gravely wounded, and meanwhile he feels secure: nobody will attack him from ambush.

Age has other physical compensations besides the nirvana of dozing in the sun. A few of the simplest needs become a pleasure to satisfy. When an old woman in a nursing home was asked what she really liked to do, she answered in one word: "Eat." She might have been speaking for many of her fellows. Meals in a nursing home, however badly cooked, serve as climactic moments of the day. The physical essence of the pensioners is being renewed at an appointed hour; now they can go back to meditating or to watching TV while looking forward to the next meal. They can also look forward to sleep, which has become a definite pleasure, not the mere interruption it once had been.

Here I am thinking of old persons under nursing care. Others ferociously guard their independence, and some of them suffer less than one might expect from being lonely and impoverished. They can be rejoiced by visits and meetings, but they also have company inside their heads. Some of them are busiest when their hands are still. What passes through the minds of many is a stream of persons, images, phrases, and familiar tunes. For some that stream has continued since childhood, but now it is deeper; it is their present and their past combined. At times they conduct silent dialogues with a vanished friend, and these are less tiring—often more rewarding—than spoken conversations. If inner resources are lacking, old persons living alone may seek comfort and a kind of companionship in the bottle. I should judge from the gossip of various neighborhoods that the outer suburbs from Boston to San Diego are full of secretly alcoholic widows. One of those widows, an old friend, was moved from her apartment into a retirement home. She left behind her a closet in which the floor was covered wall to wall with whiskey bottles. "Oh, those empty bottles!" she explained. "They were left by a former tenant."

Not whiskey or cooking sherry but simply giving up is the great- *
est temptation of age. It is something different from a stoical acceptance of infirmities, which is something to be admired. At 63, when

he first recognized that his powers were failing, Emerson wrote one of his best poems, "Terminus":

It is time to be old,
To take in sail: —
The god of bounds,
Who sets to seas a shore,
Came to me in his fatal rounds,
And said, "No more!
No farther shoot
Thy broad ambitious branches, and thy root.
Fancy departs, no more invent;
Contract thy firmament
To compass of a tent."

Emerson lived in good health to the age of 79. Within his narrowed firmament, he continued working until his memory failed; then he consented to having younger editors and collaborators. The givers-up see no reason for working. Sometimes they lie in bed all day when moving about would still be possible, if difficult. I had a friend, a distinguished poet, who surrendered in that fashion. The doctors tried to stir him to action, but he refused to leave his room. Another friend, once a successful artist, stopped painting when his eyes began to fail. His doctor made the mistake of telling him that he suffered from a fatal disease. He then lost interest in everything except the splendid Rolls-Royce, acquired in his prosperous days, that stood in the garage. Daily he wiped the dust from its hood. He couldn't drive it on the road any longer, but he used to sit in the driver's seat, start the motor, then back the Rolls out of the garage and drive it in again, back twenty feet and forward twenty feet; that was his only distraction.

I haven't the right to blame those who surrender, not being able to put myself inside their minds or bodies. Often they must have compelling reasons, physical or moral. Not only do they suffer from a variety of ailments, but also they are made to feel that they no longer have a function in the community. Their families and neighbors don't ask them for advice, don't really listen when they speak, don't call on them for efforts. One notes that there are not a few recoveries from apparent senility when that situation changes. If it doesn't change, old persons may decide that efforts are useless. I sympathize with their problems, but the men and women I envy are those who accept old   * age as a series of challenges.

For such persons, every new infirmity is an enemy to be outwitted, an obstacle to be overcome by force of will. They enjoy each little victory over themselves, and sometimes they win a major success. Renoir was one of them. He continued painting, and magnificently, for years after he was crippled by arthritis; the brush had to be strapped to his arm. "You don't need your hand to paint," he said. Goya was another of the unvanquished. At 72 he retired as an official painter of the Spanish court and decided to work only for himself. His later years were those of the famous "black paintings" in which he let his imagination run (and also of the lithographs, then a new technique). At 78 he escaped a reign of terror in Spain by fleeing to Bordeaux. He was deaf and his eyes were failing; in order to work he had to wear several pairs of spectacles, one over another, and then use a magnifying glass; but he was producing splendid work in a totally new style. At 80 he drew an ancient man propped on two sticks, with a mass of white hair and beard hiding his face and with the inscription "I am still learning."

Giovanni Papini said when he was nearly blind, "I prefer martyrdom to imbecility." After writing sixty books, including his famous *Life of Christ*, he was at work on two huge projects when he was stricken with a form of muscular atrophy. He lost the use of his left leg, then of his fingers, so that he couldn't hold a pen. The two big books, though never to be finished, moved forward slowly by dictation; that in itself was a triumph. Toward the end, when his voice had become incomprehensible, he spelled out a word, tapping on the table to indicate letters of the alphabet. One hopes never to be faced with the need for such heroic measures.

"Eighty years old!" the great Catholic poet Paul Claudel wrote in his journal. "No eyes left, no ears, no teeth, no legs, no wind? And when all is said and done, how astonishingly well one does without them!"

Thinking about Writing

Words

Powerful words both depend on and help shape their context. In what way does each word in the list below depend on its context for strength? What does each contribute to its context? Can you think of any other word the author might have used in its place? How does the word strike you, and how do you respond to the sentence or passage because of the word?

succumbed
temptation
envy

Thinking

1. Cowley quotes the French writer André Gide talking about an old person as an actor who plays a role. What in the writing of either Cowley or Gide explains why the old person plays a role? Why is the play improvised?
2. Cowley mentions a number of new attributes: a new role, new vices, new compensations, and new virtues. Since he is talking about old age, why does he see so much new? What does his calling these "new" tell you about Cowley's view of old age?
3. As a rule, Cowley seems most tolerant and understanding when he is talking about the ways old people behave. Why do you think he abandons his tolerant attitude when he discusses "those who surrender"? What does this single intolerance tell you about Cowley?
4. Cowley says not only do the old ail, but they "no longer have a function in the community." To what extent do you agree? What do you see as the popular image of old age: what we as a nation think about our old people? (You might consider how the old are portrayed in advertisements on television and in magazines, what fashions are marketed to them, what euphemisms we use for *age* and for *old*, or what roles they play in movies, television programs, or ads.)

Writing

1. Both André Gide here in Cowley's essay and George Orwell in "Shooting an Elephant" in chapter 4 talk about playing a role. Consider how the two writers refer to roles. Write an essay in which you compare and contrast the two roles. You might begin by considering what generates a need for a role in the first place, and ask yourself what could be the advantages the role player has in playing a certain role.

2. Write an essay based on observations of your own playing a part as you were growing up. What were the virtues and the vices of your role? Do you see growing up as a shifting of roles?

3. Write about your oldest relative or acquaintance, describing his or her appearance, disposition and personality, likes, dislikes, and wishes, if you know them. In what ways do you assume old age has been satisfying for this person? What have been its apparent disappointments? If you can, interview your subject.

Annie Dillard

Annie Dillard (b. 1945) was born in Pittsburgh and educated at Hollins College. A writer, a teacher of creative writing and poetry, and a contributing editor for *Harper's*, Dillard won the Pulitzer Prize for her book *Pilgrim at Tinker Creek*. Writing in the tradition of Henry David Thoreau's *Walden*, Dillard is never far from nature, even when she is describing social behavior. The selection here comes from a collection of her essays, *Teaching a Stone to Talk*. In this piece, Dillard says she values solitude but, although she was seeking it when she chanced upon the little boy playing by himself, she sees a great difference between solitude and loneliness. She is so moved by the child's desperate desire for company that she stops in her tracks to thank God for having given her sisters and friends when she was a child.

On a Hill Far Away

In Virginia, late one January afternoon while I had a leg of lamb in the oven, I took a short walk. The idea was to exercise my limbs and rest my mind, but these things rarely work out as I plan.

It was sunset by the time I crossed Tinker Creek by hopping from stone to stone and inching up a fallen tree trunk to the bank. On the far side of the creek I followed a barbed-wire fence through steers' pasture and up to a high grassy hill. I'd never been there before. From the hill the distant creek looked still and loaded with sky.   *

On the hilltop, just across the barbed-wire fence, were three outbuildings: a fenced horse barn, around which a dun mare and a new foal were nervously clattering; a cyclone-fenced dog pen with a barking shepherd and a barking bird dog; and a frame toolshed under whose weedy eaves a little boy was pretending to write with a stone.

The little boy didn't see me. He looked to be about eight, thin, wearing a brown corduroy jacket with darker brown pile on the collar and a matching beaked corduroy cap with big earflaps. He alternated between pretending to write big letters on the toolshed wall and fooling with the dogs from outside their pen. The dogs were going crazy at their fence because of me, and I wondered why the boy didn't turn around; he must be too little to know much about dogs. When he did see me, by accident, his eyebrows shot up. I smiled and hollered and he came over to the barbed wire.

We watched the horses. "How old's the foal?" I asked him. The golden foal looked like a test model in a patent office—jerky, its eyes not set quite right, a marvel. It ran to keep from falling.

"That one is just one. You'd have to say he was *one.* . . ."[1]

Boy, I thought. I sure don't know anything about horses.

". . .he was just *born* six days ago."

The foal wanted to approach. Every time it looked at us, the mare ran interference and edged the foal away.

The boy and I talked over the barbed wire. The dogs' names were Barney and Duke. "Luke?" I said. The boy was shocked. "Duke," * he said. He was formal and articulate; he spoke in whole sentences, choosing his words. "I haven't yet settled on a name for the foal, although Father says he is mine." When he spoke this way, he gazed up at me through meeting eyebrows. His dark lips made a projecting circle. He looked like a nineteenth-century cartoon of an Earnest Child. This kid is a fraud, I thought. Who calls his father "Father"? But at other times his face would loosen; I could see then that the accustomed gesture of his lips resembled that of a person trying not to cry. Or he would smile, or look away shyly, like now: "Actually, I've been considering the name Marky Sparky."

"Marky Sparky," I repeated, with as much warmth as I could * muster. The sun was down. What was I doing chatting with a little kid? Wasn't there something I should be reading?

Then he paused. He looked miserably at his shoetops, and I looked at his brown corduroy cap. Suddenly the cap lifted, and the little face said in a rush, "Do you know the Lord as your personal savior?"

[1]One: a foal's age is counted from January 1 of the year it is born, so even a foal born in January is called a one-year-old immediately. —Ed.

"Not only that," I said, "I know your mother."
It all came together. She had asked me the same question.

Until then I had not connected this land, these horses, and this little boy with the woman in the big house at the top of the hill, the house I'd approached from the other direction, to ask permission to walk the land. That was about a year ago. There had been a very long driveway from the highway on the other side of the hill. The driveway made a circle in front of the house, and in the circle stood an eight-foot aluminum cross with a sign underneath it reading CHRIST THE LORD IS OUR SALVATION. Spotlights in the circle's honeysuckle were trained up at the cross and the sign. I rang the bell.

The woman was very nervous. She was dark, pretty, hard, with the same trembling lashes as the boy. She wore a black dress and one brush roller in the front of her hair. She did not ask me in.

My explanation of myself confused her, but she gave permission. Yes, I could walk their property. (She did not add, as others have, "But I don't want no kids in here roughhousing.") She did not let me go; she was worried about something else. She worked her hands. I waited on the other side of the screen door until she came out with it:

"Do you know the Lord as your personal savior?"

My heart went out to her. No wonder she had been so nervous. She must have to ask this of everyone, absolutely everyone, she meets. That is Christian witness. It makes sense, given its premises. I wanted to make her as happy as possible, reward her courage, and run.   *

She was stunned that I knew the Lord, and clearly uncertain whether we were referring to the same third party. But she had done   *
her bit, bumped over the hump, and now she could relax. She told me about her church, her face brightening. She was part of the Reverend Jerry Falwell's congregation. He is the powerful evangelist in Lynchburg, Virginia, who has recently taken to politics. She drove, I inferred, 120 miles round trip to go to church. While I waited behind the screen door she fetched pamphlets, each a different color. I thanked her kindly; I read them later. The one on the Holy Spirit I thought was good.

So this was her son. She had done a good job. He was a nice little kid. He was glad now his required speech was over; he was glad that I was talking easily, telling about meeting his mother. That I had met her seemed to authenticate me to him and dissolve some wariness.

The wind that follows sunset was blowing from the western ridge, across our hill and down. There had been ice in the creek. The boy moved closer to the barbed-wire fence; he jammed his fists in his pockets. Whenever I smiled or laughed he looked at me disbelieving, and lifted his eyes from beneath his cap's bill again and again to my face.

He never played at the creek, he said. Because he might be down there, and Father might come home not knowing he was there, and let all the horses out, and the horses would trample him. I had noticed that he quailed whenever the mare in her pen jerked his way.

Also there were snakes down there—water moccasins, he said. He seemed tired, old even, weary with longings, solemn. Caution passes for wisdom around here, and this kid knew all the pitfalls. In fact, there are no water moccasins this far north, except out on the coast, but there are some copperheads; I let it go. "They won't hurt you," I said. "I play at the creek," I said. "Lots." How old are you? Eight? Nine? How could you not play at the creek? Or: Why am I trying to force this child to play at the creek? What do I do there alone that he'd want to do? What do I do there at all?

The distant creek looked like ice from the hill, lightless and unmoving. The bare branches of sycamores on its banks met soundlessly. When was spring coming? The sky was purpling. Why would anyone in his right mind play at the creek?

"You're cold," I said to the boy. His lips were blue. He tried to keep his corduroy shoulders against his bare neck. He pretended not to hear. "I have to go," I said.

"Do you know how to catch a fish when you haven't got a rod, or a line, or a hook?" He was smiling, warming up for a little dialect, being a kid in a book. He must read a lot. "First, you get you a *stick*. . . ." He explained what sort of stick. "Then you pull you a thread of honeysuckle . . . and if you need you a *hook* . . ."

We talked about fishing. "I've got a roast in the oven," I said. "I've got to go." He had to go too; Father would be home, and the boy had to set the table for dinner. His mother was fasting. I said so long, so long, and turned. He called, "One more thing!" I looked back; he hesitated a second and began loudly, "Did you ever step on a big old snake?"

All right, then. I thanked God for the sisters and friends I had had when I was little; I have not been lonely yet, but it could come at any time. I pulled my jacket collar up as high as I could. He described stepping on the snake; he rolled his eyes and tried to stir me. "I felt it just . . . *move* under my foot. It was so . . . *slimy*. . . ." I bided my time. His teeth were chattering. "We were walking through the field beneath the cemetery. I called, 'Wait, Father, wait!' I couldn't lift my foot." I wondered what they let him read; he spoke in prose, like *le bourgeois gentilhomme*.[2]

"Gee," I kept saying, "you must have been scared."

"Well, I was *about* knee-deep in honeysuckle."

Oh! That was different. Probably he really *had* stepped on a snake. I would have been plenty scared myself, knee-deep in honeysuckle, but there was no way now to respond to his story all over again, identically but sincerely. Still, it was time to go. It was dark. The mare had nosed her golden foal into the barn. The creek below held a frail color still, the memory of a light that hadn't yet been snuffed.

We parted sadly, over the barbed-wire fence. The boy lowered his enormous, lighted eyes, lifted his shoulders, and went into a classic trudge. He had tried again to keep me there. But I simply had to go. It was dark, it was cold, and I had a roast in the oven, lamb, and I don't like it too well done.

Thinking about Writing

Words

Powerful words both depend on and help shape their context. In what way does each word in the list below depend on its context for strength? What does each contribute to its context? Can you

2*le bourgeois gentilhomme*: this character in a play by Molière, a seventeenth-century French dramatist, always wanted to speak prose—Ed.

think of any other word the author might have used in its place? How does the word strike you, and how do you respond to the sentence or passage because of the word?

loaded
shocked
warmth
run
third party

Thinking

1. Dillard calls the little boy a "fraud" and says, "He seemed tired, old even, weary with longings, solemn." What do you imagine are the boy's relations with his parents? Why do you think Dillard says of the mother, "She had done a good job"? In what sense had the mother done a good job?
2. "I thanked God for the sisters and friends I had had when I was little." Recognizing the little boy's loneliness, Dillard stays and talks, long after she means to leave. How do you think she felt as the boy kept trying to keep her? How did you feel at these moments? How did you feel toward the boy? Why do you think Dillard says she doesn't like lamb too well done?
3. Dillard's thinking jumps around as she spends time with the boy. Point out any indications of her liking or disliking him. How does she feel about him at the start and at the end of the encounter? How do you feel about her giving us her thoughts?

Writing

1. Write about some aspect of your childhood from the standpoint of what company you had: parents, siblings, friends. How did the presence (or absence) of others help shape you? Use incidents to illustrate your description.
2. Have you ever had an experience which, although moving in itself, was actually significant because some related realization followed it? Write about your experience after considering how Dillard has treated hers. Notice how she has given her experience, her coming

upon the little boy, the greater share of her writing, while her recognition, realizing how fortunate her childhood had been, is relatively short and comes late in the piece.

3. Both Dillard here and Bambara earlier in "What It Is I Think I'm Doing Anyhow" use their words unconventionally. Dillard interjects her thoughts as she narrates the episode; Bambara creates words and uses sentence fragments. They both seem confronted with situations that are just too "uptight," too stiff and formal, situations that appear to threaten their happiness, and so they remedy the situations by using unconventional language.

Write a paper in which you explore the use of off-beat techniques in these two writers' work, adding examples if you want from other writers who, in your opinion, succeed in the same ways.

Pablo Neruda

Pablo Neruda (1904–73) was born in Chile where he was educated. He was only twenty when he adopted this pen name—his real name was Neftali Basualto—and published a book of poems entitled *Twenty Love Songs*. After graduation, Neruda entered the diplomatic service, first as Chilean consul to such places as Burma, Ceylon (Sri Lanka), and Cambodia and later as ambassador to Mexico and France. He always considered himself the voice of Chile, its people, its nature, and its artists. During the years of the Spanish civil war, when writers in Spain were repressed, Neruda became the voice for all Spanish writers. Urging his fellow Latin American artists toward expressions of political awareness, he felt himself blessed by his native land. Although he traveled widely, he always came home joyously. In 1971, he won the Nobel Prize for literature. In the selection here, which comes from a collection of his prose writings called *Passions and Impressions*, Neruda remembers various New Year's Eves he has celebrated, deciding that his own, the Chilean, is the best.

Universal Night

More than thirty years ago I happened to arrive in Saigon in an automobile—a black limousine—of supreme elegance, lacquered like a coffin. I was driven by an impeccable French chauffeur attired in an imposing uniform.

Once in the center of the city, I asked him: "What's the best hotel in the city?"

"The Grand Hotel," he replied.

"And what's the worst?" He looked at me, surprised.

203

"A hotel I know in the Chinese district," he said. "It has every discomfort you could want."

"Take me to that one," I directed.

Vexed, he changed direction and drove toward the Chinese quarter. He deposited my dusty suitcase at the door, dumping it upside down, thus indicating his disdain. Mistakenly, he had taken me for a gentleman.   *

The room, though shabby, was spacious and pleasant. There was a bed covered with mosquito netting, and a night table. At the opposite end of the room was a wooden platform with a porcelain pillow.

"What's that for?" I asked the Chinese bellboy.

"For smoking opium. Shall I bring you a pipe?"

"Not right now," I replied, giving him some expectation of increasing his clientele.

So I was right in the heart of Saigon's China. The cities of the East—from Calcutta to Singapore, from Penang to Batavia—consist of the vaguely official European establishments of the colonizers, surrounded by enormous rings of Chinese banking, working, and residential districts.

It is a sacred principle with me that in every new city I immediately go out into the streets, through markets, up and down through sun and shadow, into the splendor of life. But that night, too exhaust-   *
ed, I lay down beneath the protective gauze of the netting and fell asleep.

It had been a difficult journey; the lurching bus had rattled my bones the length of the peninsula of Indochina.[1] Finally, the rickety vehicle could go no farther; it had stopped, paralyzed, in the middle of the jungle, and there, wide awake in the darkness of a foreign land, I'd been picked up by a passing automobile. It turned out to be the car of the French governor himself. Which explains my glorious and majestic entrance into Saigon.

In that Chinese bed I slipped into infinity, peering through the windows of dream at the rivers of the South of Chile, the rain of

[1]Indochina: the name for the Vietnam peninsula when it belonged to France

Boroa, my sparse obsessions. Suddenly I was awakened by cannon fire.   *
The odor of gunpowder drifted through the netting. Another cannon
blast, and another—ten thousand detonations. Bugles, jingling bells,
horns, tolling bells, fanfare, howls. A revolution? The end of the
world?

It was something much simpler: the Chinese New Year.

Tons of deafening, blinding gunpowder. I went out to the street.
Fireworks, rockets, and Roman candles scattered blue, yellow, and
amaranth stars. What truly amazed me was a tower shooting cascades
of multicolor fire; as the shower cleared, you could see an acrobat
dancing in the middle of a fiery, spherical cage. The contortionist
was dancing amid burning sparks, thirty-five meters in the air.

One New Year's Eve years later, I experienced danger as I walked
through the streets of Naples. Fireworks, rockets, Roman candles,
erupted from every window of every Neapolitan house. An unprece-
dented contest in phosphorescent madness! What seriously affected
me, a passerby lost in those streets, was that in the ensuing silence,
after the explosions of light had subsided, all manner of indescribable
objects began to fall about my head: wobbly tables, large books and
bottles, sprung sofas, peeling picture frames containing mustachioed
photographs, battered pots and pans. The Neapolitans throw from
their balconies their year's odds and ends. Joyfully, they shed their
useless junk, and with the birth of each new year assume the duty of
uncompromising cleanliness.

But when it comes to enjoying a New Year's Eve, there's
no place like Valparaiso. It is a luminous seaport spectacle. Among
the firebedecked ships, the tiny *Esmeralda* is the jewel of sailing ships:
her masts are crosses of diamonds that blend with the celestial
necklace of the festival night. On that night, the ships not only radi-
ate fire, they speak in their secret voices: all the foghorns of Nep-
tune, ordinarily reserved for the dangers of the sea, fill that night
with hoarse joy.

Yet the marvel is the hills, which blink on and off in the
encircling illumination, reflecting in light and shadow the fervor of
marine brilliance. It is a moving sight to see these twinkling hills,
every eye winking in response to the ships' greetings.

A New Year's Eve embrace in Valparaiso is unforgettable. There, too, in a way, we burn the remnants of the year and in the flashing of light and fire await, cleansed, the days ahead.

Thinking about Writing

Words

Powerful words both depend on and help shape their context. In what way does each word in the list below depend on its context for strength? What does each contribute to its context? Can you think of any other word the author might have used in its place? How does the word strike you, and how do you respond to the sentence or passage because of the word?

gentleman
splendor
sparse obsessions

Thinking

1. What do all celebrations have in common? Why do we celebrate, and would we know certain events had passed if we didn't? Do you think all celebrations are happy affairs? Is mourning, for instance, a celebration? In what way are celebrations important, even necessary, to our equilibrium? Can you imagine why many celebrations originated in religious rites?
2. Neruda writes about the explosions in Saigon and the old furniture in Naples. "But," he says, "there's no place like Valparaiso." Why are celebrations best when they take place in your homeland? If you disagree, why do you?
3. What effect does Neruda's strategy of introducing the taxi driver have on us? How does this incident set the scene for his talking about various New Year's Eves? Consider how he avoids merely listing types of celebrations by having established himself through the incident with the taxi driver. What does this strategy add?

Writing

1. Write an essay on celebrations, comparing them, considering their social significance, telling why you think they exist, or explaining which is your favorite and why this is so.

2. Have you ever been away from home for any celebration, your birthday or a national holiday, that you would have observed in a special way at home? How did you feel? How did you celebrate? Were you intrigued by whatever happened there, or did you long to be back home? Write about your experience.

6

Considering

Although other people's problems never bother us the way our own do, we still want to know about them. We may even derive pleasure from knowing, not because we see others suffer but because we know that life is composed of frustrations as well as joys. There is therapeutic value in defining concerns without necessarily finding solutions, for even the unsolved problem implies its absence. Moreover, talking is a way of drawing the concern outside, observing it, and putting it into perspective.

In the form of letters, the writers in this chapter address their concerns to others. For them, writing is a way of coming to terms with conditions over which they have little or no control but which cause them discomfort. Writing will not remove the conditions but it will clarify them and perhaps make them bearable.

Abigail Adams, as wife of the second president of the United States, finds herself burdened by family duties and responsibilities to the state. She must raise a family, care for two houses—the family

farm in Massachusetts and the official residence in Philadelphia—
and attend to the social duties incumbent on the president's office.
In a letter to her sister, Adams recognizes these obligations to both
family and state.

Richard Selzer, an experienced physician recalling the early
days of learning surgery, discusses a problem common to the novice
surgeon: fainting in the operating room. He offers some advice—
practice—but he urges young doctors never to lose the respect and
awe with which they approach the human body.

Lord Chesterfield advises his son that some of the best learning about life comes from casual conversation but warns that it must
be sought. He encourages his son not to underestimate the value
of casual acquaintance and advises him to ask questions whenever
he falls into conversation with strangers.

In a letter to his father, Franz Kafka describes some of the
pains he suffered during his childhood, a childhood where he constantly fell short of his father's expectations and where his father
constantly criticized him.

In an open letter, Martin Luther King, Jr., describes the
inequities in the lives of blacks and seeks to explain what course
of action must be followed to erase these inequities. The letter is
addressed not to racists but to the moderates who accuse King of
too hasty action.

Abigail Adams

Abigail Adams (1744–1818) was born Abigail Smith in Massachusetts and educated at home by her maternal grandmother. If Adams had not been the wife of the second president of the United States—John Adams—and the mother of the sixth—John Quincy Adams—today we might not have her letters. Certainly, they were not originally meant to be printed. Fortunately, we do have them, and we can read her social commentary, her political wisdom, and her domestic observations. A capable woman of sharp mind, Adams managed a farm, raised five children, and traveled both here and abroad as much as any woman could at the time. She took enormous interest in the political scene, albeit through others' actions, and was an early advocate of women's suffrage. In the selection here, which comes from the *New Letters of Abigail Adams*, she weaves domestic and political comment, moving from concern for a friend's health to wondering how she can manage a large reception, from a domestic problem to a final political comment. Together, these observations form a solid picture of not only the woman Adams was but the times in which she lived.

To Her Sister

Philadelphia, June 23, 1797

My dear Sister:

I received your Letter of June 13th and thank you for it. The account you give me respecting my House and the Farm are very pleasing. I like your proposal of going to it and taking tea with my good Neighbours very much. I am very sorry to hear that Mrs. Beal is so unwell. I have feared that she would fall into a decline, for she has appeard to me, to look very unwell for many Months. She was a good Neighbour, and would be a very heavy loss to her Family.

I do flatter myself with the prospect of comeing to Quincy to pass *
the Months of August and Sepbr. I know it will be a tedious Journey, but I fear it will be more tedious here, and the President really suffers for want of a journey, or rather for want of some Relaxation. To day will be the 5th great dinner I have had, about 36 Gentlemen to day, as many more next week, and I shall have got through the whole of Congress, with their apendages. Then comes the 4 July which is a *
still more tedious day, as we must then have not only all Congress, but all the Gentlemen of the city, the Governour and officers and companies, all of whom the late President[1] used to treat with cake, punch and wine. What the House would not hold used to be placed at long tables in the yard. As we are here we cannot avoid the trouble nor the expence. I have been informd the day used to cost the late President 500 dollors. More than 200 wt of cake used to be expended, and 2 quarter casks of wine besides spirit. You will not wonder that I dread it, or think President Washington to blame for introducing the custom, if he could have avoided it. Congress never were present here before on the day, so that I shall have a Hundred & 50 of them in addition to the other company. Long tables are sit in the House with similar entertainment. I hope the day will not be Hot. I am like to be favour with a cool one to day at which I rejoice, for it is no small task to be sit at table with 30 Gentlemen.

Judge Dana declines his appointment. I feard he would as the state of his Health has been infirm. The President has now nominated Mr. Gerry. This I know will be cavilled at by some, and he will be blamed for it, but the responsibility rest with him, and he must bear it. He would not have nominated him if he had not thought him an honest Man and a Friend to his Country, who will neither be deceived nor warped. I hope he will not refuse. *

The task of the President is very arduous, very perplexing and very hazardous. I do not wonder Washington wishd to retire from it, or rejoiced at seeing an old oak in his place. He has manifested his intire approbation of the measures persued by the Executive.

[1]the late President: George Washington. —Ed.

I thank you for your care of my things. Let Mrs. Hunt know that Nabby is well and I believe contented and that I shall want Betsy if I come as I expect, and I shall stand in need of some more female help, particuliarly a cook. I might here of some black woman in Boston perhaps who would undertake for two Months. I wish you would inquire.

I want to have the House white washed. I will thank you to see a little about it. It will be well to have the Garden attended to.

I inclose you a Ribbon I met with the other day, and I sent Cousin Betsy a short Gown to show her the fashion, by Mrs. Douse who was to send it to Boston to Mr. Smiths. I hope it will fit her. Adieu my dear Sister.

> I am most affectionately yours
> A. Adams

I have not seen a speech more to the point than Genll Shepards, but old men do not take so much pains to circulate their Fame as young ones. I enclose it for Mr. Cranch.

Thinking about Writing

Words

Powerful words both depend on and help shape their context. In what way does each word in the list below depend on its context for strength? What does each contribute to its context? Can you think of any other word the author might have used in its place? How does the word strike you, and how do you respond to the sentence or passage because of the word?

flatter myself
apendages
warped

Thinking

1. Writing of a Mrs. Beal, Adams says her death "would be a very heavy loss to her Family," without mentioning the word *death*. Why do you think she does this? Is Adams merely using a polite convention, or has she already felt the imminent end to Mrs. Beal? (Adams also says Mrs. Beal "*was* a good Neighbour.")
2. Adams has a life full of political and domestic obligations. Does anything in this letter hint at which she prefers?
3. Adams is addressing a very specific audience, her sister. What do we learn about her sister from this letter? What do we learn about the relationship between the sisters?

Writing

1. Adams is frankly bothered because George Washington entertained so lavishly in previous years that she and President Adams have no choice but to follow suit. Have you ever been in a situation in which a predecessor had behaved in so decided a fashion that people assumed you would carry on in the tradition? Did you wish to do otherwise?

   Write about what happened, whether you decided to repeat what your predecessor had done or whether you decided to break away.
2. What can you tell about Adams from her letter? What kind of person is she? Write a "Possible Portrait" of Adams, using the letter as the source of your impressions and quoting her words to support your impressions of her. You might begin with her sense of family or her need to feel informed about her "House and the Farm," while living officially in Philadelphia. See how much you can extrapolate from the letter's words in order to create your own picture of Adams's interests, and, if possible, even her personality.

Richard Selzer

Richard Selzer (b. 1928) was born in Troy, New York, and educated at Union College and Albany Medical College. A physician who teaches at Yale University School of Medicine, Selzer is also a writer of short stories, essays, and "letters." Having begun his writing career with descriptions of surgical procedures and human anatomy, Selzer has also explored the psychological side of healing. He has been accused of trying to shock. If this accusation is true, this essay suggests that Selzer might well respond that the human body inspires awe. In the following selection, which is taken from *Letters to a Young Doctor*, a collection of Selzer's essays, he offers the reader a glimpse into a surgeon's training.

Letter to a Young Surgeon III

All right. You fainted in the operating room, had to go sit on the floor in a corner and put your head down. You are making altogether too much of it. You have merely announced your humanity. Only the gods do not faint at the sight of the *mysterium tremendum*; they have too jaded a glance. At the same place in the novitiate I myself more than once slid ungracefully to the floor in the middle of things. It is less a sign of weakness than an expression of guilt. A flinching in the face of the forbidden.

The surgeon is an explorer in the tropical forest of the body. Now and then he reaches up to bring closer one of the wondrous fruits he sees there. Before he departs this place, he knows that he must pluck one of them. He knows, too, that it is forbidden to do

215

so. But it is a trophy, no, a *spoil* that has been demanded of him by   *
his patron, the patient, who has commissioned and outfitted him for
this exploration. At last the surgeon holds the plucked organ in his
hand, but he is never wholly at ease. For what man does not grow
shy, fearful, before the occult uncovered?

Don't worry. The first red knife is the shakiest. This is as true
for the assassin as it is for the surgeon. The assassin's task is easier, for
he is more likely to be a fanatic. And nothing steadies the hand like
zeal. The surgeon's work is madness icily reined in to a good purpose.
Still I know that it is perverse to relieve pain by inflicting it. This
requires that the patient give over to you his free will and his trust.
It is too much to ask. Yet we do every day, and with the arrogance   *
born of habit and custom, and grown casual, even charming.

"Come, lie down on this table," you say, and smile. Your voice
is soft and reasonable.

"Where will you cut me open?" the patient asks. And he grips
his belly as though he and it were orphan twins awaiting separate
adoption. The patient's voice is *not* calm; it trembles and quavers.

"From here . . . to here," you reply, and you draw a fingernail
across his shuddering flesh. His navel leaps like a flushed bird. Oh,
God! He has heard the knell of disembowelment. You really *do* mean
to do it! And you do, though not with the delectation that will be   *
attributed to you by those who do not do this work.

The cadaver toward which I have again and again urged you is
like an abundant nest from which the birds have long since flown.
It is a dry, uninhabited place—already dusty. It is a "thing" that the
medical student will pull apart and examine, seeking evidence, clues
from which he can reconstruct the life that once flourished there. The
living patient is a nest in which a setting bird huddles. She quivers,
but does not move when you press aside leaves in order to see better.
Your slightest touch frightens her. You hold your breath and let the
leaves spring back to conceal her. You want so much for her to trust
you.

In order to do good works throughout his lifetime, a man must
strive ever higher to carry out his benefices; he must pray, defer   *
pleasure and steel himself against temptation. And against fainting.
The committing of surgery grows easier and easier, it seems, until the

practice is second nature. Come, come! You fainted! Why don't you admit that you are imperfect, and that you strain to appeal to yourself and to others? Surgery is, in one sense, a judicious contrivance, like poetry. But . . . it is an elect life, here among the ranting machinery   *
and brazen lamps of the operating room, where on certain days now the liquidity of the patient reminds me of the drought that is attacking my own flesh. Listen, I will tell you what you already know: There is nothing like an honest piece of surgery. Say what you will, there is nothing more satisfying to the spirit than . . . the lancing of a boil!

Behold the fierce, hot protuberance compressing the howling nerves about it. You sound it with your fingers. A light tap brings back a malevolent answering wave, and a groan from the patient. Now the questing knife rides in your hand. Go! And across the swelling gallops a thin red line. Again! Deeper, plowing. All at once there lifts a wave of green mud. Suddenly the patient's breathing comes more easily, his tense body relaxes, he smiles. For him it is like being touched by the hand of God. It is a simple act, requiring not a flicker of intellect nor a whisker of logic. To outwit disease it takes a peasant's cunning, not   *
abstract brilliance. It is like the felling of a tree for firewood. Yet not poetry, nor music nor mathematics can bring such gladness, for riding out upon that wave of pus has come the black barque of pain. Just so will you come to love the boils and tumors of your patients.

I shall offer you two antidotes to fainting in the operating room.

1.   Return as often as possible to the Anatomy Laboratory. As the sculptor must gain unlimited control over his marble, the surgeon must "own" the flesh. As drawing is to the painter, so is anatomy to the surgeon. You must continue to dissect for the rest of your life. To raise a flap of skin, to trace out a nerve to its place of confluence, to carry a tendon to its bony insertion, these are things of grace and beauty. They are simple, nontheoretical, workaday acts which, if done again and again, will give rise to that profound sense of structure that is the birthplace of intuition.

It is only at the dissecting table that you can find the models of your art. Only there that you will internalize the structure and form of the body so that any variations or anomalies or unforeseen circumstances are not later met with dismay and surprise. Unlike the face, the internal organs bear a remarkable sameness to one another. True, there are differences in the size of normal kidneys, livers and spleens, and there are occasional odd lobulations and unusual arrangements of ducts and vessels, but by and large, one liver is very like another. A kidney is a kidney. Unlike a face, it bears no distinctive mark or expression that would stamp it as the kidney of Napoleon Bonaparte, say, or Herman Melville. It is this very sameness that makes of surgery a craft that can be perfected by repetition and industry. Therefore, return to the Anatomy Laboratory. Revere and follow your prosector. [1] The worship and awe you show the cadavers will come back to you a thousandfold. Even now, such an old knife as I goes to that place   * to dissect, to probe, to delve. What is an operating room but a prosectorium that has been touched into life?

   2.   Do not be impatient to wield the scalpel. To become a surgeon is a gradual, imperceptible, subtle transformation. Do not hurry from the side of the one who instructs you, but stay with your "master" until he bids you to go. It is his office to warm you with his words, on rounds and in the operating room, to color the darkness and shade the brilliance of light until you have grown strong enough to survive. Then, yes, leave him, for no sapling can grow to fullness in the shade of a big tree.

   Do these things that I have told you and you will not faint in the operating room. I do not any longer faint, nor have I for thirty years. But now and then, upon leaving the hospital after a long and dangerous operation has been brought to a successful close, I stroke the walls of the building as though it were a faithful animal that has behaved itself well.

Thinking about Words

Words

   Powerful words both depend on and help shape their context. In what way does each word in the list below depend on its context

[1]prosector: one who demonstrates dissection. —Ed.

for strength? What does each contribute to its context? Can you think of any other word the author might have used in its place? How does the word strike you, and how do you respond to the sentence or passage because of the word?

spoil
arrogance
delectation
defer pleasure
ranting
whisker
old knife

Thinking

1. How does Selzer, as he gives advice, avoid being condescending toward either you the reader or, presumably, you the novice surgeon? What instances of his humor can you find? Does this humor include him, or is he laughing at others?
2. Selzer begins writing by assigning guilt as the cause of fainting. Why do you think he prescribes treatment for the fainting without trying to cure its cause?
3. Why do you think Selzer refers to the body as the "occult"? What are some other images he uses when he refers to the body? How does his imagery affect you as a reader? What is the effect of "A kidney is a kidney"?
4. How did the lancing of a boil strike you? Why do you think Selzer mentions it?

Writing

1. This essay is full of contrasts: life and death, experience and innocence, fear and confidence. Despite these contrasts, what constant force do you feel holds the essay together? In other words, with all this dramatic contrast, why doesn't the piece fall apart? What is the writing, finally, about? Write an essay in which you explore Selzer's use of contrast and continuity.

2. Selzer readily admits that he returns to basic observations gained from dissecting. He also seems anxious to clear away any false notions we might have about surgery. Using his writing—his words, his figures of speech, and his ideas—as evidence, write an essay in which you explore what Selzer thinks of his profession. Consider any evidence in his writing that tells us whether he likes it or not.

3. Selzer's "antidotes" are not preventions. What does his attitude toward fainting in the operating room reveal about his commitment to the practice of surgery? What does he suggest to make this painful experience tolerable? Write an essay that discusses the pleasures he takes in "committing" surgery, that might help outweigh the discomforts. Try to include why you think he wants to cure fainting, but accept the guilt that causes fainting.

Philip Dormer Stanhope, Lord Chesterfield

Philip Dormer Stanhope, Lord Chesterfield (1694–1773) was born in London and educated at Cambridge University. He was to become a statesman and diplomat in later life, but his early interest in politics led him unwisely to deliver a speech in Parliament while he was underage. In consequence, he was forced to flee the country for his life. Fortunately, his rashness in Parliament was balanced by his wisdom in selecting France as a haven. While there, he perfected his French and absorbed as much culture and civilization as possible. On his return to England, he was not only older but also ready to enter diplomatic life. While serving as ambassador from England to various countries, Chesterfield wrote numerous speeches and letters, all of which are excellent descriptions of the manners and expectations of the time. This selection is one of a large group of letters to his son. In it, Chesterfield instructs the youth who is living in France, as he himself had done, preparing for his own career in the diplomatic service.

To His Son

London, January 2, 1752.

My Dear Friend:

Laziness of mind, or inattention, are as great enemies to knowledge, as incapacity; for, in truth, what difference is there between a man who will not, and a man who cannot be informed? This difference only, that the former is justly to be blamed, the latter to

221

be pitied. And yet how many there are, very capable of receiving knowledge, who from laziness, inattention, and incuriousness, will not so much as ask for it, much less take the least pains to acquire it! Our young English travellers generally distinguish themselves by   *
a voluntary privation of all that useful knowledge for which they   *
are sent abroad; and yet, at that age, the most useful knowledge is the most easy to be acquired; conversation being the book, and the best book in which it is contained. The drudgery of dry grammatical learning is over, and the fruits of it are mixed with, and adorned by, the flowers of conversation. How many of our young men have been a year at Rome, and as long at Paris, without knowing the meaning and institution of the Conclave in the former, and of the Parliament in the latter? and this merely for want of asking the first people they met with in those several places, who could at least have given them some general notions of those matters.

You will, I hope, be wiser, and omit no opportunity (for opportunities present themselves every hour of the day) of acquainting yourself with all those political and constitutional particulars of the kingdom and government of France. For instance, when you hear people mention *le Chancelier*, or *le Garde des Sceaux*,[1] is it any great trouble for you to ask, or for others to tell you, what is the nature, the powers, the objects, and the profits of those two employments, either when joined together, as they often are, or when separate, as they are at present? When you hear of a *Gouverneur*, a *Lieutenant du Roi*, a *Commandant*, and an *Intendant*[2] of the same province, is it not natural, is it not becoming, is it not necessary, for a stranger to inquire into their   *
respective rights and privileges? And yet, I dare say, there are very few Englishmen who know the difference between the civil department of the Intendant, and the military powers of the others. When you hear (as I am persuaded you must) every day of the *Vingtième*,[3] which is one in twenty, and consequently five per cent, inquire upon what that tax is laid, whether upon lands, money, merchandise, or upon all three; how levied, and what it is supposed to produce.

[1]*le Garde des Sceaux*: for us, the Attorney General. —Ed.
[2]*Intendant*: a mayor, or a state senator. —Ed.
[3]*Vingtième*: sales tax. —Ed.

When you find in books (as you will sometimes) allusions to particular laws and customs, do not rest till you have traced them to their source.

I do not mean that you should be a French lawyer; but I would not have you unacquainted with the general principles of their law, in matters that occur every day. Such is the nature of their descents; that is, the inheritance of lands: Do they all go to the eldest son, or are they equally divided among the children of the deceased? In England, all lands unsettled descend to the eldest son, as heir-at-law, unless otherwise disposed of by the father's will, except in the county of Kent, where a particular custom prevails, called Gavelkind, by which, if the father dies intestate, all his children divide his lands equally among them. In Germany, as you know, all lands that are not fiefs, are equally divided among all the children, which ruins those families; but all male fiefs of the empire descend unalienably to the next male heir, which preserves those families. In France, I believe, descents vary in different provinces.

The nature of marriage contracts deserves inquiry. In England, the general practice is, the husband takes all of the wife's fortune; and, in consideration of it, settles upon her a proper pin-money, as it is called; that is, an annuity during his life, and a jointure after his death. In France, it is not so, particularly at Paris; where *la communauté des biens*[4] is established. Any married woman at Paris (*if you are acquainted with one*) can inform you of all these particulars.

These and other things of the same nature, are the useful and rational objects of the curiosity of a man of sense and business. Could they only be atttained by laborious researches in folio-books, and worm-eaten manuscripts, I should not wonder at a young fellow's being ignorant of them; but as they are the frequent topics of conversation, and to be known by a very little degree of curiosity, inquiry and attention, it is unpardonable not to know them.

How often, and how justly, have I since regretted negligences ＊ of this kind in my youth! And how often have I since been at great trouble to learn many things which I could then have learned without any! Save yourself now, then, I beg of you, that regret and trouble

---

[4]*la communauté des biens*: goods sharing. —Ed.

hereafter. Ask questions, and many questions; and leave nothing till you are thoroughly informed of it. Such pertinent questions are far from being ill-bred or troublesome to those of whom you ask them; on the contrary, they are a tacit compliment to their knowledge; and people have a better opinion of a young man, when they see him desirous to be informed.

I have by last post received your two letters of the 1st and 5th of January, N.S. I am very glad that you have been at all the shows at Versailles: frequent the courts. I can conceive the murmurs of the French at the poorness of the fire-works, by which they thought their king or their country degraded; and, in truth, were things always as they should be, when kings give shows they ought to be magnificent.

I thank you for the *Thèse de la Sorbonne*, which you intend to send me, and which I am impatient to receive. But pray read it carefully yourself first; and inform yourself what the Sorbonne is, by whom founded, and for what purposes.

Since you have time, you have done very well to take an Italian and a German master; but pray take care to leave yourself time enough for company; for it is in company only that you can learn what will be much more useful to you than either Italian or German; I mean *la politesse, les manières et les grâces*, without which, as I told you long ago, and I told you true, *ogni fatica è vana.*[5] Adieu.

Pray make my compliments to Lady Brown.

Thinking about Writing

Words

Powerful words both depend on and help shape their context. In what way does each word in the list below depend on its context for strength? What does each contribute to its context? Can you think of any other word the author might have used in its place? How does the word strike you, and how do you respond to the sentence or passage because of the word?

[5]*ogni fatica è vana:* every effort is futile. —Ed.

distinguish
voluntary privation
becoming
negligences

Thinking

1. Why do you think Lord Chesterfield calls conversation a book? Today, with the media offering so many sources of information, how might his comment be taken? What are our "books" today?
2. From reading this letter, what can you tell about information communication in the middle of the eighteenth century? Where does the letter itself fit?
3. Why do you think Lord Chesterfield puts so many comments into parentheses? What is the difference between putting these comments into parentheses and marking them off by commas?
4. Why has Lord Chesterfield underlined the parenthetic comment following "Any married woman at Paris"? What does this comment tell the reader about social custom at the time of the letter?
5. What do you think is the relation between father and son here? What gives you this impression? Can you tell, from the father's writing, what the son is like (as the father sees him, of course)?

Writing

1. Assume the father here is worried that his son may be wasting time during his months on the European continent. Write an essay in which you examine the various ways the father has given his son advice. For example, the father may use the Others/ You contrast, the loaded parenthesis, or a double negation, as in "not . . . unacquainted." What pattern is there to the father's strategies, or does he just use them randomly?
2. Write a short letter to a younger sibling or friend who wishes to attend college, either yours or another, offering advice on a number of topics such as dress, study, types of people to be avoided or sought, wasting time, spending money (or spending time and wasting money), or any other points of interest to you.

3. "How often, and how justly, have I since regretted negligences of this kind in my youth!" What do you regret *not* doing, either when you were still in high school or when you first arrived at college? Why do you wish you had done what you did not? Write about your regret, including how you realized your mistake.

4. Write a short essay in which you examine sources of information other than books, not necessarily as a substitute for reading, but as an addition to it. What can books supply that nothing else can? Conversely, what can books not supply?

Franz Kafka

Franz Kafka (1883–1924) was born to a German-Jewish family in Prague (now in Czechoslovakia, but then a city in the Austrian empire). He was educated in law and, following his family's expectations, entered a life of business. However, a strong antipathy to the business world convinced him he must devote his serious energies to writing. Kafka used his writing to explain the human condition which he saw as alienated and isolated within a chaotic, contradictory, and puzzling world. He is the author of several works that explore this theme of alienation in an irrational world, among them *The Castle*, *The Trial*, and "Metamorphosis." In the selection here, from a collection of stories and other writings called *Dearest Father*, Kafka tries to explain his ambivalence toward his father, a man who seemed always disappointed that his son wasn't tougher and more businesslike.

To His Father

Dearest Father:

You asked me recently why I maintain that I am afraid of you. As usual, I was unable to think of any answer to your question, partly for the very reason that I am afraid of you, and partly because an explanation of the grounds for this fear would mean going into far more details than I could even approximately keep in mind while talking. And if I now try to give you an answer in writing, it will still be very incomplete, because even in writing this fear and its consequences hamper me in relation to you and because [anyway] the magnitude of the subject goes far beyond the scope of my memory and power of reasoning.

Oddly enough you have some sort of notion of what I mean. For instance, a short time ago you said to me: "I have always been fond of you, even though outwardly I didn't act towards you as other fathers generally do, and this precisely because I can't pretend as other   * people can." Now, Father, on the whole I have never doubted your goodness towards me, but this remark is one I consider wrong. You can't pretend, that's a fact, but merely for that reason to maintain that other fathers pretend is either mere opinionatedness, and as such beyond discussion, or on the other hand—and this in my view is what it really is—a veiled expression of the fact that something is wrong in our relationship and that you have played your part in causing it to be so, but without its being your fault. If you really mean that, then we are in agreement.

Compare the two of us: I, to put it in a very much abbreviated form, a Löwy with a certain basis of Kafka, which, however, is not set in motion by the Kafka will to life, business, and conquest, but by a Löwyish spur that urges more secretly, more diffidently, and in another direction, and which often fails to work entirely. You, on the other hand, a true Kafka in strength, health, appetite, loudness of voice, eloquence, self-satisfaction, worldly dominance, endurance, presence of mind, knowledge of human nature, a certain way of doing things on a grand scale, of course also with all the defects and weaknesses that go with all these advantages and into which your temperament and sometimes your hot temper drive you.

However it was, we were so different and in our difference so dangerous to each other that, if anyone had tried to calculate in advance how I, the slowly developing child, and you, the full-grown man, would stand to each other, he could have assumed that you would simply trample me underfoot so that nothing was left of me. Well, that didn't happen. Nothing alive can be calculated. But perhaps something worse happened. And in saying this I would all the time beg of you not to forget that I never, and not even for a single moment, believe any guilt to be on your side. The effect you had on me was the effect you could not help having. But you should stop considering it some particular malice on my part that I succumbed to   * that effect.

I was a timid child. For all that, I am sure I was also obstinate, as children are. I am sure that Mother spoilt me too, but I cannot believe I was particularly difficult to manage; I cannot believe that a kindly word, a quiet taking of me by the hand, a friendly look, could not have got me to do anything that was wanted of me. Now you are after all at bottom a kindly and softhearted person (what follows will not be in contradiction to this, I am speaking only of the impression you made on the child), but not every child has the endurance and   *
fearlessness to go on searching until it comes to the kindliness that lies beneath the surface. You can only treat a child in the way you yourself are constituted, with vigor, noise, and hot temper, and in this case this seemed to you, into the bargain, extremely suitable, because you wanted to bring me up to be a strong brave boy. . . .

There is only one episode in the early years of which I have a direct memory. You may remember it, too. Once in the night I kept on whimpering for water, not, I am certain, because I was thirsty, but probably partly to be annoying, partly to amuse myself. After several vigorous threats had failed to have any effect, you took me out of bed, carried me out onto the *pavlatche* and left me there alone for a while in my nightshirt, outside the shut door. I am not going to say that this was wrong—perhaps at that time there was really no other way of getting peace and quiet that night—but I mention it as typical of your methods of bringing up a child and their effect on me. I dare say I was quite obedient afterwards at that period, but it did me inner harm. What was for me a matter of course, that senseless asking for water, and the extraordinary terror of being carried outside were two things that I, my nature being what it was, could never properly connect with each other. Even years afterwards I suffered from the tormenting fancy that the huge man, my father, the ultimate authority, would come almost for no reason at all and take me out of bed in the night and carry me out onto the *pavlatche*, and that therefore I was such a mere nothing for him.

That then was only a small beginning, but this sense of nothingness that often dominates me (a feeling that is in another respect, admittedly, also a noble and fruitful one) comes largely from your influence. What I would have needed was a little encouragement, a little friendliness, a little keeping open of my road, instead of which you blocked it for me, though of course with the good intention of making me go another road. But I was not fit for that. . . .

At that time, and at that time everywhere, I would have needed encouragement. I was, after all, depressed even by your mere physical presence. I remember, for instance, how we often undressed together in the same bathing hut. There was I, skinny, weakly, slight; you strong, tall, broad. Even inside the hut I felt myself a miserable *
specimen, and what's more, not only in your eyes but in the eyes of the whole world, for you were for me the measure of all things. But then when we went out of the bathing hut before the people, I with you holding my hand, a little skeleton, unsteady, barefoot on the boards, frightened of the water, incapable of copying your swimming strokes, which you, with the best of intentions, but actually to my profound humiliation, always kept on showing me, then I was frantic with desperation and all my bad experiences in all spheres at such moments fitted magnificently together. What made me feel best was when you sometimes undressed first and I was able to stay behind in the hut alone and put off the disgrace of showing myself in public until at length you came to see what I was doing and drove me out of the hut. I was grateful to you for not seeming to notice my extremity, and besides, I was proud of my father's body. For the rest, this difference between us remains much the same to this very day.

In keeping with that, furthermore, was your intellectual domination. You had worked your way up so far alone, by your own energies, and as a result you had unbounded confidence in your opinion. For me as a child that was not yet so dazzling as later for the boy growing up. From your armchair you ruled the world. Your opinion was correct, every other was mad, wild, *meshugge*, [1] not normal. With all this your self-confidence was so great that you had no need to be consistent at all and yet never ceased to be in the right. It did sometimes happen that you had no opinion whatsoever about a matter and as a result all opinions that were at all possible with respect to the matter were necessarily wrong, without exception. You were capable, for instance, of running down the Czechs, and then the Germans, and

[1]*meshugge*: crazy. —Ed.

then the Jews, and what is more, not only selectively but in every respect, and finally nobody was left except yourself. For me you took on the enigmatic quality that all tyrants have whose rights are based on their person and not on reason. At least so it seemed to me.

This applied to thoughts as well as to people. It was enough that I should take a little interest in a person—which in any case did not happen often, as a result of my nature—for you, without any consideration for my feelings or respect for my judgment, to butt in with abuse, defamation, and denigration. Innocent, childlike people, such as, for instance, the Yiddish actor Löwy, had to pay for that. Without knowing him you compared him, in a dreadful way that I have now forgotten, to vermin and as was so often the case with people I was fond of you were automatically ready with the proverb of the dog and its fleas. I here particularly recall the actor because at that time I made a note of your pronouncements about him, with the comment: "This is how my father speaks of my friend (whom he does not even know), simply because he is my friend. I shall always be able to bring this up against him whenever he reproaches me with the lack of a child's affection and gratitude." What was always incomprehensible to me was your total lack of feeling for the suffering and shame you could inflict on me with your words and judgments. It was as though you had no notion of your power. I too, I am sure, often hurt you with what I said, but then I always knew, and it pained me, but I could not control myself, could not keep the words back, I was sorry even while I was saying it. But you struck out with your words without more ado, you weren't sorry for anyone, either during or afterwards, one was utterly defenseless against you.   *

But that was what your whole method of upbringing was like. You have, I think, a gift for bringing up children; you could, I am sure, have been of use to a human being of your own kind with your methods; such a person would have seen the reasonableness of what you told him, would not have troubled about anything else, and would quietly have done things the way he was told. But for me as a child everything you shouted at me was positively a heavenly command- ment, I never forgot it, it remained for me the most important means of forming a judgment of the world, above all of forming a judgment of you yourself, and there you failed entirely. Since as a child I was together with you chiefly at meals, your teaching was to a large extent teaching about proper behavior at table. What was brought to the table had to be eaten up, there could be no discussion of the goodness of the food—but you yourself often found the food uneatable, called it "this swill," said "that brute" (the cook) had ruined it. Because in accordance with your strong appetite and your particular habit you ate everything fast, hot and in big mouthfuls, the child had to hurry, there was a somber silence at table, interrupted by admonitions: "Eat first, talk afterwards," or "faster, faster, faster," or "there you are, you see, I finished ages ago." Bones mustn't be cracked with the teeth, but you could. Vinegar must not be sipped noïsily, but you could. The main thing was that the bread should be cut straight. But it didn't matter that you did it with a knife dripping with gravy. One had to take care that no scraps fell on the floor. In the end it was under your chair that there were most scraps. At table one wasn't allowed to do anything but eat, but you cleaned and cut your fingernails, sharpened pencils, cleaned your ears with the toothpick. Please, Father, understand me rightly: these would in themselves have been utterly insignificant details, they only became depressing for me because you, the man who was so tremendously the measure of all things for me, yourself did not keep the commandments you imposed on me. Hence the world was for me divided into three parts: into one in which I, the slave, lived under laws that had been invented only for me and which I could, I did not know why, never completely comply with; then into a second world, which was infinitely remote from mine, in which you lived, concerned with government, with the issuing of orders and with annoyance about their not being obeyed; and finally into a third world where everybody else lived happily and free from orders and from having to obey. . . .

The impossibility of getting on calmly together had one more result, actually a very natural one: I lost the capacity to talk. I dare say I would never have been a very eloquent person in any case, but I would, after all, have had the usual fluency of human language at my command. But at a very early stage you forbade me to talk. Your threat: "Not a word of contradiction!" and the raised hand that accompanied it have gone with me ever since. What I got from you—

and you are, as soon as it is a matter of your own affairs, an excellent talker—was a hesitant, stammering mode of speech, and even that was still too much for you, and finally I kept silent, at first perhaps from defiance, and then because I couldn't either think or speak in your presence.

I can't recall your ever having abused me directly and in down-right abusive terms. Nor was that necessary; you had so many other methods, and besides, in talk at home and particularly at business the words of abuse went flying around me in such swarms, as they were flung at other people's heads, that as a little boy I was sometimes almost stunned and had no reason not to apply them to myself too, for the people you were abusing were certainly no worse than I was and you were certainly not more displeased with them than with me. And here again, too, was your enigmatic innocence and inviolability; you cursed and swore without the slightest scruple about it; indeed you condemned cursing and swearing in other people and would not have it. . . .

You put special trust in bringing children up by means of irony, and this was most in keeping with your superiority over me. An admonition from you generally took this form: "Can't you do it in such-and-such a way? That's too hard for you, I suppose. You haven't the time, of course?" and so on. And each such question would be accompanied by malicious laughter and a malicious face. One was so to speak already punished before one even knew that one had done something bad. What was also maddening were those rebukes when one was treated as a third person, in other words accounted not worthy   *
even to be spoken to angrily: that is to say, when you would speak in form to Mother but in fact to me, sitting there at the same time. For instance: "Of course, that's too much to expect of our worthy son" and the like.

Fortunately there were, I admit, exceptions to all these things, mostly when you suffered in silence, and affection and kindliness by their own strength overcame all obstacles, and moved me immediately. Admittedly this was rare, but it was wonderful. For instance, when in earlier times, in hot summers, when you were tired after lunch, I saw you having a nap at the office, your elbow on the desk; or when you joined us in the country, in the summer holidays, on Sundays, worn out from work at the office; or the time when Mother was gravely ill and you stood holding on to the bookcase, shaking with sobs; or when, during my last illness, you came tiptoeing to Ottla's room to see me, stopping in the doorway, craning your neck to see me. At such times one would lie back and weep for happiness, and one weeps again now, writing it down. . . .

It was true that Mother was illimitably good to me, but all that was for me in relation to you, that is to say, in no good relation. Mother unconsciously played the part of a beater during a hunt. Even if your method of upbringing might in some unlikely case have set me on my own feet by means of producing defiance, dislike, or even hate in me, Mother canceled that out again by kindness, by talking sensibly (in the maze and chaos of my childhood she was the very pattern of good sense and reasonableness), by pleading for me, and I was again driven back into your orbit, which I might perhaps otherwise have broken out of, to your advantage and to my own. Or it was so that no real reconciliation ever came about, that Mother merely shielded me from you in secret, secretly gave me something, or allowed me to do something, and then where you were concerned I was again the furtive creature, the cheat, the guilty one, who in his worthlessness could only pursue backstairs methods even to get the things he regarded as right. Of course, I then became used to taking such courses also in quest of things to which, even in my own view, I had no right. This again meant an increase in the sense of guilt.

The next eternal result of this whole method of upbringing was that I fled from everything that even remotely reminded me of you. First there was the business. In itself, particularly in my childhood, so long as it was a shop, I ought to have liked it very much, it was so animated, the lights lit at evening, so much to see and hear, being able to help now and then and to distinguish oneself, but above all to admire you for your magnificent commercial talents, the way you sold things, managed people, made jokes, were untiring, knew the right decision to make at once in doubtful cases, and so forth; even the way you wrapped up a parcel or opened a crate was a spectacle worth watching, and all this was certainly not the worst school for a child. But since you gradually began to terrify me on all sides and the business and you became one for me, the business too made me feel uneasy. Things that had a first been a matter of course for me there now began to torment and shame me, particularly the way you treated the staff. . . .

If I was to flee from you, I had to flee from the family as well, even from Mother. True, one could always get protection from her, but only in relation to you. She loved you too much and was too devoted and loyal to you to have been able to constitute an independent spiritual force, in the long run, in the child's struggle. It was, incidentally, a true instinct the child had, for with the passing of years Mother became ever more closely allied to you; while, where she herself was concerned, she always kept her independence, within the narrowest limits, delicately and beautifully, and without ever essentially hurting you, still, with the passing of the years she did more and more completely, emotionally rather than intellectually, blindly adopt your judgments and your condemnations with regard to the children. . . .

Thinking about Writing

Words

Powerful words both depend on and help shape their context. In what way does each word in the list below depend on its context for strength? What does each contribute to its context? Can you think of any other word the author might have used in its place? How does the word strike you, and how do you respond to the sentence or passage because of the word?

pretend
succumbed
endurance
a miserable specimen
defenseless
a third person

Thinking

1. What does Kafka think of his father? How does the writing give you this impression?
2. Do you think Kafka the adult is still unhappy? Where in the writing do you have an impression of how he feels now? Can you tell how he felt when he was a child? How does the writing tell you?
3. Assuming the Kafkas are typical, middle-class people of the period and place (turn-of-the-century Prague), what does the writing tell you about the way children were brought up then? What were the roles of the parents?
4. We often think, when we consider childhood, that if things had been different then, we might be different adults today. (Richard Rodriguez considers this possibility in his essay "Running in the Sun" in chapter 3.) Why do you think Kafka has written this piece? Do you think he wishes for a different adulthood or merely a different childhood?
5. Where would you place Kafka's mother in all this tension between father and son? Does the writing give you a sense of her personality? Why do you think Kafka calls her "a beater during a hunt"? (Beaters are peasants who run through the underbrush with sticks in order to flush birds for hunters to shoot.)

Writing

1. From this letter, try to construct a picture of the boy Kafka, as you assume he was. You will have to extrapolate from Kafka's comments about failing or not pleasing his father to construct a picture of the boy. Quote from the essay to support your assumptions about both his personality and his constitution.
2. Write a letter from Kafka's father to his son, in reply to this one. Since yours will not be a real letter but an essay based on the letter form, you should write it as an essay directed from the father to the son. Feel free to explain why you behaved as you did. Consider saying something about your wife and reacting to being called a tyrant.

3. Write about the need to form friendships for ourselves, to make our own decisions, while we still seek the approval of our parents. Have you ever had a friend your parents disliked? What happened finally to your relations with your parents and the friend? Did one get sacrificed to keep the other? How do you think your parents evaluate your friendships? Why are we bothered when our parents don't like our friends? Write about this experience, if you have ever undergone it.

Martin Luther King, Jr.

Martin Luther King, Jr., (1929–68) was born in Atlanta, Georgia, and educated at Morehouse College, Crozer Theological Seminary, and Boston University. While he was pastor of Ebenezer Baptist Church in Atlanta, King was constantly active in the civil rights movement. As president of the Southern Christian Leadership Conference, he traveled and lectured widely. One such trip took him to India, where he was able to explore the teachings of Mahatma Gandhi, whose principles and practice of nonviolence appealed to him. An advocate of nonviolence, King was often criticized, even by moderates, for encouraging peaceful marches, sit-ins, and demonstrations. In this selection, drafted while King was serving a jail sentence for civil disobedience, he explains why "we can't wait" in answer to moderates' criticism of King's actions. A tireless worker for desegregation and for civil rights, he received the Nobel Peace Prize. King was assassinated in 1968. This essay comes from his longer work, *Why We Can't Wait*.

Letter from Birmingham Jail

My Dear Fellow Clergymen:[1]

While confined here in the Birmingham city jail, I came across your recent statement calling my present activities "unwise and untimely." Seldom do I pause to answer criticism of my work and ideas. If I sought to answer all the criticisms that cross my desk, my

[1]This response to a published statement by eight fellow clergymen from Alabama (Bishop C.C.J. Carpenter, Bishop Joseph A Durick, Rabbi Milton L. Grafman, Bishop Paul Hardin, Bishop Holan B. Harmon, the Reverend George M. Murray, the Reverend Edward V. Ramage and the Reverend Earl Stallings) was composed under somewhat

secretaries would have little time for anything other than such correspondence in the course of the day, and I would have no time for constructive work. But since I feel that you are men of genuine good will and that your criticisms are sincerely set forth, I want to try to answer your statement in what I hope will be patient and reasonable terms.

I think I should indicate why I am here in Birmingham, since you have been influenced by the view which argues against "outsiders coming in." I have the honor of serving as president of the Southern Christian Leadership Conference, an organization operating in every southern state, with headquarters in Atlanta, Georgia. We have some eighty-five affiliated organizations across the South, and one of them is the Alabama Christian Movement for Human Rights. Frequently we share staff, educational, and financial resources with our affiliates. Several months ago the affiliate here in Birmingham asked us to be on call to engage in a nonviolent direct-action program if such were deemed necessary. We readily consented, and when the hour came we lived up to our promise. So I, along with several members of my staff, am here because I was invited here. I am here because I have organizational ties here.

But more basically, I am in Birmingham because injustice is here. Just as the prophets of the eighth century B.C. left their villages and carried their "thus saith the Lord" far beyond the boundaries of their home towns, and just as the Apostle Paul left his village of Tarsus and carried the gospel of Jesus Christ to the far corners of the Greco-Roman world, so am I compelled to carry the gospel of freedom beyond my own home town. Like Paul, I must constantly respond to the Macedonian call for aid.

Moreover, I am cognizant of the interrelatedness of all communities and states. I cannot sit idly by in Atlanta and not be concerned about what happens in Birmingham. Injustice anywhere is a threat to justice everywhere. We are caught in an inescapable network of mutuality, tied in a single garment of destiny. Whatever affects

---

constricting circumstances. Begun on the margins of the newspaper in which the statement appeared while I was in jail, the letter was continued on scraps of writing paper supplied by a friendly Negro trusty, and concluded on a pad my attorneys were eventually permitted to leave me. Although the text remains in substance unaltered, I have indulged in the author's prerogative of polishing it for publication.

one directly, affects all indirectly. Never again can we afford to live with the narrow, provincial "outside agitator" idea. Anyone who lives inside the United States can never be considered an outsider anywhere within its bounds. You deplore the demonstrations taking place in Birmingham. But your statement, I am sorry to say, fails to express a similar concern for the conditions that brought about the demonstrations. I am sure that none of you would want to rest content with the superficial kind of social analysis that deals merely with effects and does not grapple with underlying causes. It is unfortunate that demonstrations are taking place in Birmingham, but it is even more unfortunate that the city's white power structure left the Negro community with no alternative.

In any nonviolent campaign there are four basic steps: collection of the facts to determine whether injustices exist; negotiation; self-purification; and direct action. We have gone through all these steps in Birmingham. There can be no gainsaying the fact that racial injustice engulfs this community. Birmingham is probably the most thoroughly segregated city in the United States. Its ugly record of brutality is widely known. Negroes have experienced grossly unjust treatment in the courts. There have been more unsolved bombings of Negro homes and churches in Birmingham than in any other city in the nation. These are the hard, brutal facts of the case. On the basis of these conditions, Negro leaders sought to negotiate with the city fathers. But the latter consistently refused to engage in good-faith negotiation.

Then, last September, came the opportunity to talk with leaders of Birmingham's economic community. In the course of the negotiations, certain promises were made by the merchants—for example, to remove the stores' humiliating racial signs. On the basis of these promises, the Reverend Fred Shuttlesworth and the leaders of the Alabama Christian Movement for Human Rights agreed to a moratorium on all demonstrations. As the weeks and months went by, we realized that we were the victims of a broken promise. A few signs, briefly removed, returned; the others remained.

As in so many past experiences, our hopes had been blasted, and the shadow of deep disappointment settled upon us. We had no alter-

native except to prepare for direct action, whereby we would present
our very bodies as a means of laying our case before the conscience *
of the local and the national community. Mindful of the difficulties
involved, we decided to undertake a process of self-purification. We
began a series of workshops on nonviolence, and we repeatedly asked
ourselves: "Are you able to accept blows without retaliating?" "Are
you able to endure the ordeal of jail?" We decided to schedule our
direct-action program for the Easter season, realizing that except for
Christmas, this is the main shopping period of the year. Knowing
that a strong economic-withdrawal program would be the by-product
of direct action, we felt that this would be the best time to bring
pressure to bear on the merchants for the needed change.

Then it occurred to us that Birmingham's mayoral election was
coming up in March, and we speedily decided to postpone action
until after election day. When we discovered that the Commissioner
of Public Safety, Eugene "Bull" Connor, had piled up enough votes to
be in the run-off, we decided again to postpone action until the day
after the run-off so that the demonstrations could not be used to cloud
the issues. Like many others, we wanted to see Mr. Connor defeated,
and to this end we endured postponement after postponement. Having
aided in this community need, we felt that our direct-action program
could be delayed longer.

You may well ask, "Why direct action? Why sit-ins, marches,
and so forth? Isn't negotiation a better path?" You are quite right
in calling for negotiation. Indeed, this is the very purpose of direct
action. Nonviolent direct action seeks to create such a crisis and
foster such a tension that a community which has constantly refused
to negotiate is forced to confront the issue. It seeks so to dramatize
the issue that it can no longer be ignored. My citing the creation
of tension as part of the work of the nonviolent-resister may sound *
rather shocking. But I must confess that I am not afraid of the word
"tension." I have earnestly opposed violent tension, but there is a type
of constructive, nonviolent tension which is necessary for growth. Just
as Socrates felt that it was necessary to create a tension in the mind so
that individuals could rise from the bondage of myths and half-truths
to the unfettered realm of creative analysis and objective appraisal,
so must we see the need for nonviolent gadflies to create the kind *

of tension in society that will help men rise from the dark depths of prejudice and racism to the majestic heights of understanding and brotherhood.

The purpose of our direct-action program is to create a situation so crisis-packed that it will inevitably open the door to negotiation. I therefore concur with you in your call for negotiation. Too long has our beloved Southland been bogged down in a tragic effort to live in   * monologue rather than dialogue.

One of the basic points in your statement is that the action that I and my associates have taken in Birmingham is untimely. Some have asked: "Why didn't you give the new city administration time to act?" The only answer that I can give to this query is that the new Birmingham administration must be prodded about as much as the outgoing one, before it will act. We are sadly mistaken if we feel that   * the election of Albert Boutwell as mayor will bring the millennium to Birmingham. While Mr. Boutwell is a much more gentle person than Mr. Connor, they are both segregationists, dedicated to maintenance of the status quo. I have hoped that Mr. Boutwell will be reasonable enough to see the futility of massive resistance to desegregation. But he will not see this without pressure from devotees of civil rights. My friends, I must say to you that we have not made a single gain in civil rights without determined legal and nonviolent pressure. Lamentably, it is an historical fact that privileged groups seldom give up their privileges voluntarily. Individuals may see the moral light and voluntarily give up their unjust posture, but, as Reinhold Niebuhr has reminded us, groups tend to be more immoral than individuals.

We know through painful experience that freedom is never voluntarily given by the oppressor; it must be demanded by the oppressed. Frankly, I have yet to engage in a direct-action campaign that was "well timed" in the view of those who have not suffered unduly from the disease of segregation. For years now I have heard the word "Wait!" It rings in the ear of every Negro with piercing familiarity. This "Wait" has almost always meant "Never." We must come to see, with one of our distinguished jurists, that "justice too long delayed is justice denied."

We have waited for more than 340 years for our constitutional and God-given rights. The nations of Asia and Africa are moving with jetlike speed toward gaining political independence, but we still creep at horse-and-buggy pace toward gaining a cup of coffee at a lunch counter. Perhaps it is easy for those who have never felt the stinging darts of segregation to say, "Wait." But when you have seen vicious mobs lynch your mothers and fathers at will and drown your sisters and brothers at whim; when you have seen hate-filled policemen curse, kick, and even kill your black brothers and sisters; when you see the vast majority of your twenty million Negro brothers smothering in an airtight cage of poverty in the midst of an affluent society; when you suddenly find your tongue twisted and your speech stammering as you seek to explain to your six-year-old daughter why she can't go to the public amusement park that has just been advertised on television, and see tears welling up in her eyes when she is told that Funtown is closed to colored children, and see ominous clouds of inferiority beginning to form in her little mental sky, and see her beginning to distort her personality by developing an unconscious bitterness toward white people; when you have to concoct an answer for a five-year-old son who is asking, "Daddy, why do white people treat colored people so mean?"; when you take a cross-country drive and find it necessary to sleep night after night in the uncomfortable corners of your automobile because no motel will accept you; when you are humiliated day in and day out by nagging signs reading "white" and "colored"; when your first name becomes "nigger," your middle name becomes "boy" (however old you are) and your last name becomes "John," and your wife and mother are never given the respected title "Mrs."; when you are harried by day and haunted by night by the fact that you are a Negro, living constantly at tiptoe stance, never quite knowing what to expect next, and are plagued with inner fears and outer resentments; when you are forever fighting a degenerating sense of "nobodiness"— then you will understand why we find it difficult to wait. There comes a time when the cup of endurance runs over, and men are no longer willing to be plunged into the abyss of despair. I hope, sirs, you can understand our legitimate and unavoidable impatience.

You express a great deal of anxiety over our willingness to break laws. This is certainly a legitimate concern. Since we so diligently urge people to obey the Supreme Court's decision of 1954 outlawing segregation in the public schools, at first glance it may seem rather paradoxical for us consciously to break laws. One may well ask: "How can you advocate breaking some laws and obeying others?" The answer lies in the fact that there are two types of laws: just and unjust. I would be the first to advocate obeying just laws. One has not only a legal but a moral responsibility to obey just laws. Conversely, one has a moral responsibility to disobey unjust laws. I would agree with St. Augustine that "an unjust law is no law at all."

Now, what is the difference between the two? How does one determine whether a law is just or unjust? A just law is a man-made code that squares with the moral law or the law of God. An unjust law is a code that is out of harmony with the moral law. To put it in the terms of St. Thomas Aquinas: An unjust law is a human law that is not rooted in eternal law and natural law. Any law that uplifts human personality is just. Any law that degrades human personality is unjust. All segregation statutes are unjust because segregation distorts the soul and damages the personality. It gives the segregator a false sense of superiority and the segregated a false sense of inferiority. Segregation, to use the terminology of the Jewish philosopher Martin Buber, substitutes an "I-it" relationship for an "I-thou" relationship and ends up relegating persons to the status of things. Hence segregation is not only politically, economically, and sociologically unsound, it is morally wrong and sinful. Paul Tillich has said that sin is separation. Is not segregation an existential expression of man's tragic separation, his awful estrangement, his terrible sinfulness? Thus it is that I can urge men to obey the 1954 decision of the Supreme Court, for it is morally right; and I can urge them to disobey segregation ordinances for they are morally wrong.

Let us consider a more concrete example of just and unjust laws. An unjust law is a code that a numerical or power majority group compels a minority group to obey but does not make binding on itself. This is *difference* made legal. By the same token, a just law is a code that a majority compels a minority to follow and that it is willing to follow itself. This is *sameness* made legal.

Let me give another explanation. A law is unjust if it is inflicted on a minority that, as a result of being denied the right to vote, had no part in enacting or devising the law. Who can say that the legislature of Alabama which set up that state's segregation laws was democratically elected? Throughout Alabama all sorts of devious methods are used to prevent Negroes from becoming registered voters, and there are some counties in which, even though Negroes constitute a majority of the population, not a single Negro is registered. Can any law enacted under such circumstances be considered democratically structured?

Sometimes a law is just on its face and unjust in its application. For instance, I have been arrested on a charge of parading without a permit. Now, there is nothing wrong in having an ordinance which requires a permit for a parade. But such an ordinance becomes unjust when it is used to maintain segregation and to deny citizens the First-Amendment privilege of peaceful assembly and protest.

I hope you are able to see the distinction I am trying to point out. In no sense do I advocate evading or defying the law, as would the rabid segregationist. That would lead to anarchy. One who breaks an unjust law must do so openly, lovingly, and with a willingness to accept the penalty. I submit that an individual who breaks a law that conscience tells him is unjust, and who willingly accepts the penalty of imprisonment in order to arouse the conscience of the community over its injustice, is in reality expressing the highest respect for law.

Of course, there is nothing new about this kind of civil disobedience. It was evidenced sublimely in the refusal of Shadrach, Meshach, and Abednego to obey the laws of Nebuchadnezzar, on the ground that a higher moral law was at stake. It was practiced superbly by the early Christians, who were willing to face hungry lions and the excruciating pain of chopping blocks rather than submit to certain unjust laws of the Roman Empire. To a degree, academic freedom is a reality today because Socrates practiced civil disobedience. In our own nation, the Boston Tea Party represented a massive act of civil disobedience.

We should never forget that everything Adolf Hitler did in Germany was "legal" and everything the Hungarian freedom fighters did in Hungary was "illegal." It was "illegal" to aid and comfort a Jew in Hitler's Germany. Even so, I am sure that, had I lived in Germany at the time, I would have aided and comforted my Jewish brothers. If today I lived in a Communist country where certain principles dear to the Christian faith are suppressed, I would openly advocate disobeying that country's antireligious laws.

I must make two honest confessions to you, my Christian and Jewish brothers. First, I must confess that over the past few years I have been gravely disappointed with the white moderate. I have almost reached the regrettable conclusion that the Negro's great stumbling block in his stride toward freedom is not the White Citizen's Counciler or the Ku Klux Klanner, but the white moderate, who is more devoted to "order" than to justice; who prefers a negative peace *
which is the absence of tension to a positive peace which is the presence of justice; who constantly says, "I agree with you in the goal you seek, but I cannot agree with your methods of direct action"; who paternalistically believes he can set the timetable for another man's freedom; who lives by a mythical concept of time and who constantly advises the Negro to wait for a "more convenient season." Shallow understanding from people of good will is more frustrating than absolute misunderstanding from people of ill will. Lukewarm acceptance is much more bewildering than outright rejection.

I had hoped that the white moderate would understand that law and order exist for the purpose of establishing justice and that when they fail in this purpose they become the dangerously structured dams that block the flow of social progress. I had hoped that the white moderate would understand that the present tension in the South is a necessary phase of the transition from an obnoxious negative peace, in which the Negro passively accepted his unjust plight, to a substantive and positive peace, in which all men will respect the dignity and worth of human personality. Actually, we who engage in nonviolent direct action are not the creators of tension. We merely bring to the surface the hidden tension that is already alive. We bring it out into the open, where it can be seen and dealt with. Like a boil that can never be cured so long as it is covered up but must be opened with all its ugliness to the natural medicines of air and light, injustice must be exposed, with all the tension its exposure creates, to the light of human conscience and the air of national opinion, before it can be cured.

In your statement you assert that our actions, even though peaceful, must be condemned because they precipitate violence. But is this a logical assertion? Isn't this like condemning a robbed man because his possession of money precipitated the evil act of robbery? Isn't this like condemning Socrates because his unswerving commitment to truth and his philosophical inquiries precipitated the act by the misguided populace in which they made him drink hemlock? Isn't this like condemning Jesus because his unique God-consciousness and never-ceasing devotion to God's will precipitated the evil act of crucifixion? We must come to see that, as the federal courts have consistently affirmed, it is wrong to urge an individual to cease his efforts to gain his basic constitutional rights because the quest may precipitate violence. Society must protect the robbed and punish the robber.

I had also hoped that the white moderate would reject the myth   *
concerning time in relation to the struggle for freedom. I have just received a letter from a white brother in Texas. He writes: "All Christians know that the colored people will receive equal rights eventually, but it is possible that you are in too great a religious hurry. It has taken Christianity almost two thousand years to accomplish what it has. The teachings of Christ take time to come to earth." Such an attitude stems from a tragic misconception of time, from   *
the strangely irrational notion that there is something in the very flow of time that will inevitably cure all ills. Actually, time itself is neutral; it can be used either destructively or constructively. More and more I feel that the people of ill will have used time much more effectively than have the people of good will. We will have to repent in this generation not merely for the hateful words and actions of the bad people, but for the appalling silence of the good people. Human progress never rolls in on wheels of inevitability; it comes through the tireless efforts of men willing to be co-workers with God, and without this hard work, time itself becomes an ally of the forces of social stagnation. We must use time creatively, in the knowledge that the time is always ripe to do right. Now is the time to make real the promise of democracy and transform our pending national elegy into a creative psalm of brotherhood. Now is the time to lift our national

policy from the quicksand of racial injustice to the solid rock of human dignity.

You speak of our activity in Birmingham as extreme. At first I was rather disappointed that fellow clergymen would see my non-violent efforts as those of an extremist. I began thinking about the fact that I stand in the middle of two opposing forces in the Negro community. One is a force of complacency, made up in part of Negroes who, as a result of long years of oppression, are so drained of self-respect and a sense of "somebodiness" that they have adjusted to segregation; and in part of a few middle-class Negroes who, because of a degree of academic and economic security and because in some ways they profit by segregation, have become insensitive to the problems of the masses. The other force is one of bitterness and hatred, and it comes perilously close to advocating violence. It is expressed in the various black nationalist groups that are springing up across the nation, the largest and best-known being Elijah Muhammad's Muslim movement. Nourished by the Negro's frustration over the continued existence of racial discrimination, this movement is made up of people who have lost faith in America, who have absolutely repudiated Christianity, and who have concluded that the white man is an incorrigible "devil."

I have tried to stand between these two forces, saying that we need emulate neither the "do-nothingism" of the complacent nor the hatred and despair of the black nationalist. For there is the more excellent way of love and nonviolent protest. I am grateful to God that, through the influence of the Negro church, the way of nonviolence became an integral part of our struggle.

If this philosophy had not emerged, by now many streets of the South would, I am convinced, be flowing with blood. And I am further convinced that if our white brothers dismiss as "rabblerousers" and "outside agitators" those of us who employ nonviolent direct action, and if they refuse to support our nonviolent efforts, millions of Negroes will, out of frustration and despair, seek solace and security in black-nationalist ideologies—a development that would inevitably lead to a frightening racial nightmare.

Oppressed people cannot remain oppressed forever. The yearning for freedom eventually manifests itself, and that is what has happened to the American Negro. Something within has reminded him of his birthright of freedom, and something without has reminded him that it can be gained. Consciously or unconsciously, he has been caught up by the *Zeitgeist*,[2] and with his black brothers of Africa and his brown and yellow brothers of Asia, South America, and the Caribbean, the United States Negro is moving with a sense of great urgency toward the promised land of racial justice. If one recognizes this vital urge that has engulfed the Negro community, one should readily understand why public demonstrations are taking place. The Negro has many pent-up resentments and latent frustrations, and he must release them. So let him march; let him make prayer pilgrimages to the city hall; let him go on freedom rides—and try to understand why he must do so. If his repressed emotions are not released in nonviolent ways, they will seek expression through violence; this is not a threat but a fact of history. So I have not said to my people, "Get rid of your discontent." Rather, I have tried to say that this normal and healthy discontent can be channeled into the creative outlet of nonviolent direct action. And now this approach is being termed extremist.

But though I was initially disappointed at being categorized as an extremist, as I continued to think about the matter I gradually gained a measure of satisfaction from the label. Was not Jesus an extremist for love: "Love your enemies, bless them that curse you, do good to them that hate you, and pray for them which despitefully use you, and persecute you." Was not Amos an extremist for justice: "Let justice roll down like waters and righteousness like an ever flowing stream." Was not Paul an extremist for the Christian gospel: "I bear in my body the marks of the Lord Jesus." Was not Martin Luther an extremist: "Here I stand; I cannot do otherwise, so help me God." And John Bunyan: "I will stay in jail to the end of my days before I make a butchery of my conscience." And Abraham Lincoln: "This nation cannot survive half slave and half free." And Thomas Jefferson: "We hold these truths to be self-evident, that all men are created equal. . . ." So the question is not whether we will be extremists, but what kind of extremists will we be. Will we be extremists for hate or for love? Will we be extremists for the preservation of injustice or for

[2]*Zeitgeist*: the spirit of the time. —Ed.

the extension of justice? In that dramatic scene on Calvary's hill three men were crucified. We must never forget that all three were crucified for the same crime—the crime of extremism. Two were extremists for immorality, and thus fell below their environment. The other, Jesus Christ, was an extremist for love, truth, and goodness, and thereby rose above his environment. Perhaps the South, the nation, and the world are in dire need of creative extremists.

I had hoped that the white moderate would see this need. Perhaps I was too optimistic; perhaps I expected too much. I suppose I should have realized that few members of the oppressor race can understand the deep groans and passionate yearnings of the oppressed race, and still fewer have the vision to see that injustice must be rooted out by strong, persistent, and determined action. I am thankful, however, that some of our white brothers in the South have grasped the meaning of this social revolution and committed themselves to it. They are still all too few in quantity, but they are big in quality. Some—such as Ralph McGill, Lillian Smith, Harry Golden, James McBridge Dabbs, Ann Braden, and Sarah Patton Boyle—have written about our struggle in eloquent and prophetic terms. Others have marched with us down nameless streets of the South. They have languished in filthy, roach-infested jails, suffering the abuse and brutality of policemen who view them as "dirty nigger-lovers." Unlike so many of their moderate brothers and sisters, they have recognized the urgency of the moment and sensed the need for powerful "action" antidotes to combat the disease of segregation.

Let me take note of my other major disappointment. I have been so greatly disappointed with the white church and its leadership. Of course, there are some notable exceptions. I am not unmindful of the fact that each of you has taken some significant stands on the issue. I commend you, Reverend Stallings, for your Christian stand on this past Sunday, in welcoming Negroes to your worship service on a nonsegregated basis. I commend the Catholic leaders of the state for integrating Spring Hill college several years ago.

But despite these notable exceptions, I must honestly reiterate that I have been disappointed with the church. I do not say this as one of those negative critics who can always find something wrong with the church. I say this as a minister of the gospel, who loves the church; who was nurtured in its bosom; who has been sustained by its spiritual blessings and who will remain true to it as long as the cord of life shall lengthen.

When I was suddenly catapulted into the leadership of the bus protest in Montgomery, Alabama, a few years ago, I felt we would be supported by the white church. I felt that the white ministers, priests, and rabbis of the South would be among our strongest allies. Instead, some have been outright opponents, refusing to understand the freedom movement and misrepresenting its leaders; all too many others have been more cautious than courageous and have remained silent behind the anesthetizing security of stained-glass windows.

In spite of my shattered dreams, I came to Birmingham with the hope that the white religious leadership of this community would see the justice of our cause and, with deep moral concern, would serve as the channel through which our just grievances could reach the power structure. I had hoped that each of you would understand. But again I have been disappointed.

I have heard numerous southern religious leaders admonish their worshipers to comply with a desegregation decision because it is the law, but I have longed to hear white ministers declare: "Follow this decree because integration is morally right and because the Negro is your brother." In the midst of blatant injustices inflicted upon the Negro, I have watched white churchmen stand on the sideline and mouth pious irrelevancies and sanctimonious trivialities. In the midst *
of a mighty struggle to rid our nation of racial and economic injustice, I have heard many ministers say: "Those are social issues, with which the gospel has no real concern." And I have watched many churches commit themselves to a completely otherworldly religion which makes a strange, un-Biblical distinction between body and soul, between the sacred and the secular.

I have traveled the length and breadth of Alabama, Mississippi, and all the other southern states. On sweltering summer days and crisp autumn mornings I have looked at the South's beautiful churches with their lofty spires pointing heavenward. I have beheld the impressive outlines of her massive religious-education buildings. Over and over I have found myself asking: "What kind of people worship here? Who is their God? Where were their voices when the lips of Governor

Barnett dripped with words of interposition and nullification? Where
were they when Governor Wallace gave a clarion call for defiance
and hatred? Where were their voices of support when bruised and
weary Negro men and women decided to rise from the dark dungeons
of complacency to the bright hills of creative protest?"
     Yes, these questions are still in my mind. In deep disappointment
I have wept over the laxity of the church. But be assured that my
tears have been tears of love. There can be no deep disappointment
where there is not deep love. Yes, I love the church. How could I
do otherwise? I am in the rather unique position of being the son,
the grandson, and the great-grandson of preachers. Yes, I see the
church as the body of Christ. But, oh! How we have blemished and
scarred that body through social neglect and through fear of being
nonconformists.
     There was a time when the church was very powerful—in the
time when the early Christians rejoiced at being deemed worthy to suffer for what they believed. In those days the church was not merely a
thermometer that recorded the ideas and principles of popular opinion;
it was a thermostat that transformed the mores of society. Whenever
the early Christians entered a town, the people in power became disturbed and immediately sought to convict the Christians for being
"disturbers of the peace" and "outside agitators." But the Christians
pressed on, in the conviction that they were "a colony of heaven,"
called to obey God rather than man. Small in number, they were big
in commitment. They were too God-intoxicated to be "astronomically
intimidated." By their effort and example they brought an end to such
ancient evils as infanticide and gladiatorial contests.
     Things are different now. So often the contemporary church
is a weak, ineffectual voice with an uncertain sound. So often it is
an archdefender of the status quo. Far from being disturbed by the
presence of the church, the power structure of the average community
is consoled by the church's silent—and often even vocal—sanction of
things as they are.
     But the judgment of God is upon the church as never before.
If today's church does not recapture the sacrificial spirit of the early
church, it will lose its authenticity, forfeit the loyalty of millions,
and be dismissed as an irrelevant social club with no meaning for the

twentieth century. Every day I meet young people whose disappointment with the church has turned into outright disgust.

Perhaps I have once again been too optimistic. Is organized religion too inextricably bound to the status quo to save our nation and the world? Perhaps I must turn my faith to the inner spiritual church, the church within the church, as the true *ekklesia*[3] and the hope of the world. But again I am thankful to God that some noble souls from the ranks of organized religion have broken loose from the paralyzing chains of conformity and joined us as active partners in the struggle for freedom. They have left their secure congregations and walked the streets of Albany, Georgia, with us. They have gone down the highways of the South on tortuous rides for freedom. Yes, they have gone to jail with us. Some have been dismissed from their churches, have lost the support of their bishops and fellow ministers. But they have acted in the faith that right defeated is stronger then evil triumphant. Their witness has been the spiritual salt that has preserved the true meaning of the gospel in these troubled times. They have carved a tunnel of hope through the dark mountains of disappointment.

I hope the church as a whole will meet the challenge of this decisive hour. But even if the church does not come to the aid of justice, I have no despair about the future. I have no fear about the outcome of our struggle in Birmingham, even if our motives are at present misunderstood. We will reach the goal of freedom in Birmingham and all over the nation, because the goal of America is freedom. Abused and scorned though we may be, our destiny is tied up with America's destiny. Before the pilgrims landed at Plymouth, we were here. Before the pen of Jefferson etched the majestic words of the Declaration of Independence across the pages of history, we were here. For more than two centuries our forebears labored in this country without wages; they made cotton king; they built the homes of their masters while suffering gross injustice and shameful humiliation—and yet out of a bottomless vitality they continued to thrive and develop. If the inexpressible cruelties of slavery could not stop us, the opposition we now face will surely fail. We will win our freedom because

[3]*ekklesia*: the Christian church of the New Testament. —Ed.

the sacred heritage of our nation and the eternal will of God are embodied in our echoing demands.

Before closing I feel impelled to mention one other point in your statement that has troubled me profoundly. You warmly commended the Birmingham police force for keeping "order" and "preventing violence." I doubt that you would have so warmly commended the police force if you had seen its dogs sinking their teeth into unarmed, nonviolent Negroes. I doubt that you would so quickly commend the policemen if you were to observe their ugly and inhumane treatment of Negroes here in the city jail; if you were to watch them push and curse old Negro women and young Negro girls; if you were to see them slap and kick old Negro men and young Negro boys; if you were to observe them, as they did on two occasions, refuse to give us food because we wanted to sing our grace together. I cannot join you in your praise of the Birmingham police department.

It is true that the police have exercised a degree of discipline in handling the demonstrators. In this sense they have conducted themselves rather "nonviolently" in public. But for what purpose? To preserve the evil system of segregation. Over the past few years I have consistently preached that nonviolence demands that the means we use must be as pure as the ends we seek. I have tried to make clear that it is wrong to use immoral means to attain moral ends. But now I must affirm that it is just as wrong, or perhaps even more so, to use moral means to preserve immoral ends. Perhaps Mr. Connor and his policemen have been rather nonviolent in public, as was Chief Pritchett in Albany, Georgia, but they have used the moral means of nonviolence to maintain the immoral end of racial injustice. As T. S. Eliot has said, "The last temptation is the greatest treason: To do the right deed for the wrong reason."

I wish you had commended the Negro sit-inners and demonstrators of Birmingham for their sublime courage, their willingness to suffer, and their amazing discipline in the midst of great provocation. One day the South will recognize its real heroes. They will be the James Merediths, with the noble sense of purpose that enables them to face jeering and hostile mobs, and with the agonizing loneliness that characterizes the life of the pioneer. They will be old, oppressed, battered Negro women, symbolized in a seventy-two-year-old woman in

Montgomery, Alabama, who rose up with a sense of dignity and with her people decided not to ride segregated buses, and who responded with ungrammatical profundity to one who inquired about her weariness: "My feets is tired, but my soul is at rest." They will be the young high school and college students, the young ministers of the gospel and a host of their elders, courageously and nonviolently sitting in at lunch counters and willingly going to jail for conscience's sake. One day the South will know that when these disinherited children of God sat down at lunch counters, they were in reality standing up for what is best in the American dream and for the most sacred values in our Judaeo-Christian heritage, thereby bringing our nation back to these great wells of democracy which were dug deep by the founding fathers in their formulation of the Constitution and the Declaration of Independence.

Never before have I written so long a letter. I'm afraid it is much too long to take your precious time. I can assure you that it would   * have been much shorter if I had been writing from a comfortable desk, but what else can one do when he is alone in a narrow jail cell, other than write long letters, think long thoughts, and pray long prayers?

If I have said anything in this letter that overstates the truth and indicates an unreasonable impatience, I beg you to forgive me. If I have said anything that understates the truth and indicates my having a patience that allows me to settle for anything less than brotherhood, I beg God to forgive me.

I hope this letter finds you strong in the faith. I also hope that circumstances will soon make it possible for me to meet each of you, not as an integrationist or a civil-rights leader but as a fellow clergyman and a Christian brother. Let us all hope that the dark clouds of racial prejudice will soon pass away and the deep fog of misunderstanding will be lifted from our fear-drenched communities, and in some not too distant tomorrow the radiant stars of love and brotherhood will shine over our great nation with all their scintillating beauty.

> Yours for the cause of Peace and Brotherhood,
> Martin Luther King, Jr.

Thinking about Writing

Words

Powerful words both depend on and help shape their context. In what way does each word in the list below depend on its context for strength? What does each contribute to its context? Can you think of any other word the author might have used in its place? How does the word strike you, and how do you respond to the sentence or passage because of the word?

bodies
tension
gadflies
tragic effort
sadly mistaken
negative peace
myth
tragic misconception
mouth
precious

Thinking

1. King defines just and unjust laws in several ways. What are his definitions? What do you think is a just law? An unjust one?
2. The timing for the direct-action program was first set for the Easter shopping season, when the "economic-withdrawal program" would force local merchants to recognize the blacks' buying power. Does this combination of the spiritual and financial surprise you? What does this timing say about hitting people "where it hurts"?
3. King mentions Reinhold Niebuhr's comment that groups tend to be more immoral than are individuals. Why do you think this is so? In what ways do you behave differently when you are alone rather than with company? How many companions—just one or more—are enough to change the way you act? What constitutes a group for you?
4. King quotes T. S. Eliot: "The last temptation is the greatest treason: To do the right deed for the wrong reason." He also adds that

it is wrong to "use immoral means to attain moral ends" as it is "to use moral means to preserve immoral ends." Give an example of each with reference to segregation.

Writing

1. One of King's rhetorical strategies consists of returning repeatedly to his critics' ideas, either those that apparently were expressed or those that King assumes his critics hold. For example, he says, "You deplore the demonstrations," referring to some public comment; he then says, "You may well ask," when his critics' actually may not have asked. How does this technique of including real or imagined arguments of his opponents help King's own writing and support his contentions? In an essay, explore this technique, quoting each instance you discuss.

2. King has throughout this letter used a number of paired words or concepts. Often these are opposites, such as "words . . . silence," but sometimes they are simply positioned pairs, such as "wait . . . never," or "quicksand . . . rock," or "you to forgive me . . . God to forgive me." Write an essay in which you examine the force of these paired words and concepts. Try to include the overall pair: justice and injustice.

3. Perhaps because King was a minister and knew about the construction of sermons, he uses the technique of announcing something and then following it up. For example, the four steps in a nonviolent campaign and the two disappointments are "given" to the reader and then explained fully. In an essay, examine the effect of this technique, including some discussion of King's narrative style to explain what has first been "given." How does he hold the reader's attention while he explains the separate steps? The two disappointments?

4. "As Reinhold Niebuhr has reminded us, groups tend to be more immoral than individuals," King says. Do you agree with Niebuhr? Have you ever witnessed, or been a part of, group harrassment? What happens to the sense of social responsibility when people act in groups? Why does a group behave differently from an individual? Write an essay in which explore the force, for good as well as evil, of group acts.

7

Engaging

All good writers work to engage their readers. Striving for this engagement helps focus the writer while at the same time it gives readers a sense of importance and participation. The writers in this chapter have discovered that recognizing their own importance in a text is one of the best ways to engage their readers. Writers understand that writing is a process, but they also know that behind the process, there is a person. Acknowledging their own importance in a text, these writers recognize an equal importance in their readers as they become engaged in the text.

Describing his early efforts to improve his writing, Benjamin Franklin says that he first designed a plan that would engage him actively in writing variations on an essay he had recently read. Later, rediscovering a favorite book, he remarks on the author's use of dialogue which he sees as "very engaging to the reader."

John McPhee, writing about a trip to the Alaskan wilderness, uses his own presence and experiences to describe some of the problems there. Having acknowledged his own importance as witness to what is happening in Alaska, he engages his readers' interests through accounts of his own experience.

Writing about the daily presence of death in El Salvador, Joan Didion defines her own presence there to such an extent that it becomes crucial to readers' understanding of the place. She engages her readers by insisting on her own importance in the text, with the result that readers, once engaged, respond to conditions in El Salvador and not simply to Joan Didion.

Similarly, Tom Wolfe and Hunter S. Thompson deliberately design the kind of writing that will, by including them, also engage their readers. Moreover, they rely on the visual impact of unorthodox punctuation, playfully breaking rules like naughty schoolboys in an engaging manner that invites the reader to join in.

Finally, George Orwell, writing of the time he spent in Spain during the civil war, describes how people had grown tired of the hardships of war. He, too, longed for decent food and clothes. Rather than excluding others from events as objective reporting tends to do, Orwell's admission of weakness draws readers into his experience and acts to engage readers' interests.

Benjamin Franklin

Benjamin Franklin (1706–90) was born in Boston but spent much of his life in Philadelphia. As a youth, he served an apprenticeship in his brother's printing business. It was here that he recognized the immense power of language. Burning ambition and a thirst for knowledge constantly pressed him to read whatever he could, to write about whatever engaged his mind, and to talk to as many people as possible. A highly creative man, Franklin was an inventor, a diplomat, a philosopher, and what we would today probably call a systems analyst. His broad interests reached from street lights to the court of France. In the selection here, which comes from his *Autobiography*, Franklin discusses how he discovered the wonders of language and practiced making words work for him. Then, he notes a clever method for capturing a reader's attention.

Words

About this time I met with an odd volume of the *Spectator*. It was the third. I had never before seen any of them. I bought it, read it over and over, and was much delighted with it. I thought the writing excellent and wished if possible to imitate it. With that view, I took some of the papers, and making short hints of the sentiment in each sentence, laid them by a few days, and then without looking at the book, tried to complete the papers again by expressing each hinted sentiment at length and as fully as it had been expressed before, in any suitable words that should occur to me. Then I compared my *Spectator* with the original, discovered some of my faults, and corrected them. But I found I wanted a stock of words or a readiness in recollecting and using them, which I thought I should have acquired before that time

if I had gone on making verses; since the continual search for words of the same import but of different length to suit the measure, or of different sound for the rhyme would have laid me under a constant necessity of searching for variety, and also have tended to fix that variety in my mind, and make me master of it. Therefore I took some of the tales in the *Spectator* and turned them into verse, and after a time, when I had pretty well forgotten the prose, turned them back again. I also sometimes jumbled my collections of hints into confusion, and after some weeks endeavoured to reduce them into the best order before I began to form the full sentences and complete the paper. This was to teach me method in the arrangement of thoughts. By comparing my work afterwards with the original, I discovered many faults and corrected them; but I sometimes had the pleasure of fancying that in certain particulars of small import I had been lucky   *
enough to improve the method or the language, and this encouraged me to think that I might possibly in time come to be a tolerable   *
English writer, of which I was extremely ambitious.

The time I allotted for these exercises and for reading, was at night after work, or before it began in the morning, or on Sundays, when I contrived to be in the printing house alone, avoiding as much as I could the common attendance on public worship which my father used to exact of me when I was under his care—and which, indeed, I still thought a duty, though I could not, as it seemed to me, afford the time to practise it.

When about sixteen years of age I happened to meet with a book written by one Tryon, recommending a vegetable diet. I determined to go into it. My brother, being yet unmarried, did not keep house but boarded himself and his apprentices in another family. My refusing to eat flesh occasioned an inconveniency, and I was frequently chid for my singularity. I made myself acquainted with Tryon's manner of   *
preparing some of his dishes, such as boiling potatoes or rice, making hasty pudding, and a few others; and then proposed to my brother that if he would give me weekly half the money he paid for my board, I would board myself. He instantly agreed to it, and I presently found that I could save half what he paid me. This was an additional fund for buying of books. But I had another advantage in it. My brother and the rest going from the printing house to their meals, I remained

there alone, and dispatching presently my light repast (which often *
was no more than a biscuit or a slice of bread, a handful of raisins or
a tart from the pastry cook's, and a glass of water) had the rest of the
time till their return for study, in which I made the greater progress
from that greater clearness of head and quicker apprehension which
generally attend temperance in eating and drinking. Now it was that
being on some occasion made ashamed of my ignorance in figures,
which I had twice failed in learning when at school, I took Cocker's
book of arithmetic, and went through the whole by myself with the
greatest of ease. I also read Seller's and Sturmy's book on navigation
and became acquainted with the little geometry it contains, but I
never proceeded far in that science. I read about this time Locke *On
Human Understanding,* and *The Art of Thinking* by Messrs. du Port
Royal.

    While I was intent on improving my language, I met with an
English grammar (I think it was Greenwood's) at the end of which
there were two little sketches on the arts of rhetoric and logic, the
latter finishing with a dispute in the Socratic method. And soon after I
procured Xenophon's *Memorable Things of Socrates,* wherein there are
many examples of the same method. I was charmed with it, adopted
it, dropped my abrupt contradiction and positive argumentation, and
put on the humble enquirer. And being then, from reading Shafts-
bury and Collins, made a doubter, as I already was in many points
of our religious doctrines, I found this method the safest for myself
and very embarrassing to those against whom I used it; therefore, I
took a delight in it, practised it continually, and grew very artful
and expert in drawing people, even of superior knowledge, into con-
cessions the consequences of which they did not foresee, entangling
them in difficulties out of which they could not extricate themselves,
and so obtaining victories that neither myself nor my cause always
deserved. I continued this method some few years but gradually left
it, retaining only the habit of expressing myself in terms of modest
diffidence, never using when I advance anything that may possibly
be disputed the words, "certainly," "undoubtedly," or any others that
give the air of positiveness to an opinion; but rather say, "I conceive
or apprehend a thing to be so or so," "It appears to me," or "I should
think it so or so, for such and such reasons," or "I imagine it to be

so," or "It is so if I am not mistaken." This habit, I believe, has been of great advantage to me when I have had occasion to inculcate my opinions and persuade men into measures that I have been from time to time engaged in promoting. And as the chief ends of conversation are to *inform*, or to *be informed*, to *please* or to *persuade*, I wish well-meaning and sensible men would not lessen their power of doing good by a positive, assuming manner that seldom fails to disgust, tends to create opposition, and to defeat every one of those purposes for which speech was given to us. In fact, if you wish to instruct others, a positive, dogmatical manner in advancing your sentiments may provoke contradiction and prevent a candid attention. If you desire instruction and improvement from the knowledge of others, you should not at the same time express yourself as firmly fixed in your present opinions; modest and sensible men, who do not love disputation, will probably leave you undisturbed in the possession of your error. In adopting such a manner you can seldom expect to please your hearers, or to persuade those whose concurrence you desire. Pope judiciously observes,

Men must be taught as if you taught them not,
And things unknown propos'd as things forgot.

     In constant disagreement with his brother, Franklin decides to leave Boston.

     I sold some of my books to raise a little money, was taken on board the sloop privately, had a fair wind, and in three days found myself at New York, near three hundred miles from my home, at the age of seventeen, without the least recommendation to or knowledge of any person in the place, and with very little money in my pocket.

     The inclination I had had for the sea was by this time done   * away, or I might now have gratified it. But having another profession and conceiving myself a pretty good workman, I offered my services to the printer of the place, old Mr. Wm. Bradford (who had been the first printer in Pennsylvania, but had removed thence in consequence of a quarrel with the Governor, Geo. Keith). He could give me no employment, having little to do and hands enough already. "But," says he, "my son at Philadelphia has lately lost his principal hand, Aquila Rose, by death. If you go thither I believe he may employ you."

Philadelphia was a hundred miles farther. I set out, however, in a boat for Amboy, leaving my chest and things to follow me round by sea. In crossing the bay we met with a squall that tore our rotten sails to pieces, prevented our getting into the kill, and drove us upon Long Island. In our way a drunken Dutchman, who was a passenger, too, fell overboard; when he was sinking, I reached through the water to his shock pate and drew him up so that we got him in again. His   *
ducking sobered him a little, and he went to sleep, taking first out of his pocket a book which he desired I would dry for him. It proved to be my old favorite author Bunyan's *Pilgrim's Progress* in Dutch, finely printed on good paper with copper cuts, a dress better than I had ever seen it wear in its own language. I have since found that it has been translated into most of the languages of Europe, and suppose it has been more generally read than any other book except, perhaps, the Bible. Honest John was the first that I know of who mixes narration and dialogue, a method of writing very engaging to the reader, who in the most interesting parts finds himself, as it were, admitted into the company and present at the conversation. Defoe has imitated him successfully in his *Robinson Crusoe*, in his *Moll Flanders*, and other pieces; and Richardson has done the same in his *Pamela*, etc.

On approaching the island, we found it was in a place where there could be no landing, there being a great surf on the stony beach. So we dropped anchor and swung out our cable towards the shore. Some people came down to the water edge and hallooed to us, as we did to them, but the wind was so high and the surf so loud that we could not understand each other. There were some canoes on the shore, and we made signs and called to them to fetch us, but they either did not comprehend us or thought it impracticable, so they went off. Night approaching, we had no remedy but to have patience till the wind abated, and in the meantime the boatman and I concluded to sleep if we could, and so we crowded into the scuttle with the Dutchman who was still wet, and the spray breaking over the head of our boat leaked through to us, so that we were soon almost as wet as he. In this manner we lay all night with very little rest, but the wind abating the next day, we made a shift to reach Amboy before night, having been thirty hours on the water without victuals or any drink but a bottle of filthy rum, the water we sailed on being salt.

In the evening I found myself very feverish and went to bed; but having read somewhere that cold water drank plentifully was good for a fever, I followed the prescription, sweat plentifully most of the night, my fever left me, and in the morning crossing the ferry, I proceeded on my journey on foot, having fifty miles to Burlington, where I was told I should find boats that would carry me the rest of the way to Philadelphia.

Thinking about Writing

Words

Powerful words both depend on and help shape their context. In what way does each word in the list below depend on its context for strength? What does each contribute to its context? Can you think of any other word the author might have used in its place? How does the word strike you, and how do you respond to the sentence or passage because of the word?

small import
tolerable
singularity
dispatching
inclination
shock pate

Thinking

1. Franklin thought well of the Socratic method of argument in which he played the "humble enquirer," pretending to know little or nothing about the subject and thus "allowing" others to discover what he wanted them to know. (For an example, see Plato's "The

Allegory of the Cave" in chapter 9.) Why do you think this relatively gentle mode of persuasion appealed to Franklin more than "a positive, assuming manner that seldom fails to disgust"? To what extent do you agree with Franklin that if you want to convince someone you should do so modestly?

2. Franklin admired the style of mixing narration and dialogue which he said was "very engaging to the reader." Do you agree with him? Why do you think Franklin doesn't use this style? In what ways do you find Franklin's writing engaging? To whom does he seem to speak?

3. Do you tend to use the same style for everything you write? When you set out to write, which influences you more: yourself as writer (and therefore as thinker, learner, and expounder), your audience, or your subject (a paper for history, a lab report for biology)?

4. Bunyan's method of combining narration and dialogue is not appropriate for all types of writing. For what types of writing do you think it would be appropriate? Which of the following do you think would benefit from Bunyan's method, and why do you think so?
   a. an account of a man seeking truth
   b. a newspaper report of a fire
   c. the report of a press conference
   d. a movie star's crash diet
   e. a boxer's headaches
   f. an account of a murder
   g. the account of a murder trial
   h. a film review
   i. an interview
   j. the report of a team's slump
   k. a test report about a new drug

Writing

1. Review Franklin's advice about persuading people, and then write two simple arguments for curbing dogs. Prepare the first argument as if it were written by an irate, hysterical citizen, the second by

a modest and sensible person who does not "love disputation" but who really wishes to convince others that curbing dogs is a dog owner's responsibility.

2. For amusement, turn a short passage from one of your science textbooks into verse. Three paragraphs from the text should be enough for this experiment. This rendering may be in free verse and need not rhyme unless you want it to. When you have finished, answer this question: in order to turn the text into verse, what did you have to do as you read the text? Hand in a copy of both the text and the poem you wrote.

3. Turn the three Shakespeare sonnets in chapter 5 into prose, adopting any style you prefer. You may find the style of New Journalism, illustrated in this chapter by the pieces by Tom Wolfe and Hunter S. Thompson, appropriate for your rendering.

4. Use the plot of a novel, film, or play as the basis for writing a newspaper article. Use a headline for your title.

John McPhee

John McPhee (b.1931) was born in Princeton, New Jersey, and educated at both Princeton and Cambridge universities. His career began with writing scripts for television programs, and then he moved to editing for *Time* magazine and staff writing for *The New Yorker*. McPhee's writing is diverse, including such topics as experimental aircraft, bears, nuclear safeguards, oranges, and the Pine Barrens of New Jersey. His writing has appeared in such varied publications as *Holiday*, *National Geographic*, *Playboy*, and *Atlantic*. He tackles cultural and geographic problems, heightening and humanizing them with realistic details that are readable and appealing. In this way, McPhee informs without being didactic. In this selection, which comes from his book about Alaska called *Coming Into the Country*, McPhee seeks to engage the reader's imagination with scenes from life in the far north.

Things Are Rough Enough in Town

Dick Cook, in his generosity, lifts from his plate a small gob of muskrat fat and gives it to me. The fat is savory, a delicacy. The lean of the "rat" could be taken for dark, strong chicken.

He is saying, "There's a pride to doing something other people can't do. My life style is what so many people dream about. What they don't dream is that it took six or eight years of hard work to get it. A lot of these people who keep coming into the country don't belong here. They have fallen in love with a calendar photo and they want to live under a beautiful mountain. When they arrive, the reality doesn't match the dream. It's too much for them. They don't want to work hard enough; they don't want to spread out—to go far enough up the streams. This is relatively poor trapping country. You need a twenty-mile radius. But they won't move away from the Yukon. My cabin is the farthest off the river. Have another cup of tea."

Tea strong enough to blacken tin. Hanging over the campfire is a No. 10 can, coated with carbon from the fire, and even blacker within, its bottom a swamp of leaves. To use his own term for what he is doing here, Cook is on vacation. In cool spring weather toward the end of ducks, we are close by three lakes near the Yukon, far downriver   * from Eagle. He is here to hunt. The vacation is from the weight of tasks at home, which is ten miles away. His shelter is only his orange canvas tarp, one side strung between spruce, the opposite stakes in the sphagnum. He finishes his duck-and-muskrat stew, and stretches out under the tarp, head propped up, taking his ease. He remarks that Nessmuk could not stand the confinement of an A-shaped or wall-sided tent and neither can he.

Cook's knowledge of wood lore is encyclopedic. Impromptu, he can, and readily will, give a thirty-minute lecture on just about any aspect of it from wolf dens to whetstones, so it is no surprise—except in a geographical way, far off in the Alaskan bush—to hear him invoke the pen name of the nineteenth-century Eastern writer George Sears, called Nessmuk, whose "Woodcraft," published in 1884, was the first American book on forest camping, and is written with so much wisdom, wit, and insight that it makes Henry David Thoreau seem alien, humorless, and French. Donna Kneeland is beside the fire, her legs folded straight beneath her. She adds wood. She is attempting to dry, possibly repair, a boot that has a two-inch rip near the sole. A parabola of wire crosses the top of the No. 10 can. She lifts it. With a short stick in her other hand, she tilts the bottom, pouring tea into my cup. I welcome it, to defray the chill, which neither Dick nor Donna seems to notice. Staked out in the woods around us are seven sled dogs. They, too, are on holiday.

When new people come in, Cook continues, he recommends that they rent a cabin in or near Eagle, somewhere close to civilization, and spend a winter there first—with the wilderness a quarter of a mile away. "That leaves some unburned bridges. Try trapping, hunting meat, getting some skills together—setting yourself up. Money will not accomplish it, but money is important. You need axes, splitting mauls, rifles, saws, winter clothing. The average person brings—or buys within a couple of years—at least ten thousand dollars' worth of gear. It helps to have a truck at the post-office town. A small boat with a kicker costs twelve hundred dollars. Bring a two-year supply of food. You won't learn enough in a year."   *

Donna, looking up from her boot, says, "Steve Ulvi, when he was here last week, wanted to know what traps to buy, and he—"

"He asked a lot of things, but that is his business," Cook says, with such sharpness that Donna falls silent.

"Why do people live in Eagle?" I ask him.

"I don't know," he says. "I've always wondered. Some of them came with the intention of going on into the bush and have never carried it out. One person in Eagle has tried three times. But a lot of people come with a desire not to work—just to be there and not to work. I've never understood that. The country and the weather are too hard just to sit."

He draws an analogy between what he has done and what the early Western settlers did. They dug makeshift houses into the dirt while concentrating on the clearing of fields and the construction of barns. That was the way settlement had to take place. "If you built a nice house first, your livestock would die." Dogs, in Cook's case, were his livestock, so fishnets came first. Then he planted a garden. Then he set traplines. He learned sleds and mushing from Indians. "There   * were several of the old ones around who knew what they were doing and were still sober enough to talk about it." He has continued to   * learn, he says, just by observing other people along the river. "Charlie Edwards *does* things. I sit and think them out. I've learned more from his mistakes than I've learned from my own. I feel at home now, after twelve years—at home on water, in the woods, in summer, in winter. I feel a part of what is here. The bush is so far beyond what anybody has been taught. The religious power here is beyond all training. There are forces here that a lot of people don't know exist."

"What are they?"

"They can't be articulated. You're out of the realm of words. *
You are close to the land here, to nature, to what the Indians called
Mother and I call Momma. Momma decides everything. The concept
is still here, but the Indians have given it up. They say the Indians
now have rights to land in which to do their subsistence hunting and
trapping. That is ridiculous. It is about time the whites got it equally.
There is just no land, no legal place to go, in Alaska. If they wipe
out the white people who are living in the bush, they wipe out the
native culture."

He shifts his weight, and for a moment I can see his arm. There
is a chamois-cloth shirt under his cotton pullover, but both are so
shredded and rent with holes that the arm is visible behind its curtain
of rags. The skin is as white as paper. A skull and crossbones is tat-
tooed there. A dagger sunk into the skull from above protrudes from
the chin like an iron Vandyke. It is flanked by the letters US and
MC. "I grew up in Lyndhurst, Ohio. My father was in the commer-
cial-industrial air-conditioning business. I helped pay my bills at the
Colorado School of Mines by going into the mountains with dynamite, blasting open pegmatite dikes and selling the crystals. Students
then all had dynamite in the trunks of their cars—like nowadays they
all wear Vibram soles and carry sheath knives." Cook's first wife was
a model. She left him, and for a time he looked after his two infant
children. When she divorced him, he lost in court a case for custody.
"Since then, I have never understood trees," he says. "They put down
roots." He has not seen his children in a great many years. One is
eighteen, and has a child of her own.

There is a small, square-ended aluminum boat—dragged in here
over riverine muskeg and rammed through hells of willow. In it now
is an armory of guns, one of which belonged to Dick's father and
grandfather. The lakes are small. Quietly, we paddle across one of
them, leave the boat, and creep through the woods. We avoid a
mound of bear scat—fairly, but not acutely, fresh. It glistens but
has stopped smoking. Approaching the shore of the next lake, Dick
motions us to get down, and we crawl toward the water without
damaging the silence. The forest cover extends to the edge. We *
lie there, behind trees, looking out. Dick lifts a shotgun. In the
beginnings of the twilight, a pair of loons are cruising. They are

beyond range. Their heads are up. Their bodies float high. They sense no danger. Their course is obliquely toward the gun. Now we can distinguish the black-and-white shingling on their necks. Silently swimming, they come nearer still. Loons. They are quick. Diving, they can suddenly be gone. He fires. He fires again. The loons elect to sprint down the surface—cacophonous, flailing—their splayfeet * spading the water. A pellet or two may have touched them, but it seems unlikely.

Dick hands one of the guns to Donna and says that he is going to skirt the lake. If the loons return, she is to fire. Silently, he is gone. We hear nothing of his movements among the trees. He is gone an hour. Donna, whispering, asks me if I know much about this gun.

"Nothing," I tell her.

"Nothing?"

"Nothing."

"Neither do I. Those loons will have to come pretty close before I'll try to hit them."

A single loon now tests that distance. It comes swimming around a peninsula of sedge and adopts a path that leads directly toward the muzzle of the gun. Serene in its ignorance, it glides steadily onward without even a slight change of course until, with the distance nearly closed, its breast seems a yard wide. Still it has not seen us. The gun is aimed and ready. If the bird swims any farther, it will hit the shore. Donna blasts. The loon's move is too quick to be called a dive. It is a complete and instant disappearance. There is no commotion, no blood in the water, no loon.

We whisper through the time. At length, more shots ring out, down the lake. It is the sound of Cook, missing. Eventually, he comes back. We now try another lake—creeping the final dozen yards through the forest to its shore. "Wait here," Cook says, and he leaves the .22. "Kill a rat if one goes by." Meanwhile, he will circle the shoreline. This lake has rats for sure, and there—he points to a far cove and a barely visible line of darning-egg heads—are ducks. In the unending twilight, another hour passes. At various distances and times, we hear half a dozen sharp reports. "You can be active in a job in town, but it doesn't seem as important," Donna whispers. "Here the important thing is—well, getting your meat." She mentions that she was a stewardess once for Reeve Aleutian. A muskrat rounds a clump of sedge, swimming before us, left to right. Donna follows it with the rifle and fires. The water jumps a foot. We cannot see the spent bullet, sinking like a pebble toward the bottom of the lake, but the muskrat probably can. There was something she particularly liked about Reeve Aleutian. The airline was always ready to ignore its schedules and serve as an emergency ambulance service for the entire island chain. And so the work was, as she phrases it, "more interesting than just coffee, tea, or me." Winds blew seventy miles an hour over the islands sometimes. A DC-3 would try to touch on a runway and have trouble setting down because its wings wished to stay in the air. In an Electra once, she was approaching Adak, winds in the seventies. Suddenly the turbulence increased and the Electra overturned. It was not just steeply banked—it was flying upside down. Donna noted with interest the silence of the passengers. She had thought that in such a situation people would scream. Objects fell to the ceiling. Toilets spilled. The plane crossed the island, and slowly rolled upright. Its second approach was successful. On the ground, after thanking the passengers for flying Reeve and wishing them a pleasant stay on Adak, Donna suggested to the other stewardess that they have a drink. "That is the only time in my life I have ever done that," she whispers now— "taken a drink, you know, in order to relax." Intense firing breaks out far down the shore, a Boone and Crockett sonata. When Cook appears again beside us, he has nothing in hand and nothing to retrieve. He says, "One trouble with this type of life is you can go hungry when you screw up." This is true in two ways, for cartridges cost a few cents apiece and shotgun shells a quarter. In effect, he has been firing grocery money into the lake. We return to the sled dogs and the lean-to, but soon Cook, frustrated, says, "If we don't get something, we're not going to eat," and, cursing Momma, he takes off once more, for a final walking circuit of the shore.

By the fire, Donna sews a patch on a pair of Dick's trousers, and remarks to me that for an Easterner I seem to be surprisingly dressed, in that my boots and vest and general gear are the sorts of things she associates with Alaska. I explain to her about the Wild East, and how I like to go out when I can, and that I always have. "But I'll tell you the difference, Donna. The difference is that pile of bear sign back there, and the absence of trails, and . . ." My thoughts race ahead of what I am trying to say. The difference is also in the winter silence, a silence that can be as wide as the country, and the dreamy, sifting slowness of the descent of the dry snow. If there were only twenty-five people in the state of New Jersey, they would then sense   * the paramount difference, which is in the unpeopled reach of this country. I may have liked places that are wild and been quickened all my days just by the sound of the word, but I see now I never knew what it could mean. I can see why people who come to Alaska are unprepared. In four decades of times beyond some sort of road, I never set foot in a place like this. It is in no way an extension of what I've known before. The constructions I have lived by ought not, and do not, apply here. Left on my own here, I would have to change in a hurry, and learn in a hurry, or I'd never last a year.

For a time, the only sound is the fire. The dogs are asleep. There's no wind. The forest is as quiet as it was, a month before, under snow. Donna tightens the thread. She says, finally, "I know what you mean. When I first came out here, I felt the same way. I saw what it was like and I thought, I'll never survive."

What would she do in a medical emergency, like a simple case of appendicitis?

"I hope this doesn't sound corny," she answers, "but things are living and dying out here all the time. If I got appendicitis, I would just die."

Cook, in half an hour's absence, fires one shot. When he comes back, he drops a muskrat on the ground with a hole above its ear. Donna says, "They're hard to skin when they've been shot in the head." She skins it out neatly, and covers the pelt with salt. The inner rat goes into the pot.

We roll out our sleeping bags side by side, remove our boots, settle in. I have before now lacked the courage to reach into my pack and take out a thing for which I feel a great need. Antithetical forces are in strife within me. What I want is my pillow. Its capacity   * to soften the coming sleep is perhaps not as great as its capacity to humiliate me before these rugged pioneers. Shame at last loses out to comfort. My hand goes into the pack. The pillow is small and white. The slip is homemade, with snaps at one end, so that it can contain a down jacket, which it does. I mumble an explanation of this, saying that nonetheless I feel a touch ridiculous—in their company, in this country—reaching into my gear for a pillow.   *

"Don't apologize," says Cook, getting up on one elbow to admire the pillow. "As Nessmuk said, we're not out here to rough it. We're here to smooth it. Things are rough enough in town."

Thinking about Writing

Words

Powerful words both depend on and help shape their context. In what way does each word in the list below depend on its context for strength? What does each contribute to its context? Can you think of any other word the author might have used in its place? How does the word strike you, and how do you respond to the sentence or passage because of the word?

ducks
learn
learned sleds
sober
words
damaging
cacophonous
twenty-five people
pillow

Thinking

1. What do you think is the main point of this selection? How has McPhee rendered the point for you? What is your reaction to McPhee's encounter with Dick Cook and Donna Kneeland? How do you feel McPhee uses the presence of these two people and domestic details as an aid in making a statement about Alaska as he sees it? Why does McPhee refer to Dick Cook sometimes as Dick and sometimes as Cook? Why is Donna always Donna?

2. What is the effect for you of McPhee's including visual details that you can picture clearly: muskrat fat, Dick's tattoo, the patch Donna is sewing, the bear droppings? How does picturing objects help you as reader to become sympathetic toward *invisible*, abstract ideas and concerns?

3. "They have fallen in love with a calendar photo," says Dick of the people who romanticize Alaska. When you think about Alaska, what do you imagine? In what ways do your ideas differ from McPhee's description?

4. Why do you think people seek the "simple life" when in fact it is anything but simple? Isn't the simple life the one the city dweller lives, rising, working, and playing all in a predictable routine? What is the simple life for you?

Writing

1. Write an account in narrative form, with conversations, in order to make a statement about some human condition you have observed. You may want to consider how people rush to copy the latest style of dress or behavior, or how being an artist often entails living frugally to pursue that art, or how people tend to become more conservative as they get older. Or think of your own human condition, and create a narrative around it. Where is McPhee's main statement about Alaska? Who makes it? Think about this strategy when you write your account.

2. Rewrite this encounter in an impersonal style, considering the same problem as McPhee did, that a novice has a difficult time adjusting to Alaska. Describe this adjustment, its success or failure, in a few paragraphs. Use impersonal phrasing like "There are," "People find," and "It is difficult" in order to flatten the writing. When you have finished, you may wish to reread McPhee to see how his style "fleshes out" what could have been a drab, albeit informative, observation.

3. To what extent do we follow our imaginations whenever we venture into any new situation? Had you fallen in love with any "calendar photo" or delicious fantasy when you decided to attend the particular college you do? In what way is going to Alaska like

going to college? Consider people you know for whom you could say college life is "too much for them. They don't want to work hard enough; they don't want to spread out—to go far enough up the streams."

Write an essay that argues for commitment and hard work in any new venture. Explain what the hard work entails, and discuss why we must have both desire and diligence to succeed.

4. Write an essay in which you explore the "simple life." Consider the current fashion for rugged outdoor clothing and wholesome foods, offering some reasons for the appeal to Americans today who seek respite from the "rat race" and the stresses of urban life. If you enjoy certain aspects of the simple life, be sure to include your own experiences and desires. Has the simple life given you the satisfactions you sought? What did you find was your greatest disappointment with it? Consider these questions when you write your essay.

Joan Didion

Joan Didion (b. 1934) was born in Sacramento, California, and educated at the University of California at Berkeley. She has written fiction, such as *Play It As It Lays* and *A Book of Common Prayer*, screenplays (with her husband, writer John Gregory Dunne), and numerous essays, collected in *The White Album* and *Slouching Toward Bethlehem*. In both her fiction and nonfiction, Didion presents the world as chaotic. Her characters and the real people she writes about in essays react to this chaos, either going mad or not, sometimes making sense, sometimes merely being brave. In the selection here, which comes from a longer work called *Salvador*, Didion again presents a chaotic world, a real one this time, with real people grasping at shreds of a calm daily life in the face of death.

Living with Death

One of the more shadowy elements of the violent scene here [is] the death squad. Existence of these groups has long been disputed, but not by many Salvadorans. . . . Who constitutes the death squads is yet another difficult question. We do not believe that these squads exist as permanent formations but rather as ad hoc vigilante groups that coalesce according to perceived need. Membership is also uncertain, but in addition to civilians we believe that both on- and off-duty members of the security forces are participants. This was unofficially confirmed by right-wing spokesman Maj. Roberto D'Aubuisson who stated in an interview in early 1981 that security force members utilize the guise of the death squad when a potentially embarrassing or odious task needs to be performed.

—*From the confidential but later declassified January 15, 1982 memo previously cited, drafted for the State Department by the political section at the embassy in San Salvador.*

The dead and pieces of the dead turn up in El Salvador everywhere, every day, as taken for granted as in a nightmare, or a horror movie. Vultures of course suggest the presence of a body. A knot of children on the street suggests the presence of a body. Bodies turn up in the brush of vacant lots, in the garbage thrown down ravines in the richest districts, in public rest rooms, in bus stations. Some are dropped in Lake Ilopango, a few miles east of the city, and wash up near the lakeside cottages and clubs frequented by what remains in San Salvador of the sporting bourgeoisie. Some still turn up at El Playón, the lunar lava field of rotting human flesh visible at one time or another on every television screen in America but characterized in June of 1982 in the *El Salvador News Gazette*, an English-language weekly edited by an American named Mario Rosenthal, as an "uncorroborated story . . . dredged up from the files of leftist propaganda." Others turn up at Puerta del Diablo, above Parque Balboa, a national *Turicentro* described as recently as the April–July 1982 issue of *Aboard TACA*, the magazine provided passengers on the national airline of El Salvador, as "offering excellent subjects for color photography."

I drove up to Puerta del Diablo one morning in June of 1982, past the Casa Presidencial and the camouflaged watch towers and heavy concentrations of troops and arms south of town, on up a narrow road narrowed further by landslides and deep crevices in the roadbed, a drive so insistently premonitory that after a while I began   *
to hope that I would pass Puerta del Diablo without knowing it, just miss it, write it off, turn around and go back. There was however no way of missing it. Puerta del Diablo is a "view site" in an older and distinctly literary tradition, nature as lesson, an immense cleft rock through which half of El Salvador seems framed, a site so romantic and "mystical," so theatrically sacrificial in aspect, that it might be a cosmic parody of nineteenth-century landscape painting. The place presents itself as pathetic fallacy: the sky "broods," the stones "weep," a constant seepage of water weighting the ferns and moss. The foliage is thick and slick with moisture. The only sound is a steady buzz, I believe of cicadas.

Body dumps are seen in El Salvador as a kind of visitors' must-do, difficult but worth the detour. "Of course you have seen El Playón," an aide to President Alvaro Magaña said to me one day, and

proceeded to discuss the site geologically, as evidence of the country's geothermal resources. He made no mention of the bodies. I was unsure if he was sounding me out or simply found the geothermal aspect of overriding interest. One difference between El Playón and Puerta del   *
Diablo is that most bodies at El Playón appear to have been killed somewhere else, and then dumped; at Puerta del Diablo the executions are believed to occur in place, at the top, and the bodies thrown over. Sometimes reporters will speak of wanting to spend the night at Puerta del Diablo, in order to document the actual execution, but at the time I was in Salvador no one had.

The aftermath, the daylight aspect, is well documented. "Nothing fresh today, I hear," an embassy officer said when I mentioned that I had visited Puerta del Diablo. "Were there any on top?" someone else asked. "There were supposed to have been three on top yesterday." The point about whether or not there had been any on top was that usually it was necessary to go down to see bodies. The way down is hard. Slabs of stone, slippery with moss, are set into the vertiginous cliff, and it is down this cliff that one begins the descent to the bodies, or what is left of the bodies, pecked and maggoty masses of flesh, bone, hair. On some days there have been helicopters circling, tracking those making the descent. Other days there have been militia at the top, in the clearing where the road seems to run out, but on the morning I was there the only people on top were a man and a woman and three small children, who played in the wet grass while the woman started and stopped a Toyota pickup. She appeared to be learning how to drive. She drove forward and then back toward the edge, apparently following the man's signals, over and over again.

We did not speak, and it was only later, down the mountain and back in the land of the provisionally living, that it occurred to   *
me that there was a definite question about why a man and a woman might choose a well-known body dump for a driving lesson. This was one of a number of occasions, during the two weeks my husband and I spent in El Salvador, on which I came to understand, in a way I had not understood before, the exact mechanism of terror.

Whenever I had nothing better to do in San Salvador I would walk up in the leafy stillness of the San Benito and Escalón districts,   *
where the hush at midday is broken only by the occasional crackle of

a walkie-talkie, the click of metal moving on a weapon. I recall a day in San Benito when I opened my bag to check an address, and heard the clicking of metal on metal all up and down the street. On the whole no one walks up here, and pools of blossoms lie undisturbed * on the sidewalks. Most of the houses in San Benito are more recent than those in Escalón, less idiosyncratic and probably smarter, but the most striking architectural features in both districts are not the houses but their walls, walls built upon walls, walls stripped of the usual copa de oro and bougainvillea, walls that reflect successive generations of violence: the original stone, the additional five or six or * ten feet of brick, and finally the barbed wire, sometimes concertina, sometimes electrified; walls with watch towers, gun ports, closed-circuit television cameras, walls now reaching twenty and thirty feet.

San Benito and Escalón appear on the embassy security maps as districts of relatively few "incidents," but they remain districts in which a certain oppressive uneasiness prevails. In the first place there are always "incidents"—detentions and deaths and disappearances—in the *barrancas*, the ravines lined with shanties that fall down behind the houses with the walls and the guards and the walkie-talkies; one day in Escalón I was introduced to a woman who kept the lean-to that served as a grocery in a *barranca* just above the Hotel Sheraton. She was sticking prices on bars of Camay and Johnson's baby soap, stopping occasionally to sell a plastic bag or two filled with crushed ice and Coca-Cola, and all the while she talked in a low voice about her fear, about her eighteen-year-old son, about the boys who had been taken out and shot on successive nights recently in a neighboring *barranca*.

In the second place there is, in Escalón, the presence of the Sheraton itself, a hotel that has figured rather too prominently in certain local stories involving the disappearance and death of Americans. The Sheraton always seems brighter and more mildly festive than either the Camino Real or the Presidente, with children in the pool and flowers and pretty women in pastel dresses, but there are usually several bulletproofed Cherokee Chiefs in the parking area, and the men drinking in the lobby often carry the little zippered purses that in San Salvador suggest not passports or credit cards but Browning 9-mm. pistols.

It was at the Sheraton that one of the few American *desaparecidos*,[1] a young free-lance writer named John Sullivan, was last seen, in December of 1980. It was also at the Sheraton, after eleven on the evening of January 3, 1981, that the two American advisers on agrarian reform, Michael Hammer and Mark Pearlman, were killed, along with the Salvadoran director of the Institute for Agrarian Transformation, José Rodolfo Viera. The three were drinking coffee in a dining room off the lobby, and whoever killed them used an Ingram MAC-10, without sound suppressor, and then walked out through the lobby, unapprehended.   *

Thinking about Writing

Words

Powerful words both depend on and help shape their context. In what way does each word in the list below depend on its context for strength? What does each word contribute to its context? Can you think of any other word the author might have used in its place? How does the word strike you, and how do you respond to the sentence or passage because of the word?

premonitory
overriding interest
provisionally
leafy stillness
pools
generations
unapprehended

Thinking

1. Didion's writing, like John McPhee's, is highly visual, but unlike him, she deliberately omits specific dialogue in this selection. What effect has this economy on you the reader? Which do you prefer,

---

[1]*desaparecidos*: disappeared ones. —Ed.

the conversations re-created in McPhee's writing or the words reported in Didion's? How does Didion indicate her own presence, other than writing, "I drove . . ."?

2. Puerta del Diablo, says Didion, "presents itself as pathetic fallacy" (that is, the assigning of human emotions to nature). How does this description help to give you Didion's picture of the place as well as its effect on her? What is its effect on you? When she says, "difficult but worth the detour," her style shifts from literary analytic to pseudotravelogue, and her mood shifts as well. What are her moods in these two places? What other moods appear elsewhere? How does her mood affect yours?

3. The president's aide discusses the attractions of El Playón in terms of its "geothermal" aspects, completely ignoring its use as a body dump. Didion wonders if he was sounding her out. What other reasons do you think he could have had for mentioning only El Playón's virtues?

4. What effect has the driving lesson on you as you read about the body dump? How does the Toyota pickup affect the mood of the scene? Do you see any particular color for the pickup? Why do you think the couple chose "a well-known body dump for a driving lesson"?

Writing

1. Didion gives two striking examples of people living with death, one in the driving lesson and the other in the crowd at the Sheraton swimming pool. Both include women and children.

    Write an essay in which you compare and contrast these two pictures, perhaps including the way in which you think each suggests "the exact mechanism of terror."

2. Read the travel section of your Sunday paper, looking for positive comments about various places to visit. (You won't find negative comments, of course.) What style can you see emerging as travel writers seek to impress us with the delights of places they visit?

    Using examples from the newspaper, write an essay that explores the style of travel writing. Look for outrageous and possibly amusing examples of making the dull seem exciting, as well as any special vocabulary, like *charming* instead of *ugly* or *awkward*.

3. Often a product connected with some negative aspect of life will be presented publicly in glowing terms, described with euphemisms whenever the negative aspects must be admitted. Reality, however, hovers around, conspicuous by its absence. For example, in a department store, the section with clothing for very large women calls itself "Women's Sizes" or the like; a television commercial for roach killer depicts whimsical creatures dancing to joyous music; and a magazine advertisement for a new brand of toilet paper emphasizes everything but its actual use.

   Write an essay in which you explore the uses of such techniques in presenting or selling any potentially unsavory product. Perhaps you have read Evelyn Waugh's *The Loved One* or Jessica Mitford's *The American Way of Death* and can refer to one of these works in your essay.

4. Write an essay in which you examine the way people, when faced with sadness or horror, carry on with daily life. Often the most ordinary routines become the greatest solace in such times of stress. Consider why, after a tragedy, we want to perform some ordinary task that reconnects us with life, such as eating and drinking after a funeral. When you are worried or distracted, do you find comfort in sorting out the papers on your desk or doing the laundry or working on some project that gives you the sense that you are still functioning, still "OK"? You might wish to refer to Didion's essay for examples of people living with death.

Tom Wolfe

Tom Wolfe (b. 1931) was born Thomas Kennerly
Wolfe, Jr., in Virginia. He was educated at Washington
and Lee University and earned a Ph.D. at Yale University.
An artist as well as a journalist, Wolfe began his writing career as a reporter, first for a newspaper in Massachusetts, then for the *Washington Post*. He eventually
found his drawings as well as articles appearing in such
magazines as *Esquire* and *Harper's*. Although he has had
numerous one-man shows of his drawings, it is for his
writing that he is best known to the general public. In
the 1960s he introduced the writing style known as New
Journalism, an innovative genre of investigative reporting
which combines "pop" language with conventional techniques of fiction writing. The results of this new style may
be seen in several works, among them *The Electric Koolaid
Acid Test* and *The Right Stuff*. In the selection here, which
comes from a longer work found in *The New Journalism*,
edited by Wolfe, he explains how he was first inspired
to write such unorthodox literature, "letting the reader,
via the narrator, talk to the characters, hector them, insult them, prod them with irony or condescension, or
whatever."

How New Journalism
Started

Yet in terms of experimenting in non-fiction, the way I worked
at that point couldn't have been more ideal. I was writing mostly for
New York, which, as I say, was a Sunday supplement. At that time,
1963 and 1964, Sunday supplements were close to being the lowest

form of periodical. Their status was well below that of the ordinary daily newspaper, and only slightly above that of the morbidity press, sheets like the *National Enquirer* in its "I Left My Babies in the Deep Freeze" period. As a result, Sunday supplements had no traditions, no pretensions, no promises to live up to, not even any rules to speak of. They were brain candy, that was all. Readers felt no guilt whatsoever about laying them aside, throwing them away or not looking at them at all. I never felt the slightest hesitation about trying any device that might conceivably grab the reader a few seconds longer. I tried to yell right in his ear: *Stick around!* . . . Sunday supplements were no place for diffident souls. That was how I started playing around with the device of point-of-view.

For example, I once did a story about the girls in jail at the Women's House of Detention in Greenwich Village at Greenwich Avenue and the Avenue of the Americas, an intersection known as Nut Heaven. The girls used to yell down to boys on the street, to all the nice free funky Village groovies they saw walking around down there. They would yell every male first name they could think of— "Bob!" "Bill!" "Joe!" "Jack!" "Jimmy!" "Willie!" "Benny!"—until they hit the right name, and some poor fool would stop and look up and answer. Then they would suggest a lot of quaint anatomical impossibilities for the kid to perform on himself and start laughing like maniacs. I was there one night when they caught a boy who looked about twenty-one named Harry. So I started the story with the girls yelling at him:

"'Hai-ai-ai-ai-ai-ai-ai-ai-ai-ai-ai-ai-ai-ai-ai-ai-ai-ai-ai-ai-ai-ai-ai-ai-ai-ai-ai-ai-ai-ai-ai-ai-ai-ai-ai-ai-ai-ai-ai-ai-ai-ai-ai-aireeeeeeeeeeeeeeeeeeeee!'"

I looked at that. I liked it. I decided I would enjoy yelling at the little bastard myself. So I started lambasting him, too, in the next sentence:

"O, dear Sweet Harry, with your French gangster-movie bangs, your Ski Shop turtleneck sweater and your Army-Navy Store blue denim shirt over it, with your Bloomsbury corduroy pants you saw in the *Manchester Guardian* airmail edition and sent away for and your sly intellectual pigeon-toed libido roaming in Greenwich Village— that siren call really for you?"

Then I let the girls have another go at it:

"'Hai-ai-ai-ai-ai-ai-ai-ai-ai-ai-ai-ai-aireeeeeeeeee!'"

Then I started in again, and so on. There was nothing subtle about such a device, which might be called the Hectoring Narrator. Quite the opposite. That was precisely why I liked it. I liked the idea of starting off a story by letting the reader, via the narrator, talk to the characters, hector them, insult them, prod them with irony or condescension, or whatever. Why should the reader be expected to just lie flat and let these people come tromping through as if his mind were a subway turnstile? But I was democratic about it, I was. Sometimes I would put myself into the story and make sport of me. I would be "the man in the brown Borsalino hat," a large fuzzy Italian fedora I wore at the time, or "the man in the Big Lunch tie." I would write about myself in the third person, usually as a puzzled onlooker or someone who was in the way, which was often the case. Once I even began a story about a vice I was also prone to, tailor-made clothes, as if someone else were the hectoring narrator . . . treating *me* in a flippant manner: "Real buttonholes. That's it! A man can take his thumb and forefinger and unbutton his sleeve at the wrist because this kind of suit has real buttonholes there. Tom, boy, it's terrible. Once you know about it, you start seeing it. All the time!". . . and so on . . . anything to avoid coming on like the usual non-fiction narrator, with a hush in my voice, like a radio announcer at a tennis match.

The voice of the narrator, in fact, was one of the great problems in non-fiction writing. Most non-fiction writers, without knowing it, wrote in a century-old British tradition in which it was understood that the narrator shall assume a calm, cultivated and, in fact, genteel voice. The idea was that the narrator's own voice should be like the off-white or putty-colored walls that Syrie Maugham popularized in interior decoration . . . a "neutral background" against which bits of color would stand out. *Understatement* was the thing. You can't imagine what a positive word "understatement" was among both journalists and literati ten years ago. There is something to be said for the notion, of course, but the trouble was that by the early 1960s understatement had become an absolute pall. Readers were bored to tears without understanding why. When they came upon that pale beige tone, it began to signal to them, unconsciously, that a well-known bore was here again, "the journalist," a pedestrian mind, a phlegmatic spirit, a

faded personality, and there was no way to get rid of the pallid little   *
troll, short of ceasing to read. This had nothing to do with objectivity
and subjectivity or taking a stand or "commitment"—it was a matter
of personality, energy, drive, bravura . . . style, in a word . . . The
standard non-fiction writer's voice was like the standard announcer's
voice . . . a drag, a droning . . .

To avoid this I would try anything. For example, I wrote a
story about Junior Johnson, a stock car racer from Ingle Hollow,
North Carolina, who had learned to drive by running moonshine
whiskey to Charlotte and other distribution points. "There ain't no
harder work in the world than making whiskey," Junior would say.
"I don't know of any other business that compels you to get up at
all times of night and go outdoors in the snow and everything else
and work. H'it's the hardest way in the world to make a living, and
I don't think anybody'd do it unless they had to." Now, as long
as Junior Johnson was explaining the corn liquor industry, there was
no problem, because (a) dialogue tends to be naturally attractive,
or involving, to the reader, and (b) Johnson's Ingle Hollow lingo
was unusual. But then I had to take over the explanation myself, in
order to compress into a few paragraphs information that had come
from several interviews. So . . . I decided I would rather talk in Ingle
Hollow accents myself, since that seemed to go over all right. There
is no law that says the narrator has to speak in beige or even New
York journalese. So I picked up the explanation myself, as follows:
"Working mash wouldn't wait for a man. It started coming to a head
when it got ready to and a man had to be there to take it off, out
there in the woods, in the brush, in the brambles, in the muck, in
the snow. Wouldn't it have been something if you could have just
set it all up inside a good old shed with a corrugated metal roof and
order those parts like you want them and not have to smuggle all that
copper and all that sugar and all that everything out here in the woods
and be a coppersmith and a plumber and a cooper and a carpenter
and a pack horse and every other goddamned thing God ever saw in
the world, all at once.

"And live decent hours—Junior and his brothers, about two
o'clock in the morning they'd head out to the stash, the place where
the liquor was hidden after it was made . . ."

I was feigning the tones of an Ingle Hollow moonshiner, in order to create the illusion of seeing the action through the eyes of someone who was actually on the scene and involved in it, rather than a beige narrator. I began to think of this device as the *downstage voice*, as if characters downstage from the protagonist himself were talking.

I would do the same thing with descriptions. Rather than just come on as the broadcaster describing the big parade, I would shift as quickly as possible into the eye sockets, as it were, of the people in the story. Often I would shift the point of view in the middle of a paragraph or even a sentence. I began a story on Baby Jane Holzer, entitled "The Girl of the Year," as follows:

"Bangs manes bouffant beehives Beatle caps butter faces brush-on lashes decal eyes puffy sweaters French thrust bras flailing leather blue jeans stretch pants stretch jeans honeydew bottoms eclair shanks elf boots ballerinas Knight slippers, hundreds of them, these flaming little buds, bobbing and screaming, rocketing around inside the Academy of Music Theater underneath that vast old moldering cherub dome up there—aren't they super-marvelous!

"'Aren't they super-marvelous!' says Baby Jane, and then: 'Hi, Isabel! Isabel! You want to sit backstage—with the Stones!'

"The show hasn't even started yet, the Rolling Stones aren't even on the stage, the place is full of a great shabby moldering dimness, and these flaming little buds.

"Girls are reeling this way and that way in the aisle and through their huge black decal eyes, sagging with Tiger Tongue Lick Me brush-on eyelashes and black appliqués, sagging like display-window Christmas trees, they keep staring at—her—Baby Jane—on the aisle."

The opening paragraph is a rush of Groovy clothes ending with the phrase "—aren't they super-marvelous!" With this phrase the point-of-view shifts to Baby Jane, and one is looking through her eyes at the young girls, "the flaming little buds," who are running around the theater. The description continues through Jane's eyes until the phrase "they keep staring at—her—Baby Jane," whereupon the point-of-view shifts to the young girls, and the reader is suddenly looking through *their* eyes at Baby Jane: "What the hell is this? She is gorgeous in the most outrageous way. Her hair rises up from her head in a huge hairy corona, a huge tan mane around a narrow face and two eyes opened—swock!—like umbrellas, with all that hair flowing down over a coat made of . . . zebra! Those motherless stripes! Oh, damn! Here she is with her friends, looking like some kind of queen bee for all flaming little buds everywhere."

In fact, three points-of-view are used in that rather short passage, the point-of-view of the subject (Baby Jane), the point-of-view of the people watching her (the "flaming little buds"), and my own. I switched back and forth between points-of-view continually, and often abruptly, in many articles I wrote in 1963, 1964, and 1965. Eventually a reviewer called me a "chameleon" who instantly took on the coloration of whomever he was writing about. He meant it negatively. I took it as a great compliment. A chameleon . . . but * exactly!

Sometimes I used point-of-view in the Jamesian sense in which fiction writers understand it, entering directly into the mind of a character, experiencing the world through his central nervous system throughout a given scene. Writing about Phil Spector ("The First Tycoon of Teen"), I began the article not only inside his mind but with a virtual stream of consciousness. One of the news magazines apparently regarded my Spector story as an improbable feat, because they interviewed him and asked him if he didn't think this passage was merely a fiction that appropriated his name. Spector said that, in fact, he found it quite accurate. This should have come as no surprise, since every detail in the passage was taken from a long interview with Spector about exactly how he had felt at the time:

"All these raindrops are *high* or something. They don't roll down the window, they come straight back, toward the tail, wobbling, like all those Mr. Cool snowheads walking on mattresses. The plane is taxiing out toward the runway to take off, and this stupid infarcted water wobbles, sideways, across the window. Phil Spector, 23 years old, the rock and roll magnate, producer of Philles Records, America's first teen-age tycoon, watches . . . this watery pathology . . . it is *sick, fatal.* He tightens his seat belt over his bowels . . . A hum rises inside the plane, a shot of air comes shooting through the vent over somebody's seat, some ass turns on a cone of light, there is a sign stuck out by the runway, a mad, cryptic, insane instruction to the pilot— Runway 4, Are Cylinder Laps Mainside DOWN?—and beyond, disoriented crop rows of sulphur blue lights, like the lights on top of a

New Jersey toothpaste factory, only spreading on and on in sulphur blue rows over Los Angeles County. It is . . . disoriented. Schizoid raindrops. The plane breaks in two on takeoff and everybody in the front half comes rushing toward Phil Spector in a gush of bodies in a thick orange—*napalm!* No, it happens aloft; there is a long rip in the side of the plane, it just rips, he can see the top ripping, folding back in sick curds, like a sick Dali egg, and Phil Spector goes sailing through the rip, dark, freezing. And the engine, it is *reedy*—

"Miss!"

"A stewardess is walking to the back to buckle herself in for the takeoff. The plane is moving, the jets are revving. Under a Lifebuoy blue skirt, her fireproof legs are clicking out of her Pinki-Kinki-Panti Fantasy—"

I had the feeling, rightly or wrongly, that I was doing things no one had ever done before in journalism. I used to try to imagine the feeling readers must have had upon finding all this carrying on and cutting up in a Sunday supplement. I liked that idea. I had no sense of being a part of any normal journalistic or literary environment. Later I read the English critic John Bayley's yearnings for an age when writers had Pushkin's sense of "looking at all things afresh," as if for the first time, without the constant intimidation of being aware of what other writer have alrady done. In the mid-1960s that was exactly the feeling I had.

I'm sure that others who were experimenting with magazine articles, such as Talese, began to feel the same way. They were moving beyond the conventional limits of journalism, but not merely in terms of technique. The kind of reporting they were doing struck them as far more than ambitious, too. It was more intense, more detailed, and certainly more time-consuming than anything that newspaper or magazine reporters, including investigative reporters, were accustomed to. They developed the habit of staying with the people they were writing about for days at a time, weeks in some cases. They had to gather all the material the conventional journalist was after—and then keep going. It seemed all-important to *be there* when dramatic scenes took place, to get the dialogue, the gestures, the facial expressions, the details of the environment. The idea was to give the full objective description, plus something that readers had always had to go to novels and short stories for: namely, the subjective or emotional life of the characters. That was why it was so ironic when both the journalistic and literary old guards began to attack this new journalism as "impressionistic." The most important things one attempted in terms of technique depended upon a depth of information that had never been demanded in newspaper work. Only through the most searching forms of reporting was it possible, in non-fiction, to use whole scenes, extended dialogue, point-of-view, and interior monologue. Eventually I, and others, would be accused of "entering people's minds". . . But exactly! I figured that was one more doorbell a reporter had to push.

Most of the people who eventually wrote about my style, however, tended to concentrate on certain mannerisms, the lavish use of dots, dashes, exclamation points, italics, and occasionally punctuation that never existed before : : : : : : : : : and of interjections, shouts, nonsense words, onomatopoeia, mimesis, pleonasms, the continual use of the historical present, and so on. This was natural enough, because many of these devices stood out even before one had read a word. The typography actually *looked* different. Referring to my use of italics and exclamation points, one critic observed, with scorn, that my work looked like something out of Queen Victoria's childhood diary. Queen Victoria's childhood diaries are, in fact, quite readable; even charming. One has only to compare them with the miles of official prose she laid on Palmerston, Wellington, Gladstone in letters and communiqués and on the English people in her proclamations to see the point I'm making. I found a great many pieces of punctuation and typography lying around dormant when I came along—and I must say I had a good time using them. I figured it was time someone violated what Orwell called "the Geneva conventions of the mind". . . a protocol that had kept journalism and non-fiction generally (and novels) in such a tedious bind for so long. I found that things like exclamation points, italics, and abrupt shifts (dashes) and syncopations (dots) helped to give the illusion not only of a person talking but of a person thinking. I used to enjoy using dots where they would be least expected, not at the end of a sentence but in the middle, creating the effect . . . of a skipped beat. It seemed to me the mind reacted—*first!* . . . in dots, dashes, and exclamation points, then rationalized, drew up a brief, with periods.

I soon found that people loved to parody my style. By 1966 the parodies began to come in a rush. I must say I read them all. I suppose it's because at the heart of every parody there is a little gold ball of tribute. Even hostile parodies admit from the start that the target has a distinct voice.

It is not very often that one comes across a new style, period. And if a new style were created not via the novel, or the short story, or poetry, but via journalism—I suppose that would seem extraordinary. It was probably that idea—more than any specific devices, such as using scenes and dialogue in a "novelistic" fashion—that began to give me very grand ideas about a new journalism. As I saw it, if a new literary style could originate in journalism, then it stood to reason that journalism could aspire to more than mere emulation of those aging giants, the novelists.

Thinking about Writing

Words

Powerful words both depend on and help shape their context. In what way does each word in the list below depend on its context for strength? What does each contribute to its context? Can you think of any other word the author might have used in its place? How does the word strike you, and how do you respond to the sentence or passage because of the word?

morbidity press
brain candy
turnstile
pall
pale
pallid
but exactly

Thinking

1. "I decided I would enjoy yelling at the little bastard myself," says Wolfe, and so he enters the narrative. What happens to you as reader when he writes himself into his own report? Do you feel excluded, outside the action, or do you feel that you can, "via the narrator, talk to the characters"? Has Wolfe made you *want* to talk to them? If so, how has he done this?
2. Wolfe knows his writing looks strange and offbeat. He says his writing confused critics when it first appeared because, "The typography actually *looked* different." How does the appearance of Wolfe's writing contribute to the writing? Where do you feel the appearance detracts from the writing or bothers you when you read it?

Writing

1. Find a human interest story in the newspaper. Try rewriting the piece in New Journalism style, following Wolfe's prescription:
   a. use whole scenes
   b. write (create) extended dialogue
   c. allow point of view to move anywhere
   d. write (create) interior monologue
2. Write an essay in which you analyze the presence of the narrator (the one who is writing) in any three of the following pieces:
   a. a newspaper report of a world news event
   b. a human interest story
   c. a lab report
   d. a film review
   e. a letter to the editor
   f. any selection in this book
   Arrange your analysis of these three items in any order. You may want to consider them in order of "warmth," by ranking narrator presence in the pieces. If you discover another relation among the pieces, tell what it is and how you discovered it.

Hunter S. Thompson

Hunter S. Thompson (b. 1939) was born in Louisville, Kentucky. After attending local public schools, at the age of seventeen he joined the U. S. Air Force. By the time he was twenty, Thompson was a Caribbean correspondent for the *New York Herald Tribune* and a few years later a South American correspondent for the *National Observer*. He spent a year with the Hell's Angels because of his interest in the subculture and then wrote his first book, *The Hell's Angels, a Strange and Terrible Saga*. Tom Wolfe, who defined the New Journalism, has called Thompson a "Gonzo Journalist," one who writes a manic, self-centered style which appeals because Thompson, "for all his surface ferocity, usually casts himself as a frantic loser, inept and half-psychotic." In the following selection, from a longer piece in *The New Journalism*, edited by Tom Wolfe, Thompson conveys personal horror at the time-honored horse race. The original essay from which this comes is titled "The Kentucky Derby Is Decadent and Depraved."

Welcome to Derbytown

I got off the plane around midnight and no one spoke as I crossed the dark runway to the terminal. The air was thick and hot, like wandering into a steam bath. Inside, people hugged each other and shook hands . . . big grins and a whoop here and there: "By God! You old *bastard! Good* to see you, boy! *Damn* good . . . and I *mean* it!"

In the air-conditioned lounge I met a man from Houston who said his name was something or other—"but just call me Jimbo"—and he was here to get it on. "I'm ready for *anything*, by God! Anything at all. Yeah, what are you drinkin?" I ordered a Margarita with ice,

but he wouldn't hear of it: "Naw, naw . . . what the hell kind of drink is that for Kentucky Derby time? What's *wrong* with you, boy?" He grinned and winked at the bartender. "Goddam, we gotta educate this *
boy. Get him some good *whiskey*. . . ."

I shrugged. "Okay, a double Old Fitz on ice." Jimbo nodded his *
approval.

"Look." He tapped me on the arm to make sure I was listening. "I know this Derby crowd, I come here every year, and let me tell you one thing I've learned—this is no town to be giving people the impression you're some kind of faggot. Not in public, anyway. Shit, they'll roll you in a minute, knock you in the head and take every goddam cent you have."

I thanked him and fitted a Marlboro into my cigarette *
holder. "Say," he said, "you look like you might be in the horse business . . . am I right?"

"No," I said. "I'm a photographer."

"Oh yeah?" He eyed my ragged leather bag with new interest. "Is that what you got there—cameras? Who you work for?"

"Playboy," I said.

He laughed. "Well goddam! What are you gonna take pictures of—nekkid horses? Haw! I guess you'll be workin' pretty hard when they run the Kentucky Oaks. That's a race just for fillies." He was laughing wildly. "Hell yes! And they'll all be nekkid too!"

I shook my head and said nothing; just stared at him for a moment, trying to look grim. "There's going to be trouble," I said. "My assignment is to take pictures of the riot."

"What riot?"

I hesitated, twirling the ice in my drink. "At the track. On Derby Day. The Black Panthers." I stared at him again. "Don't you read the newspapers?"

The grin on his face had collapsed. "What the *hell* are you talkin about?"

"Well . . . maybe I shouldn't be telling you. . . ." I shrugged. *
"But hell, everybody else seems to know. The cops and the National Guard have been getting ready for six weeks. They have 20,000 troops on alert at Fort Knox. They've warned us—all the press and photographers—to wear helmets

and special vests like flak jackets. We were told to expect shooting. . . ."

"No!" he shouted; his hands flew up and hovered momentarily between us, as if to ward off the words he was hearing. Then he whacked his fist on the bar. "Those sons of bitches! God Almighty! The Kentucky Derby!" He kept shaking his head. "No! *Jesus!* That's almost too bad to believe!" Now he seemed to be jagging on the stool, and when he looked up his eyes were misty. "Why? Why *here?* Don't they respect *anything?*"

I shrugged again. "It's not just the Panthers. The FBI says bus-   *
loads of white crazies are coming in from all over the country — to mix with the crowd and attack all at once, from every direction. They'll be dressed like everybody else. You know — coats and ties and all that. But when the trouble starts . . . well, that's why the cops are so worried."

He sat for a moment, looking hurt and confused and not quite able to digest all this terrible news. Then he cried out: "Oh . . . Jesus! What in the name of God is happening in this country? Where can you get away from it?"

"Not here," I said, picking up my bag. "Thanks for the drink . . . and good luck."

He grabbed my arm, urging me to have another, but I said I was overdue at the Press Club and hustled off to get my act together for the awful spectacle. At the airport newsstand I picked up a Courier-Journal and scanned the front page headlines: "Nixon Sends GI's into Cambodia to Hit Reds" . . . "B-52's Raid, then 2,000 GI's Advance 20 Miles" . . . "4,000 U.S. Troops Deployed Near Yale as Tension Grows Over Panther Protest." At the bottom of the page was a photo of Diane Crump, soon to become the first woman jockey ever to ride in the Kentucky Derby. The photographer had snapped her "stopping in the barn area to fondle her mount, Fathom." The rest of the paper was spotted with ugly war news and stories of "student unrest." There was no mention of any protest action at a small Ohio school called Kent State.

I went to the Hertz desk to pick up my car, but the moon-faced young swinger in charge said they didn't have any. "You can't rent   *
one anywhere," he assured me. "Our Derby reservations have been

booked for six weeks." I explained that my agent had confirmed a white Chrysler convertible for me that very afternoon but he shook his head. "Maybe we'll have a cancellation. Where are you staying?" I shrugged. "Where's the Texas crowd staying? I want to be with *
my people."
    He sighed. "My friend, you're in trouble, This town is flat *full*. Always is, for the Derby."
    I leaned closer to him, half-whispering: "Look, I'm from Playboy. How would you like a job?"
    He backed off quickly. "What? Come on, now. What kind of a job?"
    "Never mind," I said. "You just blew it." I swept my bag off the *
counter and went to find a cab. The bag is a valuable prop in this kind of work; mine has a lot of baggage tags on it—SF, LA, NY, Lima, Rome, Bangkok, that sort of thing—and the most prominent tag of all is a very official, plastic-coated thing that says "Photog. Playboy Mag." I bought it from a pimp in Vail, Colorado, and he told me how to use it. "Never mention Playboy until you're sure they've seen this thing first," he said. "Then, when you see them notice it, that's the time to strike. They'll go belly up every time. This thing is magic, I tell you. Pure magic."
    Well . . . maybe so. I'd used it on the poor geek in the bar, and *
now, humming along in a Yellow Cab toward town, I felt a little guilty about jangling the poor bugger's brains with that evil fantasy. But what the hell? Anybody who wanders around the world saying, "Yes, I'm from Texas," deserves whatever happens to him. And he had, after all, come here once again to make a 19th century ass of *
himself in the midst of some jaded, atavistic freakout with nothing to recommend it except a very saleable "tradition." Early in our chat, Jimbo had told me that he hasn't missed a Derby since 1954. "The little lady won't come anymore," he said. "She just grits her teeth and turns me loose for this one. And when I say 'loose' I do mean *loose!* I toss ten-dollar bills around like they were goin' outa-style! Horses, whiskey, women . . . shit, there's women in this town that'll do *anything* for money."
    Why not? Money is a good thing to have in these twisted times. Even Richard Nixon is hungry for it. Only a few days before the Derby

he said, "If I had any money I'd invest it in the stock market." And the market, meanwhile, continued its grim slide.

Thinking about Writing

Words

Powerful words both depend on and help shape their context. In what way does each word in the list below depend on its context for strength? What does each contribute to its context? Can you think of any other word the author might have used in its place? How does the word strike you, and how do you respond to the sentence or passage because of the word?

winked
shrugged
thanked
shrugged
shrugged
swinger
shrugged
swept
geek
19th century ass

Thinking

1. What is this selection about? Why do you think Thompson pauses in his narrative to comment on the political climate at that time? Why does he focus on the Derby rather than, say, on the World Series? What binds the Derby tradition to the political state for Thompson? What American tradition, in sports or the arts, acts for you as a reflection of political malaise the way the Derby acts for Thompson?
2. What do you think of Jimbo? Do you feel sorry for him? How does Thompson feel about Jimbo? How do you know?

3. What is the effect of Thompson telling us about his bag and its baggage tags, the *Playboy* tag in particular? Why do you think he refers to the tag as "a very official, plastic-coated thing"?

Writing

1. Both Thompson here and Orwell in either of his essays in this book ("Shooting an Elephant" or "Barcelona") use a strategy that seems to invite the reader's sympathy—that of admitting their weaker sides, their being guilty or imperfect, even as they are describing other people's weaknesses.

   Write an essay that explores the two writers' uses of this strategy. How do they appeal to your emotions? Do you find their frankness endearing and believable? Consider these questions as you write your essay. You may have noticed other writers who employ this strategy; mention them as well, including your reaction to their techniques.

2. The title of Thompson's essay from which this selection comes is "The Kentucky Derby Is Decadent and Depraved." How has Thompson used vocabulary and details to support this contention? How does his making himself a liar affect your reaction to his contention?

   Write an essay in which you explore the ways Thompson conveys ideas of decadence and depravity—in himself and in others.

George Orwell

George Orwell (1903–50) was born Eric Blair in India and was educated in England. After a university education he served with the British police in Burma, an experience that confirmed his wish to become a journalist. Orwell hoped to use the position of writer to speak out against oppression, loneliness, totalitarian government, and political coercion. In Spain as a journalist during the Spanish civil war, he observed how people behaved under the pressures of war, especially as the initial excitement began to wane. In the essay here, he remarks how easily people revert to earlier habits, once the glow of the first fight has died down and the harsh realities of wartime living become apparent. Never one to preach, Orwell includes himself in this group of people who initially could tolerate any hardship, only to wish fervently later on for a good dinner and decent bottle of wine. Orwell was to return to his theme of old habits when he wrote *Animal Farm*, his anti-Stalinist satire. The selection here comes from a longer work, *Homage to Catalonia*, his account of the Spanish civil war.

Barcelona

Everyone who has made two visits, at intervals of months, to Barcelona during the war has remarked upon the extraordinary changes that took place in it. And curiously enough, whether they went there first in August and again in January, or, like myself, first in December and again in April, the thing they said was always the same: that the revolutionary atmosphere had vanished. No doubt to anyone who had been there in August, when the blood was scarcely dry in the

302

streets and militia were quartered in the smart hotels, Barcelona in December would have seemed bourgeois; to me, fresh from England, it was liker to a workers' city than anything I had conceived possible. Now the tide had rolled back. Once again it was an ordinary city, a little pinched and chipped by war, but with no outward sign of working-class predominance.

The change in the aspect of the crowds was startling. The militia uniform and the blue overalls had almost disappeared; everyone seemed to be wearing the smart summer suits in which Spanish tailors specialize. Fat prosperous men, elegant women, and sleek cars were everywhere. (It appeared that there were still no private cars; nevertheless, anyone who "was anyone" seemed able to command a car.) The officers of the new Popular Army, a type that had scarcely existed when I left Barcelona, swarmed in surprising numbers. The Popular Army was officered at the rate of one officer to ten men. A certain number of these officers had served in the militia and been brought back from the front for technical instruction, but the majority were young men who had gone to the School of War in preference to joining the militia. Their relation to their men was not quite the same as in a bourgeois army, but there was a definite social difference, expressed by the difference of pay and uniform. The men wore a kind of coarse brown overalls, the officers wore an elegant khaki uniform with a tight waist, like a British Army officer's uniform, only a little more so. I do not suppose that more than one in twenty of them had yet been to the front, but all of them had automatic pistols strapped to their belts; we, at the front, could not get pistols for love or money. As we made our way up the street I noticed that people were staring at our dirty exteriors. Of course, like all men who have been several months in the line, we were a dreadful sight. I was conscious of looking like a scarecrow. My leather jacket was in tatters, my woollen cap had lost its shape and slid perpetually over one eye, my boots consisted of very little beyond splayed-out uppers. All of us were in more or less the same state, and in addition we were dirty and unshaven, so it was no wonder that the people stared. But it dismayed me a little, and brought it home to me that some queer things had been happening in the last three months.

During the next few days I discovered by innumerable signs that my first impression had not been wrong. A deep change had come over the town. There were two facts that were the keynote of all else. One was that the people—the civil population—had lost much of their interest in the war; the other was that the normal division of society into rich and poor, upper class and lower class, was reasserting itself.

The general indifference to the war was surprising and rather disgusting. It horrified people who came to Barcelona from Madrid or even from Valencia. Partly it was due to the remoteness of Barcelona from the actual fighting; I noticed the same thing a month later in Tarragona, where the ordinary life of a smart seaside town was continuing almost undisturbed. But it was significant that all over Spain voluntary enlistment had dwindled from about January onwards. In Catalonia, in February, there had been a wave of enthusiasm over the first big drive for the Popular Army, but it had not led to any great increase in recruiting. The war was only six months old or thereabouts when the Spanish Government had to resort to conscription, which would be natural in a foreign war, but seems anomalous in a civil war. Undoubtedly it was bound up with the disappointment of the revolutionary hopes with which the war had started. The trade union members who formed themselves into militias and chased the Fascists back to Zaragoza in the first few weeks of war had done so largely because they believed themselves to be fighting for working-class control; but it was becoming more and more obvious that working-class control was a lost cause, and the common people, especially the town proletariat, who have to fill the ranks in any war, civil or foreign, could not be blamed for a certain apathy. Nobody wanted to lose the war, but the majority were chiefly anxious for it to be over. You noticed this wherever you went. Everywhere you met with the same perfunctory remark: "This war—terrible, isn't it? When is it going to end?" Politically conscious people were far more aware of the internecine struggle between Anarchist and Communist than of the fight against Franco. To the mass of the people the food-shortage was the most important thing. "The front" had come to be thought of as a mythical far-off place to which young men disappeared and either did not return or returned after three or four months with vast sums

of money in their pockets. (A militiaman usually received his back pay when he went on leave.) Wounded men, even when they were hopping about on crutches, did not receive any special consideration. To be in the militia was no longer fashionable. The shops, always the   *
barometers of public taste, showed this clearly. When I first reached Barcelona the shops, poor and shabby though they were, had specialized in militiamen's equipment. Forage-caps, zipper jackets, Sam Browne belts, hunting-knives, water-bottles, revolver-holsters were displayed in every window. Now the shops were markedly smarter, but the war had been thrust into the background. As I discovered later, when buying my kit before going back to the front, certain things that one badly needed at the front were very difficult to procure.

But besides all this there was the startling change in the social atmosphere—a thing difficult to conceive unless you had actually experienced it. When I first reached Barcelona I had thought it a town where class distinctions and great differences of wealth hardly existed. Certainly that was what it looked like. "Smart" clothes were an abnormality, nobody cringed or took tips, waiters and flower-women and   *
bootblacks looked you in the eye and called you "comrade." I had not grasped that this was mainly a mixture of hope and camouflage. The working class believed in a revolution that had been begun but never consolidated, and the bourgeoisie were scared and temporarily disguising themselves as workers. In the first months of revolution there must have been many thousands of people who deliberately put on overalls and shouted revolutionary slogans as a way of saving their   *
skins. Now things were returning to normal. The smart restaurants and hotels were full of rich people wolfing expensive meals, while   *
for the working-class population food-prices had jumped enormously without any corresponding rise in wages. Apart from the expensiveness of everything, there were recurrent shortages of this and that, which, of course, always hit the poor rather than the rich. The restaurants and hotels seemed to have little difficulty in getting whatever they wanted, but in the working-class quarters the queues for bread, olive oil, and other necessaries were hundreds of yards long. Previously in Barcelona I had been struck by the absence of beggars; now there were quantities of them. Outside the delicatessen shops at the top of the Ramblas gangs of barefooted children were always waiting to swarm

round anyone who came out and clamour for scraps of food. The "revolutionary" forms of speech were dropping out of use. Strangers seldom addressed you as *tú* and *camarada* nowadays; it was usually *señor* and *usted*. *Buenos días* was beginning to replace *salud*. The waiters were back in their boiled shirts and the shop-walkers were cringing in the familiar manner. My wife and I went into a hosiery shop on the Ramblas to buy some stockings. The shopman bowed and rubbed his hands as they do not do even in England nowadays, though they used to do it twenty or thirty years ago. In a furtive indirect way the practice of tipping was coming back. The workers' patrols had been ordered to dissolve and the pre-war police forces were back in the streets. One result of this was that the cabaret show and high-class brothels, many of which had been closed by the workers' patrols, had promptly re-opened. A small but significant instance of the way in which everything was now orientated in favor of the wealthier classes could be seen in the tobacco shortage. For the mass of the people the shortage of tobacco was so desperate that cigarettes filled with sliced liquorice-root were being sold in the streets. I tried some of these once. * (A lot of people tried them once.) Franco held the Canaries, where all the Spanish tobacco is grown; consequently the only stocks of tobacco left on the Government side were those that had been in existence before the war. These were running so low that the tobacconists' shops only opened once a week; after waiting for a couple of hours in a queue you might, if you were lucky, get a three-quarter-ounce packet of tobacco. Theoretically the Government would not allow tobacco to be purchased from abroad, because this meant reducing the gold-reserves, which had got to be kept for arms and other necessities. Actually there was a steady supply of smuggled foreign cigarettes of the more expensive kinds, Lucky Strikes and so forth, which gave a grand opportunity for profiteering. You could buy the smuggled cigarettes openly in the smart hotels and hardly less openly in the streets, provided that you could pay ten pesetas (a militiaman's daily wage) for a packet. The smuggling was for the benefit of the wealthy people, and therefore connived at. If you had enough money there was nothing that you could not get in any quantity, with the possible exception of bread, which was rationed fairly strictly. This open contrast of wealth and poverty would have been impossible a few months earlier, when the working class still were or seemed to be in control. But it would not be fair to attribute it solely to the shift of political power. Partly it was a result of the safety of life in Barcelona, where there was little to remind one of the war except an occasional air-raid. Everyone who had been in Madrid said that it was completely different there. In Madrid the common danger forced people of almost all kinds into some sense of comradeship. A fat man eating quails while children are begging for bread is a disgusting sight, but you are less likely to see it when you are within sound of the guns.

A day or two after the street-fighting I remember passing through one of the fashionable streets and coming upon a confectioner's shop with a window full of pastries and bon-bons of the most elegant kinds, at staggering prices. It was the kind of shop you see in Bond Street or the Rue de la Paix.[1] And I remember feeling a vague horror and amazement that money could still be wasted upon such things in a hungry war-stricken country. But God forbid that I should pretend to any personal superiority. After several months of discomfort I had a ravenous desire for decent food and wine, cocktails, American cigarettes, and so forth, and I admit to having wallowed in every   * luxury that I had money to buy. During that first week, before the street-fighting began, I had several preoccupations which interacted upon one another in a curious way. In the first place, as I have said, I was busy making myself as comfortable as I could. Secondly, thanks to over-eating and over-drinking, I was slightly out of health all that week. I would feel a little unwell, go to bed for half a day, get up and eat another excessive meal, and then feel ill again. At the same time I was making secret negotiations to buy a revolver. I badly wanted a revolver—in trench-fighting much more useful than a rifle—and they were very difficult to get hold of. The Government issued them to policemen and Popular Army officers, but refused to issue them to the militia; you had to buy them, illegally, from the secret stores of the Anarchists. After a lot of fuss and nuisance an Anarchist friend managed to procure me a tiny 26-inch automatic pistol, a wretched weapon, useless at more than five yards, but better than nothing. And

---

[1]Bond Street or the Rue de la Paix: fashionable shopping streets in London and Paris respectively. —Ed.

besides all this I was making preliminary arrangements to leave the P.O.U.M. militia and enter some other unit that would ensure my being sent to the Madrid front.

Thinking about Writing

Words

.   Powerful words both depend on and help shape their context. In what way does each word in the list below depend on its context for strength? What does each contribute to its context? Can you think of any other word the author might have used in its place? How does the word strike you, and how do you respond to the sentence or passage because of the word?

exteriors
fashionable
cringed
overalls
wolfing
once
wallowed

Thinking

1. In this piece of writing, as in his "Shooting an Elephant," Orwell is both participant and observer. As such, he includes himself when he comments on changes in Barcelona. How does he tell us the city has changed? How do you know he has changed as well?
2. When Orwell comments on his own behavior, how does he speak for everyone in the same situation? That is, in what way does he use himself to speak for general behavior?
3. How do you react to his admitting "ravenous desire" for luxuries such as food, alcohol, and cigarettes? In "Shooting an Elephant," his essay in chapter 4, Orwell admits he'd like to drive a bayonet into a Buddhist priest's guts. What is the effect of this frankness?

4. "In Madrid the common danger forced people of almost all kinds into some sense of comradeship," says Orwell, speaking of the way people behaved in the capital city of Spain where battles were raging even as Barcelona was settling down. Why do you think people of almost all kinds tend to pull together in adversity when, if there were no emergency, they might not exchange two words? Why do people help one another during fires, floods, and wars when they don't during happier times?

Writing

1. Write your observations about some situation in which behavior, yours too, was not exactly noble. This might have been during a crowded sale, a group harrassment, a cruel joke, or the like.

   After describing what happened, make some comment on the experience, not to excuse the behavior but to indicate what you learned from the situation, especially from your own participation. Were you surprised that you, too, could behave this way? How does presenting yourself as less than perfect offer your readers a sympathetic atmosphere in a way that picturing yourself as following "good" behavior wouldn't? How can "good" behavior exclude readers? Consider these questions as you write.

2. Both George Orwell and John McPhee use everyday objects such as food and clothing to describe life situations: Orwell talks about a city changed in war, while McPhee describes a life in the wilderness. In an essay, quoting from both writers, examine the use of essential, familiar objects which are easily visualized to describe some abstract condition such as the hardship of life in the wilderness or life during a war.

8

Explaining

Archimedes, the Greek mathematician, is said to have leapt from his bath dripping wet to share his discoveries about the purity of gold. Whether this story is true is not important. Explaining ideas to others clarifies perceptions, and Archimedes is likeable for his spontaneous nature. The writers in this chapter explain discoveries they have made about the way people think. The thinking is concerned with some aspect of imagination, fancy, or misconception which ultimately affects the way people behave.

Joan Didion explains that as a writer she doesn't want to lose track of her former selves, even those selves that displease her today. The reason that these former selves are important is that they are clues about how things appeared to her at various times in her life. As a writer and an observer, she wants always to be able to define her own reality, to *remember what it was to be me.*

E. M. Forster explains that the search for a pure race is a vain one, although there are many people who believe a pure race can

311

be found and who base judgments of human behavior on what they see as racial qualities. To illustrate his explanations, Forster offers himself as guinea pig in a fruitless racial exercise.

Animals, explains scientist Jacob Bronowski, have only a limited memory and are consequently bound to the present, while humans have highly developed facilities to remember and to anticipate. Human imagination is the function of this looking backward and forward. Unlike animals, says Bronowski, humans are not bound to the present, and when they move back and forth in imagination they make great discoveries.

When Eugen Herrigel, a German philosopher, went to Japan in the early part of this century to study Zen, the Eastern philosophy, he found it almost impossible to understand. As he explains, he had been so well trained in the rational thinking of European education that he had to struggle to accept the mystical quality of Zen.

Margaret Fuller, a journalist writing in the first half of the nineteenth century, also explains a reaction to a foreign culture as she writes of Americans traveling to Europe. She groups these travelers according to the attitudes they had before they left America and their reactions to European culture.

And finally writer Mary McCarthy explains how during her adolescence she changed her personality to meet other people's expectations. This chameleon-like behavior was the result of her desire not to disappoint her elders, who saw her as an innocent young creature, or her peers, whom she wished to impress as a sophisticated woman of the world.

Joan Didion

Joan Didion (b. 1934) was born in California and educated at the University of California at Berkeley. A journalist, a novelist, a writer of screenplays and essays, Didion frames her work as a reaction to the world around her and her place in it. For her, this world is often chaotic, but the writer in her strives to come to terms with the chaos. In the essay here, which comes from a collection called *Slouching Towards Bethlehem*, Didion tells how she keeps notebooks—not diaries—filled with cryptic words that trigger old memories and often bring her face-to-face with some of the characters she used to be. For Didion, the notes must always lead back to her. She is the common denominator. When her family denies that it snowed on a particular day, Didion says for her it did. This response is not a lie, for her need is always to remember "*how it felt to me.*"

On Keeping
a Notebook

" 'That woman Estelle,' " the note reads, " 'is partly the reason why George Sharp and I are separated today.' *Dirty crepe-de-Chine wrapper, hotel bar, Wilmington RR, 9:45 A.M. August Monday morning.*"

Since the note is in my notebook, it presumably has some meaning to me. I study it for a long while. At first I have only the most general notion of what I was doing on an August Monday morning in the bar of the hotel across from the Pennsylvania Railroad station in

Wilmington, Delaware (waiting for a train? missing one? 1960? 1961? why Wilmington?), but I do remember being there. The woman in the dirty crepe-de-Chine wrapper had come down from her room for a beer, and the bartender had heard before the reason why George Sharp and she were separated today. "Sure," he said, and went on mopping the floor. "You told me." At the other end of the bar is a girl. She is talking, pointedly, not to the man beside her but to a cat lying in the triangle of sunlight cast through the open door. She is wearing a plaid silk dress from Peck & Peck, and the hem is coming down.

Here is what it is: the girl has been on the Eastern Shore, and now she is going back to the city, leaving the man beside her, and all she can see ahead are the viscous summer sidewalks and the 3 A.M. long-distance calls that will make her lie awake and then sleep drugged through all the steaming mornings left in August (1960? 1961?). Because she must go directly from the train to lunch in New York, she wishes that she had a safety pin for the hem of the plaid silk dress, and she also wishes that she could forget about the hem and the lunch and stay in the cool bar that smells of disinfectant and malt and make friends with the woman in the crepe-de-Chine wrapper. She is afflicted by a little self-pity, and she wants to compare Estelles. That is what that was all about.

Why did I write it down? In order to remember, of course, but exactly what was it I wanted to remember? How much of it actually happened? Did any of it? Why do I keep a notebook at all? It is easy to deceive oneself on all those scores. The impulse to write things down is a peculiarly compulsive one, inexplicable to those who do not share it, useful only accidentally, only secondarily,   * in the way that any compulsion tries to justify itself. I suppose that it begins or does not begin in the cradle. Although I have felt compelled to write things down since I was five years old, I doubt that my daughter ever will, for she is a singularly blessed and accepting child, delighted with life exactly as life presents itself to her, unafraid to go to sleep and unafraid to wake up. Keepers of private notebooks are a different breed altogether, lonely and resistant rearrangers of things, anxious malcontents, children afflicted apparently at birth with some presentiment of loss.

My first notebook was a Big Five tablet, given to me by my mother with the sensible suggestion that I stop whining and learn to amuse myself by writing down my thoughts. She returned the tablet to me a few years ago; the first entry is an account of a woman who believed herself to be freezing to death in the Arctic night, only to find, when day broke, that she had stumbled onto the Sahara Desert, where she would die of the heat before lunch. I have no idea what turn of a five-year-old's mind could have prompted so insistently "ironic" and exotic a story, but it does reveal a certain predilection for the extreme which has dogged me into adult life; perhaps if I were analytically inclined I would find it a truer story than any I might   *
have told about Donald Johnson's birthday party or the day my cousin Brenda put Kitty Litter in the aquarium.

So the point of my keeping a notebook has never been, nor is it now, to have an accurate factual record of what I have been doing or thinking. That would be a different impulse entirely, an instinct for reality which I sometimes envy but do not possess. At no point have I ever been able successfully to keep a diary; my approach to daily life ranges from the grossly negligent to the merely absent, and on those few occasions when I have tried dutifully to record a day's events, boredom has so overcome me that the results are mysterious at best. What is this business about "shopping, typing piece, dinner with E, depressed"? Shopping for what? Typing what piece? Who is E? Was this "E" depressed, or was I depressed? Who cares?

In fact I have abandoned altogether that kind of pointless entry; instead I tell what some would call lies. "That's simply not true," the members of my family frequently tell me when they come up against my memory of a shared event. "The party was *not* for you, the spider was *not* a black widow, *it wasn't that way at all.*" Very likely they are right, for not only have I always had trouble distinguishing between what happened and what merely might have happened, but I remain unconvinced that the distinction, for my purposes, matters.   *
The cracked crab that I recall having for lunch the day my father came home from Detroit in 1945 must certainly be embroidery, worked into the day's pattern to lend verisimilitude; I was ten years old and would not now remember the cracked crab. The day's events did not turn

on cracked crab. And yet it is precisely that fictitious crab that makes me see the afternoon all over again, a home movie run all too often, the father bearing gifts, the child weeping, an exercise in family love and guilt. Or that is what it was to me. Similarly, perhaps it never did snow that August in Vermont; perhaps there never were flurries in the night wind, and maybe no one else felt the ground hardening and summer already dead even as we pretended to bask in it, but that was how it felt to me, and it might as well have snowed, could have snowed, did snow.

How it felt to me: that is getting closer to the truth about a notebook. I sometimes delude myself about why I keep a notebook, imagine that some thrifty virtue derives from preserving everything observed. See enough and write it down, I tell myself, and then some morning when the world seems drained of wonder, some day when I am only going through the motions of doing what I am sup- posed to do, which is write—on that bankrupt morning I will simply   * open my notebook and there it will all be, a forgotten account with accumulated interest, paid passage back to the world out there: dia- logue overheard in hotels and elevators and at the hat-check counter in Pavillon (one middle-aged man shows his hat check to another and says, "That's my old football number"); impressions of Bettina Aptheker and Benjamin Sonnenberg and Teddy ("Mr. Acapulco") Stauffer; careful *aperçus* about tennis bums and failed fashion models and Greek shipping heiresses, one of whom taught me a significant lesson (a lesson I could have learned from F. Scott Fitzgerald, but perhaps we all must meet the very rich for ourselves) by asking, when I arrived to interview her in her orchid-filled sitting room on the second day of a paralyzing New York blizzard, whether it was snowing outside.

I imagine, in other words, that the notebook is about other people. But of course it is not. I have no real business with what one stranger said to another at the hat-check counter in Pavillon; in fact I suspect that the line "That's my old football number" touched not my own imagination at all, but merely some memory of something once read, probably "The Eighty-Yard Run." Nor is my concern with a woman in a dirty crepe-de-Chine wrapper in a Wilmington bar. My stake is always, of course, in the unmentioned girl in the plaid silk   * dress. *Remember what it was to be me:* that is always the point.

It is a difficult point to admit. We are brought up in the ethic that others, any others, all others, are by definition more interesting than ourselves; taught to be diffident, just this side of self-effacing. ("You're the least important person in the room and don't forget it," Jessica Mitford's governess would hiss in her ear on the advent of any social occasion; I copied that into my notebook because it is only recently that I have been able to enter a room without hearing some such phrase in my inner ear.) Only the very young and the very old may recount their dreams at breakfast, dwell upon self, interrupt with memories of beach picnics and favorite Liberty lawn dresses and the rainbow trout in a creek near Colorado Springs. The rest of us are expected, rightly, to affect absorption in other people's favorite dresses, other people's trout.

And so we do. But our notebooks give us away, for however dutifully we record what we see around us, the common denominator of all we see is always, transparently, shamelessly, the implacable "I." We are not talking here about the kind of notebook that is patently for public consumption, a structural conceit for binding together a series of graceful *pensées;* we are talking about something private, about bits of the mind's string too short to use, an indiscriminate and erratic assemblage with meaning only for its maker.

And sometimes even the maker has difficulty with the meaning. There does not seem to be, for example, any point in my knowing for the rest of my life that, during 1964, 720 tons of soot fell on every square mile of New York City, yet there it is in my notebook, labeled "FACT." Nor do I really need to remember that Ambrose Bierce liked to spell Leland Stanford's name "£eland $tanford" or that "smart women almost always wear black in Cuba," a fashion hint without much potential for practical application. And does not the relevance of these notes seem marginal at best?:

> In the basement museum of the Inyo County Courthouse in Independence, California, sign pinned to a mandarin coat: "This MANDARIN COAT was often worn by Mrs. Minnie S. Brooks when giving lectures on her TEAPOT COLLECTION."

> Redhead getting out of car in front of Beverly Wilshire Hotel, chinchilla stole, Vuitton bags with tags reading:

MRS. LOU FOX
HOTEL SAHARA
VEGAS

Well, perhaps not entirely marginal. As a matter of fact, Mrs. Minnie S. Brooks and her MANDARIN COAT pull me back into my own childhood, for although I never knew Mrs. Brooks and did not visit Inyo County until I was thirty, I grew up in just such a world, in houses cluttered with Indian relics and bits of gold ore and ambergris and the souvenirs my Aunt Mercy Farnsworth brought back from the Orient. It is a long way from that world to Mrs. Lou Fox's world, where we all live now, and is it not just as well to remember that? Might not Mrs. Minnie S. Brooks help me to remember what I am? Might not Mrs. Lou Fox help me to remember what I am not?

But sometimes the point is harder to discern. What exactly did I have in mind when I noted down that it cost the father of someone I know $650 a month to light the place on the Hudson in which he lived before the Crash? What use was I planning to make of this line by Jimmy Hoffa: "I may have my faults, but being wrong ain't one of them"? And although I think it interesting to know where the girls who travel with the Syndicate have their hair done when they find themselves on the West Coast, will I ever make suitable use of it? Might I not be better off just passing it on to John O'Hara? What is a recipe for sauerkraut doing in my notebook? What kind of magpie keeps this notebook? "*He was born the night the Titanic went down.*" That seems a nice enough line, and I even recall who said it, but is it not really a better line in life than it could ever be in fiction? But of course that is exactly it: not that I should ever use the line, but that I should remember the woman who said it and the afternoon I heard it. We were on her terrace by the sea, and we were finishing the wine left from lunch, trying to get what sun there was, a California winter sun. The woman whose husband was born the night the *Titanic* went down wanted to rent her house, wanted to go back to her children in Paris. I remember wishing that I could afford the house, which cost $1,000 a month. "Someday you will," she said lazily. "Someday it all comes." There in the sun on her terrace it seemed easy to believe in someday, but later I had a low-

grade afternoon hangover and ran over a black snake on the way to
the supermarket and was flooded with inexplicable fear when I heard
the checkout clerk explaining to the man ahead of me why she was
really divorcing her husband. "He left me no choice," she said over
and over as she punched the register. "He has a little seven-month-
old baby by her, he left me no choice." I would like to believe that
my dread then was for the human condition, but of course it was for
me, because I wanted a baby and did not then have one and because
I wanted to own the house that cost $1,000 a month to rent and
because I had a hangover.

It all comes back. Perhaps it is difficult to see the value in having
one's self back in that kind of mood, but I do see it; I think we are
well advised to keep on nodding terms with the people we used to be,
whether we find them attractive company or not. Otherwise they turn
up unannounced and surprise us, come hammering on the mind's door
at 4 A.M. of a bad night and demand to know who deserted them,
who betrayed them, who is going to make amends. We forget all too
soon the things we thought we could never forget. We forget the
loves and the betrayals alike, forget what we whispered and what we
screamed, forget who we were. I have already lost touch with a couple
of people I used to be; one of them, a seventeen-year-old, presents
little threat, although it would be of some interest to me to know
again what it feels like to sit on a river levee drinking vodka-and-
orange-juice and listening to Les Paul and Mary Ford and their echoes
sing "How High the Moon" on the car radio. (You see I still have the
scenes, but I no longer perceive myself among those present, no longer
could even improvise the dialogue.) The other one, a twenty-three-
year-old, bothers me more. She was always a good deal of trouble,
and I suspect she will reappear when I least want to see her, skirts
too long, shy to the point of aggravation, always the injured party,
full of recriminations and little hurts and stories I do not want to hear
again, at once saddening me and angering me with her vulnerability
and ignorance, an apparition all the more insistent for being so long
banished.

It is a good idea, then, to keep in touch, and I suppose that
keeping in touch is what notebooks are all about. And we are all
on our own when it comes to keeping those lines open to ourselves:
your notebook will never help me, nor mine you. "*So what's new in the*

whiskey business?" What could that possibly mean to you? To me it means a blonde in a Pucci bathing suit sitting with a couple of fat men by the pool at the Beverly Hills Hotel. Another man approaches, and they all regard one another in silence for a while. "So what's new in the whiskey business?" one of the fat men finally says by way of welcome, and the blonde stands up, arches one foot and dips it in the pool, looking all the while at the cabaña where Baby Pignatari is talking on the telephone. That is all there is to that, except that several years later I saw the blonde coming out of Saks Fifth Avenue in New York with her California complexion and a voluminous mink coat. In the harsh wind that day she looked old and irrevocably tired to me, and even the skins in the mink coat were not worked the way they were doing them that year, not the way she would have wanted them done, and there is the point of the story. For a while after that I did not like to look in the mirror, and my eyes would skim the newspapers and pick out only the deaths, the cancer victims, the premature coronaries, the suicides, and I stopped riding the Lexington Avenue IRT because I noticed for the first time that all the strangers I had seen for years—the man with the seeing-eye dog, the spinster who read the classified pages every day, the fat girl who always got off with me at Grand Central—looked older than they once had.

It all comes back. Even that recipe for sauerkraut: even that brings it back. I was on Fire Island when I first made that sauerkraut, and it was raining, and we drank a lot of bourbon and ate the sauerkraut and went to bed at ten, and I listened to the rain and the Atlantic and felt safe. I made the sauerkraut again last night and it did not make me feel any safer, but that is, as they say, another story.

Thinking about Writing

Words

Powerful words both depend on and help shape their context. In what way does each word in the list below depend on its context for strength? What does each contribute to its context? Can you think of

any other word the author might have used in its place? How does the word strike you, and how do you respond to the sentence or passage because of the word?

accidentally
truer
distinction
bankrupt
unmentioned

Thinking

1. Didion remembers *"how it felt to me"* and *"what it was to be me."* What do you feel is the difference between these two ways of thinking? How does Didion illustrate each? Although they are both personal ways of remembering, to what extent are they equally personal for Didion? What in her writing tells us about Didion's need to return to what is most meaningful for her? Is there anything in the writing that explains why Didion is interested in others only when they remind her of something about herself?
2. How does Didion explain her preference for notebooks over diaries? In what way does she tell us that she prefers fiction to fact?
3. What tells us how Didion makes the leap from notes to (her) reality? For example, how does the first note, the one about Estelle, tie in with Didion's own experience of that weekend? What was her experience then, and how do we know about it?
4. How do you think a diary note, a factual account, might sound if Didion had written one for her weekend on the Eastern Shore instead of the note on Estelle?
5. Didion says that "it might as well have snowed, could have snowed, did snow" to explain her "lies," accepting details that exist in her imagination only. What is the difference between possibility and probability? Between probability and truth? Between truth and "truth"? When her family says, "That's simply not true," why does Didion answer, "but that was how it felt to me"?

Writing

1. Keep a notebook for a week, and write in it anything that strikes your fancy, remembering that the notebook must be your own, to

serve only you. At the end of the week, write a few comments about your experience. Consider how your entries help you to "*remember what it was to be me,*" in the sense that two or three words could evoke how you felt at the moment you recorded the words in your notebook.

Then, write a brief essay based on Didion's concept of note-books, her idea that "your notebook will never help me, nor mine you." Refer to your own notes if you wish, but you need not hand in the notes with your essay unless you wish to.

2. Write about one of the people you used to be. You may find "them attractive company or not." Rather than simply composing a laundry list of your past people, you might try evoking an episode from your past and allowing the person you were to color the episode as you remember it. Ask yourself, "How was I then? Who was I?" When you think of that moment, what details do you remember?

3. Go into a public place—the cafeteria, the library, a restaurant, a supermarket—where you can observe a few strangers and, if possible, catch a line or two of a conversation. Note what words interest you. Write a dozen key words or phrases in a notebook. Do this three times, in three different places if you can (or in the same place if you must). Later, read through your three lists, trying to find a pattern in what interests you. Still later, bring your lists to class and compare them with the lists of one or two other students. Does each list have its own character? Can you draw any conclusions about the way you react to overheard words? In what ways does a classmate's list appeal to you, or do you find it basically uninteresting when you compare it with one of your own?

Write a brief essay in which you explore the character of your lists, especially after you have seen others' lists. Consider the "common denominator of all we see is always, transparently, shameless-ly, the implacable 'I'," be it Didion's "I," yours, or someone else's. Who is your "implacable 'I'"?

E. M. Forster

E. M. Forster (1879–1970) was born in London and educated at Cambridge University where he studied classics and history. After his university education, Forster embarked on a career of writing and lecturing. One lecture trip took him to India, where he found inspiration for his novel of East meeting West, *A Passage to India*. As a novelist, a critic, and an essayist, Forster was concerned with the complexities of human nature and human interaction. In addition to *A Passage to India*, Forster wrote *Howard's End* and *A Room With a View*. The essay here, which comes from a collection of Forster's nonfiction, *Two Cheers for Democracy*, was written on the eve of World War II, just as Hitler and the Nazi party were beginning to implement their racial policies towards the Jews in Germany.

Racial Exercise

Let us do some easy exercises in Racial Purity.

And let me offer myself for dissection-purposes.

If I go the right way about it, I come of an old English family, but the right way is unfortunately a crooked one. It is far from easy going in the branches of my genealogical tree. I have to proceed via my father to his mother, thence to her mother, and thence to her father. If I follow this zigzag course I arrive in the satisfactory bosom of a family called Sykes, and have a clear run back through several centuries. The Sykes' go right away ever so far, right back to a certain Richard of Sykes Dyke who flourished somewhere about the year 1400. Whether inside their dyke, which lay in Cumberland, or outside it, which was Yorkshire, this family never did anything earthshaking,

still they did keep going in the documentary sense, they made money   *
and married into it, they became mayors of Pontefract or Hull, they
employed Miss Anna Seward as a governess, and, in the seventeenth
century, one of them, a Quaker, was imprisoned on account of his
opinions in York Castle, and died there. I come of an old English
family, and I am proud of it.

Unfortunately, in other directions the prospect is less extensive.   *
If I take a wrong turning and miss the Sykes', darkness descends on
my origins almost at once. Mrs. James is a case in point, and a very
mortifying one. Mrs. James was a widow who not so very long ago
married one of my great-grandfathers. I am directly descended from
her, know nothing whatever about her, and should like at all events
to discover her maiden name. Vain quest. She disappears in the mists
of antiquity, like Richard of Sykes Dyke, but much too soon. She
might be anyone, she may not even have been Aryan. When her
shadow crosses my mind, I do not feel to belong to an old family at
all.

After that dissection, let us proceed to do our easy Racial Exercise.

It is this: Can you give the names of your eight great-
grandparents?

The betting is eight to one that you cannot. The Royal Family
could, some aristocrats could, and so could a few yeomen who have
lived undisturbed in a quiet corner of England for a couple of hundred
years. But most of the people I know (and probably most of the
people who read these words) will fail. We can often get six or seven,
seldom the whole eight. And the human mind is so dishonest and
so snobby, that we instinctively reject the eighth as not mattering,
and as playing no part in our biological make-up. As each of us
looks back into his or her past, doors open upon darkness. Two
doors at first—the father and the mother—through each of these
two more, then the eight great-grandparents, the sixteen great-greats,
then thirty-two ancestors . . . sixty-four . . . one hundred and twenty-
eight . . . until the researcher reels. Even if the stocks producing us
interbred, and so reduced the total of our progenitors by using some
of them up on us twice, even if they practised the strict domestic
economy of the Ptolemies, the total soon becomes enormous,

and the Sykes' in it are nothing beside the Mrs. James'. On such a shady past as this—our common past—do we erect the ridiculous doctrine of Racial Purity.

In the future the situation will be slightly less ridiculous. Registers of marriage and birth will be kept more carefully, bastardy more cunningly detected, so that in a couple of hundred years millions of people will belong to Old Families. This should be a great comfort to them. It may also be a convenience, if governments continue to impose racial tests. Citizens will be in a position to point to an Aryan ancestry if their government is Aryan, to a Cretinist ancestry if it is Cretin, and so on, and if they cannot point in the direction required, they will be sterilized. This should be a great discomfort to them. Nor will the sterilization help, for the mischief has already been done in our own day, the mess has been made, miscegenation has already taken place. Whether there ever was such an entity as a "pure race" is debatable, but there certainly is not one in Europe today—the internationalisms of the Roman Empire and of the Middle Ages have seen to that. Consequently there never can be a pure race in the future. Europe is mongrel forever, and so is America.

How extraordinary it is that governments which claim to be realistic should try to base themselves on anything so shadowy and romantic as race! A common language, a common religion, a common culture all belong to the present, evidence about them is available, they can be tested. But race belongs to the unknown and unknowable past. It depends upon who went to bed with whom in the year 1400, not to mention Mrs. James, and what historian will ever discover that? Community of race is an illusion. Yet belief in race is a growing psychological force, and we must reckon with it. People like to feel that they are all of a piece, and one of the ways of inducing that feeling is to tell them that they come of pure stock. That explains the ease with which the dictators are putting their pseudo-science across. No doubt they are not cynical about it, and take themselves in by what they say. But they have very cleverly hit on a weak spot in the human equipment—the desire to feel a hundred per cent, no matter what the percentage is in.

A German Professor was holding forth the other day on the subject of the origins of the German people. His attitude was that the purity of the Nordic stock is not yet proved and should not be spoken of as proved. But it should be spoken of as a fact, because it is one, and the proofs of its existence will be forthcoming as soon as scholars are sufficiently energetic and brave. He spoke of "courage" in research. According to his own lights, he was a disinterested research- er, for he refused to support what he knew to be true by arguments which he held to be false. The truth, being *a priori*,[1] could afford to wait on its mountain top until the right path to it was found: the truth of Nordic purity which every German holds by instinct in his blood. In India I had friends who said they were descended from the Sun and looked down on those who merely came from the Moon, but they were not tense about it and seemed to forget about it between times, nor did they make it a basis for political violence and cruelty; it takes the west to do that.

Behind our problem of the eight great-grandparents stands the civilizing figure of Mendel. I wish that Mendel's name was mentioned in current journalism as often as Freud's or Einstein's. He embodies a salutary principle, and even when we are superficial about him, he helps to impress it in our minds. He suggests that no stock is pure, and that it may at any moment throw up forms which are unexpected, and which it inherits from the past. His best-known experiments were with the seeds of the pea. It is impossible that human beings can be studied as precisely as peas — too many factors are involved. But they too keep throwing up recessive characteristics, and cause us to question the creed of racial purity. Mendel did not want to prove anything. He was not a "courageous" researcher, he was merely a researcher. Yet he has unwittingly put a valuable weapon into the hands of civilized people. We don't know what our ancestors were like or what our descendants will be like. We only know that we are all of us mongrels, dark haired and light haired, who must learn not to bite one another. Thanks to * Mendel and to a few simple exercises we can see comparatively clearly into the problem of race, if we choose to look, and can do a little to combat the pompous and pernicious rubbish that is at present being prescribed in the high places of the earth.

[1]*a priori*: working forward deductively from known causes to effects. —Ed.

Thinking about Writing

Words

Powerful words both depend on and help shape their context. In what way does each word in the list below depend on its context for strength? What does each contribute to its context? Can you think of any other word the author might have used in its place? How does the word strike you, and how do you respond to the sentence or passage because of the word?

documentary
prospect
romantic
holding forth
bite

Thinking

1. How would you describe Forster's tone and style, his way of writing? What words or kinds of words does he tend to repeat? What do you think of his vocabulary, particularly such expressions as "vain quest" and "the betting is eight to one," given that he is, after all, writing about a very serious subject? What's the effect of his using himself as a guinea pig? How does the final reference to Gregor Mendel contribute to the selection?

2. Forster calls Europe and America "mongrel forever." What do you think when you hear the word *mongrel*? What makes a mongrel? Have you ever had a mongrel dog? In what way was the animal a survivor, even attractive in its own special way?

3. Forster says there are no pure races. If you agree with him, what reasons can you think of to support this claim? How do you think the concept of a pure race came about in the first place? What factors tend to alter the concept?

4. Forster says, "People like to feel that they are all of a piece," and they become "so dishonest and so snobby" that they actually

believe in some sort of racial purity. Why do you think racists offer rationales for their prejudice?

Writing

1. Write an essay that explores the strengths of being a "mongrel" nation, for both society and government. What are the advantages to a society of having new blood from many backgrounds? Can you think of disadvantages?

2. Write an essay, including pictures if possible, that explores the changing images of a particular stereotype. If you cannot include actual pictures, use full descriptions. You may want to speculate about why images change and whether it is people themselves, or the images of people, that change.

3. In a brief essay, consider what motivates people toward rationalizing their prejudices. Consider how good old-fashioned patriotism, or nationalism, may by its selectivity actually foster the ideas of prejudice toward other people. Include any personal or observed experiences that illustrate your argument.

4. How can lack of prejudice indicate lack of judgment? Write an essay in which you examine and defend the need for strong preferences to develop taste and judgment.

Jacob Bronowski

Jacob Bronowski (1908–74) was born in Poland and educated there and at Cambridge University. He was a mathematician, a physicist, a biologist, and a philosopher. A trip to Japan after World War II to study the effects of the atomic bomb prompted him to turn his energies to exploring science as culture and to defining the link between art and science. While still living in England, he wrote science programs for the BBC, entitled "The Ascent of Man," and worked as a statistician for the British government. Later, in America, he worked as a biologist in human affairs for the Salk Institute. In the essay here, from the *Proceedings of the American Academy of Arts and Letters*, Bronowski explores human creativity, which he sees as a function of memory and anticipation, the ways we look back and look forward to experiences.

The Reaches of Imagination

For three thousand years, poets have been enchanted and moved and perplexed by the power of their own imagination. In a short and summary essay I can hope at most to lift one small corner of that mystery; and yet it is a critical corner. I shall ask, What goes on in the mind when we imagine? You will hear from me that one answer to this question is fairly specific: which is to say, that we can describe the working of the imagination. And when we describe it as I shall do, it becomes plain that imagination is a specifically *human* gift. To imagine is the characteristic act, not of the poet's mind, or the painter's, or the scientist's, but of the mind of man.

My stress here on the word *human* implies that there is a clear difference in this between the actions of men and those of other animals. Let me then start with a classical experiment with animals and children which Walter Hunter thought out in Chicago about 1910. That was the time when scientists were agog with the success of Ivan Pavlov in forming and changing the reflex actions of dogs, which Pavlov had first announced in 1903. Pavlov had been given a Nobel prize the next year, in 1904; although in fairness I should say that the award did not cite his work on the conditioned reflex, but on the digestive gland.

Hunter duly trained some dogs and other animals on Pavlov's lines. They were taught that when a light came on over one of three tunnels out of their cage, that tunnel would be open; they could escape down it, and were rewarded with food if they did. But once he had fixed that conditioned reflex, Hunter added to it a deeper idea: he gave the mechanical experiment a new dimension, literally—the dimension of time. Now he no longer let the dog go to the lighted tunnel at once; instead, he put out the light, and then kept the dog waiting a little while before he let him go. In this way Hunter timed how long an animal can remember where he has last seen the signal light to his escape route.

The results were and are staggering. A dog or a rat forgets which one of three tunnels has been lit up within a matter of seconds—in Hunter's experiment, ten seconds at most. If you want such an animal to do much better than this, you must make the task much simpler: you must face him with only two tunnels to choose from. Even so, the best that Hunter could do was to have a dog remember for five minutes which one of two tunnels had been lit up.

I am not quoting these times as if they were exact and universal: they surely are not. Hunter's experiment, more than fifty years old now, had many faults of detail. For example, there were too few animals, they were oddly picked, and they did not all behave consistently. It may be unfair to test a dog for what he saw, when he commonly follows his nose rather than his eyes. It may be unfair to test any animal in the unnatural setting of a laboratory cage. And there are higher animals, such as chimpanzees and other primates, which certainly have longer memories than the animals that Hunter tried.

Yet when all these provisos have been made (and met, by more modern experiments) the facts are still startling and characteristic. An animal cannot recall a signal from the past for even a short fraction of the time that a man can—for even a short fraction of the time that a child can. Hunter made comparable tests with six-year-old children, and found, of course, that they were incomparably better than the best of his animals. There is a striking and basic difference between a man's ability to imagine something that he saw or experienced, and an animal's failure.

Animals make up for this by other and extraordinary gifts. The salmon and the carrier pigeon can find their way home as we cannot: they have, as it were, a practical memory that man cannot match. But their actions always depend on some form of habit: on instinct or on learning, which reproduce by rote a train of known responses. They do not depend, as human memory does, on calling to mind the recollection of absent things.

Where is it that the animal falls short? We get a clue to the answer, I think, when Hunter tells us how the animals in his experiment tried to fix their recollection. They most often pointed themselves at the light before it went out, as some gun dogs point rigidly at the game they scent—and get the name *pointer* from the posture. The animal makes ready to act by building the signal into its action. There is a primitive imagery in its stance, it seems to me; it is as if the animal were trying to fix the light on its mind by fixing it in its body. And indeed, how else can a dog mark and (as it were) name one of three tunnels, when he has no such words as *left* and *right*, and no such numbers as *one, two, three?* The directed gesture of attention and readiness is perhaps the only symbolic device that the dog commands to hold on to the past, and thereby to guide himself into the future.

I used the verb *to imagine* a moment ago, and now I have some ground for giving it a meaning. *To imagine* means to make images and to move them about inside one's head in new arrangements. When you and I recall the past, we imagine it in this direct and homely sense. *

The tool that puts the human mind ahead of the animal is imagery. For us, memory does not demand the preoccupation that it demands in animals, and it lasts immensely longer, because we fix it in images or other substitute symbols. With the same symbolic vocabulary we spell out the future—not one but many futures, which we weigh one against another.

I am using the word *image* in a wide meaning, which does not restrict it to the mind's eye as a visual organ. An image in my usage is what Charles Peirce called a *sign*, without regard for its sensory quality. Peirce distinguished between different forms of signs, but there is no reason to make his distinction here, for the imagination works equally with them all, and that is why I call them all images.

Indeed, the most important images for human beings are simply   *
words, which are abstract symbols. Animals do not have words, in our sense: there is no specific center for language in the brain of any animal, as there is in the human being. In this respect at least we know that the human imagination depends on a configuration in the brain that has only evolved in the last one or two million years. In the same period, evolution has greatly enlarged the front lobes in the human brain, which govern the sense of the past and the future; and it is a fair guess that they are probably the seat of our other images. (Part of the evidence for this guess is that damage to the front lobes in primates reduces them to the state of Hunter's animals.) If the guess turns out to be right, we shall know why man has come to look like a highbrow or an egghead: because otherwise there would not be room   *
in his head for his imagination.

The images play out for us events which are not present to our sense, and thereby guard the past and create the future—a future that does not yet exist, and may never come to exist in that form. By contrast, the lack of symbolic ideas, or their rudimentary poverty, cuts off an animal from the past and the future alike, and imprisons him in the present. Of all the distinctions between man and animal, the characteristic gift which makes us human is the power to work with symbolic images: the gift of imagination.

This is really a remarkable finding. When Philip Sidney in 1580 defended poets (and all unconventional thinkers) from the Puritan charge that they were liars, he said that a maker must imagine things that are not. Halfway between Sydney and us, William Blake said, "What is now proved was once only imagined." About the same time, in 1796, Samuel Taylor Coleridge for the first time distinguished between the passive fancy and the active imagination, "the living

Power and prime Agent of all human Perception." Now we see that they were right, and precisely right: the human gift is the gift of imagination—and that is not just a literary phrase.

Nor is it just a literary gift; it is, I repeat, characteristically human. Almost everything that we do that is worth doing is done in the first place in the mind's eye. The richness of human life is that we have many lives; we live the events that do not happen (and some that cannot) as vividly as those that do; and if thereby we die a thousand deaths, that is the price we pay for living a thousand lives. (A cat, of course, has only nine). Literature is alive to us because we live its images, but so is any play of the mind—so is chess: the lines of play that we foresee and try in our heads and dismiss are as much a part of the game as the moves that we make. John Keats said that the unheard melodies are sweeter, and all chess players sadly recall that the combinations that they planned and which never came to be played were the best.

    I make this point to remind you, insistently, that imagination is the manipulation of images in one's head; and that the rational manipulation belongs to that, as well as the literary and artistic manipulation. When a child begins to play games with things that stand for other things, with chairs or chessmen, he enters the gateway to reason and imagination together. For the human reason discovers new relations between things not by deduction, but by that unpredictable blend of speculation and insight that scientists call induction, which—like other forms of imagination—cannot be formalized. We see it at work when Walter Hunter inquires into a child's memory, as much as when Blake and Coleridge do. Only a restless and original mind would have asked Hunter's questions and could have conceived his experiments, in a science that was dominated by Pavlov's reflex arcs and was heading toward the behaviorism of John Watson.

    Let me find a spectacular example for you from history. What is the most famous experiment that you had described to you as a child? I will hazard that it is the experiment that Galileo is said to have made in Sidney's age, in Pisa about 1590, by dropping two unequal balls from the Leaning Tower. There, we say, is a man in the modern mold, a man after our own hearts: he insisted on questioning the authority of Aristotle and St. Thomas Aquinas, and seeing with his own eyes whether (as they said) the heavy ball would reach the ground before the light one. Seeing is believing.

Yet seeing is also imagining. Galileo did challenge the authority of Aristotle, and he did look at his mechanics. But the eye that Galileo used was the mind's eye. He did not drop balls from the Leaning Tower of Pisa—if he had, he would have got a very doubtful answer. Instead, Galileo made an imaginary experiment in his head, which I will describe as he did years later in the book he wrote after the Holy Office silenced him: the *Discorsi . . . intorno a due nuove scienze*, which was smuggled out to be printed in the Netherlands in 1638.

Suppose, said Galileo, that you drop two unequal balls from the tower at the same time. And suppose that Aristotle is right—suppose that the heavy ball falls faster, so that it steadily gains on the light ball, and hits the ground first. Very well. Now imagine the same experiment done again, with only one difference: this time the two unequal balls are joined by a string between them. The heavy ball will again move ahead, but now the light ball holds it back and acts as a drag or brake. So the light ball will be speeded up and the heavy ball will be slowed down; they must reach the ground together because they are tied together, but they cannot reach the ground as quickly as the heavy ball alone. Yet the string between them has turned the two balls into a single mass which is heavier than either ball—and surely (according to Aristotle) this mass should therefore move faster than either ball? Galileo's imaginary experiment has uncovered a contradiction; he says trenchantly, "You see how, from your assumption that a heavier body falls more rapidly than a lighter one, I infer that a (still) heavier body falls more slowly." There is only one way out of the contradiction: the heavy ball and the light ball must fall at the same rate, so that they go on falling at the same rate when they are tied together.

This argument is not conclusive, for nature might be more subtle (when the two balls are joined) than Galileo has allowed. And yet it is something more important: it is suggestive, it is stimulating, it opens a new view—in a word, it is imaginative. It cannot be settled without an actual experiment, because nothing that we imagine can become knowledge until we have translated it into, and backed it by, real experience. The test of imagination is experience. But then, that is as true of literature and the arts as it is of science. In science, the imaginary experiment is tested by confronting it with physical experience; and in literature, the imaginative conception is tested by confronting it with human experience. The superficial speculation in science is dismissed because it is found to falsify nature; and the shallow work of art is discarded because it is found to be untrue to our own nature. So when Ella Wheeler Wilcox died in 1919, more people were reading her verses than Shakespeare's; yet in a few years her work was dead. It had been buried by its poverty of emotion and its trivialness of thought: which is to say that it had been proved to be as false to the nature of man as, say, Jean Baptiste Lamarck and Trofim Lysenko were false to the nature of inheritance. The strength of the imagination, its enriching power and excitement, lies in its interplay with reality—physical and emotional.

I doubt if there is much to choose here between science and the arts: the imagination is not much more free, and not much less free, in one than in the other. All great scientists have used their imagination freely, and let it ride them to outrageous conclusions without crying "Halt!" Albert Einstein fiddled with imaginary experiments from boyhood, and was wonderfully ignorant of the facts that they were supposed to bear on. When he wrote the first of his beautiful papers on the random movement of atoms, he did not know that the Brownian motion which it predicted could be seen in any laboratory. He was sixteen when he invented the paradox that he resolved ten years later, in 1905, in the theory of relativity, and it bulked much larger in his mind than the experiment of Albert Michelson and Edward Morley which had upset every other physicist since 1881. All his life Einstein loved to make up teasing puzzles like Galileo's, about falling lifts and the detection of gravity; and they carry the nub of the problems of general relativity on which he was working.

Indeed, it could not be otherwise. The power that man has over nature and himself, and that a dog lacks, lies in his command of imaginary experience. He alone has the symbols which fix the past and play with the future, possible and impossible. In the Renaissance, the symbolism of memory was thought to be mystical, and devices that were invented as mnemonics[1] (by Giordano Bruno, for example, and by Robert Fludd) were interpreted as magic signs. The symbol is the

---

[1]mnemonics: memory aids, catch words that help a person remember something. —Ed.

tool which gives man his power, and it is the same tool whether the symbols are images or words, mathematical signs or mesons. And the symbols have a reach and a roundness that goes beyond their literal and practical meaning. They are the rich concepts under which the mind gathers many particulars into one name, and many instances into one general induction. When a man says *left* and *right*, he is outdistancing the dog not only in looking for a light; he is setting in * train all the shifts of meaning, the overtones and the ambiguities, between *gauche* and *adroit* and *dexterous*, between *sinister* and the sense of right. When a man counts *one*, *two*, *three*, he is not only doing mathematics; he is on the path to the mysticism of numbers in Pythagoras and Vitruvius and Kepler, to the Trinity and the signs of the Zodiac.

I have described imagination as the ability to make images and to move them about inside one's head in new arrangements. This is the faculty that is specifically human, and it is the common root from which science and literature both spring and grow and flourish together. For they do flourish (and languish) together; the great ages of science are the great ages of all the arts, because in them powerful minds have taken fire from one another, breathless and higgledy-piggledy, without asking too nicely whether they ought to tie their imagination to falling balls or a haunted island. Galileo and Shakespeare, who were born in the same year, grew into greatness in the same age; when Galileo was looking through his telescope at the moon, Shakespeare was writing *The Tempest* and all Europe was in ferment, from Johannes Kepler to Peter Paul Rubens, and from the first table of logarithms by John Napier to the Authorized Version of the Bible.

Let me end with a last and spirited example of the common inspiration of literature and science, because it is as much alive today as it was three hundred years ago. What I have in mind is man's ageless fantasy, to fly to the moon. I do not display this to you as a high scientific enterprise; on the contrary, I think we have more important discoveries to make here on earth than wait for us, beckoning, at the horned surface of the moon. Yet I cannot belittle the fascination which that ice-blue journey has had for the imagination of men, long before it drew us to our television screens to watch the tumbling astronauts. Plutarch and Lucian, Ariosto and Ben Jonson wrote about it, before the days of Jules Verne and H.G. Wells and science fiction. The seventeenth century was heady with new dreams and fables about voyages to the moon. Kepler wrote one full of deep scientific ideas, which (alas) simply got his mother accused of witchcraft. In England, Francis Godwin wrote a wild and splendid work, *The Man in the Moone*, and the astronomer John Wilkins wrote a wild and learned one, *The Discovery of a New World*. They did not draw a line between science and fancy; for example, they all tried to guess just where in the journey the earth's gravity would stop. Only Kepler understood that gravity has no boundary, and put a law to it—which happened to be the wrong law.

All this was a few years before Isaac Newton was born, and it was all in his head that day in 1666 when he sat in his mother's garden, a young man of twenty-three, and thought about the reach of gravity. This was how he came to conceive his brilliant image, that the moon is like a ball which has been thrown so hard that it falls exactly as fast as the horizon, all the way round the earth. The image will do for any satellite, and Newton modestly calculated how long therefore an astronaut would take to fall round the earth once. He made it ninety minutes, and we have all seen now that he was right; but Newton had no way to check that. Instead he went on to calculate how long in that case the distant moon would take to round the earth, if indeed it behaves like a thrown ball that falls in the earth's gravity, and if gravity obeyed a law of inverse squares. He found that the answer would be twenty-eight days.

In that telling figure, the imagination that day chimed with nature, and made a harmony. We shall hear an echo of that harmony on the day when we land on the moon, because it will be not a technical but an imaginative triumph, that reaches back to the beginning of modern science and literature both. All great acts of imagination are like this, in the arts and in science, and convince us because they fill out reality with a deeper sense of rightness. We start with the simplest vocabulary of images, with *left* and *right* and *one*, *two*, *three*, and before we know how it happened the words and the numbers have conspired to make a match with nature: we catch in them the pattern of mind and matter as one.

Thinking about Writing

Words

Powerful words both depend on and help shape their context. In what way does each word in the list below depend on its context for strength? What does each contribute to its context? Can you think of any other word the author might have used in its place? How does the word strike you, and how do you respond to the sentence or passage because of the word?

homely
simply
room
only
dominated
beautiful
outdistancing

Thinking

1. Why do you think mnemonics were considered magical or mystical during the Renaissance? How would the appearance of the printed word have affected this concept of memory? What mnemonic devices do we still use?

2. Bronowski says that "we live in the events that do not happen (and some that cannot) as vividly as those that do, and if thereby we die a thousand deaths, that is the price we pay for living a thousand lives. (A cat, of course, has only nine.)" Why do you think he says this? If, as Bronowski reports, animals have exceptionally short memories, can we conclude that they do not fear? In what ways is memory responsible for anticipation and, hence, fear?

3. Bronowski reminds us that Galileo and Shakespeare were born in the same year. How does this juxtaposition of names affect you as you read? How do you *imagine* "powerful minds have taken fire from one another," if one of them was in England writing plays and the other was in Italy looking through a telescope? How do minds take fire from each other today?

Writing

1. Write an essay on mnemonic devices in which you explore how they function. Try to include a few of your own, and ask family or friends for some of theirs. If you can, ask a speaker of a foreign language if there are any common mnemonic devices in that language. Why do you think we can remember these devices? What are the different types of mnemonic devices, or do they all function the same way?

2. Write a brief essay describing how your imagination works for you on a daily basis, perhaps as you make choices, as you experience fear or happiness, as you "intend," as you study and learn, as you play, or as you plan. For instance, how does your imagination function when you are either solving a difficult mathematical problem or reading a difficult poem or deciding where to eat on Friday?

3. Bronowski says we discover new relations between things not by deduction but by induction. Deduction says:

> All men are cowards.
> Tom is a man.
> Therefore, Tom is a coward.

Induction moves from a particular observation to a general conclusion: For example, you might notice that all the women in your sociology class are wearing jeans, and from this you might conclude that skirts have gone out of fashion on your campus. This kind of reasoning, as you can see, has all kinds of holes, and such thinking could be as incorrect as correct. In deduction, there are fewer chances to be incorrect.

Consider how Bronowski supports the value of mental exercises like those involved in induction. Write an essay in which you explore Bronowski's contention that induction leads to our discoveries of new relations. Use quotes from his essay to support your ideas.

Eugen Herrigel

Eugen Herrigel (1884–1955) was born and educated in Germany, where he studied philosophy and eventually became a professor. Although trained in the tradition of Western thinkers, especially the ancient Greeks and the Germans, Herrigel became interested in the Eastern philosophy of Zen. While teaching in Japan at the University of Tokyo, he began to study Zen in order to become a mystic—that is, one who understands the theory and practice of Zen philosophy. Through long, arduous hours of study, which took the form of archery lessons, he tried to learn the principles of Zen. But he found *un*learning the conditioning of our traditional Western education almost impossible. He had been taught, as we have been, that hard work and diligent application bring success—a formula that does not apply in Zen. When his shots were poor, Herrigel thought the fault lay in the way he held the bow, and so he tried to correct his grip. Eventually he understood that the perfect shot would have to come from somewhere beyond the self if he wished to succeed. This account of Herrigel's experience comes from a longer work, his *Zen in the Art of Archery*.

"It" Shoots

"Stop thinking about the shot!" the Master called out. "That way it is bound to fail." "I can't help it," I answered, "the tension gets too painful."

"You only feel it because you haven't really let go of yourself. It is all so simple. You can learn from an ordinary bamboo leaf what ought to happen. It bends lower and lower under the weight of snow. Suddenly the snow slips to the ground without the leaf having stirred.

340

Stay like that at the point of highest tension until the shot falls from you. So, indeed, it is: when the tension is fulfilled, the shot *must* fall, it must fall from the archer like snow from a bamboo leaf, before he even thinks it."

In spite of everything I could do or did not do, I was unable to wait until the shot "fell." As before, I had no alternative but to loose it on purpose. And this obstinate failure depressed me all the more since I had already passed my third year of instruction. I will not deny that I spent many gloomy hours wondering whether I could justify this waste of time, which seemed to bear no conceivable relationship to anything I had learned and experienced so far. The sarcastic remark of a countryman of mine, that there were important pickings to be *
made in Japan besides this beggarly art, came back to me, and though I had dismissed it at the time, his query as to what I intended to do with my art if ever I learned it no longer seemed to me so entirely absurd.

The Master must have felt what was going on in my mind. He had, so Mr. Komachiya told me later, tried to work through a Japanese introduction to philosophy in order to find out how he could help me from a side I already knew. But in the end he had laid the book down with a cross face, remarking that he could now understand that a person who interested himself in such things would naturally find the art of archery uncommonly difficult to learn.

We spent our summer holidays by the sea, in the solitude of a quiet, dreamy landscape distinguished for its delicate beauty. We had taken our bows with us as the most important part of our equipment. Day out and day in I concentrated on loosing the shot. This had become an *idée fixe*,[1] which caused me to forget more and more the Master's warning that we should not practice anything except self-detaching immersion. Turning all the possibilities over in my mind, I came to the conclusion that the fault could not lie where the Master suspected it: in lack of purposelessness and egolessness, but in the fact that the fingers of the right hand gripped the thumb too *
tight. The longer I had to wait for the shot, the more convulsively I pressed them together without thinking. It was at this point, I told

[1] *idée fixe*: an obsession. —Ed.

myself, that I must set to work. And ere long I had found a simple   *
and obvious solution to this problem. If, after drawing the bow, I
cautiously eased the pressure of the fingers on the thumb, the moment
came when the thumb, no longer held fast, was torn out of position
as if spontaneously: in this way a lightning loose could be made
and the shot would obviously "fall like snow from a bamboo leaf."
This discovery recommended itself to me not least on account of its
beguiling affinity with the technique of rifle-shooting. There the index   *
finger is slowly crooked until an ever diminishing pressure overcomes
the last resistance.

     I was able to convince myself very quickly that I must be on the
right track. Almost every shot went off smoothly and unexpectedly,
to my way of thinking. Naturally I did not overlook the reverse side of
this triumph: the precision work of the right hand demanded my full
attention. But I comforted myself with the hope that this technical
solution would gradually become so habitual that it would require no
further notice from me, and that the day would come when, thanks
to it, I would be in a position to loose the shot, self-obliviously and
unconsciously, at the moment of highest tension, and that in this case
the technical ability would spiritualize itself. Waxing more and more   *
confident in this conviction I silenced the protest that rose up in me,
ignored the contrary counsels of my wife, and went away with the
satisfying feeling of having taken a decisive step forward.

     The very first shot I let off after the recommencement of the
lessons was, to my mind, a brilliant success. The loose was smooth,
unexpected. The Master looked at me for a while and then said
hesitantly, like one who can scarcely believe his eyes: "Once again,
please!" My second shot seemed to me even better than the first.
The Master stepped up to me without a word, took the bow from my
hand, and sat down on a cushion, his back towards me. I knew what
that meant, and withdrew.

     The next day Mr. Komachiya informed me that the Master
declined to instruct me any further because I had tried to cheat him.
Horrified beyond measure by this interpretation of my behavior, I
explained to Mr. Komachiya why, in order to avoid marking time
forever, I had hit upon this method of loosing the shot. On his
interceding for me, the Master was finally prepared to give in, but

made the continuation of the lessons conditional upon my express promise never to offend again against the spirit of the "Great Doctrine."

If profound shame had not cured me, the Master's behavior would certainly have done so. He did not mention the incident by so much as a word, but only said quite quietly: "You see what comes of not being able to wait without purpose in the state of highest tension. You cannot even learn to do this without continually asking yourself: Shall I be able to manage it? Wait patiently, and see what comes — and how it comes!"

I pointed out to the Master that I was already in my fourth year and that my stay in Japan was limited.

"The way to the goal is not to be measured! Of what importance are weeks, months, years?"

"But what if I have to break off half way?" I asked.

"Once you have grown truly egoless you can break off at any time. Keep on practicing that."

And so we began again from the very beginning, as if everything I had learned hitherto had become useless. But the waiting at the point of highest tension was no more successful than before, as if it were impossible for me to get out of the rut.

One day I asked the Master: "How can the shot be loosed if 'I' do not do it?"

" 'It' shoots," he replied.

"I have heard you say that several times before, so let me put it another way: How can I wait self-obliviously for the shot if 'I' am no longer there?"

" 'It' waits at the highest tension."

"And who or what is this 'It'?"

"Once you have understood that, you will have no further need of me. And if I tried to give you a clue at the cost of your own experience, I would be the worst of teachers and would deserve to be sacked! So let's stop talking about it and go on practicing."

Weeks went by without my advancing a step. At the same time I discovered that this did not disturb me in the least. Had I grown tired of the whole business? Whether I learned the art or not, whether I experienced what the Master meant by 'It' or not, whether I found the way to Zen or not—all this suddenly seemed to have become so remote, so indifferent, that it no longer troubled me. Several times I made up my mind to confide in the Master, but when I stood before him I lost courage; I was convinced that I would never hear anything but the monotonous answer: "Don't ask, practice!" So I stopped asking, and would have liked to stop practicing, too, had not the Master held me inexorably in his grip. I lived from one day to the next, did my professional work as best I might, and in the end ceased to bemoan the fact that all my efforts of the last few years had become meaningless.

Then, one day, after a shot, the Master made a deep bow and broke off the lesson. "Just then 'It' shot!" he cried, as I stared at him bewildered. And when I at last understood what he meant I couldn't suppress a sudden whoop of delight.   *

"What I have said," the Master told me severely, "was not praise, only a statement that ought not to touch you. Nor was my bow meant for you, for you are entirely innocent of this shot. You remained this time absolutely self-oblivious and without purpose in the highest tension, so that the shot fell from you like a ripe fruit. Now go on practicing as if nothing had happened."

Only after a considerable time did more right shots occasionally come off, which the Master signalized by a deep bow. How it happened that they loosed themselves without my doing anything, how it came about that my tightly closed right hand suddenly flew back wide open, I could not explain then and I cannot explain today. The fact remains that it did happen, and that alone is important. But at least I got to the point of being able to distinguish, on my own, the right shots from the failures. The qualitative difference is so great that it cannot be overlooked once it has been experienced. Outwardly, for the observer, the right shot is distinguished by the cushioning of the right hand as it is jerked back, so that no tremor runs through the body. Again, after wrong shots the pent-up breath is expelled explosively, and the next breath cannot be drawn quickly enough. After right shots the breath glides effortlessly to its end, whereupon air is unhurriedly breathed in again. The heart continues to beat evenly and quietly, and with concentration undisturbed one can go straight on to the next shot. But inwardly, for the archer himself, right shots have the effect of making him feel that the day has just begun. He feels in the mood for all right doing, and, what is perhaps even more important, for all right not-doing. Delectable indeed is this state. But he who has it, said the Master with a subtle smile, would do well to have it as though he did not have it. Only unbroken equanimity can accept it in such a way that it is not afraid to come back.

"Well, at least we've got over the worst," I said to the Master, when he announced one day that we were going on to some new exercises. "He who has a hundred miles to walk should reckon ninety as half the journey," he replied, quoting the proverb. "Our new exercise is shooting at a target."

Thinking about Writing

Words

Powerful words both depend on and help shape their context. In what way does each word in the list below depend on its context for strength? What does each contribute to its context? Can you think of any other word the author might have used in its place? How does the word strike you, and how do you respond to the sentence or passage because of the word?

pickings
fact
work
beguiling
waxing
whoop

Thinking

1. Herrigel's sensible European education intrudes when he is trying to loose the shot. Why do you think he concentrates on technique so much, on the fingers gripping the thumb? What comfort do you think he may have gained from thinking about his grip? Why do you think he compares archery with rifle-shooting?

2. Rebuffed by the Master, Herrigel tries to explain to Mr. Komachiya why "I had hit upon this method" for shooting. Why do you think Herrigel had been so pleased with himself? What offense had Herrigel committed?

3. The Master did not explain exactly to Herrigel how the shot would fall because the experience, if it was pure and correct, was beyond words. Why then does Herrigel, after admitting he "could not explain" how it happened, proceed to describe to the reader in words the qualitative difference between good and bad shots? To what extent is all criticism—for example, a movie review—constrained by the words the reviewer must use?

Writing

1. When Herrigel concentrated on his grip, he hoped that "technical ability would spiritualize itself," a hope that might well be shared by someone practicing the violin or a basketball shot. When you practice a musical instrument or a sport, at what point do you operate mechanically? What is the spiritual essence of playing a musical instrument, shooting a basket, or playing football? If you could have either technique or spiritual fulfillment as you pursued some art, which would you choose? How would the choice affect the way you practiced your art?

     Write an essay that argues for some combination of technique and spirit in an art or sport, based on your experience and your view of the balance or relationship that is satisfying.

2. Is there such a state of effort as "trying too hard"? Write about some experience you have had when you made enormous efforts to accomplish something, such as solving a mathematical problem or playing a difficult piece of music, when "It" finally succeeded without you. How did you feel? Did you experience joy or help-lessness? Were you proud? Did you have "unbroken equanimity," or did you worry about being able to repeat the experience?

3. Herrigel's experience confuses him because it cannot be explained. Write an essay in which you compare Herrigel's experience with John McPhee's in Chapter 7, "Things Are Rough Enough in Town." How does each author write about the inadequacy of lan-guage? Do they have anything in common?

Margaret Fuller

Margaret Fuller (1810–50) was born near Boston to an intellectual family. A precocious child, she was largely educated at home by her father. As a young adult, she organized "conversations" with other intellectual women to discuss philosophy, politics, and the role of women. She turned to journalism in order to write reviews and articles, and was sent to Europe as a journalist for the *New York Tribune*. From Europe, where she met leading writers and political figures, Fuller sent articles back to New York for publication. The selection here, one of the articles she wrote for the *Tribune*, analyzes Americans as she saw them in Europe.

American Abroad

The American in Europe, if a thinking mind, can only become more American. In some respects it is a great pleasure to be here. * Although we have an independent political existence, our position toward Europe, as to literature and the arts, is still that of a colony, and one feels the same joy here that is experienced by the colonist in returning to the parent home. What was but picture to us becomes reality; remote allusions and derivations trouble no more: we see the pattern of the stuff, and understand the whole tapestry. There is a gradual clearing up on many points, and many baseless notions and crude fancies are dropped. Even the post-haste passage of the business American through the great cities, escorted by cheating couriers and ignorant *valets de place*, unable to hold intercourse with the natives of the country, and passing all his leisure hours with his countrymen, who know no more than himself, clears his mind of some mistakes, — lifts some mists from his horizon.

There are three species. First, the servile American—a being utterly shallow, thoughtless, worthless. He comes abroad to spend his money and indulge his tastes. His object in Europe is to have fashionable clothes, good foreign cookery, to know some titled persons, and furnish himself with coffee-house gossip, by retailing which among those less travelled and as uninformed as himself he can win importance at home. I look with unspeakable contempt on this class—a class which has all the thoughtlessness and partiality of the exclusive   * classes in Europe, without any of their refinement, or the chivalric feeling which still sparkles among them here and there. However, though these willing serfs in a free age do some little hurt, and cause   * some annoyance at present, they cannot continue long; our country is fated to a grand, independent existence, and, as its laws develop, these parasites of a bygone period must wither and drop away.

Then there is the conceited American, instinctively bristling and proud of—he knows not what. He does not see, not he, that the history of Humanity for many centuries is likely to have produced results it requires some training, some devotion, to appreciate and profit by. With his great clumsy hands, only fitted to work on a steam-engine, he seizes the old Cremona violin, makes it shriek with anguish in his grasp, and then declares he thought it was all humbug before he came, and now he knows it; that there is not really any music in these old things; that the frogs in one of our swamps make much finer, for they are young and alive. To him the etiquettes of courts and camps, the ritual of the Church, seem simply silly,—and no wonder, profoundly ignorant as he is of their origin and meaning. Just so the legends which are the subjects of pictures, the profound myths which are represented in the antique marbles, amaze and revolt him; as,   * indeed, such things need to be judged of by another standard than that of the Connecticut Blue-Laws. He criticizes severely pictures, feeling quite sure that his natural senses are better means of judgment than the rules of connoisseurs,—not feeling that, to see such objects, mental vision as well as fleshly eyes are needed, and that something is aimed at in Art beyond the imitation of the commonest forms of Nature. This is Jonathan[1] in the sprawling state, the booby truant,

[1]Jonathan: Yankee.— Ed.

not yet aspiring enough to be a good schoolboy. Yet in his folly there *
is meaning; add thought and culture to his independence, and he will
be a man of might: he is not a creature without hope, like the thick-
skinned dandy of the class first specified.

The artistes form a class by themselves. Yet among them, though
seeking special aims by special means, may also be found the linea-
ments of these two classes, as well as of the third, of which I am now
to speak.

This is that of the thinking American, —a man who, recognizing
the immense advantage of being born to a new world and on a virgin
soil, yet does not wish one seed from the past to be lost. He is anxious
to gather and carry back with him every plant that will bear a new
climate and new culture. Some will dwindle; others will attain a bloom
and stature unknown before. He wishes to gather them clean, free
from noxious insects, and to give them a fair trial in his new world.
And that he may know the conditions under which he may best place
them in that new world, he does not neglect to study their history in
this.

Thinking about Writing

Words

Powerful words both depend on and help shape their context. In
what way does each word in the list below depend on its context for
strength? What does each contribute to its context? Can you think of
any other word the author might have used in its place? How does the
word strike you, and how do you respond to the sentence or passage
because of the word?

American
partiality
serfs
revolt
schoolboy

Thinking

1. Fuller says a thinking American in Europe "can only become more American." Why do you think she says, *only*? What does *only* do to the words that follow, "become more American"?
2. Fuller describes three species of Americans in Europe. Does anything in the writing tell us which is Fuller? How does the writing indicate her favorite of the three?
3. Both Fuller in this essay and Neruda in "Universal Night" in chapter 5 use the strategy of classification. Neruda describes three types of New Year's Eves; Fuller talks about three types of Americans. Neruda concludes with a comment about being home for the celebration. What is Fuller's conclusion? What do these two essays suggest about writing about types? What keeps each essay from appearing merely as a list of types? Which essay do you prefer?

Writing

1. Fuller discusses several types of travelers. Write an essay in which you describe certain favorable traits of any traveler, either here or abroad. You might include yourself or people you have observed. Rather than simply listing the traits ("A good traveler keeps an open mind, learns to eat anything," and so on), you might narrate incidents that show how these traits are useful for those who possess them.
2. If you have ever traveled outside the United States, write about how you felt as an American abroad. Did you suffer any painful moments? Were you ever treated badly because you were American? Were you ever honored? How did you feel when you returned?
3. Many people think that travel is supposed to be broadening. If you agree, write an essay that defends this idea. If you think, on the other hand, that travel is not broadening, or that it oughtn't be, write an essay to defend a contrary assertion.

Mary McCarthy

Mary McCarthy (b. 1912) was born to an affluent middle-class family in Seattle and educated at Vassar College. Orphaned when she was only six, McCarthy was raised by various relatives. She spent her adolescence, the period of this selection, with her grandparents. Verbally quick and socially adroit, she thought at first that she would like to prepare for a career on stage, but she soon discovered that writing was a stronger and more reliable talent than acting. While still at college, she founded a literary magazine, and upon graduation she began her long career as a novelist, a critic, and a political commentator. A contributor to *The Nation*, *New Republic*, and *Partisan Review*, McCarthy is as well known for her political comments as for her fiction. In the selection here, taken from her autobiographical *Memoirs of a Catholic Girlhood*, McCarthy describes herself as a rather facile adolescent, always shaping her personality to fit her companions' expectations.

Yellowstone

The summer I was fifteen I was invited to go to Montana by Ruth and Betty Bent, a pair of odd sisters who had come that year to our boarding school in Tacoma from a town called Medicine Springs, where their father was a federal judge. The answer from my grandparents was going to be no, I foresaw. I was too young (they would say) to travel by train alone, just as I was too young (they said) to go out with boys or accept rides in automobiles or talk to male callers on the telephone. This notion in my grandparents' minds was poisoning my life with shame, for mentally I was old for my age—as I was also accustomed to hearing from grownups in the family circle. I was so much older in worldly wisdom than *they* were that when my grandmother and my great-aunt read *The Well of Loneliness*, they had to come to ask me what the women in the book "did." "Think of it," nodded my great-aunt, reviewing the march of progress, "nowadays a fifteen-year-old girl knows a thing like that." At school, during study hall, I wrote stories about prostitutes with "eyes like dirty dishwater," which my English teacher read and advised me to send to H. L. Mencken for criticism. Yet despite all this—or possibly because of it—I was still being treated as a child who could hardly be trusted to take a streetcar without a grownup in attendance. The argument that "all the others did it" cut no ice with my grandfather, whose lawyer's mind was too precise to deal in condonation. He conceived that he had a weighty trust in my upbringing, since I had come to him as an orphan, the daughter of his only daughter.

Yet like many old-fashioned trustees, he had a special, one might say an occupational, soft spot. Anything educational was a lure to him. Salesmen of encyclopedias and stereopticon sets and Scribner's classics found him an easy prey in his Seattle legal offices, where he rose like a trout to the fly or a pickerel to the spoon. He reached with alacrity for his pocketbook at the sight of an extra on the school bill. I had had music lessons, special coaching in Latin, tennis lessons, riding lessons, diving lessons; that summer, he was eager for me to have golf lessons. Tickets for civic pageants, theater and concert subscription series, library memberships were treated by him as necessities, not to be paid for out of my allowance, which I was free to devote to freckle creams and Christmas Night perfume. Some of the books I read and plays I saw made other members of the family raise their eyebrows, but my grandfather would permit no interference. He looked tolerantly   *
over his glasses as he saw me stretched out on the sofa with a copy of *Count Bruga* or *The Hard-Boiled Virgin*. I had been styling myself an atheist and had just announced, that spring, that I was going east to college. The right of the mind to develop according to its own lights was a prime value to my grandfather, who was as rigid in applying this principle as he was strait-laced in social matters.

The previous summer had been made miserable for me by his outlandish conduct. At the resort we always went to in the Olympic   *

Mountains (my grandmother, who did not care for the outdoors, always stayed home in Seattle), he and I had suddenly become a center of attention. The old judges and colonels, the young married women whose husbands came up for the week end, the young college blades, the hostess with the Sweetheart haircut who played the piano for dancing, the very prep-school boys were looking on me, I knew, with pity because of the way my grandfather was acting—never letting me out of his sight, tapping me on the dance floor to tell me it was my bedtime, standing on the dock with a pair of binoculars when a young man managed to take me rowing for fifteen clocked minutes on the lake. One time, when a man from New York named Mr. Jones wanted me to take his picture with a salmon, my grandfather had leapt up from the bridge table and thundered after us down the woodland path. And what did he discover?—me snapping Mr. Jones' picture on a rustic bridge, that was all. What did he think could have happened, anyway, at eleven o'clock in the morning, fifty feet from the veranda where he and his cronies were playing cards? The whole hotel knew what he thought and was laughing at us. A boy did imitations of Mr. Jones holding the salmon with one hand and hugging me with the other, then dropping the salmon and fleeing in consternation when my grandfather appeared.

My grandfather did not care; he never cared what people thought of him, so long as he was doing his duty. And he expected me to be perfectly happy, taking walks up to the waterfall with him and the judges' and colonels' ladies; measuring the circumference of Douglas firs; knocking the ball around the five-hole golf course; doing the back dive from the springboard while he looked on, approving, with folded arms; playing the player piano by myself all afternoon: torn rolls of "Tea for Two" and "Who" and one called "Sweet Child" that a young man with a Marmon roadster had sung into my radiant ear on the dance floor until my grandfather scared him off.

Sweet child, indeed! I felt I could not stand another summer like that. I had to go to Montana, and my grandfather, I knew, would let me if only I could persuade him that the trip would be broadening and instructive; that is, if in my eyes it would be profoundly boring.

It did not take divination on my part to guess what would fit these requirements: Yellowstone Park. The very yawn I had to stifle at the thought of geysers, Old Faithful, colored rock formations, Indians, grizzly bears, pack horses, tents, rangers, parties of tourists with cameras and family sedans, told me I had the bait to dangle before his kindly-severe grey eyes. It was too bad, I remarked casually, in the course of my last school letter home, that the trip was out of the question: the girls had been planning to take me on a tour of Yellowstone Park. That was all that was needed. It was as simple as selling him a renewal of his subscription to the *National Geographic*. The ease of it somehow depressed me, casting a pall over the adventure; one of the most boring things about adolescence is the knowledge of how people can be worked.

I *ought* to go to Montana, said my grandfather decidedly, after he had looked up Judge Bent in a legal directory and found that he really existed: a thing which slightly surprised me, for in my representations to my grandparents, I always had the sensation of lying. Whatever I told them was usually so blurred and glossed, in the effort to meet their approval (for, aside from anything else, I was fond of them and tried to accommodate myself to their perspective), that except when answering a direct question I hardly knew whether what I was saying was true or false. I really tried, or so I thought, to avoid lying, but it seemed to me that they forced it on me by the difference in their vision of things, so that I was always transposing reality for them into terms they could understand. To keep matters straight with my *
conscience, I shrank, whenever possible, from the lie absolute, just as, from a sense of precaution, I shrank from the plain truth. Yellowstone Park was a typical instance. I had not utterly lied when I wrote that sentence. I entertained, let us say, a vague hope of going there and had spoken to the Bent girls about it in a tentative, darkling manner, *i.e.*, "My family hopes we can see Yellowstone." To which the girls replied, with the same discreet vagueness, "Ummm."

At home, it was settled for me to entrain with the girls shortly after school closed, stay three weeks, which would give us time to "do" the Park, and come back by myself. It would only be two nights, my grandfather pointed out to my grandmother; and Judge Bent could put me on the train in care of the conductor. The two girls nodded demurely, and Ruth, the elder, winked at me, as my grandfather repeated these instructions.

I was mortified. As usual, my grandfather's manner seemed calculated to expose me in front of my friends, to whom I posed as a   *
practiced siren. My whole life was a lie, it often appeared to me, from
beginning to end, for if I was wilder than my family knew, I was far
tamer than my friends could imagine, and with them, too, as with
my family, I was constantly making up stories, pretending that a ring
given me by a great-aunt was a secret engagement ring, that I went
out dancing regularly to the Olympic Hotel, that a literary boy who
wrote to me was in love with me—the usual tales, but I did not know
that. All I knew was that there was one central, compromising fact
about me that had to be hidden from my friends and that burned me
like the shirt of the Centaur: I could not bear to have anyone find
out that I was considered too young to go out with boys.

But every word, every gesture of my grandfather's seemed
designed to proclaim this fact. I perceived an allusion to it in the
fussy way he saw us off at the Seattle depot, putting us in our drawing room with many cautions not to speak to strangers, tipping the
Pullman porter and having a "word" with the conductor, while my
grandmother pressed a lacy handkerchief to her eyes and my uncle
grinned and the old family gardener and handy man advised me not to   *
take any wooden nickels. During this degrading ordeal, the Bent girls   *
remained polite and deferential, agreeing to everything (it was always
my tendency to argue). But as soon as the train pulled out of the station, Ruth Bent coolly summoned the conductor and exchanged our
drawing room for two upper berths. They always did this on boarding
the train, she explained; two could fit very comfortably into an upper,
and the money they got back was clear profit.

Thinking about Writing

Words

Powerful words both depend on and help shape their context. In
what way does each word in the list below depend on its context for
strength? What does each contribute to its context? Can you think of

any other word the author might have used in its place? How does the word strike you, and how do you respond to the sentence or passage because of the word?

tolerantly
conduct
understand
expose . . . posed
grinned
wooden nickels

Thinking

1. "I always had the sensation of lying," says McCarthy, claiming that she was forced to fiddle with reality in order to please her grandparents. Later she says, "My whole life was a lie." In what ways does the essay give you the impression that she was or was not responsible for her behavior? Do you feel that she thinks of herself as a liar? Why do you think this?
2. Does McCarthy's admission of misconduct make her less convincing as a writer, or do you find her more human for owning up to it? What information in this selection do you use as a basis for judging her conduct and her admission? If McCarthy can say that her "whole life was a lie," are you able to believe her now?
3. From what view does McCarthy write this piece? Is she referring to the present or the past when she says, "One of the most boring things about adolescence is the knowledge of how people can be worked"? When was McCarthy bored by this knowledge? Why was she bored? Later, she refers to "the usual tales, but I did not know that." What does she mean by "that"? What is McCarthy saying about adolescents or about making up stories?

Writing

1. How did you "reconstruct" yourself when you were younger, presenting a self that would please others? What conflict did you feel between pleasing peers and pleasing family? Write about your experience.

2. After looking at some magazine advertisements and television commercials designed for the teen-age audience, write an essay that explores the image presented by the media to readers and viewers in this age group.

   In what ways is the media's advice sound in urging certain choices of diet, dress, music, sports, education, jobs, and general expectations? In what ways does the advice mislead young people? How does this happen? Do you think that most teenagers feel that they must conform to patterns they don't like in order to please others? Consider these questions when you write your essay.

9

Taking
a Stand

The writers in this chapter are concerned with beliefs and issues. They have constructed powerful arguments for readers. Most readers think that the best argument is the one they believe. Chances are they come to it already convinced of its truth and respond favorably because it agrees with them rather than the other way around. However, when readers have little information to begin with, or they haven't thought enough about a subject to support either side of an argument, or they are still undecided although they have thought about the issue, a powerful argument can help clarify thinking. Although much of the thinking comes from the argument itself, readers come away from reading such arguments more confident about their own ideas. To understand an issue is to hear both sides of an argument. The writers in this chapter present only one side, of course, but within the text of any powerful argument may be found ideas for debate, against which these writers construct their arguments.

Mary Wollstonecraft argues against preparing women merely for the marriage market, proposing that women be considered rational creatures. She sees women's preparation for marriage as a mis-education for both women and men.

Adrienne Rich argues that novice writers need to trust those who instruct them so that they do not feel threatened as they take their first, tentative steps in learning to control language. Rich sees their fear as the natural result of language having been used against them.

James Baldwin argues against the cruelties of racism as he remembers the days when restaurants refused to serve blacks. He seeks in his argument to explain the anger that explodes when a person is humiliated in this way.

Virginia Woolf maintains that a creative woman must clarify her position if she wishes to lead a creative, productive life. Woolf argues for doing away with the myth of the self-sacrificing female. This myth will destroy women if they don't destroy it first.

Carey Thomas argues for educating women. Carey, writing in the nineteenth century, insists that women are mentally and physically strong enough to attend college.

Barbara Grizzuti Harrison, writing about abortion, argues for a calm approach when we debate this explosive subject. But, human nature being what it is, we need to be provoked into debating the issue in the first place.

Bertrand Russell maintains there is no God, refuting several arguments offered by believers. He argues that this thinking is inconsistent as he explains his own views on the subject.

Henry S. Salt argues that humans must speak against animals being used for hunting or for scientific research. Salt claims that people should protect creatures that lack voices of their own.

Alice Walker argues that the creative woman should have one child — at most — if she is to remain free to work. But, Walker maintains, the creative woman should have a child only if this is of interest to her.

Plato argues that people live in a dark cave, believing that shadows are real objects, but that they can be led up toward the light by education. However, once they have seen the light, Plato argues, they can't return to the darkness.

Samuel Johnson argues against procrastination. He recognizes that, although getting the work done would be infinitely less painful than thinking about it, people nonetheless choose the thornier path.

Joseph Wood Krutch argues that if governments are cruel it is because they tend to seek the greatest good for the greatest number. Then, Krutch maintains, there's hope only in the individual, for governments are too efficient to love.

And finally, Jonathan Swift argues that Irish economic problems are so dire that only drastic measures can be taken. Realizing that economic independence and political prestige go hand in hand, Swift offers a solution to the problem.

Mary Wollstonecraft

Mary Wollstonecraft (1759–97) was born in London. The combination of need to support herself and an admiration for learning led her to become first a teacher, then a writer and translator. Through her wit and intelligence, she gained admission to London literary circles where she was able to meet and talk with other radical intellectuals. She wrote on political and cultural affairs, reading and translating from the French publications of the day. Moved by the French Revolution, she strove to define liberty, especially for women, whom she saw as victims of a political and social arrangement that fostered marriage over any other possible occupation. She herself was against the institution, which she felt belittled women and made of them badly educated objects of barter, given to "nickname God's creatures" and to become "propagators of fools." In this selection, from a longer work called *Vindication of the Rights of Women*, she addresses the problem of sexist stereotyping of women as mindless objects, blaming the miseducation of men and women for the deplorable state.

The Frivolous Sex

My own sex, I hope, will excuse me, if I treat them like rational *
creatures, instead of flattering their fascinating graces, and viewing them as if they were in a state of perpetual childhood, unable to stand alone. I earnestly wish to point out in what true dignity and human happiness consists—I wish to persuade women to endeavor to acquire strength, both of mind and body, and to convince them that the soft phrases, susceptibility of heart, delicacy of sentiment, and refinement of taste, are almost synonymous with epithets of weakness,

and that those beings who are only the objects of pity and that kind of love, which has been termed its sister, will soon become objects of contempt.

Dismissing, then, those pretty feminine phrases, which the men condescendingly use to soften our slavish dependence, and despising that weak elegancy of mind, exquisite sensibility, and sweet docility of manners, supposed to be the sexual characteristics of the weaker vessel, I wish to show that elegance is inferior to virtue, that the first object of laudable ambition is to obtain a character as a human being, regardless of the distinction of sex; and that secondary views should be brought to this simple touchstone.

This is a rough sketch of my plan; and should I express my conviction with the energetic emotions that I feel whenever I think of the subject, the dictates of experience and reflection will be felt by some of my readers. Animated by this important object, I shall disdain to cull my phrases or polish my style; I aim at being useful, and   *
sincerity will render me unaffected; for, wishing rather to persuade by the force of my arguments, than dazzle by the elegance of my language, I shall not waste my time in rounding periods, or in fabricating the turgid bombast of artificial feelings, which, coming from the head, never reach the heart. I shall be employed about things, not words! and, anxious to render my sex more respectable members of society, I shall try to avoid that flowery diction which has slided from essays into novels, and from novels into familiar letters and conversation.

These pretty superlatives, dropping glibly from the tongue, viti- ate the taste, and create a kind of sickly delicacy that runs away from simple unadorned truth; and a deluge of false sentiments and over- stretched feelings, stifling the natural emotions of the heart, render the domestic pleasures insipid, that ought to sweeten the exercise of those severe duties, which educate a rational and immortal being for   *
a nobler field of action.

The education of women has, of late, been more attended to than formerly; yet they are still reckoned a frivolous sex, and ridiculed or pitied by the writers who endeavor by satire or instruc- tion to improve them. It is acknowledged that they spend many of the first years of their lives in acquiring a smattering of accomplish- ments; meanwhile strength of body and mind are sacrificed to libertine notions of beauty, to the desire of establishing themselves—the only way women can rise in the world — by marriage. And this desire making mere animals of them, when they marry they act as such children may be expected to act — they dress; they paint, and nickname God's creatures. Surely these weak beings are only fit for a seraglio![1] — Can they be expected to govern a family with judgment, or take care of the poor babes whom they bring into the world?

If then it can be fairly deduced from the present conduct of the sex, from the prevalent fondness for pleasure which takes place of ambition, and those nobler passions that open and enlarge the * soul; that the instruction which women have hitherto received has only tended, with the constitution of civil society, to render them insignificant objects of desire — mere propagators of fools! — if it can * be proved that in aiming to accomplish them, without cultivating their understandings, they are taken out of their sphere of duties, and made ridiculous and useless when the short-lived bloom of beauty is over.[2] I presume that *rational* men will excuse me for endeavoring to * persuade them to become more masculine and respectable.

Indeed the word masculine is only a bugbear: there is little reason to fear that women will acquire too much courage or fortitude; for their apparent inferiority with respect to bodily strength, must render them, in some degree, dependent on men in the various relations of life; but why should it be increased by prejudices that give a sex to virtue, and confound simple truths with sensual reveries?

Women are, in fact, so much degraded by mistaken notions of female excellence, that I do not mean to add a paradox when I assert, that this artificial weakness produces a propensity to tyrannize, and gives birth to cunning, the natural opponent of strength, which leads them to play off those contemptible infantine airs that undermine esteem even whilst they excite desire. Let men become more chaste and modest, and if women do not grow wiser in the same ratio, it will be clear that they have weaker understandings. It seems scarcely necessary to say, that I now speak of the sex in general. Many individuals have more sense than their male relatives; and, as nothing preponderates where there is a constant struggle for an equilibrium, without it

[1]seraglio: harem. — Ed.

[2]A lively writer, I cannot recollect his name, asks what business women turned of forty have to do in the world? — [Wollstonecraft]

has naturally more gravity, some women govern their husbands without degrading themselves, because intellect will always govern.

Thinking about Writing

Words

Powerful words both depend on and help shape their context. In what way does each word in the list below depend on its context for strength? What does each word contribute to its context? Can you think of any other word the author might have used in its place? How does the word strike you, and how do you respond to the sentence or passage because of the word?

rational
useful
immortal
ambition
fools
rational

Thinking

1. Wollstonecraft rejects "fabricating the turgid bombast of artificial feelings, which, coming from the head, never reach the heart." Wouldn't you think artificial feelings come from the heart and never reach the head? Why do you think Wollstonecraft locates artifice in the head? What do you think Wollstonecraft would say about the source of true feelings?
2. Why must marriage as Wollstonecraft describes it here depend on women's weakness rather than strength? Do you agree with her when she says a weak woman is likely to tyrannize and resort to cunning? In what ways has education failed women, both in Wollstonecraft's day and our own?
3. How does Wollstonecraft see men in relation to women? What would happen to women if men changed? How do women, as

described by Wollstonecraft, affect men? What would happen to men if women changed?

Writing

1. Go into a card shop, locate some frankly sentimental cards, and copy down a dozen or so messages that supposedly come from the heart. Write an analysis of this artificial language, adding your own comments or those you think Wollstonecraft might have offered as you react to the messages from the card. You may prefer to role-play, pretending to be Wollstonecraft reacting to the cards' messages.

2. Wollstonecraft mentions writers who "endeavor by satire or instruction to improve" women. Examine some current women's magazines or romantic novels to discover how these publications contribute to the education and improvement of women. Read the words, and also look at the illustrations. How are women pictured in fiction, nonfiction, and advertisements? How are the writers endeavoring to improve women? Write an essay in which you examine the effects, as you see them, of such publications.

3. What kind of person is Mary Wollstonecraft? How can you tell from her writing what she is like and what her views might be concerning, for example, men, women, and marriage? Can you guess what she might think about beauty, which she says is short-lived? Write an essay that describes the author as you see her through her writing. Quote Wollstonecraft's own words for support.

Adrienne Rich

Adrienne Rich (b. 1929) was born in Baltimore and educated at Radcliffe College. Even before graduating, she was recognized as a major talent among American poets. She has received numerous prizes and awards for her writing, among them an award from the National Institute of Arts and Letters and the National Book Award. Writer and teacher, she has served as poet-in-residence at various colleges and universities. In this essay, she recalls teaching at the City College of New York when students were being admitted under open enrollment. She maintains that her students, accustomed to language being used against them, needed an atmosphere of trust in which to read and to write. This selection is part of a longer work, "Teaching Language in Open Admissions," written in 1972, which appears in her prose collection *On Lies, Secrets, and Silence.*

Teaching Language in Open Admissions

Sometimes as I walk up 133rd Street, past the glass-strewn doorways of P.S. 161, the graffiti-sprayed walls of tenements, the uncollected garbage, through the iron gates of South Campus and up the driveway to the prefab hut which houses the English department, I think wryly of John Donne's pronouncement that "the University is a Paradise; rivers of Knowledge are there; Arts and Sciences flow from thence." I think that few of our students have this Athenian notion of what college is going to be for them; their first introduction to it is a many hours' wait in line at registration, which only reveals that the courses they have been advised or wanted to take are filled, or conflict in hours with a needed job; then more hours at the cramped, heavily guarded bookstore; then perhaps, a semester in courses which they never chose, or in which the pace and allusions of a lecturer are daunting or which may meet at opposite ends of an elongated campus stretching for six city blocks and spilling over into a former warehouse on Broadway. Many have written of their first days at C.C.N.Y.: "I only knew it was different from high school." What was different, perhaps, was the green grass of early September with groups of young people in dashikis and gelés, jeans and tie-dye, moving about with the unquenchable animation of the first days of the fall semester; the encounter with some teachers who seem to respect them as individuals; something at any rate less bleak, less violent, less mean-spirited, than the hall of Benjamin Franklin or Evander Childs or some other school with the line painted down the center of the corridor and a penalty for taking the short-cut across that line. In all that my students have written about their high schools, I have found bitterness, resentment, satire, black humor; never any word of nostalgia for the school, though sometimes a word of affection for a teacher "who really tried."

The point is that, as Mina Shaughnessy, the director of the Basic Writing Program at City, has written: "the first stage of Open Admissions involves *openly admitting* that education has failed for too many students."[1] . . .

Meeting some of the so-called ethnic students in class for the first time in September 1970, I began to realize that: there *are* still poor Jews in New York City; they teach English better to native speakers of Greek on the island of Manhattan; the Chinese student with acute English-language difficulties is stereotyped as "nonexpressive" and channeled into the physical sciences before anyone has a chance to find out whether he or she is a potential historian, political theorist, or psychologist; and (an intuition, more difficult to prove) white, ethnic working-class young women seem to have problems of self–

---

[1]Mina P. Shaughnessy, "Open Admissions —A Second Report," in *The City College Department of English Newsletter*, vol. II, no. 1., January 1972. A. R., 1978: See also Shaughnessy's *Errors and Expectations: A Guide for the Teacher of Basic Writing* (New York: Oxford, 1977), a remarkable study in the methodology of teaching language.

reliance and of taking their lives seriously that young black women students as a group do not seem to share . . .

Confronted with these individuals, this city, these life situations, these strengths, these damages, there are some harsh questions that * have to be raised about the uses of literature. I think of myself as a teacher of language: that is, as someone for whom language has implied freedom, who is trying to aid others to free themselves through the written word, and above all through learning to write it for themselves. I cannot know for them what it is they need to free, or what words they need to write; I can only try with them to get an approximation of the story they want to tell. I have always assumed, and I do still assume, that people come into the freedom of language through reading, before writing; that the differences of tone, rhythm, vocabulary, intention, encountered over years of reading are, whatever else they may be, suggestive of many different possible modes of being. But my daily life as a teacher confronts me with young men and women who have had language and literature *used against* them, to keep them in their place, to mystify, to bully, to * make them feel powerless. Courses in great books or speed-reading are not an answer when it is the meaning of literature itself that is in question. Sartre says: "the literary object has no other substance than the reader's subjectivity; Raskolnikov's waiting is *my* waiting which I lend him. . . . His hatred of the police magistrate who questions him is my hatred, which has been solicited and wheedled out of me by signs. . . . Thus, the writer appeals to the reader's freedom to collaborate in the production of his work."[2] But what if it is these very signs, or ones like them, that have been used to limit the reader's freedom or to convince the reader of his or her unworthiness to "collaborate in the production of the work"?

I have no illuminating answers to such questions. I am sure we must revise, and are revising, our notion of the "classic," which has come to be used as a term of unquestioning idolatry instead of in the meaning which Sartre gives it: a book written by someone who "did not have to decide with each work what the meaning and value of literature were, since its meaning and value were fixed by tradition."[3]

[2]Jean-Paul Sartre, *What Is Literature?* (New York: Harper Colophon Books, 1965). pp. 39–40.

[3]Ibid., p. 85.

And I know that the action from the other side, of becoming that person who puts signs on paper and invokes the collaboration of a reader, encounters a corresponding check: in order to write I have to believe that there is someone willing to collaborate subjectively, as opposed to a grading machine out to get me for mistakes in spelling and grammar. (Perhaps for this reason, many students first show the writing they are actually capable of in an uncorrected journal rather than in a "theme" written "for class.") The whole question of *trust* as a basis for the act of reading or writing has only opened up since we began trying to educate those who have every reason to mistrust literary culture. For young adults trying to write seriously for the first time in their lives, the question "Whom can I trust?" must be an underlying boundary to be crossed before real writing can occur. We   * who are part of literary culture come up against such a question only when we find ourselves writing on some frontier of self-determination, as when writers from an oppressed group *within* literary culture, such as black intellectuals, or, most recently, women, begin to describe and analyze themselves as they cease to identify with the dominant * culture. Those who fall into this category ought to be able to draw on it in entering into the experience of the young adult for whom writing itself—as reading—has been part of the not-me rather than one of the natural activities of the self.

At this point the question of method legitimately arises: How to do it? How to develop a working situation in the classroom where trust becomes a reality, where the students are writing with belief in their own validity, and reading with belief that what they read has validity for them? The question is legitimate—How to do it?—but I am not sure that a description of strategies and exercises, readings, and writing topics can be, however successful they have proven for one teacher. When I read such material, I may find it stimulating and heartening as it indicates the varieties of concern and struggle going on in other classrooms, but I end by feeling it is useless to me. X is not myself and X's students are not my students, nor are my students of this fall the same as my students of last spring. A couple of years ago I decided to teach *Sons and Lovers*,[4] because of my sense that the novel touched on facts of existence crucial to people in their late teens, and my belief that it dealt with certain aspects of family

---

[4]*Sons and Lovers*: a novel by D. H. Lawrence. —Ed.

life, sexuality, work, anger, and jealousy which carried over to many cultures. Before the students began to read, I started talking about the time and place of the novel, the life of the mines, the process of industrialization and pollution visible in the slag heaps; and I gave the students (this was an almost all-black class) a few examples of the dialect they would encounter in the early chapters. Several students challenged the novel sight unseen: it had nothing to do with them, it was about English people in another era, why should they expect to find it meaningful to them, and so forth. I told them I had asked them to read it because I believed it was meaningful for them; if it was not, we could talk and write about why not and how not. The following week I reached the classroom door to find several students already there, energetically arguing about the Morels, who was to blame in the marriage, Mrs. Morel's snobbery, Morel's drinking and violence—taking sides, justifying, attacking. The class never began; it simply continued as other students arrived. Many had not yet read the novel, or had barely looked at it; these became curious and interested in the conversation and did go back and read it because they felt it must have something to have generated so much heat. That time, I felt some essential connections had been made, which carried us through several weeks of talking and writing about and out of *Sons and Lovers*, trying to define our relationships to its people and theirs to each other. . . .

Thinking about Writing

Words

Powerful words both depend on and help shape their context. In what way does each word in the list below depend on its context for strength? What does each contribute to its context? Can you think of any other word the author might have used in its place? How does the word strike you, and how do you respond to the sentence or passage because of the word?

damages
mystify
real
analyze

Thinking

1. Rich refers to Sartre's statement about a reader being free to collaborate in the production of a work. How do you collaborate when you read? How are your responses "solicited and wheedled"? When you write, what do you expect of your reader? To what extent do you feel there is a "grading machine" out to get you "for mistakes in spelling and grammar"? What does this feeling do to your writing? To your sense of yourself?
2. Rich claims her college students had no nostalgia for high school, and many, when asked to write about college, would say "I only knew it was different from high school." Why do you imagine nostalgia and its absence are so important to Rich, especially for students new to college? How does this selection show Rich's attitude toward her students?

Writing

1. For Rich, language implied freedom in that writers *should* be able to collaborate with whatever they read, and *should* want someone to collaborate with their own writing, but she knows that people often "have had language *used against* them, to keep them in their place, to mystify, to bully, to make them feel powerless."

   Write an essay in which you argue against language that seeks power for the user while it leaves others feeling powerless. You'll find this kind of language in political writing, in the talk of many physicians, and in advertising and "sales pitches." Look especially for examples of hidden coercion in which the reader *appears* to have freedom while actually being deprived of power.
2. When we design plans for action, we have two sources of impressions, our own feelings about the action and evidence of the feelings of others concerned. Ideally, a good plan will meet the requirements of our own understanding and please others. In this way,

Rich presents her plan for teaching, using *Sons and Lovers*, the novel by D. H. Lawrence.

Write an essay in which you use Rich's writing to examine what she wanted and what her students wanted in the classroom. You need not have read or heard of *Sons and Lovers*. What you are seeking are indications of her own and her students' needs, her attitude toward her students, and any clues that led her to make her teaching plan.

James Baldwin

James Baldwin (b. 1924) was born in New York City, the son of a Harlem preacher. Baldwin became a preacher himself while still in high school, as he has written in his largely autobiographical novel, *Go Tell It on the Mountain*. He soon gave up this occupation to devote himself to his writing, supporting himself with odd jobs until recognition brought financial reward and the freedom to work only on his writing. He has produced numerous novels and essays since then. Although he has lived most of his adult life in France, Baldwin often writes of being black in America. In the account here, which comes from one of his essay collections, *Notes of a Native Son*, Baldwin tells of the mounting rage he felt as, totally helpless, he was refused service in restaurants. He argues in this piece that helplessness and frustration of this sort create an anger that never disappears.

Rage

. . . The year which preceded my father's death had made a great change in my life. I had been living in New Jersey, working in defense plants, working and living among southerners, white and black. I knew about the south, of course, and about how southerners treated Negroes and how they expected them to behave, but it had never entered my mind that anyone would look at me and expect *me* to behave that way. I learned in New Jersey that to be a Negro meant, precisely, that one was never looked at but was simply at the mercy of the reflexes the color of one's skin caused in other people. I acted in New Jersey as I had always acted, that is as though I thought a great deal of myself—I had to *act* that way—with results that were, simply, unbelievable. I had scarcely arrived before I had earned the enmity,

375

which was extraordinarily ingenious, of all my superiors and nearly   *
all my co-workers. In the beginning, to make matters worse, I simply
did not know what was happening. I did not know what I had done,
and I shortly began to wonder what *anyone* could possibly do, to bring
about such unanimous, active, and unbearably vocal hostility. I knew
about jim-crow but I had never experienced it. I went to the same self-
service restaurant three times and stood with all the Princeton boys
before the counter, waiting for a hamburger and coffee; it was always
an extraordinarily long time before anything was set before me, but it
was not until the fourth visit that I learned that, in fact, nothing had
ever been set before me: I had simply picked something up. Negroes
were not served there, I was told, and they had been waiting for me
to realize that I was always the only Negro present. Once I was told
this, I determined to go there all the time. But now they were ready
for me and, though some dreadful scenes were subsequently enacted
in that restaurant, I never ate there again.

It was the same story all over New Jersey, in bars, bowling alleys,
diners, places to live. I was always being forced to leave, silently,
or with mutual imprecations. I very shortly became notorious and
children giggled behind me when I passed and their elders whispered
or shouted—they really believed that I was mad. And it did begin to
work on my mind, of course; I began to be afraid to go anywhere and
to compensate for this I went places to which I really should not have
gone and where, God knows, I had no desire to be. My reputation
in town naturally enhanced my reputation at work and my working
day became one long series of acrobatics designed to keep me out of   *
trouble. I cannot say that these acrobatics succeeded. It began to seem
that the machinery of the organization I worked for was turning over,
day and night, with but one aim: to eject me. I was fired once, and
contrived, with the aid of a friend from New York, to get back on
the payroll; was fired again, and bounced back again. It took a while
to fire me for the third time, but the third time took. There were
no loopholes anywhere. There was not even any way of getting back
inside the gates.

That year in New Jersey lives in my mind as though it were
the year during which, having an unsuspected predilection for it, I
first contracted some dread, chronic disease, the unfailing symptom
of which is a kind of blind fever, a pounding in the skull and fire

in the bowels. Once this disease is contracted, one can never be really carefree again, for the fever, without an instant's warning, can recur at any moment. It can wreck more important things than race relations. There is not a Negro alive who does not have this rage in his blood—one has the choice, merely, of living with it consciously or surrendering to it. As for me, this fever has recurred in me, and does, and will until the day I die.

My last night in New Jersey, a white friend from New York took me to the nearest big town, Trenton, to go to the movies and have a few drinks. As it turned out, he also saved me from, at the very least, a violent whipping. Almost every detail of that night stands out very clearly in my memory. I even remember the name of the movie we saw because its title impressed me as being so patly ironical. It was a movie about the German occupation of France, starring Maureen O'Hara and Charles Laughton and called *This Land Is Mine*. I remember the name of the diner we walked into when the movie ended: it was the "American Diner." When we walked in the counterman asked what we wanted and I remember answering with the casual sharpness which * had become my habit: "We want a hamburger and a cup of coffee, what do you think we want?" I do not know why, after a year of such rebuffs, I so completely failed to anticipate his answer, which was, of course, "We don't serve Negroes here." This reply failed to discompose me, at least for the moment. I made some sardonic comment about the name of the diner and we walked out into the streets.

This was the time of what was called the "brown-out," when the lights in all American cities were very dim. When we re-entered the streets something happened to me which had the force of an optical illusion, or a nightmare. The streets were very crowded and I was facing north. People were moving in every direction but it seemed to me, in that instant, that all of the people I could see, and many more than that, were moving toward me, against me, and that everyone was white. I remember how their faces gleamed. And I felt, like a physical sensation, a *click* at the nape of my neck as though some interior string connecting my head to my body had been cut. I began to walk. I heard my friend call after me, but I ignored him. Heaven only knows what was going on in his mind, but he had the good sense not to touch me —I don't know what would have happened if he had —and to keep me in sight. I don't know what was going on in my mind, either; I certainly had no conscious plan. I wanted to do something to crush these white faces, which were crushing me. I walked for perhaps a block or two until I came to an enormous, glittering, and fashionable restaurant in which I knew not even the intercession of the Virgin would cause me to be served. I pushed through the doors and took the first vacant seat I saw, at a table for two, and waited.

I do not know how long I waited and I rather wonder, until today, what I could possibly have looked like. Whatever I looked like, I frightened the waitress who shortly appeared, and the moment she appeared all of my fury flowed towards her. I hated her for her white face, and for her great, astounded, frightened eyes. I felt that if she found a black man so frightening I would make her fright worthwhile.

She did not ask me what I wanted, but repeated, as though she had learned it somewhere, "We don't serve Negroes here." She did not say it with the blunt, derisive hostility to which I had grown so accustomed, but, rather, with a note of apology in her voice, and fear. This made me colder and more murderous than ever. I felt I had to do something with my hands. I wanted her to come close enough for me to get her neck between my hands.

So I pretended not to have understood her, hoping to draw her closer. And she did step a very short step closer, with her pencil poised incongruously over her pad, and repeated the formula: ". . . don't serve Negroes here."

Somehow, with the repetition of that phrase, which was already ringing in my head like a thousand bells of a nightmare, I realized that she would never come any closer and that I would have to strike from a distance. There was nothing on the table but an ordinary water-mug half full of water, and I picked this up and hurled it with all my strength at her. She ducked and it missed her and shattered against the mirror behind the bar. And, with that sound, my frozen blood abruptly thawed, I returned from wherever I had been, I *saw*, for the first time, the restaurant, the people with their mouths open, already, as it seemed to me, rising as one man, and I realized what I had done, and where I was, and I was frightened. I rose and began running for the door. A round, potbellied man grabbed me by the nape of the neck just as I reached the doors and began to beat me about the face. I kicked him and got loose and ran into the streets. My friend whispered, "*Run!*" and I ran.

My friend stayed outside the restaurant long enough to misdirect my pursuers and the police, who arrived, he told me, at once. I do not know what I said to him when he came to my room that night. I could not have said much. I felt, in the oddest, most awful way, that I had somehow betrayed him. I lived it over and over and over again, the way one relives an automobile accident after it has happened and one finds oneself alone and safe. I could not get over two facts, both equally difficult for the imagination to grasp, and one was that I could have been murdered. But the other was that I had been ready to commit murder. I saw nothing very clearly but I did see this: that my life, my *real* life, was in danger, and not from anything other people might do but from the hatred I carried in my own heart.

Thinking about Writing

Words

Powerful words both depend on and help shape their context. In what way does each word in the list below depend on its context for strength? What does each contribute to its context? Can you think of any other word the author might have used in its place? How does the word strike you, and how do you respond to the sentence or passage because of the word?

ingenious
acrobatics
casual
betrayed
real

Thinking

1. Why do you think Baldwin begins this piece of writing with so many contrasts and opposites? What effect has this on you as you

read? How does this strategy make you feel toward Baldwin at this point? How do you think he felt?

2. Throughout his account, Baldwin is never alone; yet, although he is constantly with others, he never tells us much about them — who they are, what they are doing, what they look like, or even their names. Why do you suppose he limits the presence of others to this extent? How does this shadowy appearance of others help us to see Baldwin as he saw himself?

3. How do you think Baldwin solves the problems of being alienated?

Writing

1. Have you ever blundered into an awkward situation when, suddenly realizing where you were and what was happening, you did not withdraw but stubbornly carried on, perhaps hating yourself or those around you? Why did you insist on continuing instead of backing off or beating a hasty retreat, even when you sank deeper into a morass, and when you may have been in psychological or physical danger? What were you trying to prove? Write about your experience in this situation.

2. Write an essay in which you defend the argument that Baldwin has posed here — that alienation throws us back on our own resources and in order to respect ourselves we must often go through gyrations that may seem counterproductive but that preserve our very souls.

3. Write about some experience you have had when you were not alone in that other people were around, but you were alone in that you had made no human contact. Although others existed, they did so for themselves, without you, for you were alienated. You may have had such an experience at a party when someone came up to you and, as you talked, looked over your shoulder and eventually drifted away, as if you had never existed. Similarly, you may remember a conversation when you have been charmed by the sound of your own voice or impressed with your own ideas, only to realize that the people you are with do not really *hear* you.

Virginia Woolf

Virginia Woolf (1882–1941) was born in London. The child of an intellectual family, she was educated at home by her father. She became a critic, a writer, and a leading member of the literary circle in London known as the Bloomsbury Group as well as cofounder with her husband, Leonard Woolf, of Hogarth Press. An interest in experimental modes of fiction led Woolf to develop a style which blended time with daily experience for her characters. *Jacob's Room* and *To the Lighthouse* are written in this mode. She also wrote essays, critical works, and translations. In the selection here, a paper read to the Women's Service League in London, Woolf responds to the women of her day—early in this century—who were just beginning to find careers for themselves. Woolf describes "killing" the popular Victorian image of the self-effacing female before she could continue to define her professional needs. This piece comes from *The Death of the Moth and Other Essays*.

Professions for Women

When your secretary invited me to come here, she told me that your Society is concerned with the employment of women and she suggested that I might tell you something about my own professional experiences. It is true I am a woman; it is true I am employed; but what professional experiences have I had? It is difficult to say. My profession is literature; and in that profession there are fewer experiences for women than in any other, with the exception of the stage —fewer, I mean, that are peculiar to women. For the road was cut many years ago —by Fanny Burney, by Aphra Behn, by Harriet Martineau, by Jane Austen, by George Eliot—many famous women, and many

more unknown and forgotten, have been before me, making the path smooth, and regulating my steps. Thus, when I came to write, there were very few material obstacles in my way. Writing was a reputable and harmless occupation. The family peace was not broken by the   *
scratching of a pen. No demand was made upon the family purse. For ten and sixpence one can buy paper enough to write all the plays of Shakespeare—if one has a mind that way. Pianos and models, Paris, Vienna and Berlin, masters and mistresses, are not needed by a writer. The cheapness of writing paper is, of course, the reason why women have succeeded as writers before they have succeeded in the other professions.

But to tell you my story—it is a simple one. You have only got to figure to yourselves a girl in a bedroom with a pen in her hand. She had only to move that pen from left to right—from ten o'clock to one. Then it occurred to her to do what is simple and cheap enough after all—to slip a few of those pages into an envelope, fix a penny stamp in the corner, and drop the envelope into the red box at the corner. It was thus that I became a journalist; and my effort was rewarded on the first day of the following month—a very glorious day it was for me—by a letter from an editor containing a cheque for one pound ten shillings and sixpence. But to show you how little I deserve to be called a professional woman, how little I know of the struggles and difficulties of such lives, I have to admit that instead of spending that sum upon bread and butter, rent, shoes and stockings, or butcher's bills, I went out and bought a cat—a beautiful cat, a Persian cat, which very soon involved me in bitter disputes with my neighbours.

What could be easier than to write articles and to buy Persian cats with the profits? But wait a moment. Articles have to be about something. Mine, I seem to remember, was about a novel by a famous man. And while I was writing this review, I discovered that if I were going to review books I should need to do battle with a certain phantom. And the phantom was a woman, and when I came to know her better I called her after the heroine of a famous poem, The Angel in the House. It was she who used to come between me and my paper when I was writing reviews. It was she who bothered me and wasted my time and so tormented me that at last I killed her. You who come of a younger and happier generation may not have heard of her— you may not know what I mean by the Angel in the House. I will

describe her as shortly as I can. She was intensely sympathetic. She was immensely charming. She was utterly unselfish. She excelled in the difficult arts of family life. She sacrificed herself daily. If there   *
was chicken, she took the leg; if there was a draught she sat in it—in short she was so constituted that she never had a mind or a wish of her own, but preferred to sympathize always with the minds and wishes of others. Above all—I need not say it—she was pure. Her purity was supposed to be her chief beauty—her blushes, her great grace. In those days—the last of Queen Victoria—every house had its Angel. And when I came to write I encountered her with the very first words. The shadow of her wings fell on my page; I heard the rustling of her skirts in the room. Directly, that is to say, I took my pen in hand to review that novel by a famous man, she slipped behind me and whispered: "My dear, you are a young woman. You are writing about a book that has been written by a man. Be sympathetic; be tender; flatter; deceive; use all the arts and wiles of our sex. Never   *
let anybody guess that you have a mind of your own. Above all, be pure." And she made as if to guide my pen. I now record the one act for which I take some credit to myself, though the credit rightly belongs to some excellent ancestors of mine who left me a certain sum of money—shall we say five hundred pounds a year?—so that it was not necessary for me to depend solely on charm for my living. I   *
turned upon her and caught her by the throat. I did my best to kill her. My excuse, if I were to be had up in a court of law, would be that I acted in self-defence. Had I not killed her she would have killed me. She would have plucked the heart out of my writing. For, as I found, directly I put pen to paper, you cannot review even a   *
novel without having a mind of your own, without expressing what you think to be the truth about human relations, morality, sex. And all these questions, according to the Angel in the House, cannot be dealt with freely and openly by women; they must charm, they must conciliate, they must—to put it bluntly—tell lies if they are to succeed. Thus, whenever I felt the shadow of her wing or the radiance of her halo upon my page, I took up the inkpot and flung it at her. She died hard. Her fictitious nature was of great assistance to her. It is far harder to kill a phantom than a reality. She was always creeping back when I thought I had despatched her. Though I flatter myself that I killed her in the end, the struggle was severe; it took much

time that had better have been spent upon learning Greek grammar; or in roaming the world in search of adventures. But it was a real experience; it was an experience that was bound to befall all women writers at that time. Killing the Angel in the House was part of the occupation of a woman writer.

But to continue my story. The Angel was dead; what then remained? You may say that what remained was a simple and common object—a young woman in a bedroom with an inkpot. In other words, now that she had rid herself of falsehood, that young woman had only * to be herself. Ah, but what is "herself"? I mean, what is a woman? I assure you, I do not know. I do not believe that you know. I do not believe that anybody can know until she has expressed herself in all the arts and professions open to human skill. That indeed is one of the reasons why I have come here —out of respect for you, who are in process of showing us by your experiments what a woman is, who are in process of providing us, by your failures and successes, with that extremely important piece of information.

But to continue the story of my professional experiences. I made one pound ten and six by my first review; and I bought a Persian cat with the proceeds. Then I grew ambitious. A Persian cat is all very well, I said; but a Persian cat is not enough. I must have a motor car. And it was thus that I became a novelist—for it is a very strange thing that people will give you a motor car if you will tell them a story. It is a still stranger thing that there is nothing so delightful in the world as telling stories. It is far pleasanter than writing reviews of famous novels. And yet, if I am to obey your secretary and tell you my professional experiences as a novelist, I must tell you about a very strange experience that befell me as a novelist. And to understand it you must try first to imagine a novelist's state of mind. I hope I am not giving away professional secrets if I say that a novelist's chief desire is to be as unconscious as possible. He has to induce in himself a state of perpetual lethargy. He wants life to proceed with the utmost quiet and regularity. He wants to see the same faces, to read the same books, to do the same things day after day, month after month, while he is writing, so that nothing may break the illusion in which he is living — so that nothing may disturb or disquiet the mysterious nosings about, feelings round, darts, dashes and sudden discoveries of that very shy and illusive spirit, the imagination. I suspect that this state is the same both for men and women. Be that as it may, I want you to imagine me writing a novel in a state of trance. I want you to figure to yourselves a girl sitting with a pen in her hand, which for minutes, and indeed for hours, she never dips into the inkpot. The image that comes to my mind when I think of this girl is the image of a fisherman lying sunk in dreams on the verge of a deep lake with a rod held out over the water. She was letting her imagination sweep unchecked round every rock and cranny of the world that lies submerged in the depths of our unconscious being. Now came the experience, the experience that I believe to be far commoner with women writers than with men. The line raced through the girl's fingers. Her imagination had rushed away. It had sought the pools, the depths, the dark places where the largest fish slumber. And then there was a smash. There was an explosion. There was foam and confusion. The imagination had dashed itself against something hard. The girl was roused from her dream. She was indeed in a state of the most acute and difficult distress. To speak without figure she had thought of something, something about the body, about the passions which it was unfitting for her as a woman to say. Men, her reason told her, would be shocked. The consciousness of what men will say of a woman who speaks the truth about her passions had roused her from her artist's state of unconsciousness. She could write no more. The trance was over. Her imagination could work no longer. This I believe to be a very common experience with women writers—they are impeded by the extreme conventionality of the other sex. For though men sensibly allow themselves great freedom in these respects, I doubt they realize or can control the extreme severity with which they condemn such freedom in women.

These then were two very genuine experiences of my own. These were two of the adventures of my professional life. The first— killing the Angel in the House —I think I solved. She died. But the second, telling the truth about my own experiences as a body, I do not think I solved. I doubt that any woman has solved it yet. The obstacles against her are still immensely powerful—and yet they are very difficult to define. Outwardly, what is simpler than to write books? Outwardly, what obstacles are there for a woman rather than for a man? Inwardly, I think, the case is very different; she has still many ghosts to fight, many prejudices to overcome. Indeed it will be a long time still, I think, before a woman can sit down to write a book without finding a phantom to be slain, a rock to be dashed against. And if this is so in literature, the freest of all professions for women, how is it in the new professions which you are now for the first time entering?

Those are the questions that I should like, had I time, to ask you. And indeed, if I have laid stress upon these professional experiences of mine, it is because I believe that they are, though in different forms, yours also. Even when the path is nominally open—when there is nothing to prevent a woman from being a doctor, a lawyer, a civil servant—there are many phantoms and obstacles, as I believe, looming in her way. To discuss and define them is I think of great value and importance; for thus only can the labor be shared, the difficulties be solved. But besides this, it is necessary also to discuss the ends and the aims for which we are fighting, for which we are doing battle with these formidable obstacles. Those aims cannot be taken for granted; they must be perpetually questioned and examined. The whole position, as I see it—here in this hall surrounded by women practicing for the first time in history I know not how many different professions—is one of extraordinary interest and importance. You have won rooms of your own in the house hitherto exclusively owned by men. You are able, though not without great labor and effort, to pay the rent. You are earning your five hundred pounds a year. But this freedom is only a beginning; the room is your own, but it is still bare. It has to be furnished; it has to be decorated; it has to be shared. How are you going to furnish it, how are you going to decorate it? With whom are you going to share it, and upon what terms? These, I think, are questions of the utmost importance and interest. For the first time in history you are able to ask them; for the first time you are able to decide for yourselves what the answers should be. Willingly would I stay and discuss those questions and answers— but not tonight. My time is up; and I must cease.

Thinking about Writing

Words

Powerful words both depend on and help shape their context. In what way does each word in the list below depend on its context for

strength? What does each contribute to its context? Can you think of any other word the author might have used in its place? How does the word strike you, and how do you respond to the sentence or passage because of the word?

harmless
difficult
our
charm
even
only
conventionality

Thinking

1. This is a nonfiction essay, yet there are moments when you might think it was part of a novel. Woolf has used certain techniques usually found in fiction in order to arrest and hold the reader's, or the listener's, attention. What are some of these techniques? Because this was originally a talk, Woolf used strategies that were designed to hold an audience's attention. Is there anything in the writing that would tell you it had been a talk if you didn't know that?

2. "The cheapness of writing paper is, of course, the reason why women have succeeded as writers before they have succeeded in the other professions," says Woolf. What other factors can you think of that might have contributed to women writing?

   What other "reputable and harmless" jobs have women chosen to pursue? Why do you imagine Woolf considers these two facets of work? Reputable for whom? Harmless in what way? Discuss the constraints on the working woman still under the shadow of Victorian home life and on today's career-oriented woman.

3. What do you see as the connection between the Angel in the House and "caretaker" jobs like nursing, teaching, and office work, jobs to which women were limited early in this century?

4. "Had I not killed her she would have killed me." Are you surprised that the phantom is a woman? If Woolf is actually concerned with male domination, what message could she be conveying through a female hovering in the background? In what ways does this

comment on her own behavior and on that of women in general? How is presenting a female phantom, rather than a male phantom, an effective strategy?

Writing

1. Why have women traditionally not held professional jobs although they have always worked? What's the difference between a job and a career?

    Write an essay in which you explore the various "phantoms and obstacles" that loom in the way of women becoming professionals in all fields today. What are today's Angels? Are they all in the house?

2. Woolf says, "It is far harder to kill a phantom than a reality." How might it also be far harder to kill a benign-appearing evil than an obviously pernicious one?

    When an evil appears benign, who says it is evil? Who says it is benign? Read again Martin Luther King, Jr.'s essay, "Letter from Birmingham Jail" in chapter 6, especially the part where he discusses unjust laws. Then, considering Woolf's Angel, write an essay that addresses the difficulty of confronting evil when it appears as a blessing.

M. Carey Thomas

M. Carey Thomas (1857–1935) was born in Baltimore. In an age that considered educating women risky and foolish, Thomas nonetheless graduated from Cornell University. When she was refused a Ph.D. from two German universities because of her sex, she went to the university in Zurich, Switzerland, where she finally earned her doctorate. Returning to America, she became first a professor of literature and, later, the president of Bryn Mawr College. A tireless worker for women's rights in education, Thomas often wrote on the subject. The selection here reminds readers of the sentiments of the day, as Thomas recalls her own bitterness when confronting those sentiments, some of which portrayed women as weak and evil. Her anger is outweighed only by her conviction that women were not evil but strong, physically and mentally. If her concern for the physical seems puzzling, one needs only to remember that hers was a time when many women died young from childbirth or tuberculosis. To compound these problems by sending women to college seemed dangerous to many, even to the women themselves. This selection comes from a longer work, *The Educated Woman in America*.

Educated Woman

The passionate desire of women of my generation for higher education was accompanied thruout its course by the awful doubt, felt by women themselves as well as by men, as to whether women as a sex were physically and mentally fit for it. I think I can best make this clear to you if I refer briefly to my own experience. I cannot remember the time when I was not sure that studying and going to college were the things above all others which I wished to do. I was always wondering whether it could be really true, as every one thought, that boys were cleverer than girls. Indeed, I cared so much that I never dared to ask any grown-up person the direct question, not even my father or mother, because I feared to hear the reply. I remember often praying about it, and begging God that if it were true that because I was a girl I could not successfully master Greek and go to college and understand things to kill me at once, as I could not bear to live in such an unjust world. When I was a little older I read the Bible entirely thru with passionate eagerness because I had heard it said that it proved that women were inferior to men. Those were not the days of the higher criticism. I can remember weeping over the account of Adam and Eve because it seemed to me that the curse pronounced on Eve might imperil girls' going to college; and to this day I can never read many parts of the Pauline epistles without feeling again the sinking of the heart with which I used to hurry over the verses referring to women's   * keeping silence in the churches and asking their husbands at home. I searched not only the Bible, but all other books I could get for light on the woman question. I read Milton with rage and indignation. Even as a child I knew him for the woman hater he was. The splendor of Shakespeare was obscured to me then by the lack of intellectual power in his greatest women characters. Even now it seems to me that only Isabella in *Measure for Measure* thinks greatly, and weighs her actions greatly, like a Hamlet or a Brutus.

I can well remember one endless scorching summer's day when sitting in a hammock under the trees with a French dictionary, blinded by tears more burning than the July sun, I translated the most indecent book I have ever read, Michelet's famous —were it not now forgotten, I should be able to say infamous —book on woman, *La femme.* I was beside myself with terror lest it might prove true that I myself was   * so vile and pathological a thing. Between that summer's day in 1874 and a certain day in the autumn in 1904, thirty years had elapsed. Altho during these thirty years I had read in every language every book on women that I could obtain, I had never chanced again upon a book that seemed to me so to degrade me in my womanhood as the seventh and seventeenth chapters on women and women's edu- cation, of President Stanley Hall's *Adolescence.* Michelet's sickening sentimentality and horrible over-sexuality seemed to me to breathe

again from every pseudo-scientific page. But how vast the difference between then and now in my feelings, and in the feelings of every woman who has had to do with the education of girls! Then I was terror-struck lest I, and every other woman with me, were doomed to live as pathological invalids in a universe merciless to women as a sex. Now we know that it is not we, but the man who believes such things about us, who is himself pathological, blinded by neurotic mists of sex, unable to see that women form one-half of the kindly race of normal, healthy human creatures in the world; that women, like men, are quick-   *
ened and inspired by the same study of the great traditions of their race, by the same love of learning, the same love of science, the same love of abstract truth; that women, like men, are immeasurably benefited, physically, mentally and morally, and are made vastly better mothers, as men are made vastly better fathers, by   *
subordinating the distracting instincts of sex to the simple human fellowship of similar education and similar intellectual and social ideals.

It was not to be wondered at that we were uncertain in those old days as to the ultimate result of women's education. Before I myself went to college I had never seen but one college woman. I had heard that such a woman was staying at the house of an acquaintance. I went to see her with fear. Even if she had appeared in hoofs and horns I was determined to go to college all the same. But it was a relief to find this Vassar graduate tall and handsome and dressed like other women. When, five years later, I went to Leipzig to study after I had been graduated from Cornell, my mother used to write me that my name was never mentioned to her by the women of her acquaintance. I was thought by them to be as much of a disgrace to my family as if I had eloped with the coachman. Now, women who have been to college are as plentiful as blackberries on summer hedges. Even my native city of Baltimore is full of them, and women who have in addition studied in Germany are regarded with becoming deference by the very Baltimore women who disapproved of me.

During the quarter of the century of the existence of the Association of Collegiate Alumnae two generations of college women have reached mature life, and the older generation is now just passing off the stage. We are therefore better prepared than ever before to give an account of what has been definitely accomplished, and to predict what will be the tendencies of women's college and university education in the future.

The curriculum of our women's colleges has steadily stiffened. Women, both in separate, and in coeducational colleges, seem to prefer the old-fashioned, so-called disciplinary studies. They disregard the so-called accomplishments. I believe that to-day more women   * than men are receiving a thoro college education, even altho in most cases they are receiving it sitting side by side with men in the same college lecture rooms.

We are now living in the midst of great and, I believe on the whole beneficent, social changes which are preparing the way for the coming economic independence of women.

In order to prepare for this economic independence, we should expect to see what is now taking place. Colleges for women and college departments of coeducational universities are attended by ever-increasing numbers of women students. In seven of the largest western universities women already outnumber men in the college departments. . . .

Just because women have shown such an aptitude for a true college education and such delight in it, we must be careful to maintain it for them in its integrity. We must see to it that its disciplinary quality is not lowered by the insertion of so-called practical courses which are falsely supposed to prepare for life. Women are rapidly coming to control women's college education. It rests with us to decide whether we shall barter for a mess of pottage the inheritance of the girls of this generation which the girls of my generation agonized to obtain for themselves and for other girls.

Thinking about Writing

Words

Powerful words both depend on and help shape their context. In what way does each word in the list below depend on its context for strength? What does each contribute to its context? Can you think of

any other word the author might have used in its place? How does the word strike you, and how do you respond to the sentence or passage because of the word?

hurry
terror
quickened
fathers
accomplishments

Thinking

1. Much of the force of Thomas's writing comes from her historical perspective and her personal way of contrasting past and present. The past is hers, of course, while the present belongs to the young women she sees being educated at the time of her writing. What does she tell you about the past? How does this account of her own past describe Thomas the child and Thomas the young adult? How is this account of her past problems useful to her making a statement about education in her day? What saves this essay from being bitter, as if she were saying "When I was young I didn't have it as good as you spoiled young things"?
2. "Even as a child I knew him for the woman hater he was," Thomas says of the poet Milton. Why do you think Thomas was so moved by discoveries in books rather than in daily life? Why do you suppose classical works were such a reality for her? Why didn't she just dismiss these works as fiction or, simply, incorrect? What does her reception of such works show about her? What modern books might reduce her to tears if she were a young woman reading today?
3. Do you think Thomas was correct in predicting "the coming economic independence of women"? How has education made changes in women's status? How has the education of women made changes in education itself?
4. Why do you think people once questioned a woman's physical ability to pursue a college education? What careers require women today to question their physical abilities when they consider embarking on those careers?

Writing

1. How do you react to false representations of women, men, children, races, or religions? Write an essay that argues the case for honesty, drawing on stereotypical representations in advertising, literature, movies, or television programs that seem to you unfair in their depiction of either sex, a couple, a family, the elderly, a race, or a religion.

2. Both Mary Wollstonecraft and M. Carey Thomas are concerned with educating women in order to improve their status. Write an argument, drawing on both these writers' views, that supports the contention that education, both formal and informal, in schools and in daily life, has changed and will continue to change the status of women. Where has education succeeded, and where has it failed? Can you discern any differences between the writers' approaches? Are the differences due to the lapse in time between Wollstonecraft's day and Thomas's? How are both women ultimately concerned with economics—the market value of a female?

3. Read a number of magazines, some devoted largely to women's concerns and some to men's, to determine what topics these publications address. These may be evident from articles, stories, or advertisements. Are there topics discussed in either men's or women's publications that are not discussed in both? Is there any topic that appears to be exclusively addressed in one or the other? Is there any topic that both discuss, but each in a separate manner?

   Write an argument that either supports or challenges the gender-specific features of publications. If you see these sources of information as part of our education, explain how you see them influencing our lives. For example, what kind of a woman would one be if she lived up to all the expectations implied in the ads and stories for women? What kind of a man is the ideal presented in men's magazines? If you find this manner of shaping our thinking helpful, argue for it. If you find it confusing, or in any way harmful, write your argument against it. You might ask yourself whether these publications tell society how to behave or reflect how it already behaves.

Barbara Grizzuti Harrison

Barbara Grizzuti Harrison (b. 1934) was born in Brooklyn, New York. A freelance writer and a journalist, Harrison has always been attracted to controversial subjects and to writing about them. Her first book was *Unlearning the Lie: Sexism in School*. A religious conversion in her own life led to her next book, *Visions of Glory: A History and a Memory of Jehovah's Witnesses*. In the writing here, which appeared originally in the *New York Times* of May 8, 1980, she tackles the difficult subject of abortion, which she has called elsewhere "the most vexing moral question of our time." In this selection, she asks for calm debate, warning that nothing will come of strident hysteria, while recognizing the need to feel discomfort about abortions, in order to talk about the subject in the first place.

Abortion

If there is one issue on which sane and reasonable people cannot agree to disagree, it is abortion. And even to say that is to make an inflammatory statement: People on both sides of the issue—pro-choice (or pro-abortion) and anti-abortion (or pro-life)—refuse, for the most part, to acknowledge that honor and decency can attach to anyone in the other camp.

You see what I mean: pro-choice/pro-abortion; anti-abortion/ pro-life—even the semantics of abortion defeat dialogue. And to occupy a middle ground, to admit to being pushed in one direction, pulled in another, by the claims of conscience, compassion, and reality, is intolerable (others would say unconscionable): People call you names.

395

Smugness or stridency overwhelms rational discourse; and the voices we hear from most frequently — the loudest voices — are often both smug and strident, which is to say arrogant. The arrogance of (some) anti-abortionists is flagrant: to burn a clinic is not an act con- *
ceived in humility. There is another kind of arrogance that expresses itself in the unwarranted assumption that anyone who takes a position against abortion is punitive, anti-sexual, lacking in compassion, or mindlessly following an imperative imposed upon her by a "patriarchal" religion.

Partly in an effort to resolve my own psychic tug of war, I sought to hear the quiet voices of conviction from whom we do not often hear.

I thought, while I was at it, that I might as well start at home. I have a 17-year-old son, a 16-year-old daughter. My daughter said: "Abortion is murder." My son said, "The woman should decide for herself." My daughter, however, added: "It's different from other murders, though, because nobody means to do evil; there isn't any desire to kill."

She was expressing — without knowing it — a sophisticated theological concept: that of subjective, as opposed to objective, sin.

Catholics who do not oppose abortion take refuge in this theological loophole: Miriam Walcott, a lay leader, formerly Catholic chaplain at Brown University, says that while she is "personally repelled by abortion, it is specifically inaccurate to ascribe sin, such as murder, where none is intended within the conscience of the individual choosing to have an abortion."

Catholics for a Free Choice, a national organization with state and local chapters, quotes the Second Vatican Council Declaration on Religious Liberty, saying that people who possess "civil rights are not to be hindered in leading their lives in accordance with their conscience." Joan Harriman, of Catholics for Alternatives, whose activities include "nonjudgmental pregnancy counseling," says that "abortion is often the lesser evil in service of the greater good. I am concerned with when 'ensoulment' takes place; and second-trimester abortions are awful to contemplate. But I can't contemplate making a choice for another woman, either."

A friend I value for her generosity as much as for her integrity says adamantly that if my daughter were to have an abortion, she would refuse to drive her to a clinic: "I couldn't aid and abet you. I'm beginning to feel immoral because I don't try to dissuade friends who are choosing to have abortions. I allow the vehemence of my feelings to embarrass me, so my protest comes out sounding like a little romantic squeak."

My friend is Jewish, and secular; and she "couldn't care less when 'ensoulment' takes place. That's splitting hairs and focusing attention away from the kind of society we're creating. I see abortion as the worst kind of denial of our bodies. We are our bodies. If we deny the limits inherent in being a physical creature, society approaches an ideal of mechanical perfection. Mongoloid children or thalidomide babies can live happy and good lives. The trouble is that they are intimations of our mortality."

Another friend of mine, an active member of a mainline Protestant church, says, "I know how terribly destructive it is for a mother to give up a child for adoption; and how much adopted children suffer from a sense of identity loss. On one side guilt, on the other side longing. When my extended family gets together, I see three faces that probably would not be here if abortion had been legal 20 years ago — three adopted children. I love those children, and I'm glad they're alive. But I think of their mothers. How terrible it must have been — how terrible it is — for them."

Elizabeth Moore is a welfare mother of six who works for Feminists for Life. When anti-abortionists brought a fetus to a National Organization for Women conference on abortion, she publicly denounced their action on the ground that it was "hurtful to dialogue." Active in the civil rights movement and in the peace movement, she is opposed to "all forms of violence—handguns, nukes, capital punishment."

Clearly not an ultraconservative, she takes issue with what has unfortunately become known as the "pro-family" line: she supports the proposed equal rights amendment, day-care centers, shelters for battered wives and sex education in the public schools. "Abortion," she says, "is not an alternative to sharing jobs and wealth. Abortion does not cure poverty."

Pam Cira, also of Feminists for Life, says, "Feminism grew out of the anger of women who did not want their value to be determined by men. How can we turn around and arbitrarily devalue the fetus?

How can I support a Nestlé boycott[1] and turn around and support the destruction of life *in utero?*"

"I wish we could talk to one another," she said. "This is a heartbreaking issue, and if we shout, the Women's Movement will be destroyed."

Some women are reluctant to speak. One very prominent religious reproaches herself for her silence: "A significant amount of blame must go to women like me who delivered the pro-life movement into the hands of people who care nothing about the hungry of the world, nothing about social justice, and who are not pro-life but merely anti-abortion."

"In talking about abortion," she continued, "we are talking about relationships: the relationship between the woman and the father, the relationship between the woman and the fetus, and our relationship to God, whose essence is creation and who calls us to be co-creators in the search for social justice. We say that a woman's body is her own, but we can't forget that moral decisions always come out of the perspective of being related. A human being is never not related."

"I was driving once with a group of poor Mexican-American women," she said, "and we passed a car with a bumper that said 'Abortion Is Murder.' By the time we reached our destination, every single woman in that car had admitted to having an abortion. They were scared to tell their husbands they were pregnant, and scared to tell them they were aborting. They had no options. Socially and economically, they saw no way out."

Like my daughter, I believe that abortion is murder. But I would drive my daughter to a clinic. I don't know how to fit this reality into a tidy moral or logical equation. But I do know that the arrogance *
one hears from the loud voices on both sides of this issue stems from the implicit assumption that the function of morality is to make one comfortable; whereas in fact the function of morality is to make one profoundly uncomfortable — it is only out of that discomfort, that spiritual or psychic itch, vexation and turmoil — that authentic ethical decisions can be made.

---

[1]Nestlé boycott: Nestlé company was accused of sending inferior powdered milk to third world countries, which prompted people in America to boycott Nestlé products. —Ed.

Thinking about Writing

Words

Powerful words both depend on and help shape their context. In what way does each word in the list below depend on its context for strength? What does each contribute to its context? Can you think of any other word the author might have used in its place? How does the word strike you, and how do you respond to the sentence or passage because of the word?

conceived
tidy

Thinking

1. Why do you think Harrison, who agrees with her daughter about abortion, would nonetheless drive her to a clinic for an abortion? What does this tell you about Harrison the mother and Harrison the woman? What does she tell you about her own views of arrogance? In what ways does this view of arrogance fit with her view of abortion? Why do you think we tend to lack rational discourse when we discuss this issue?

2. Consider the difference between the statement that "Catholics who do not oppose abortion take refuge in this theological loophole" and the statement that "Catholics who support free choice find support in this religious concept." Can you infer anything about Harrison from the first statement (hers, from the essay) through her choice of words? Would you be able to tell *from this statement* if she was for or against abortion? Could you infer if she is Catholic? Do you know how she feels about theological loopholes?

3. What is the difference between moral right and legal right? How has the abortion issue become a political one? Do you believe the abortion issue should be solved by the church or the state? How would you describe abortion in order for it to be a legal, and not a moral, issue?

Writing

1. Look at the language surrounding the issue of abortion or any issue that interests you (nuclear power, star wars, affirmative action, censorship). Read Adrienne Rich's essay "Teaching Language in Open Admissions" in this chapter, especially where she discusses the language of power. If you can, read George Orwell's essay "Politics and the English Language."

   Write an essay that takes a stand against "power language," against word choice being deliberately used by those desiring power to confuse and coerce others into submission and agreement.

2. Write two brief but passionate arguments, one for and one against abortion. Find words and expressions that convey the sentiments for which you argue in each, such as "free choice," "moral commitment," "ensoulment," and so forth, trying to fit the most apt words to the slant of the argument.

   When you have written the arguments, ask someone who doesn't know you well to read them and to decide, from the evidence you cite, the structure of your arguments, and your choice of words, which side of the issue you support.

   This exchange could be conducted in class. If you would rather not discuss your own opinion on this sensitive issue, you need not, but you will find interesting a stranger's assumptions based on your language. When a number of people have exchanged papers and speculated about the writers' positions, discuss the terminology that various students use in their arguments.

3. The Reverend Martin Luther King, Jr., argues in "Letter from Birmingham Jail" that an unjust law is no law at all (see chapter 6). He then defines the unjust law.

   Read his essay, and then write an essay comparing King's discussion of a just law with the issues set forth in Harrison's essay, presenting an argument for or against taking the law into your own hands. Use any examples from either of the essays or your own observations to support your argument.

Bertrand Russell

Bertrand Russell (1872–1970) was born in England and educated at Cambridge University. A mathematician and philosopher, Russell devoted his life to exploring logical thought. With another mathematician-philosopher, Alfred North Whitehead, he wrote *Principia Mathematica*, long recognized as a major work in symbolic logic. An outspoken and active pacifist who was arrested for antinuclear demonstration when he was eighty-nine, Russell sought to apply logical principles to all phases of life. His writings on the philosphy of politics, of religion, and of education reflect this turn of mind. He won the Nobel Prize for literature in 1950, awarded for the broad scope of his writings. In the selection here, which comes from a longer work called *Why I Am Not a Christian*, he quite casually and almost conversationally rejects common explanations for God's existence.

The Existence of God

To come to this question of the existence of God: it is a large and serious question, and if I were to attempt to deal with it in any adequate manner I should have to keep you here until Kingdom Come, so that you will have to excuse me if I deal with it in a somewhat summary fashion. You know, of course, that the Catholic Church has laid it down as a dogma that the existence of God can be proved by the unaided reason. That is a somewhat curious dogma, but * it is one of their dogmas. They had to introduce it because at one time the freethinkers adopted the habit of saying that there were such and such arguments which mere reason might urge against the existence * of God, but of course they knew as a matter of faith that God did exist. The arguments and the reasons were set out at great length,

401

and the Catholic Church felt that they must stop it. Therefore they laid it down that the existence of God can be proved by the unaided reason and they had to set up what they considered were arguments to prove it. There are, of course, a number of them, but I shall take only a few.

The First-cause Argument

Perhaps the simplest and easiest to understand is the argument of the First Cause. (It is maintained that everything we see in this world has a cause, and as you go back in the chain of causes further and further you must come to a First Cause, and to that First Cause you give the name of God.) That argument, I suppose, does not carry very much weight nowadays, because, in the first place, cause is not quite what it used to be. The philosophers and the men of science have got going on cause, and it has not anything like the vitality it used to have; but, apart from that, you can see that the argument that there must be a First Cause is one that cannot have any validity. I may say that when I was a young man and was debating these questions very seriously in my mind, I for a long time accepted the argument of the First Cause, until one day, at the age of eighteen, I read John Stuart Mill's Autobiography, and I there found this sentence: "My father taught me that the question 'Who made me?' cannot be answered, since it immediately suggests the further question 'Who made God?'" That very simple sentence showed me, as I still think, the fallacy in the argument of the First Cause. If everything must have a cause, then God must have a cause. If there can be anything without a cause, it may just as well be the world as God, so that there cannot be any validity in that argument. It is exactly of the same nature as the Hindu's view, that the world rested upon an elephant and the elephant rested upon a tortoise; and when they said, "How about the tortoise?" the Indian said, "Suppose we change the subject." The argument is really no better than that. There is no reason why the world could not have come into being without a cause; nor, on the other hand, is there any reason why it should not have always existed. There is no reason to suppose that the world had a beginning at all.

The idea that things must have a beginning is really due to the poverty *
of our imagination. Therefore, perhaps, I need not waste any more
time upon the argument about the First Cause.

The Natural-law Argument

Then there is a very common argument from natural law. That was
a favorite argument all through the eighteenth century, especially
under the influence of Sir Isaac Newton and his cosmogony. People
observed the planets going around the sun according to the law of
gravitation, and they thought that God had given a behest to these
planets to move in that particular fashion, and that was why they
did so. That was, of course, a convenient and simple explanation
that saved them the trouble of looking any further for explanations
of the law of gravitation. Nowadays we explain the law of gravitation
in a somewhat complicated fashion that Einstein has introduced. I
do not propose to give you a lecture on the law of gravitation, as
interpreted by Einstein, because that again would take some time; at
any rate, you no longer have the sort of natural law that you had
in the Newtonian system, where, for some reason that nobody could
understand, nature behaved in a uniform fashion. We now find that
a great many things we thought were natural laws are really human
conventions. You know that even in the remotest depths of stellar
space there are still three feet to a yard. That is, no doubt, a very
remarkable fact, but you would hardly call it a law of nature. And
a great many things that have been regarded as laws of nature are
of that kind. On the other hand, where you can get down to any
knowledge of what atoms actually do, you will find they are much less
subject to law than people thought, and that the laws at which you
arrive are statistical averages of just the sort that would emerge from
chance. There is, as we all know, a law that if you throw dice you will
get double sixes only about once in thirty-six times, and we do not
regard that as evidence that the fall of the dice is regulated by design;
on the contrary, if the double sixes came every time we should think
that there was design. The laws of nature are of that sort as regards
a great many of them. They are statistical averages such as would

emerge from the laws of chance; and that makes this whole business of natural law much less impressive than it formerly was. Quite apart from that, which represents the momentary state of science that may change tomorrow, the whole idea that natural laws imply a lawgiver is due to a confusion between natural and human laws. Human laws are   *
behests commanding you to behave in a certain way, in which way you may choose to behave, or you may choose not to behave; but natural laws are a description of how things do in fact behave, and being a mere description of what they in fact do, you cannot argue that there must be somebody who told them to do that, because even supposing that there were, you are then faced with the question "Why did God issue just those natural laws and no others?" If you say that he did it simply from his own good pleasure, and without any reason, you then find that there is something which is not subject to law, and so your train of natural law is interrupted. If you say, as more orthodox theologians do, that in all the laws which God issues he had a reason for giving those laws rather than others—the reason, of course, being to create the best universe, although you would never think it to look at it—if there were a reason for the laws which God gave, then God himself was subject to law, and therefore you do not get any advantage by introducing God as an intermediary. You have really a law outside and anterior to the divine edicts, and God does not serve your purpose, because he is not the ultimate lawgiver. In short, this whole argument about natural law no longer has anything like the strength it used to have. I am traveling on in time in my review of the arguments. The arguments that are used for the existence of God change their character as time goes on. They were at first hard intellectual arguments embodying certain quite definite fallacies. As we come to modern times they become less respectable intellectually and more and more affected by a kind of moralizing vagueness.

The Argument from Design

The next step in this process brings us to the argument from design. You all know the argument from design: everything in the world is made just so that we can manage to live in the world,

and if the world was ever so little different, we could not manage to live in it. That is the argument from design. It sometimes takes a rather curious form; for instance, it is argued that rabbits have white   *
tails in order to be easy to shoot. I do not know how rabbits would view that application. It is an easy argument to parody. You all know   *
Voltaire's remark, that obviously the nose was designed to be such as to fit spectacles. That sort of parody has turned out to be not nearly so wide of the mark as it might have seemed in the eighteenth century, because since the time of Darwin we understand much better why living creatures are adapted to their environment. It is not that their environment was made to be suitable to them but that they grew to be suitable to it, and that is the basis of adaptation. There is no evidence of design about it.

When you come to look into this argument from design, it is a most astonishing thing that people can believe that this world, with all the things that are in it, with all its defects, should be the best that omnipotence and omniscience have been able to produce in millions of years. I really cannot believe it. Do you think that, if you were granted omnipotence and omniscience and millions of years in which to perfect your world, you could produce nothing better than the Ku Klux Klan or the Fascists? Moreover, if you accept the ordinary laws of science, you have to suppose that human life and life in general on this planet will die out in due course: it is a stage in the decay of the solar system; at a certain stage of decay you get the sort of conditions of temperature and so forth which are suitable to protoplasm, and there is life for a short time in the life of the whole solar system. You see in the moon the sort of thing to which the earth is tending — something dead, cold, and lifeless.

I am told that that sort of view is depressing, and people will sometimes tell you that if they believed that, they would not be able to go on living. Do not believe it; it is all nonsense. Nobody really worries much about what is going to happen millions of years hence. Even if they think they are worrying much about that, they are really deceiving themselves. They are worried about something much more mundane, or it may merely be a bad digestion; but nobody is really seriously rendered unhappy by the thought of something that is going to happen to this world millions and millions of years hence. Therefore, although it is of course a gloomy view to suppose that life will die out—at least I suppose we may say so, although sometimes when I contemplate the things that people do with their lives I think it is almost a consolation—it is not such as to render life miserable. It merely makes you turn your attention to other things.

The Moral Arguments for Deity

Now we reach one stage further in what I shall call the intellectual descent that the Theists have made in their argumentations, and we come to what are called the moral arguments for the existence of God. You all know, of course, that there used to be in the old days three * intellectual arguments for the existence of God, all of which were disposed of by Immanuel Kant in the *Critique of Pure Reason*, but no sooner had he disposed of those arguments than he invented a new one, a moral argument, and that quite convinced him. He was like many people: in intellectual matters he was skeptical, but in moral matters he believed implicitly in the maxims that he had imbibed at his mother's knee. That illustrates what the psychoanalysts so much * emphasize—the immensely stronger hold upon us that our very early associations have than those of later times.

Kant, as I say, invented a new moral argument for the existence of God, and that in varying forms was extremely popular during the nineteenth century. It has all sorts of forms. One form is to say that there would be no right or wrong unless God existed. I am not for the moment concerned with whether there is a difference between right and wrong, or whether there is not: that is another question. The point I am concerned with is that, if you are quite sure there is a difference between right and wrong, you are then in this situation: Is that difference due to God's fiat or is it not? If it is due to God's fiat, then for God himself there is no difference between right and wrong, and it is no longer a significant statement to say that God is good. If you are going to say, as theologians do, that God is good, you must then say that right and wrong have some meaning which is independent of God's fiat, because God's fiats are good and not bad independently of the mere fact that he made them. If you are going to say that, you will then have to say that it is not only through God that right and wrong came into being, but that they are in their essence logically anterior to God. You could, of course, if you liked, say that there was a superior deity who gave orders to the God who made this world, or could take up the line that some of the gnostics took up — a line which I often thought was a very plausible one — that as a matter of fact this world that we know was made by the devil at a moment when God was not looking. There is a good deal to be said for that, and I am not concerned to refute it.

The Argument for the Remedying of Injustice

Then there is another very curious form of moral argument, which is this: they say that the existence of God is required in order to bring justice into the world. In the part of this universe that we know there is great injustice, and often the good suffer, and often the wicked prosper, and one hardly knows which of those is the more annoying; but if you are going to have justice in the universe as a whole you have to suppose a future life to redress the balance of life here on earth. So they say that there must be a God, and there must be heaven and hell in order that in the long run there may be justice. That is a very curious argument. If you looked at the matter from a scientific point of view, you would say, "After all, I know only this world. I do not know about the rest of the universe, but so far as one can argue at all on probabilities one would say that probably this world is a fair sample, and if there is injustice here the odds are that there is injustice elsewhere also." Supposing you got a crate of oranges that you opened, and you found all the top layer of oranges bad, you would not argue, "The underneath ones must be good, so as to redress the balance." You would say, "Probably the whole lot is a bad consignment"; and that is really what a scientific person would argue about the universe. He would say, "Here we find in this world a great deal of injustice, and so far as that goes that is a reason for supposing that justice does not rule in the world; and therefore so far as it goes it affords a moral argument against deity and not in favor of one." Of course I know that the sort of intellectual arguments that I have been talking to you about are not what really moves people.

What really moves people to believe in God is not any intellectual argument at all. Most people believe in God because they have been taught from early infancy to do it, and that is the main reason.

Then I think that the next most powerful reason is the wish for safety, a sort of feeling that there is a big brother who will look after you. That plays a very profound part in influencing people's desire for a belief in God.

Thinking about Writing

Words

Powerful words both depend on and help shape their context. In what way does each word in the list below depend on its context for strength? What does each contribute to its context? Can you think of any other word the author might have used in its place? How does the word strike you, and how do you respond to the sentence or passage because of the word?

curious (used three times)
mere
poverty
confusion
you all know (used twice)
knee

Thinking

1. Russell gives a cause for God's existence and then rejects it. Is there anything in his writing that tells you what he thinks of the people who hold with these causes, or has he depersonalized his attacks, aiming for ideas only?
2. Russell was considered outspoken and often overbold in his political and social statements. Is there anything in this essay to which you could point if you wished to criticize him on such grounds?

3. If Russell's writing here consists of his offering a cause only to reject it, what keeps the writing moving along? Why isn't there a sameness to the writing about causes? Or is there? How does Russell hold the reader's interest?

4. How did you react to this piece? Are you annoyed? Shocked? Amused? Offended?

Writing

1. Russell has said, "the church has chosen to label as morality a certain narrow set of rules of conduct which have nothing to do with human happiness". When you think of morality, what do you think of? Barbara Grizutti Harrison in her essay in this chapter says "the function of morality is to make one profoundly uncomfortable."

   Using ideas from both essayists, as well as from your own observation and experience, write an essay on morality. Consider in your essay what you think is the purpose of morality and to what extent it leads to personal happiness. Consider how much of the moral code — the rules for conduct by which we live — is left to individual interpretation. You might find it helpful to compare the way a law functions with the way a moral principle does. For example, we obey the law that tells us to stop at a red light. We don't interpret this law: red is red and stop is stop. A moral principle might be to avoid greed. But people can interpret *greed* in various ways. And what exactly does *avoid* mean? You might consider what punishment is inflicted on the person who breaks a law and what punishment on the one who disregards a moral principle.

2. Present an argument based on one of the following popularly held concepts, choosing one with which you cannot concur or writing one of your own. First present the commonly held argument in its favor, and then give your reasons for disagreeing with it.

   a. Putting a criminal in jail for a certain period of time will produce a person fit to function in society.

   b. Making certain that every major power in the world has a supply of nuclear weapons will assure world peace.

   c. Withdrawing economic support from South Africa will produce massive unemployment for South African blacks.

   d. Any argument about doing X to produce Y with which you cannot concur.

3. In talking about the arguments used for the existence of God, Russell says, "As we come to modern times they become less respectable intellectually and more and more affected by a kind of moralizing vagueness."

    Trace Russell's various arguments. Then, in an essay which explores these arguments, decide whether or not the later arguments are, in your view, "more and more affected by a kind of moralizing vagueness." What evidence has Russell offered to substantiate his claim? What do you mean by moralizing vagueness? What does Russell seem to mean? Consider these points when you write your essay. Be sure to quote from Russell.

Henry S. Salt

Henry S. Salt (1851–1939) was born in India and educated at Cambridge University. Almost immediately after college, he began to take an active part in debating moral and human issues of his day. He devoted his life to arguing and writing about such issues as ecology, vanishing species, vegetarianism, cruelty to animals, and the practice then quite common of beating school children. He served as secretary to a concerned-citizens group called the Humanitarian League, and he often wrote about their causes. An admirer of the American pacifist philosopher Henry David Thoreau, Salt wrote a biography of this influential figure. In the selection here, which comes from *Animals' Rights*, Salt argues against using helpless animals in scientific experiments.

Animals' Rights

Let us assume (a large assumption, certainly, controverted as it is by some most weighty medical testimony) that the progress of surgical science is assisted by the experiments of the vivisector. What then? Before rushing to the conclusion that vivisection is justifiable on that account, a wise man will take into full consideration the other, the moral side of the question—the hideous injustice of torturing an innocent animal, and the terrible wrong thereby done to the humane sense of the community.

The wise scientist and the wise humanist are identical. A true science cannot possibly ignore the solid incontrovertible fact, that the practice of vivisection is revolting to the human conscience, even among the ordinary members of a not over-sensitive society. The so-called "science" (we are compelled unfortunately, in common parlance, to use the word in this specialized technical meaning) which deliberately overlooks this fact, and confines its view to the material aspects of the problem, is not science at all, but a one-sided assertion of the views which find favor with a particular class of men.

Nothing is necessary which is abhorrent, revolting, intolerable, to the general instincts of humanity. Better a thousand times that science should forego or postpone the questionable advantage of certain problematical discoveries, than that the moral conscience of the community should be unmistakably outraged by the confusion of right and wrong. The short cut is not always the right path; and to perpetrate a cruel injustice on the lower animals, and then attempt to excuse it on the ground that it will benefit posterity, is an argument which is as irrelevant as it is immoral. Ingenious it may be (in the way of hoodwinking the unwary) but it is certainly in no true sense scientific.

It is fully admitted that experiments on men would be far more valuable and conclusive than experiments on animals; yet scientists usually disavow any wish to revive these practices, and indignantly deny the rumors, occasionally circulated, that the poorer patients in hospitals are the subjects of such anatomical curiosity. Now here, it will be observed, in the case of men, the *moral* aspect of vivisection is admitted by the scientist as a matter of course, yet in the case of animals it is allowed no weight whatever! How can this strange inconsistency be justified, unless on the assumption that men have rights, but animals have no rights—in other words, that animals are mere *things*, possessed of no purpose, and no claim on the justice and forbearance of the community?

One of the most notable and ominous features in the apologies offered for vivisection is the assertion, so commonly made by scientific writers, that is is "no worse" than certain kindred practices. When the upholders of any accused institution begin to plead that it is "no worse" than other institutions, we may feel quite assured that the case is a very bad one indeed—it is the drowning man catching at the last straw and shred of argument. Thus the advocates of experimental torture are reduced to the expedient of laying stress on the cruelties ✻ of the butcher and the herdsman, and inquiring why, if pole-axing and castration are permissible, vivisection may not also be permitted. Sport, also, is a practice which has greatly shocked the susceptibilities of the humane vivisector.

Let us admit, however, that, in contrast with the childish bru- *
tality of the sportsman, the undoubted seriousness and conscientious- ness of the vivisector (for I do not question that he acts from consci- entious motives) may be counted to his advantage. But then we have to remember, on the other hand, that the conscientious man, when he goes wrong, is far more dangerous to society than the knave or the fool; indeed, the special horror of vivisection consists precisely in this fact, that it is not due to mere thoughtlessness and ignorance, but represents a deliberate, avowed, conscientious invasion of the very principle of animals' rights.

I have already said that it is idle to speculate which is the worst form of cruelty to animals, for certainly in this subject, if anywhere, we must "reject the lore of nicely calculated less or more." Vivisection, if there be any truth at all in the principle for which I am contending, is not the root, but the fine flower and consummation of barbarity and injustice — the *ne plus ultra*[1] of iniquity in man's dealings with the lower races. The root of the evil lies, as I have throughout asserted, in *
that detestable assumption (detestable equally whether it be based on pseudo-religious or pseudo-scientific grounds) that there is a gulf, an impassable barrier, between man and the animals, and that the moral instincts of compassion, justice, and love, are to be as sedulously *
repressed and thwarted in the one direction as they are to be fostered and extended in the other.

Thinking about Writing

Words

Powerful words both depend on and help shape their context. In what way does each word in the list below depend on its context for strength? What does each contribute to its context? Can you think of any other word the author might have used in its place? How does the

---

[1]*ne plus ultra*: highest state. —Ed.

Henry S. Salt

word strike you, and how do you respond to the sentence or passage because of the word?
cruelties
childish
lower
instincts

Thinking

1. What difference, if any, is there between hunters killing for sport and scientists killing for others' eventual benefit? To what extent do you agree with Salt when he claims, "the conscientious man, when he goes wrong, is far more dangerous to society than the knave or the fool"? Discuss the moral implications of the conscientious man's actions; when they go wrong, who is to judge?
2. Why do you think Salt calls the animals "innocent" rather than, for example, "helpless" or "dumb"? What does Salt's choice of vocabulary tell about his thinking? The thinking of the time? Why do you think Salt humanizes animals when he describes what he sees as their plight?
3. If treatment of animals is *our* problem — that is, a moral problem — then why shouldn't Salt use a vocabulary that reflects society behaving in a certain manner rather than one that reflects the way he thinks animals feel? What words in Salt's essay reflect Salt speaking for the animals (for example, he says they are *innocent*) and what words reflect Salt speaking for people (for example, he says they act with *brutality*)?

Writing

1. What is your own position about human responsibility toward animals? Consider one of the following, and write a logical argument either for or against it:
   a. eating meat
   b. being a vegetarian
   c. killing for sport
   d. using animals in laboratory experiments
   e. killing animals for fur, hides, or feathers

2. Write an essay in which you explore how we often interpret animals' feelings in our own terms. Have you ever watched people at the zoo? Observed someone with a pet? You might want to consider the value of pets for people living alone, or for the elderly, *because* they interact with the animals on human terms, talking to them and caring about them. Consider cartoons and comics with animal characters.

3. Read again Jacob Bronowski's essay "The Reaches of Imagination," in chapter 8. Consider both Bronowski's and Salt's views of animal behavior, and then write an essay in which you argue for or against the idea that animals, having no imagination, therefore have no fear, and that humans, with imagination, have fear which they project onto animals, imagining they suffer when they are used in laboratory experiments. Quote from both Bronowski and Salt to support your argument.

Alice Walker

Alice Walker (b. 1944) was born in Georgia and educated at Sarah Lawrence College. A poet, a writer, and a teacher, Walker has been writer-in-residence at numerous universities, where she has taught Afro-American studies and black studies. An editor of the feminist magazine, *Ms*, she is perhaps best known for her novel *The Color Purple*, for which she won a Pulitzer Prize. In the selection here, which comes from Janet Sternburg's collection *The Writer on Her Work*, Walker explains quite dramatically and explicitly her need for having a child, as she tells how her creative life—the writing—has been affected by R's presence.

One Child of One's Own: A Meaningful Digression within the Work(s)

Someone asked me once whether I thought women artists should have children, and, since we were beyond discussing why this question is never asked artists who are men, I gave my answer promptly.

"Yes," I said, somewhat to my surprise. And, as if to amend my rashness, I added: "They should have children—*assuming this is of interest to them*—but only one."

In the work of this essay, and beyond this essay, I am indebted to the courageous and generous spirits of Tillie Olsen, Barbara Smith, and Gloria Steinem.

"Why only one?" this Someone wanted to know.

"Because with one you can move," I said. "With more than one you're a sitting duck."

The year after my only child, R, was born, my mother offered me uncharacteristically bad advice: "You should have another one soon," said she, "so that R will have someone to play with, and so you can get it all over with faster."

Such advice does not come from what a woman recalls of her own experience. It comes from a pool of such misguidance women have collected over the millennia to help themselves feel less foolish for having more than one child. This pool is called, desperately, pitiably, "Women's Wisdom." In fact it should be called "Women's Folly."

The rebellious, generally pithy advice that comes from a woman's own experience more often resembles my mother's automatic response to any woman she meets who pines for children but has been serenely blessed with none: "If the Lord sets you free, be free indeed." This crafty justification of both nonconformity and a shameless reveling in the resultant freedom is what women and slaves everywhere and in every age since the Old Testament have appropriated from the Bible.

"No, thank you," I replied. "I will never have another child out of this body again."

"But why do you say that?" she asked breathlessly, perhaps stunned by my redundancy. "You married a man who's a wonderful fatherly type. He has so much love in him he should have fifty children running around his feet."

I saw myself stamping them out from around his feet like so many ants. If they're running around his feet for the two hours between the time he comes home from the office and the time we put them to bed, I thought, they'd be underneath my desk all day. Stamp, Stamp.

My mother continued: "Why," she said, "until my fifth child I was like a young girl. I could pick up and go anywhere I wanted to." She *was* a young girl. She was still under twenty-five when her fifth child was born, my age when I became pregnant with R. Besides, since I am the last child in a family of eight, this image of nimble flight is not the one lodged forever in my mind. I remember a woman struggling to get everyone else dressed for church on Sunday and only with the greatest effort being able to get ready on time herself. But, since I am not easily seduced by the charms of painful past experience, recalled in present tranquility, I did not bring this up.

At the time my mother could "pick up and go" with five children, she and my father traveled, usually, by wagon. I can see how that would have been pleasant: it is pleasant still in some countries — in parts of China, Cuba, Jamaica, Mexico, Greece, etc., etc. A couple of slow mules, ambling along a bright southern road, the smell of pine and honeysuckle, absence of smog, birds chirping. Those five dear little voices piping up in back of the wagon seat, healthy from natural foods: Plums! Bird! Tree! Flowers! Scuppernongs! Enchanting. *

"The other reason I will never have another child out of this body is because having a child *hurts*, even more than toothache (and I am sure no one who has had toothache but not childbirth can imagine this), and it changes the body."

Well, there are several responses from the general supply of Women's Folly my mother could have chosen to answer this. She chose them all.

"*That* little pain," she scoffed. (*Although from her own experience, which, caught in a moment of weakness for truth she has let slip, she has revealed that during my very own birth the pain was so severe she could not speak, not even to tell the midwife I had been born, and that because of the pain she was sure she would die—a thought that no doubt, under the circumstances, afforded relief. Instead, she blacked out, causing me to be almost smothered by the bedclothes.*) "That pain is over before you know it." That is response #1. #2 is, "The thing about that kind of pain is that it does a funny thing to a woman (*Uh-oh, I thought, this is going to be the Women's Folly companion to the 'women sure are funny creatures,' stuff*); looks like the more it hurts you to give birth, the more you love the child." (*Is that why she loves me so much, I wonder. Naturally, I had wanted to be loved for myself, not for her pain.*) #3. "Sometimes the pain, they say, isn't even real. Well, not as real as it feels at the time." (*This one deserves comment made only with blows, and is one of the reasons women sometimes experience muscle spasms around their mothers.*) And then, #4, the one that angers me most of all: "Another thing about the pain, you soon forget it."

Am I mistaken in thinking I have never forgotten a pain in my life. Even those at parties, I remember.

"I remember every moment of it perfectly," I said. "Furthermore, I don't like stretch marks. I hate them, especially on my thighs" (which are otherwise gorgeous, and of which I am vain). Nobody had told me that my body, after bearing a child, would not be the same. I had heard things like: "Oh, your figure, and especially your breasts [of which I am also vain] will be better than ever." They sagged.

Well, why did I have a child in the first place?

Curiosity. Boredom. Avoiding the draft. Of these three reasons, I am redeemed only by the first. Curiosity is my natural state and has led me headlong into every worthwhile experience (never mind the others) I have ever had. It justifies itself. Boredom, in my case, means a lull in my writing, emotional distance from whatever political movement I am involved in, inability to garden, read, or daydream—easily borne if there are at least a dozen good movies around to attract me. Alas, in Jackson, Mississippi, where my husband, M, and I were living in 1968, there were few. About the draft we had three choices: the first, C.O. status for M, was immediately denied us, as was "alternative service to one's country," which meant, in his case, legally desegregating a violent, frightening, rigidly segregated Mississippi; the second was to move to Canada, which did not thrill me, but which I would gladly have done rather than have M go to prison. (Vietnam was never one of our choices.) The third was, if M could not become twenty-six years old in time, to make of him "a family man."

My bad days were spent in depression, anxiety, rage against the war and a state of apprehension over the amount of rainfall there is annually in Vancouver, and the slow rate of racial "progress" in Mississippi. (Politicians were considered "progressive" if they announced they were running for a certain office as candidates "for *all* the people;" this was a subtle—they thought—announcement to blacks that their existence was acknowledged.) I was also trying to become pregnant.

My good days were spent teaching, writing a simple history pamphlet for use in black day-care centers in Jackson, recording black women's autobiographies, making a quilt (African fabrics, Mississippi string pattern), completing my second book, a novel, and trying to become pregnant.

Three days after I finished the novel, R was born. The pregnancy: the first three months I vomited. The middle three I felt fine and
flew off to look at ruins in Mexico. The last three I was so huge—I
looked like someone else, which did not please me.

What is true about giving birth is . . . that it is miraculous. It
might even be the one genuine miracle in life (which is, by the
way, the basic belief of many "primitive" religions). The "miracle"
of nonbeing, death, certainly pales, I would think, beside it. So to
speak.

For one thing, though my stomach was huge and the baby (?!)
constantly causing turbulence within it, I did not believe a baby, a
person, would come out of me. I mean, look what had gone *in*. (Men
have every right to be envious of the womb. I'm envious of it myself,
and I have one.) But there she was, coming out, a black, curling lock
of hair the first part to be seen, followed by nearly ten pounds of—a
human being!

Reader, I *stared*.

But this hymn of praise I, anyhow, have heard before, and will
not permit myself to repeat it, since there are, in fact, very few
variations, and these have become boring and shopworn. They were   *
boring and shopworn even at the birth of Christ, which is no doubt
why "Virgin Birth" and "Immaculate Conception" were all the rage.

The point is, I was changed forever. From a woman whose
"womb" had been, in a sense, her head; that is to say, certain small
seeds had gone in, rather different if not larger or better "creations"
had come out, to a woman who had "conceived" books in her head,
and had also engendered at least one human being in her body.

Well, I wondered, with great fear, where is the split in me now?   *
What is the damage? Was it true, as "anonymous"—so often a woman
with distressing observations—warned: "Women have not created as
fully as men because once she has a child a woman can not give herself
to her work the way a man can . . . etc, etc?" Was I, as a writer, *done
for*? So much of Women's Folly, literary and otherwise, makes us feel
constricted by experience rather than enlarged by it. Curled around
my baby, feeling more anger and protectiveness than love, I thought
of at least two sources of folly resistance Women's Folly lacks. It lacks
all conviction that women have the ability to plan their lives for

periods longer than nine months, and it lacks the courage to believe that experience, and the expression of that experience, may simply be different, *unique*, rather than "greater" or "lesser." The art or literature that saves our lives *is great to us*, in any case: more than that, as a Grace Paley character might say, we do not need to know.

I was suddenly a mother. Combating the Women's Folly in my own head was the first thing. The urge was primal: the desire to live *and to appreciate my own unique life, as no one other than—myself.

It helped tremendously that by the time R was born I had no doubts about being a writer (doubts about making a *living* by writing, always). Write I did, night and day, *something*, and it was not even a choice, as having a baby was a choice, but a necessity. When I didn't write I thought of making bombs and throwing them. Of shooting racists. Of doing away—as painlessly and neatly as possible (except when I indulged in kamikaze tactics of rebellion in my daydreams) with myself. Writing saved me from the sin and *inconvenience* of violence—as it saves most writers who live in "interesting" oppressive times and are not afflicted by personal immunity.

I began to see, during a period when R and I were both ill— we had moved to Cambridge for a year and a half because I needed a change from Mississippi—that her birth, and the difficulties it pro- *vided us, joined me to a body of experience and a depth of commit- ment to my own life, hard to comprehend, otherwise. Her birth was the incomparable gift of seeing the world at quite a different angle than before, and judging it by standards that would apply far beyond my natural life. It also forced me to understand, viscerally, women's *need for a store of Women's Folly and yet feel on firm ground in my rejection of it. But rejection also has its pain. . . .

I feel very little guilt (most days) about the amount of time "taken from my daughter" by my work. I was amazed to discover I could read a book and she could exist at the same time. And how soon she learned that there are other things to enjoy besides myself. Between an abstracted, harassed adult and an affectionate sitter or neighbor's child who can be encouraged to return a ball, there is no contest, as one knows.

There *was* a day, when, finally after five years of writing *Meridian* (a book "about" the civil rights movement, feminism, socialism, the

shakiness of revolutionaries and the radicalization of saints—the kind
of book out of the political sixties that white feminist scholar Francine
du Plessix Gray declared recently in the *New York Times Book Review*
did not exist) I felt a pang.

I wrote this self-pitying poem:

Now that the book is finished,
now that I know my characters will live,
I can love my child again.
She need sit no longer
at the back of my mind
the lonely sucking of her thumb
a giant stopper in my throat

But this was as much celebration as anything. After all, the book
was finished, the characters *would* live, and of course I'd loved my
daughter all along. As for "the giant stopper in my throat," perhaps
it is the fear of falling silent, *mute*, writers have from time to time.
This fear is a hazard of the work itself, which requires a *severity* toward
the self that is often overwhelming in its discomfort, more than it is
the existence of one's child, who, anyway, by the age of seven, at
the latest, is one's friend, and can be told of the fears one has, that
she can, by listening to one, showing one a new dance step, perhaps,
sharing a coloring book, or giving one a hug, help allay.

In any case, it is not my child who tells me I have no femaleness
white women must affirm. Not my child who says I have no rights
black men or black women must respect.

It is not my child who has purged my face from history and
herstory and left mystory just that, a mystery; my child loves my face
and would have it on every page, if she could, as I have loved my
own parents' faces above all others, and have refused to let them be
denied, or myself to let them go.

Not my child, who in a way *beyond* all this, but really of a piece
with it, destroys the planet daily, and has begun on the universe.   *

We are together, my child and I. Mother and child, yes, but   *
sisters really, against whatever denies us all that we are.

For a long time I had this sign, which I constructed myself, deliberately, out of false glitter, over my desk:

Dear Alice,

Virginia Woolf had madness;
George Eliot had ostracism,
somebody else's husband,
and did not dare to use
her own name.
Jane Austen had no privacy
and no love life.
The Brontë sisters never went anywhere
and died young
and dependent on their father.
Zora Hurston (ah!) had no money
and poor health.

You have R—who is
much more delightful
and less distracting
than any of the calamities
above.

Thinking about Writing

Words

Powerful words both depend on and help shape their context. In what way does each word in the list below depend on its context for strength? What does each contribute to its context? Can you think of any other word the author might have used in its place? How does the word strike you, and how do you respond to the sentence or passage because of the word?

enchanting
boring and shopworn
split
primal
body
viscerally
destroys
together

Thinking

1. Walker says, "So much of Women's Folly, literary and otherwise, makes us feel constricted by experience rather than enlarged by it." Do you agree with Walker? If you do, can you think of any cultural or historical reasons why women should be made to feel constricted by experience? Do you think women mask the effects of experience, as society dictates, in order to conform with expectations, so that if they do have experience they pretend otherwise? Are little girls allowed the free range of experience that little boys are? Does society, in fact, encourage males to have experience while it discourages females? Does your own life reflect Walker's statement?

2. Why do you think Walker includes conversations with her mother here? What does the mother's presence represent in this dialogue? What do you gather Women's Folly is? Is there an equivalent Men's Folly?

3. How does Walker play on the word, *work(s)*? When something is "in the works," what is happening? What's the difference between *work* and *works*? Why do you think Walker wants to be free to move and not be a "sitting duck"? Do you think the "sitting duck" concept belongs to all women or only to women artists? What does "sitting duck" imply?

Writing

1. Walker asks, "Was I, as a writer, *done for?*" after R, her daughter, was born. Why don't men ask this kind of question after the birth of their children? Do you think they should?

Write an essay in which you present an argument for what you consider is the best way of arranging parenting and career(s). If you can, offer some examples from your own observation of couples with a child or children. If you believe women should not combine a career outside the home with motherhood, frame your argument to defend this position. If you think fathers should raise children, tell why you think so. Try to include economic evidence as well as moral judgment in your essay.

2. Walker says having R was a choice made through curiosity, boredom, and the wish for M to avoid the draft. She then says that her writing was a necessity, not a choice. "Write I did, night and day, *something*, and it was not even a choice, as having a baby was a choice, but a necessity."

   Write about two experiences you have had, one the result of carefully weighing options and finally making a choice to act and the other a "necessity," in the sense that it had to be. Explain the forces behind the necessity as well as the reasons for the choice. Which of the two experiences has been most meaningful for you? If you find that the "necessity" has been, what can you say about choice?

   Were the two experiences connected or related in any way? For example, you might have chosen a particular college, but along the way as you took various courses you became aware of the "necessity" to pursue one line of study—you simply had to.

Samuel Johnson

Samuel Johnson (1709–84) was born in England into a family of poor but educated booksellers. Johnson was, in spite of his own education and recognition, to remain poor for most of his life. However, he read widely, even as a child, and claimed that he knew as much at eighteen as he did at fifty-two. A willing patron helped him attend Oxford University for a few years, but poverty eventually forced him back into the working world, where he began to live "by literature and wit," writing, translating, teaching, and selling books. He taught Latin, which he insisted on speaking in France, and Greek. He contributed to two magazines of the day, the *Idler* and the *Rambler*. His great work, *A Dictionary of the English Language*, appeared in 1755. A few years later, he met the young James Boswell, who would write Johnson's biography. In the selection here, which appeared in the *Rambler*, Johnson argues that laziness is a human weakness, and although "to act is far easier than to suffer," we all procrastinate.

Idleness a Miserable State

Quis scit, an adjiciant hodiernae crastina summae Tempora Di superi!

Horace

Who knows if Heav'n, with ever-bounteous pow'r,
Shall add to-morrow to the present hour?

Francis

I sat yesterday morning employed in deliberating on which, among the various subjects that occurred to my imagination, I should bestow the paper of to-day. After a short effort of meditation by which nothing was determined, I grew every moment more irresolute, my ideas wandered from the first intention, and I rather wished to think, than thought, upon any settled subject; till at last I was awakened from this dream of study by a summons from the press; the time was come for which I had been thus negligently purposing to provide, and, however dubious or sluggish, I was now necessitated to write.

Though to a writer whose design is so comprehensive and mis-   *
cellaneous, that he may accommodate himself with a topick from every scene of life, or view of nature, it is no great aggravation of his task to be obliged to a sudden composition; yet I could not forbear to reproach myself for having so long neglected what was unavoidably to be done, and of which every moment's idleness increased the difficulty. There was however some pleasure in reflecting that I, who had only trifled till diligence was necessary, might still congratulate myself upon my superiority to multitudes, who have trifled till diligence is vain; who can by no degree of activity or resolution recover the opportunities which have slipped away; and who are condemned by their own carelessness to hopeless calamity and barren sorrow.   *

The folly of allowing ourselves to delay what we know cannot be finally escaped, is one of the general weaknesses, which, in spite of the instruction of moralists, and the remonstrances of reason, prevail to a greater or less degree in every mind; even they who most steadily withstand it, find it, if not the most violent, the most pertinacious of their passions, always renewing its attacks, and though often vanquished, never destroyed.

It is indeed natural to have particular regard to the time present, and to be most solicitous for that which is by its nearness enabled to make the strongest impressions. When therefore any sharp pain is to be suffered, or any formidable danger to be incurred, we can scarcely exempt ourselves wholly from the seducements of imagination; we readily believe that another day will bring some support or advantage which we now want; and are easily persuaded, that the moment of necessity which we desire never to arrive, is at a great distance from us.

Thus life is languished away in the gloom of anxiety, and con- *
sumed in collecting resolutions which the next morning dissipates; in
forming purposes which we scarcely hope to keep, and reconciling
ourselves to our own cowardice by excuses, which, while we admit
them, we know to be absurd. Our firmness is, by the continual contemplation of misery, hourly impaired; every submission to our fear
enlarges its dominion; we not only waste that time in which the evil
we dread might have been suffered and surmounted, but even, where
procrastination produces no absolute increase of our difficulties, make
them less superable to ourselves by habitual terrors. When evils cannot be avoided, it is wise to contract the interval of expectation; to
meet the mischiefs which will overtake us if we fly; and suffer only
their real malignity, without the conflicts of doubt, and anguish of
anticipation.

To act is far easier than to suffer; yet we every day see the
progress of life retarded by the *vis inertiae*,[1] the mere repugnance to
motion, and find multitudes repining at the want of that which nothing but idleness hinders them from enjoying. The case of Tantalus, in
the region of poetick punishment, was somewhat to be pitied, because
the fruits that hung about him retired from his hand; but what tenderness can be claimed by those who, though perhaps they suffer the
pains of Tantalus, will never lift their hands for their own relief?

There is nothing more common among this torpid generation
than murmurs and complaints; murmurs at uneasiness which only
vacancy and suspicion expose them to feel, and complaints of dis-
tresses which it is in their own power to remove. Laziness is commonly
associated with timidity. Either fear originally prohibits endeavours by
infusing despair of success; or the frequent failure of irresolute struggles, and the constant desire of avoiding labour, impress by degrees
false terrours on the mind. But fear, whether natural or acquired,
when once it has full possession of the fancy, never fails to employ it
upon visions of calamity, such as, if they are not dissipated by useful
employment, will soon overcast it with horrors, and embitter life not
only with those miseries by which all earthly beings are really more
or less tormented, but with those which do not yet exist; and which
can only be discerned by the perspicacity of cowardice. *

[1] *vis inertiae*: the force of inertia. — Ed.

Among all who sacrifice future advantage to present inclination, scarcely any gain so little as those that suffer themselves to freeze   *
in idleness. Others are corrupted by some enjoyment of more or less power to gratify the passions; but to neglect our duties, merely to avoid the labour of performing them, a labour which is always punctually rewarded, is surely to sink under weak temptations. Idleness never can secure tranquillity; the call of reason and of conscience will pierce the closest pavilion of the sluggard, and though it may not have force to drive him from his down, will be loud enough to hinder him from sleep. Those moments which he cannot resolve to make useful by devoting them to the great business of his being, will still be usurped by powers that will not leave them to his disposal; remorse and vexation will seize upon them, and forbid him to enjoy what he is so desirous to appropriate.

There are other causes of inactivity incident to more active faculties and more acute discernment. He to whom many objects of pursuit arise at the same time, will frequently hesitate between different desires, till a rival has precluded him, or change his course as new attractions prevail, and harass himself without advancing. He who sees different ways to the same end, will, unless he watches carefully over his own conduct, lay out too much of his attention upon the comparison of probabilities, and the adjustment of expedients, and pause in the choice of his road till some accident intercepts his journey. He whose penetration extends to remote consequences, and who, whenever he applies his attention to any design, discovers new prospects of advantage, and possibilities of improvement, will not easily be persuaded that his project is ripe for execution; but will superadd one contrivance to another, endeavor to unite various purposes in one operation, multiply complications, and refine niceties, till he is entangled in his own scheme, and bewildered in the perplexity of   *
various intentions. He that resolves to unite all the beauties of situation in a new purchase, must waste his life in roving to no purpose from province to province. He that hopes in the same house to obtain every convenience, may draw plans and study Palladio, but will never lay a stone. He will attempt a treatise on some important subject, and amass materials, consult authours, and study all the dependant and collateral parts of learning, but never conclude himself qualified to write. He that has abilities to conceive perfection, will not easily

be content without it; and since perfection cannot be reached, will lose the opportunity of doing well in the vain hope of unattainable excellence.

The certainty that life cannot be long, and the probability that it will be much shorter than nature allows, ought to awaken every man to the active prosecution of whatever he is desirous to perform. It is true, that no diligence can ascertain success; death may intercept the swiftest career; but he who is cut off in the execution of an honest undertaking, has at least the honour of falling in his rank, and has fought the battle though he missed the victory.

Thinking about Writing

Words

Powerful words both depend on and help shape their context. In what way does each word in the list below depend on its context for strength? What does each contribute to its context? Can you think of any other word the author might have used in its place? How does the word strike you, and how do you respond to the sentence or passage because of the word?

design
barren
gloom
perspicacity of cowardice
freeze
bewildered in

Thinking

1. Do you find Johnson's reminder that "perfection cannot be reached" acceptable? Does this idea depress you? When you write a paper or take an examination, do you try to aim for an A, or can you produce good work when you admit you'll probably not get the A? Does aiming for B or C produce inferior work?

2. Johnson says that we should shorten the interval of expectation, "when evils cannot be avoided," and meet the mischiefs, suffering only real discomfort. We *should*, but we frequently don't. Do you think the reason we don't get right to work on an assignment is that we want to avoid discomfort? Which do you feel is the greater discomfort, working or avoiding work?

3. Do you agree with Johnson when he says, "To act is far easier than to suffer"? When you procrastinate, are you an idler, a sluggard in your pavilion of sleep, or someone who gets so entangled in schemes and bewildered "in the perplexity of various intentions that you can't get started working"?

4. What is the pleasure in putting off work? Why do you think we suffer from *vis inertiae*?

Writing

1. Assuming we all procrastinate at one time or another, can you conclude that the pleasure of not working is, for whatever strange reasons, stronger than the imagined discomforts of actual work?

   Write an essay in which you argue that procrastination with all its tensions is nonetheless a pleasure. Because the imagination influences our thinking at these times, you might want to look again at Jacob Bronowski's essay, "The Reaches of Imagination", in chapter 8, as well as rereading Johnson's essay. Give evidence from your own experience to support your argument.

2. According to Johnson, the folly of allowing ourselves to delay required work is, "if not the most violent, the most pertinacious" of our passions, and although we often vanquish it, we never destroy it. Read again Virginia Woolf's essay, "Professions for Women," where she recalls killing the Angel, with great difficulty, as "She died hard." One of the reasons the Angel died hard was her pertinacious nature.

   Write an essay in which you argue that intrusions to work are of two sorts, the ones we devise for ourselves in our idleness and the ones that exist outside us as dangerous interferences. Argue that those outside us may be killed, but those of our own design are merely vanquished periodically but never totally destroyed. Quote from both Woolf and Johnson, and draw on your own observations and experience.

Plato

Plato (428–347 B.C.) was born in Athens to a prosperous family. His being wellborn not only allowed him
to be educated but also placed a burden of responsibility on him, that of upholding the traditions of Periclean
democracy and public service. He became the pupil of the
philosopher Socrates, whose thought Plato recorded for
us to read today. Plato wrote this philosophy in the form
of dialogues, conversations between Socrates and others,
discussing various issues within the structure of questions
and responses. In this selection, which comes from Plato's *Republic*, Socrates is talking with someone named
Glaucon. They are discussing, within a larger framework of
the ideal state, the subject of education. Using the image
of a dark cave with light at the top to represent levels of
enlightenment, they discover what happens when people
either remain uneducated or else become educated to various levels. Those people who are left "in the dark" behave
in their particular fashion, just as those who are enlight-
ened behave in theirs. To render readable and understand-
able what could, after all, be a complicated discussion,
Plato uses the combination of dialogue and allegory—the
cave image with an account of people who either remain
or who climb out.

The Allegory
of the Cave

"Then after this," I said, "liken our nature in its education and
want of education to a condition which I may thus describe. Picture
men in an underground cave-dwelling, with a long entrance reaching
up towards the light along the whole width of the cave; in this they lie
from their childhood, their legs and necks in chains, so that they stay

where they are and look only in front of them, as the chain prevents their turning their heads round. Some way off, and higher up, a fire is burning behind them, and between the fire and the prisoners is a road on higher ground. Imagine a wall built along this road, like the screen which showmen have in front of the audience, over which they show the puppets."

"I have it," he said.

"Then picture also men carrying along this wall all kinds of articles which overtop it, statues of men and other creatures in stone and wood and other materials; naturally some of the carriers are speaking, others are silent."

"A strange image and strange prisoners," he said.

"They are like ourselves," I answered. "For in the first place do you think that such men would have seen anything of themselves or of each other except the shadows thrown by the fire on the wall of the cave opposite to them?"

"How could they," he said, "if all their life they had been forced to keep their heads motionless?"

"What would they have seen of the things carried along the wall? Would it not be the same?"

"Surely."

"Then if they were able to talk with one another, do you not think that they would suppose what they saw to be the real things?"

"Necessarily."

"Then what if there were in their prison an echo from the opposite wall? When any one of those passing by spoke, do you imagine that they could help thinking that the voice came from the shadow passing before them?"

"No, certainly not," he said.

"Then most assuredly," I said, "the only truth that such men would conceive would be the shadows of those manufactured articles?" *

"That is quite inevitable," he said.

"Then consider," I said, "the manner of their release from their bonds and the cure of their folly, supposing that they attained their natural destiny in some such way as this. Let us suppose one of them *
released, and forced suddenly to stand up and turn his head, and walk and look towards the light. Let us suppose also that all these actions gave him pain, and that he was too dazed to see the objects whose

shadows he had been watching before. What do you think he would say if he were told by someone that before he had been seeing mere foolish phantoms, while now he was nearer to being, and was turned to what in a higher degree is, and was looking more directly at it? And further, if each of the several figures passing by were pointed out to him, and he were asked to say what each was, do you not think that he would be perplexed, and would imagine that the things he had seen before were truer than those pointed out to him?"

"Yes, much truer," he said.

"Then if he were forced to look at the light itself, would not his eyes ache, and would he not try to escape, and turn back to things which he could look at, and think that they were really more distinct than the things shown him?"

"Yes," he said.

"But," I said, "if someone were to drag him out up the steep *
and rugged ascent, and did not let go till he had been dragged up to the light of the sun, would not his forced journey be one of pain and annoyance; and when he came to the light, would not his eyes be so full of the glare that he would not be able to see a single one of the objects we now call true?"

"Certainly, not all at once," he said.

"Yes, I fancy that he would need time before he could see things in the world above. At first he would most easily see shadows, then the reflections in water of men and everything else, and, finally, the things themselves. After that he could look at the heavenly bodies and the sky itself by night, turning his eyes to the light of the stars and the moon more easily than to the sun or to the sun's light by day?"

"Surely."

"Then, last of all, I fancy he would be able to look at the sun and observe its nature, not its appearances in water or on alien material, *
but the very sun itself in its own place?"

"Inevitably," he said.

"And that done, he would then come to infer concerning it *
that it is the sun which produces the seasons and years, and controls everything in the sphere of the visible, and is in a manner the author of all those things which he and his fellow-prisoners used to see?"

"It is clear that this will be his next conclusion," he said.

"Well, then, if he is reminded of his original abode and its wisdom, and those who were then his fellow-prisoners, do you not think he will pity them and count himself happy in the change?"

"Certainly."

"Now suppose that those prisoners had had among themselves a system of honors and commendations, that prizes were granted to the man who had the keenest eye for passing objects and the best memory for which usually came first, and which second, and which came together, and who could most cleverly conjecture from this what was likely to come in the future, do you think that our friend would think longingly of those prizes and envy the men whom the prisoners honor and set in authority? Would he not rather feel what Homer describes, and wish earnestly

To live on earth a swain,
Or serve a swain for hire,[1]

or suffer anything rather than be so the victim of seeming and live in their way?"

"Yes," he said, "I certainly think that he would endure anything rather than that."

"Then consider this point," I said. "If this man were to descend again and take his seat in his old place, would not his eyes be full of darkness because he had just come out of the sunlight?"

"Most certainly," he said.

"And suppose that he had again to take part with the prisoners there in the old contest of distinguishing between the shadows, while his sight was confused and before his eyes had got steady (and it might take them quite a considerable time to get used to the darkness), would not men laugh at him, and say that having gone up above he had come back with his sight ruined, so that it was not worth while even to try to go up? And do you not think that they would kill him who tried to release them and bear them up, if they could lay hands on him, and slay him?"

"Certainly," he said.

"Now this simile, my dear Glaucon, must be applied in all its parts to what we said before; the sphere revealed by sight being

[1]swain: peasant; serve a swain for hire: be a peasant's servant. —Ed.

contrasted with the prison dwelling, and the light of the fire therein with the power of the sun. If you will set the upward ascent and the seeing of the things in the upper world with the upward journey of the soul to the intelligible sphere, you will have my surmise; and that is what you are anxious to have. Whether it be actually true, God knows. But this is how it appears to me. In the world of knowledge the Form of the good is perceived last and with difficulty, but when it is seen it must be inferred that it is the cause of all that is right and beautiful in all things, producing in the visible world light and the lord of light, and being itself lord in the intelligible world and the giver of truth and reason, and this Form of the good must be seen by whosoever would act wisely in public or in private."

"I agree with you," he said, "so far as I am capable."

"Come, then," I said, "and agree with me in this also; and don't be surprised that they who have come thus far are unwilling to trouble themselves with mortal affairs, and that their souls are ever eager to dwell above. For this is but natural if the image we have related is true."

"It is," he said.

"Then do you think it at all surprising," I said, "if one who has come from divine visions to human miseries plays a sorry part and appears very ridiculous when, with eyes still confused and before he has got properly used to the darkness that is round him, he is compelled to contend in law courts or elsewhere concerning the shadows of the just or the images which throw those shadows, or to dispute concerning the manner in which those images are conceived by men who have never seen real justice?"

"No, it is anything but surprising," he said.

"Yes," I said, "a sensible man would remember that the eyes may be confused in two ways, and for two reasons—by a change from light to darkness, or from darkness to light. He will consider that the same may happen with the soul, and when he sees a soul in trouble and unable to perceive, he will not laugh without thinking; rather he will examine whether it has come from a brighter light and is dim because it is not accustomed to the darkness, or whether it is on its way from ignorance to greater brightness and is dazzled with the greater brilliance; and so he will count the first happy in its condition and its life, but the second he will pity, and if he please to laugh at it, his laughter will be less ridiculous than that of him who laughs at the soul that has come from the light above."

"You speak with great fairness," he said.

"Then," I said, "if these things be true, we must think thus on the subject before us — that education is not what certain of its professors declare it to be. They say, if you remember, that they put knowledge in the soul where no knowledge has been, if men put sight into blind eyes."

"Yes, they do," he said.

"But our present argument," I said, "shows that there resides in each man's soul this faculty and the instrument wherewith he learns, and that it is just as if the eye could not turn from darkness to light unless the whole body turned with it; so this faculty and instrument must be wheeled round together with the whole soul away from that which is becoming, until it is able to look upon and to endure being and the brightest blaze of being; and that we declare to be the good. Do we not?"

"Yes."

"Education, then," I said, "will be an art of doing this, an art of conversion, and will consider in what manner the soul will be turned round most easily and effectively. Its aim will not be to implant vision in the instrument of sight. It will regard it as already possessing that, but as being turned in a wrong direction, and not looking where it ought, and it will try to set this right."

"That seems probable," he said.

Thinking about Writing

Words

Powerful words both depend on and help shape their context. In what way does each word in the list below depend on its context for strength? What does each contribute to its context? Can you think of any other word the author might have used in its place? How does the word strike you, and how do you respond to the sentence or passage because of the word?

manufactured
natural.
drag
nature
infer

Thinking

1. Why do you think the Form of the good is perceived last and with
   much difficulty? Wouldn't education and life be more pleasant if
   the good could be taught, and learned, first with everything else
   to follow? Why isn't good taught first?
2. Do you agree with Plato that we know only what we perceive?
   That education must not be a filling up of an empty brain but
   rather a turning toward the right direction? That if we perceive
   only shadows, we believe those are real objects?
3. Why do you suppose people "still in the dark" resent anyone who'd
   try to take them up to the light, so much that they'd kill this person
   if they could? Why do people resent any disruption of what they
   see as an adequate life? Why do you think people feel threatened
   when their "adequate" lives are questioned?
4. Plato says when the man who comes out of the cave looks at the
   light his eyes ache. In what way is "ignorance bliss" and knowledge
   disruptive?

Writing

1. "The only truth that such men would conceive would be the
   shadows of those manufactured articles." Socrates asks Glaucon,
   referring to people still chained in the cave. In what way are we
   "kept in the dark" about politics, power, health issues, pollution,
   acts of terrorism, civil rights, so that we tend to believe shadows
   are truths? How does the language of media and of those "in the
   know" tend to keep people in caves? If the people chained in caves
   believe shadows are truths, then do you think they should be told
   the truth or left where they are, presumably, quite contented?

   Write an essay in which you present an argument supporting
   or opposing keeping people "in the dark."

2. Why do people who have "seen the light" resent troubling themselves about mortal affairs? Why do people who are still in the dark resent those who have gone up to the light coming back down and telling them about shadows and truth?

   Read again Norman Mailer's essay, "Channel 6," in chapter 4, especially the part where he defends his conversation on the television program as reflecting too good an education. How is Mailer reflecting Plato's suggestion that people in the cave strongly resent anyone's trying to drag them up to the light? How is Mailer also telling us that once a person has been up to the light he or she would do anything rather than return to darkness?

   Write an essay that argues in support of this Platonic idea of resentment as it comes from both sides, the one that has seen the light and the one that is still in the dark.

3. Write an essay in which you argue that the purpose of education today does not concern the Form of the good but rather the Form of the most efficient, with power and money as its end, rewarding "the keenest eye for passing objects." Or argue that education does concern the Form of the good.

Jonathan Swift

Jonathan Swift (1667–1745) was born of English parents in Dublin and educated at Trinity College, Dublin, and later at Oxford University. Swift's nonconformist outlook became the basis for a brilliant intellectual life in which he wrote histories and political pamphlets. His most compelling style was to be satire, through which he displayed the evils of humanity as he saw them. *Gulliver's Travels*, recognized as a savage attack on "the vices of all men in all countries," was an instant success. As Dean of St. Patrick's cathedral in Dublin, Swift observed with dismay the oppressed Irish, whom he saw as politically insignificant even as he sympathized with them. In an effort to raise the Irish economic status, and with it their political prestige, he strove to place their manufactures on the competitive world market. As to English oppression of the Irish, Swift saw government without consent of the governed as "the very definition of slavery." In the essay here, written in 1729, Swift scorns the English treatment of the Irish and offers a solution to the problem.

A Modest Proposal

It is a melancholy object to those who walk through this great town or travel in the country, when they see the streets, the roads, and cabin doors, crowded with beggars of the female sex, followed by three, four, or six children, all in rags and importuning every passenger for an alms. These mothers, instead of being able to work for their honest livelihood, are forced to employ all their time in strolling to beg sustenance for their helpless infants, who, as they grow up, either turn thieves for want of work, or leave their dear native country to fight for the Pretender in Spain, or sell themselves to the Barbados.

I think it is agreed by all parties that this prodigious number of children in the arms, or on the backs, or at the heels of their mothers, and frequently of their fathers, is in the present deplorable state of the kingdom a very great additional grievance; and therefore whoever could find out a fair, cheap, and easy method of making these children sound, useful members of the commonwealth would deserve so well of the public as to have his statue set up for a preserver of the nation.

But my intention is very far from being confined to provide only for the children of professed beggars; it is of a much greater extent, and shall take in the whole number of infants at a certain age who are born of parents in effect as little able to support them as those who demand our charity in the streets.

As to my own part, having turned my thoughts for many years upon this important subject, and maturely weighed the several schemes of other projectors, I have always found them grossly mistaken in their computation. It is true, a child just dropped from its *
dam may be supported by her milk for a solar year, with little other nourishment; at most not above the value of two shillings, which the mother may certainly get, or the value in scraps, by her lawful occupation of begging; and it is exactly at one year that I propose to provide for them in such a manner as instead of being a charge upon their parents or the parish, or wanting food and raiment for the rest of their lives, they shall on the contrary contribute to the feeding, and partly to the clothing, of many thousands.

There is likewise another great advantage in my scheme, that it will prevent those voluntary abortions, and that horrid practice of women murdering their bastard children, alas, too frequent among us, sacrificing the poor innocent babes, I doubt, more to avoid the expense than the shame, which would move tears and pity in the most savage and inhuman breast.

The number of souls in this kingdom being usually reckoned one million and a half, of these I calculate there may be about two hundred thousand couples whose wives are breeders; from which number I *
subtract thirty thousand couples who are able to maintain their own children, although I apprehend there cannot be so many under the present distress of the kingdom; but this being granted, there will remain an hundred and seventy thousand breeders. I again subtract fifty thousand for those women who miscarry, or whose children die

by accident or disease within the year. There only remain an hundred and twenty thousand children of poor parents annually born. The question therefore is, how this number shall be reared and provided for, which, as I have already said, under the present situation of affairs, is utterly impossible by all the methods hitherto proposed. For we can neither employ them in handicraft or agriculture; we neither build houses (I mean in the country) nor cultivate land. They can very seldom pick up a livelihood by stealing till they arrive at six years old, except where they are of towardly parts; although I confess they learn the rudiments much earlier, during which time they can however be looked upon only as probationers, as I have been informed by a principal gentleman in the county of Cavan, who protested to me that he never knew above one or two instances under the age of six, even in a part of the kingdom so renowned for the quickest proficiency in that art.   *

I am assured by our merchants that a boy or a girl before twelve years old is no salable commodity; and even when they come to this age they will not yield above three pounds, or three pounds and a half a crown at most on the Exchange; which cannot turn to account either to the parents of the kingdom, the charge of nutriment and rags having been at least four times that value.

I shall now therefore humbly propose my own thoughts, which I hope will not be liable to the least objection.

I have been assured by a very knowing American of my acquaintance in London, that a young healthy child well nursed is at a year old a most delicious, nourishing, and wholesome food, whether stewed, roasted, baked, or boiled; and I make no doubt that it will equally serve in a fricassee or a ragout.

I do therefore humbly offer it to public consideration that of the hundred and twenty thousand children, already computed, twenty thousand may be reserved for breed, whereof only one fourth part to be males, which is more than we allow sheep, black cattle, or swine; and my reason is that these children are seldom the fruits of marriage, a circumstance not much regarded by our savages,   * therefore one male will be sufficient to serve four females. That the remaining hundred thousand may at a year old be offered in sale to the persons of quality and fortune through the kingdom, always advising the mother to let them suck plentifully in the last month, so as to render them plump and fat for a good table. A child will make two dishes at an entertainment for friends; and when the family dines alone, the fore or hind quarter will make a reasonable dish, and seasoned with a little pepper or salt will be very good boiled on the fourth day, especially in winter.

I have reckoned upon a medium that a child just born will weigh twelve pounds, and in a solar year if tolerably nursed increaseth to twenty-eight pounds.

I grant this food will be somewhat dear, and therefore very proper for landlords, who, as they have already devoured most of the *
parents, seem to have the best title to the children.

Infant's flesh will be in season throughout the year, but more plentiful in March, and a little before and after. For we are told by a grave author, an eminent French physician, that fish being a prolific diet, there are more children born in Roman Catholic countries about nine months after Lent than at any other season; therefore, reckoning a year after Lent, the markets will be more glutted than usual, because the number of popish infants is at least three to one in this kingdom; *
and therefore it will have one other collateral advantage, by lessening the number of Papists among us.

I have already computed the charge of nursing a beggar's child (in which list I reckon all cottagers, laborers, and four-fifths of the farmers) to be about two shillings per annum, rags included; and I believe no gentleman would repine to give ten shillings for the carcass of a good fat child, which, as I have said, will make four dishes of excellent nutritive meat, when he hath only some particular friend or his own family to dine with him. Thus the squire will learn to be a good landlord, and grow popular among the tenants; and the mother will have eight shillings net profit, and be fit for work till she produces another child.

Those who are more thrifty (as I must confess the times require) may flay the carcass; the skin of which artificially dressed will make admirable gloves for ladies, and summer boots for fine gentlemen.

As to our city of Dublin, shambles[1] may be appointed for this purpose in the most convenient parts of it, and butchers we may be assured will not be wanting; although I rather recommend buying

[1]shambles: slaughterhouses. —Ed.

the children alive, and dressing them hot from the knife as we do roasting pigs.

A very worthy person, a true lover of his country, and whose virtues I highly esteem, was lately pleased in discoursing on this matter to offer a refinement upon my scheme. He said that many gentlemen of his kingdom, having of late destroyed their deer, he conceived that the want of venison might be well supplied by the bodies of young lads and maidens, not exceeding fourteen years of age nor under twelve, so great a number of both sexes in every county being now ready to starve for want of work and service; and these to be disposed of by their parents, if alive, or otherwise by their nearest relations. But with due deference to so excellent a friend and so deserving a patriot, I cannot be altogether in his sentiments; for as to the males, my American acquaintance assured me from frequent experience that their flesh was generally tough and lean, like that of our schoolboys, by continual exercise, and their taste disagreeable; and to fatten them would not answer the charge. Then as to the females, it would, I think with humble submission, be a loss to the public, because they soon would become breeders themselves; and besides, it is not improbable that some scrupulous people might be apt to censure such a practice (although indeed very unjustly) as a little bordering upon cruelty; * which, I confess, hath always been with me the strongest objection against any project, how well soever intended.

But in order to justify my friend, he confessed that this expedient was put into his head by the famous Psalmanazar, a native of the island Formosa, who came from thence to London above twenty years ago, and in conversation told my friend that in his country when any young person happened to be put to death, the executioner sold the carcass to persons of quality as a prime dainty; and that in his time the body of a plump girl of fifteen, who was crucified for an attempt to poison the emperor, was sold to his Imperial Majesty's prime minister of state, and other great mandarins of the court, in joints from the gibbet, at four hundred crowns. Neither indeed can I deny that if the same use were made of several plump young girls in this town, who without one single groat to their fortunes cannot stir abroad without a chair, and appear at the playhouse and assemblies in foreign fineries which they never will pay for, the kingdom would not be the worse.

Some persons of a desponding spirit are in great concern about   *
that vast number of poor people who are aged, diseased, or maimed,
and I have been desired to employ my thoughts what course may be
taken to ease the nation of so grievous an encumbrance. But I am
not in the least pain upon that matter, because it is very well known
that they are every day dying and rotting by cold and famine, and
filth and vermin, as fast as can be reasonably expected. And as to the
younger laborers, they are now in almost as hopeful a condition. They
cannot get work, and consequently pine away for want of nourishment
to a degree that if any time they are accidentally hired to common
labor, they have not strength to perform it; and thus the country and
themselves are happily delivered from the evils to come.

I have too long digressed, and therefore shall return to my
subject. I think the advantages by the proposal which I have made
are obvious and many, as well as of the highest importance.

For first, as I have already observed, it would greatly lessen
the number of Papists, with whom we are yearly overrun, being the
principal breeders of the nation as well as our most dangerous enemies;
and who stay at home on purpose to deliver the kingdom to the
Pretender, hoping to take their advantage by the absence of so many
good Protestants, who have chosen rather to leave their country than   *
to stay at home and pay tithes against their conscience to an Episcopal
curate.

Secondly, the poorer tenants will have something valuable of
their own, which by law may be made liable to distress, and help to
pay their landlord's rent, their corn and cattle being already seized
and money a thing unknown.

Thirdly, whereas the maintenance of an hundred thousand children, from two years old and upwards, cannot be computed at less
than ten shillings a piece per annum, the nation's stock will be thereby
increased fifty thousand pounds per annum, besides the profit of a new
dish introduced to the tables of all gentlemen of fortune in the kingdom who have any refinement in taste. And the money will circulate
among ourselves, the goods being entirely of our own growth and
manufacture.

Fourthly, the constant breeders, besides the gain of eight
shillings sterling per annum by the sale of their children, will be rid
of the charge of maintaining them after the first year.

Fifthly, this food would likewise bring great custom to taverns, where the vintners will certainly be so prudent as to procure the best receipts for dressing it to perfection, and consequently have their houses frequented by all the fine gentlemen, who justly value themselves upon their knowledge in good eating; and a skillful cook, who understands how to oblige his guests, will contrive to make it as expensive as they please.

Sixthly, this would be a great inducement to marriage, which all wise nations have either encouraged by rewards or enforced by laws and penalties. It would increase the care and tenderness of mothers toward their children, when they were sure of a settlement for life to the poor babes, provided in some sort by the public, to their annual profit instead of expense. We should see an honest emulation among the married women, which of them could bring the fattest child to the market. Men would become as fond of their wives during the time of their pregnancy as they are now of their mares in foal, their cows in calf, or sows when they are ready to farrow; nor offer to beat or kick them (as is too frequent a practice) for fear of a miscarriage.

Many other advantages might be enumerated. For instance, the addition of some thousand carcasses in our exportation of barreled beef, the propagation of swine's flesh, and improvements in the art of making good bacon, so much wanted among us by the great destruction of pigs, too frequent at our tables, which are no way comparable in taste or magnificence to a well-grown, fat, yearling child, which roasted whole will make a considerable figure at a lord mayor's feast or any other public entertainment. But this and many others I omit, being studious of brevity.

Supposing that one thousand families in this city would be constant customers for infants' flesh, besides others who might have it at merry meetings, particularly weddings and christenings, I compute that Dublin would take off annually about twenty thousand carcasses, and the rest of the kingdom (where probably they will be sold somewhat cheaper) the remaining eighty thousand.

I can think of no one objection that will possibly be raised against this proposal, unless it should be urged that the number of people will be thereby much lessened in the kingdom. This I freely own, and it was indeed one principal design in offering it to the world. I desire the reader will observe, that I calculate my remedy for this one individual kingdom of Ireland and for no other that ever was, is, or I think ever can be upon earth. Therefore let no man talk to me of other expedients: of taxing our absentees at five shillings a pound: of using neither clothes nor household furniture except what is of our own growth and manufacture: of utterly rejecting the materials and instruments that promote foreign luxury: of curing the expensiveness of pride, vanity, idleness, and gaming in our women: of introducing a vein of parsimony, prudence, and temperance: of learning to love our country, in the want of which we differ even from Laplanders and the inhabitants of Topinamboo: of quitting our animosities and factions, nor acting any longer like the Jews, who were murdering one another at the very moment their city was taken: of being a little cautious not to sell our country and conscience for nothing: of teaching landlords to have at least one degree of mercy toward their tenants: lastly, of putting a spirit of honesty, industry, and skill into our shopkeepers: who, if a resolution could now be taken to buy only our native goods, would immediately unite to cheat and exact upon us in the price, the measure, and the goodness, nor could ever yet be brought to make one fair proposal of just dealing, though often and earnestly invited to it.

Therefore I repeat, let no man talk to me of these and the like expedients, till he hath at least some glimpse of hope that there will ever be some hearty and sincere attempts to put them in practice.

But as to myself, having been wearied out for many years with offering vain, idle, visionary thoughts, and at length utterly despairing of success, I fortunately fell upon this proposal, which, as it is wholly new, so it hath something solid and real, of no expense and little trouble, full in our own power, and whereby we can incur no danger in disobliging England. For this kind of commodity will not bear exportation, the flesh being of too tender a consistence to admit a long continuance in salt, although perhaps I could name a country which would be glad to eat up our whole nation without it.

After all, I am not so violently bent upon my own opinion as to reject any offer proposed by wise men, which shall be found equally innocent, cheap, easy, and effectual. But before something of that kind shall be advanced in contradiction to my scheme, and offering a better, I desire the author or authors will be pleased maturely to consider two points. First, as things now stand, how they will be

able to find food and raiment for an hundred thousand useless mouths *
and backs. And secondly, there being a round million of creatures
in human figure throughout this kingdom, whose sole subsistence put
into a common stock would leave them in debt two millions of pounds
sterling, adding those who are beggars by profession to the bulk of
farmers, cottagers, and laborers, with their wives and children who
are beggars in effect; I desire those politicians who dislike my overture,
and may perhaps be so bold to attempt an answer, that they will first
ask the parents of these mortals whether they would not at this day
think it a great happiness to have been sold for food at a year old in this
manner I prescribe, and thereby have avoided such a perpetual scene
of misfortunes as they have since gone through by the oppression of
landlords, the impossibility of paying rent without money or trade, the
want of common sustenance, with neither house nor clothes to cover
them from the inclemencies of the weather, and the most inevitable
prospect of entailing the like or greater miseries upon their breed
forever.

I profess, in the sincerity of my heart, that I have not the
least personal interest in endeavoring to promote this necessary work,
having no other motive than the public good of my country, by
advancing our trade, providing for infants, relieving the poor, and
giving some pleasure to the rich. I have no children by which I can
propose to get a single penny; the youngest being nine years old, and
my wife past childbearing.

Thinking about Writing

Words

Powerful words both depend on and help shape their context. In
what way does each word in the list below depend on its context for
strength? What does each contribute to its context? Can you think of
any other word the author might have used in its place? How does the
word strike you, and how do you respond to the sentence or passage
because of the word?

dropped . . . dam
breeders
proficiency
our savages
devoured
popish infants
cruelty
desponding
good
mouths and backs

Thinking

1. Irony is a simulation of innocence. Swift's speaker, under the guise of innocence, proposes eating Irish babies as a solution to Irish economic woes. Not every sentence is written in irony, however. Sometimes Swift's speaker is perfectly serious and straightforward. Point out where he is most ironic and where he is being perfectly serious. How can you tell which writing is ironic and which is not?
2. How does Swift's use of numbers and mathematical terms affect you and your perception of his subject? Why do you think he uses such vocabulary?
3. How does Swift's introducing "a very knowing American" and "the famous Psalmanazar" tell you something about the author's sense of humor?
4. Why do you think Swift calls his proposal "modest"? What is his proposal, and what does he really want?

Writing

1. If irony tends to be funny, how can it be used effectively to discuss serious subjects? This essay seriously examines the poverty and subjugation of the Irish. The irony is so outrageous that while nobody would take it at face value, the writing as a whole remains forceful and convincing. How does Swift propose something so absurd that, while people would not begin to roast Irish babies, they would nonetheless think seriously about the plight of the Irish as a result of reading this essay? Is the force found only in the unironic

parts of the writing or is there powerful argument beneath the irony as well? Write an essay in which you explore the combination of irony with straightforward writing, in order to determine how Swift has used both to convey his concern. Quote from the essay to support your observations.

2. You need not have read eighteenth-century history to appreciate this essay. Assuming you, like most of us, have a limited knowledge of what was happening when Swift wrote "A Modest Proposal," what clues and references to conditions then can you gather from his writing? In short, what do you know from this essay about life at the time? Where are the clues? Are they embedded in the irony, or are they in all parts of the essay?

Quoting from the essay, write a brief description of the times. You should extrapolate freely, making inferences from Swift's information. You might find it helpful to begin your thinking by making a list of conditions, as they appear in the text. Then, when you have listed a number of them, you can structure your own essay.

Joseph Wood Krutch

Joseph Wood Krutch (1893–1970) was born in Nashville, Tennessee, and educated at the University of Tennessee and Columbia University. Abandoning an early plan to become an engineer, Krutch pursued a career in literature, becoming a scholar and writer. He taught at various universities before eventually finding himself at his own alma mater, Columbia. In addition, Krutch served *The Nation* as its drama critic and was a member of the National Institute of Arts and Letters. A deep concern, bordering on pessimism, for the human condition inspired many of his essays. In his later years, Krutch lived in Arizona, close to nature and far from the stress of city life. There, he speculated on human behavior which he deplored even as he found nature "herself" lacking in compassion. Krutch found only one consolation: the individual. While nature is cruel and governments likewise, individuals alone are capable of love. In the following essay, which comes from a collection of Krutch's essays entitled *The Desert Year*, he deplores the way modern bureaucratic states mimic the impersonal efficiency of nature, aiming for the common good while disregarding the individual. Krutch argues that the only hope lies in this individual.

The Individual
and the Species

A few mornings ago I rescued a bat from a swimming pool. The man who owned the pool—but did not own the bat—asked me why. That question I do not expect ever to be able to answer, but it involves a good deal. If even I myself could understand it, I would know

451

what it is that seems to distinguish man from the rest of nature, and why, despite all she has to teach him, there is also something he would like to teach her if he could.

It is true that I like bats better than most people do. Though the fact that they fly without feathers is a heterodoxy held against them since ancient times, I find it easy to forgive. Moreover, and though I was exposed at an early age to Gustave Doré's illustrations for the *Inferno*, I do not associate leathery wings with Satan. I know that their owners have no special predilection for female tresses and "like a bat out of hell" is not, for me, an especially expressive metaphor. But that is not the reason why I took the trouble to rescue one from drowning.

Nature books always explain—for the benefit of utilitarians—that bats are economically important because they destroy many insects. For the benefit of those more interested in the marvelous than in the profitable, they also usually say something about the bat's wonderful invention of a kind of sonar by the aid of which he can fly in the blackest night without colliding with even so artificial an obstruction as a piano wire strung across his path. But before lifting my particular bat out of the swimming pool, I did not calculate his *
economic importance and I did not rapidly review in my mind the question whether or not his scientific achievement entitled him to life.

Still less could I pretend that he was a rare specimen or that one bat more or less would have any perceptible effect on the balance of nature. There were plenty of others just like him, right here where I live and throughout this whole area. Almost every night I have seen several of his fellows swooping down to the swimming pool for a drink before starting off for an evening of economically useful activity. A few weeks before I had, as a matter of fact, seen near Carlsbad, New Mexico, several hundred thousand of this very species in a single flight. That had seemed like enough bats to satisfy one for a normal lifetime. Yet here I was, not only fishing a single individual from *
the water, but tending him anxiously to see whether or not he could recover from an ordeal which had obviously been almost too much for him.

Probably he had fallen in because he had miscalculated in the course of the difficult maneuver involved in getting a drink on the

wing. Probably, therefore, he had been in the water a good many hours and would not have lasted much longer. But he looked as though he wanted to live and I, inexplicably, also hoped that he would. And that would seem to imply some sort of kindliness more detached, more irrational, and more completely gratuitous than any nature herself is capable of. "So careful of the type she seems, so *
careless of the single life."

At Carlsbad, so it seemed to me, I had seen bats as nature sees them. Here by the swimming pool, I had seen an individual bat as only man can see him. It was a neat coincidence which arranged the two experiences so close together, and I shall always think of them in that way.

At the cave, I had, of course, plenty of company, since the bats constitute one of the official sights of a National Park. Biologists from distant countries often come specially to see them; but to the ordinary tourist their flight is only a side show, to be taken in after a day underground among the twenty-three miles of explored passages in possibly the most extensive cave in the world. Like Old Faithful in the Yellowstone, the bat eruption is reliably predictable and those unwilling to spend much time on nature can attend a scheduled performance.   *

About sunset, the very miscellaneous crowd begins to gather, rather nervously uncertain whether it is exhibiting a cultural interest or just being silly. Presently, the park ranger assigned the job of speaking the prologue that evening climbs a boulder to make a little *
speech, artfully compounded of information and simple, harmless jokes. Tonight, he says, the flight will not be a very large one — probably between two and three hundred thousand bats. Ten years ago, there would have been at least two million, though for once man is not responsible for the declining animal population. The last decade has been unusually dry; that has meant fewer insects and, therefore, fewer bats. Perhaps a relatively wet part of the cycle is about due and the numbers may go up again. But even now there are more than most visitors will care to stay to see.

The bats, he continues, are of the kind called the Mexican free-tailed because the tips of their tails project, as those of most bats do not, a little beyond the leathery membrane which stretches between the hind legs and helps the wings in flight. This bat is the smaller of the two species common in the region, and no one knows how long it has been living in the cave. At least it has been there long enough to lay down vast quantities of guano and hundreds of tons of it were mined out a short generation ago, before chemical fertilizers made the operation unprofitable. Indeed, it was the bats which led to the discovery, within this century, of the caves themselves. Some cowboys went to investigate what they thought was a cloud of smoke from a forest fire, discovered that it was a cloud of bats, instead, and thus were led into the caverns which have not yet been explored to their end.

The ranger pauses, and says that it probably won't be long now. The crowd peers down into a black hole which descends very steeply into the ground. Presently someone, like an excited spectator at the race track, shouts "Here they come," as a single bat rises out of the darkness. Less than a quarter of a second later this first-man-out is followed by another, and another, and another until the air is filled by a vast flying squadron. The bats rise, spiraling in a counterclockwise direction up to the rim of the pit, and then disappear as a long stream headed southward. They will all, says the ranger, take a preliminary drink at a stream a mile or so away and then scatter for the night's foraging, to return one by one after a number of hours which depends on how good the hunting is. By morning at the latest, all will have come back to hang, head downward, from the cave wall. And since the young were left behind, each mother must find her way back in the darkness to her particular place among the hundreds of thousands of her fellows.

Every now and then there is a break of a second or two in the steady stream. Then bats begin to erupt again, as though the mouth * of the cave were some sort of biological volcano spewing Mexican free-tailed bats in endless number. But no, on second thought, that metaphor will not do, for there is none of the undisciplined confusion of an inanimate explosion. In what order they come I do not know. Perhaps simply in the order of their nearness to the mouth of the cave. Neither, for that matter, do I know how, hanging in darkness, they know that outside the sun has gone down. But in any event, this is not the pell-mell of a mob. In New York, the crowds released from the skyscrapers do not make their way out of their canyons or into the caves of their subway in any such orderly fashion. There is no pushing, no shoving, no collision. It is like the relentless, disciplined advance of some armada of the air which makes the boasted thousand-plane raids of the latest world war seem puny indeed.

Presently, the spectators begin to drift away in the order of their conscientiousness in "doing" the sights. Poor as the show is said to be by comparison with the good old days when the Carlsbad bats were really flourishing, it will go on for several hours. Being a medium good sight-seer, I depart at about the time when half of my fellows have already left. As I walk away, I cast my eye back over my shoulder to see that the bats are still coming. For, as Dr. Johnson says, there is a horror in all last things and it may very well be that I shall never see them again.

It is only weeks later that I suddenly remember to ask myself "Why counterclockwise"? Who decided that they should adopt that direction for their spiral, and when did he decide it? Here is a perfect example which Pascal should have known about when he was discussing the fact that it is sometimes less important what a convention is than simply that there should be one. Bat individualists — if, and I doubt it, there are any such things — sensibly confine their protestant behavior to matters significant in themselves and never undertake to demonstrate that there is more than one way of getting out of this cave.

Or is, perhaps, their apparently sensible behavior really a score for the mechanist? In our part of the world, the water that leaves our bathtubs in a miniature whirlpool also spirals counterclockwise because the direction of the earth's rotation tips the otherwise neutral balance in that direction. I have read that in the Southern Hemisphere the normal direction of a vortex is clockwise. Are there bat caves in Africa or in South America and, if there are, then do the bats, I wonder, come out of them clockwise? What would happen if a bat conditioned in the Southern Hemisphere were transported to the north? On all these questions, I had better, I suppose, consult some experts, though I imagine there aren't many. Technically, of course, bats belong to the mammalogists, but because bats are the only mammals which actually fly they don't really fit in anywhere.

456 *Joseph Wood Krutch*

Nature abhors a vacuum—in more senses than one. At Carlsbad she found a good place for bats and so she put a great many of them there. In fact, as the recent decline in their numbers neatly illustrates, she filled the place right up to—and no doubt a little beyond—what the food supply could support. If this method of making sure that there will always be as many as possible means that a few of the weaker will always go to the wall that is to her a matter of indifference.   *

Even I find it difficult to love, in my special human way, as many bats as I saw at Carlsbad. Nature is content to love them in her way and makes no attempt here to love them in the way that even I would fail at. She loves bats in general and as a species. For that reason she can never get enough of them. But as long as there are plenty in the world, she is unconcerned with any particular bat. She gives him his chance (or sometimes his lack of it) and if he does not, or cannot, take it, others will. A margin of failure is to be expected. The greatest good of the greatest number is a ruling principle so absolute that it is not even tempered with regret over those who happen not to be included within the greatest number.

Thus nature discovered, long before the sociologists did, the statistical criterion. Bureaucratic states which accept averages and curves of distribution as realities against which there is no appeal represent a sort of "return to nature" very different from what that phrase is ordinarily taken to imply. Insofar as the great dictators can be assumed to be in any sense sincere when they profess a concern with the welfare of their people or even with that of mankind, their concern is like nature's— indifferent to everything except the statistically measurable result. If they really love men, then they love them only as nature loves bats. She never devised anything so prompt and effective as the gas chamber, but her methods are sometimes almost equally unscrupulous. For she also has her methods—not always pretty ones—of getting rid of what she considers the superfluous. She seems to agree, in principle, with those who maintain that any decisive concern with a mere individual is unscientific, sentimental, and ultimately incompatible with the greatest good of the greatest number.

But one bat in a swimming pool is not the same thing as two or three hundred thousand at Carlsbad. Because there is only one of him and only one of me, some sort of relationship, impossible in the presence of myriads, springs up between us. I no longer take toward him the attitude of nature or the dictator. I become a man again, aware of feelings which are commonly called humane but for which I prefer the stronger word, human.

It was the barking of two young police dogs taking a natural, unsentimental interest in an individual in distress which first called my attention to what I still think of as "my" bat, though I am sure nothing in nature prepared him to believe that I would assume any responsibility for his welfare. At first, I did not know what he was because a fish out of water looks no less inexplicable than a bat in it. The enormous wings attached to his tiny mouse body had helped, no doubt, to keep him afloat, but they were preposterously unmanageable in a dense, resistant medium. The little hooks on his arms by means of which he climbs clumsily on a rough surface were useless on the vertical, tiled sides of the pool. When I lifted him out with a flat wire net, he lay inertly sprawled, his strange body so disorganized as   * to have lost all functional significance, like a wrecked airplane on a mountainside which does not look as though it had ever been able to take to the air.

A slight shiver which shook his body when I leaned over him was the only sign of life. The situation did not look promising, for I knew that a live bat is very much alive, with a heart which sometimes beats more than seven times as fast as mine. Since he obviously needed — if he was not too far gone to need anything — to be dry and to be warm I spread him on top of a wall in the full sun to which he had never, perhaps, been exposed before. Every now and then the tremor recurred; and as his fur dried, I began to be aware of a heart beating furiously. Possibly, I began to say, he may survive. When I bent closer, he raised his head and hissed in my face, exposing a gleaming set of little white teeth before he collapsed exhausted again.

By now his leathery wings were dry and his fur hardly more than damp. But he still seemed incapable of any except the feeblest movements. I thought that at best it would be hours before he would be able to fly. I put a stone beside him to cast a semishadow and was turning away when I caught sight of something out of the corner of my eye. I looked, just in time to see him raise himself suddenly onto his bony elbows and take off. He half-circled the pool to get his bearings and, flying strongly now, he disappeared from my sight over the desert, not permanently the worse, I hope, for a near escape from the death which would not have been very important so far as the total welfare of the bat community is concerned. Inevitably, I have wondered whether he has since been among the bats I see drinking at the pool at evening. Or has he, perhaps, found some body of water with less unpleasant associations?

But why had I done more than, like the dogs, peer at him with curiosity? Why had I felt sad when I thought he would never recover, really joyful when I saw him fly away? He is not economically important, however much his tribe may be. If he had drowned, there would have been others left to catch insects as well as to demonstrate for the benefit of science the bat's sonar. Who am I that I should exhibit a concern which, apparently, the Great Mother of bats (and of men) does not share? What did I accomplish for bats, for myself, or for humanity at large when I fished my bat from the water?

These are not rhetorical questions. They probably have several answers, but there is one of which I am especially aware. What I had done was to keep alive an attitude, an emotion, or better yet a strong passion, of which only the faint beginnings are observable in any creature except man and which, moreover, appear in danger of extinction because of two powerful enemies. This sort of concern with a mere individual is scorned alike by the frank apostles of violent unreason and by those proponents of the greatest good for the greatest number who insist upon being what they call scientific rather than what they call sentimental.

Very often I have wondered over the fact that love for humanity seems so often incompatible with love for individual men and women. It seems almost as though most people have to choose one or the other, and it is an often-observed fact, that those who believe themselves great humanitarians are frequently ruthless with acquaintances and dependents alike. They, however, can at least give the specious explanation that concern with the mere individual must not be allowed to confuse the main issue. But what of the less explicable fact that often the kindest and most considerate people seem little concerned with government and politics? Swift boasted his contempt for humanity and his love for John, Tom, and Harry. Anatole France offered the explanation that to love humanity meant to idealize it and therefore to hate most men for not realizing the ideal. But I have sometimes wondered if the paradox were not rooted in something even more fundamental.

It was nature which loved the race, and it was man who added to that a love for the individual as such. Perhaps those two things, though not really incompatible under all circumstances, become so when one accepts also nature's passion for mere numbers. Perhaps, in other words, there really is something incompatible between the value which we put on the individual and nature's insatiable appetite for more and more of every kind of creature, at no matter what cost either to other species or to the individuals of any one species. Perhaps we have retained too much of her immoderate desire for multiplication while developing our own concern for the individual, whom we think of as rare or irreplaceable. Perhaps in other words, it is easiest to love both man and men when there are not too many (or even not too obviously enough) of the last. Perhaps men should not be too common if they are to have value.

One thing is certain. However many of us there may be or come to be, no man and no group of men should have too much power over $*$ too many of us. It makes such men or such groups feel too much as $**$ though they were nature herself. So careful of the type they are — or claim to be; so careless of the single life they indubitably become.

Thinking about Writing

Words

Powerful words both depend on and help shape their context. In what way does each word in the list below depend on its context for strength? What does each contribute to its context? Can you think of any other word the author might have used in its place? How does the word strike you, and how do you respond to the sentence or passage because of the word?

owned
own

my
single individual
capable
performance
prologue
erupt
go to the wall
disorganized
too (three times in final paragraph)

Thinking

1. Who do you think is the "Individual" of the title? What is the "Species"?
2. How does Krutch use these episodes, the one at the pool and the one at the cave, to introduce and support his argument?
3. Some people say that nature is kind but that humans are not. Krutch reverses this precept. What effect has this reversal on you, the reader?
4. How do both facts and myths about bats contribute to their suitability as subjects for this essay? Could Krutch have used any other animal in place of bats? A snake? A bird?
5. How can you tell from the vocabulary Krutch uses that he prefers the pool bat to the cave bats?
6. Why do you think Krutch personifies nature? Why do you think he doesn't refer to nature simply as a system or a force? Try reading a sentence or two where Krutch refers to nature, but substitute scientific terms for the writer's human ones. What is the result? Which do you prefer? Do you agree that nature is best presented through personification?

Writing

1. According to Krutch, nature is indifferent to the loss of a few when there are so many left. He likens bureaucratic states to nature when they seek the greatest good for the greatest number. Write a brief argument that either supports or refutes this idea. You may wish to read again Mark Twain's essay, "A Campaign That Failed," in chapter 4, which examines one person's reaction to the loss of one

man's life. Perhaps you can find another example of the tendency to seek the common good, often at the expense of the individual. If your sympathy lies with the state rather than with the individual, find examples to support your argument.

2. Joseph Wood Krutch and Jonathan Swift both write arguments that concern humane attitudes toward people. One writes about the individual, the other about government. Each uses a special style to express his sentiments. Each uses a device to whet our appetite as readers and to hold our attention. Both are caring. You can find many other similarities and differences.

   Write an essay comparing and contrasting these two writers, their methods and their messages. At the conclusion of your essay, you may wish to say which essay you prefer or to defend each as apt for itself.

3. Krutch refers to Swift's "contempt for humanity and his love for John, Tom, and Harry." Read again both essays, Swift's and Krutch's, with an eye to discovering what elements in Swift might have appealed to Krutch or inspired him in his own writing. For example, Krutch has written elsewhere that social planners try to design a better world based on what they observe and tell themselves about human behavior, without being true to themselves and their own consciousness. In other words, the place to start social action is in the individual. Swift's writing could easily have inspired this idea. There are other debts to Swiftian thought in Krutch's essay. Try to discover some for yourself; then, write a brief essay based on Krutch's debt to Swift.

Acknowledgments (continued)

Malcolm Cowley, "The View from 80," from THE VIEW FROM 80 by Malcolm Cowley. Copyright © 1976, 1978, 1980. Reprinted by permission of Viking Penguin Inc.

Joan Didion, "Living with Death," from SALVADOR by Joan Didion. Copyright © 1983 by Joan Didion. Reprinted by permission of Simon & Schuster, Inc.

Joan Didion, "On Keeping a Notebook," from SLOUCHING TOWARDS BETHLEHEM by Joan Didion. Copyright © 1961, 1964, 1965, 1966, 1967, 1968 by Joan Didion. Reprinted by permission of Farrar, Straus, and Giroux, Inc.

Annie Dillard, "On a Hill Far Away," from TEACHING A STONE TO TALK by Annie Dillard. Copyright © 1982 by Annie Dillard. Reprinted by permission of Harper & Row, Publishers, Inc.

Peter S. Feibleman, "Paella," from EATING TOGETHER: RECOLLECTIONS AND RECIPES by Lillian Hellman and Peter S. Feibleman. Copyright © 1984 by Left Leg, Inc. and Frog Jump, Inc.

M. F. K. Fisher, "The Changeover," from AS THEY WERE, by M. F. K. Fisher. Copyright © 1982 by M. F. K. Fisher. Reprinted by permission of Alfred A. Knopf, Inc.

M. F. K. Fisher, "I Was Really Very Hungry," from AS THEY WERE, by M. F. K. Fisher. Copyright © 1982 by M. F. K. Fisher. Reprinted by permission of Alfred A. Knopf, Inc.

E. M. Forster, "Racial Exercise," from TWO CHEERS FOR DEMOCRACY, copyright 1951 by E. M. Forster; renewed 1979 by Donald Parry. Reprinted by permission of Harcourt Brace Jovanovich, Inc. and Edward Arnold, Publishers, Ltd.

Benjamin Franklin, "Words," from THE AUTOBIOGRAPHY AND OTHER WRITINGS, edited by L. Jesse Lemisch (N.Y.: The New American Library).

Margaret Fuller, "American Abroad," excerpt from MARGARET FULLER: AMERICAN ROMANTIC edited by Perry Miller. Copyright © 1963 by Perry Miller. Reprinted by permission of Doubleday & Company, Inc.

Barbara Grizzuti Harrison, "Abortion," reprinted by permission of the author. Copyright © 1980 by Barbara Grizzuti Harrison.

Eugen Herrigel, "It Shoots," from ZEN IN THE ART OF ARCHERY by Eugen Herrigel. Copyright © 1953 by Pantheon Books, Inc. Reprinted by permission of Pantheon Books, a division of Random House, Inc.

Franz Kafka, "Letter to His Father," excerpted from LETTER TO HIS FATHER by Franz Kafka, translated by Ernst Kaiser and Eithne Wilkins. Copyright © 1953, 1954, 1966 by Schocken Books Inc. Copyright renewed by Schocken Books Inc.

Joseph Wood Krutch, "The Individual and the Species," from THE DESERT YEAR. Reprinted with permission of The Trustees of Columbia University in the City of New York. All rights reserved.

Martin Luther King, Jr., "Letter from Birmingham Jail, April 16, 1963," from WHY WE CAN'T WAIT by Martin Luther King, Jr. Copyright © 1963 by Martin Luther King, Jr. Reprinted by permission of Harper & Row, Publishers, Inc.

Norman Mailer, "Channel 6," from PIECES AND PONTIFICATIONS by Norman Mailer. Reprinted by permission of the author and the author's agents, Scott Meredith Literary Agency, Inc., 845 Third Avenue, New York, New York, 10022.

Katherine Mansfield, "Illness," from THE JOURNAL OF KATHERINE MANSFIELD, edited by John Middleton Murray. Copyright © 1927 by Alfred A. Knopf, Inc. and renewed 1955 by John Middleton Murray. Reprinted by permission of the publisher.

Mary McCarthy, "Yellowstone Park" Copyright 1955, 1983 by Mary McCarthy. Reprinted from "Yellowstone Park" in her volume MEMORIES OF A CATHOLIC GIRLHOOD by permission of Harcourt Brace Jovanovich, Inc.

462

John McPhee, "Things are Rough Enough in Town," excerpt from COMING INTO THE COUNTRY by John McPhee. Copyright ©1976, 1977 by John McPhee. Originally appeared in THE NEW YORKER. Reprinted by permission of Farrar, Straus and Giroux, Inc.

Margaret Mead, "Preparing for the Field," excerpted from BLACKBERRY WINTER by Margaret Mead. Copyright ©1972 by Margaret Mead. By permission of William Morrow & Company.

Vladimir Nabokov, "Cousin Yuri," reprinted by permission of Article 3B Trust under the will of Vladimir Nabokov from SPEAK, MEMORY by Vladimir Nabokov. Copyright ©1966 by Vladimir Nabokov.

Pablo Neruda, "Universal Night," from PASSIONS AND IMPRESSIONS by Pablo Neruda, edited by Mathilde Neruda and Miguel Otero Silva, translated by Margaret Sayers Peden. Copyright ©1980, 1981, 1983 by Farrar, Straus and Giroux, Inc. Reprinted by permission of Farrar, Straus and Giroux, Inc.

George Orwell, "Barcelona," from HOMAGE TO CATALONIA by George Orwell. Copyright ©1952, 1980 by Sonia Brownell Orwell. Reprinted by permission of Harcourt Brace Jovanovich and the Estate of the late Sonia Brownell Orwell and Secker Warburg Ltd.

George Orwell, "Shooting an Elephant," from SHOOTING AN ELEPHANT AND OTHER ESSAYS by George Orwell. Copyright 1950 by Sonia Brownell Orwell; renewed 1978 by Sonia Pitt-Rivers. Reprinted by permission of Harcourt Brace Jovanovich, Inc. and the Estate of the late Sonia Brownell Orwell and Secker and Warburg Ltd.

Plato, "Allegory of the Cave," Book VII of THE REPUBLIC by Plato, translated by A. D. Lindsay, Everyman Library Series. By permission of J. M. Dent & Sons Ltd., Publishers.

Adrienne Rich, "Teaching Language in Open Admissions," is reprinted from ON LIES, SECRETS AND SILENCE, Selected Prose, 1966–1978, by Adrienne Rich, by permission of W. W. Norton & Company, Inc. Copyright ©1979 by W. W. Norton & Company, Inc.

Richard Rodriguez, "Running in the Sun," from HUNGER OF MEMORY by Richard Rodriguez. Copyright ©1982 by Richard Rodriguez. Reprinted by permission of David R. Godine, Publisher, Inc.

Bertrand Russell, "The Existence of God," from WHY I AM NOT A CHRISTIAN. Copyright ©1957, 1985 by Allen and Unwin. Reprinted by permission of Simon & Schuster, Inc. and by Allen and Unwin (Publishers) Ltd.

Henry S. Salt, "Animals' Rights," from Henry S. Salt, ANIMALS' RIGHTS CONSIDERED IN RELATION TO SOCIAL PROGRESS (Clarks Summit, PA, 1980) by permission of Society for Animal Rights, Inc.

Richard Selzer, "Letter to a Young Surgeon," from LETTERS TO A YOUNG DOCTOR by Richard Selzer. Copyright ©1982 by David Goldman and Janet Selzer, Trustees. Reprinted by permission of Simon & Schuster, Inc.

Lewis Thomas, "On Warts," from THE MEDUSA AND THE SNAIL by Lewis Thomas. Copyright ©1979 by Lewis Thomas. Reprinted by permission of Viking Penguin Inc.

M. Carey Thomas, "Educated Woman," reprinted by permission of the publisher from Thomas, "Motives and Future of the Educated Woman" in Cross, ed. THE EDUCATED WOMAN IN AMERICA. (N.Y.: Teachers College Press ©1965 by Teachers College, Columbia University. All rights reserved.), pp. 158–165.

Hunter S. Thompson, "The Kentucky Derby," reprinted by permission of International Creative Management. Copyright ©1970 by Hunter S. Thompson.

Henry David Thoreau, from WALDEN (N.Y.: Modern Library).

Calvin Trillin, "Mao and Me," from ALICE, LET'S EAT: FURTHER ADVENTURES OF A HAPPY EATER, by Calvin Trillin. Copyright ©1978 by Calvin Trillin. Reprinted by permission of Random House, Inc.

Alice Walker, "One Child of One's Own: A Meaningful Digression Within the Work(s)" from IN SEARCH OF OUR MOTHERS' GARDENS by Alice Walker. Copyright ©1979 by Alice Walker. Reprinted from "One Child of One's Own: A Meaningful Digression Within the Work(s)" in her volume IN SEARCH OF OUR MOTHERS' GARDENS by permission of Harcourt Brace Jovanovich.

Alice Waters, "What I Believe about Cooking," from THE CHEZ PANISSE MENU COOKBOOK, by Alice Waters. Copyright ©1982 by Alice L. Waters. Reprinted by permission of Random House, Inc.

Eudora Welty, "A Little Life," from ONE WRITER'S BEGINNINGS. Copyright ©1983, 1984 by Eudora Welty. Reprinted by permission of the publisher, Harvard University Press.

E. B. White, "Once More to the Lake," from ESSAYS OF E. B. WHITE by E. B. White. Copyright ©1941, by E. B. White. Reprinted by permission of Harper & Row, Publishers, Inc.

William Carlos Williams, "The Use of Force," from THE FARMER'S DAUGHTER. Copyright ©1938 by William Carlos Williams. Reprinted by permission of New Directions Publishing Corporation.

Tom Wolfe, "The New Journalism," reprinted by permission of International Creative Management. First appeared in *New York Magazine.* Copyright ©1972 by Tom Wolfe.

Virginia Woolf, "Professions for Women," from THE DEATH OF THE MOTH AND OTHER ESSAYS by Virginia Woolf, copyright 1942 by Harcourt Brace Jovanovich, Inc.; renewed 1970 by Marjorie T. Parson, Executrix. Reprinted by permission of the publisher.

Index of Authors and Titles

465

YELLOW	GREEN/BROWN	WHITE	
Within yellow are included a few flowers that are orange.	Green flowers may have green petals or may lack petals altogether or drop them so soon after the flower opens that the overall impression is green or, occasionally, brownish.	White flowers include those with a tinge of pink, those predominantly white or cream.	
Wood Spurge 107 xv	Common Orache 47 xii	Enchanter's-nightshade 93 viii	0–2 petals irregular flowers
Yellow Horned-poppy 11 xv	Procumbent Pearlwort 39 xii	Hedge-bedstraw 167 viii	4 petals regular flowers
Yellow Corydalis 13 xv-xvi	Wild Liquorice 69 xii	White Dead-nettle 159 viii	4 petals irregular flowers
Yellow Iris 211 xvi	Curled Dock 111 xii	Star-of-Bethlehem 207 ix	3 or 6 petals regular flowers
Small Balsam 57 xvi	Frog Orchid 215 xiii	Lesser Butterfly-orchid 217 ix	3 or 6 petals irregular flowers
Perforate St John's-wort 31 xvi-xvii	Stinking Hellebore 3 xiii	Upright Hedge-parsley 97 ix-x	5 or 7 petals regular flowers
Yellow Toadflax 137 xvii	Common Figwort 139 xiv	Sweet Violet 27 x	5 or 7 petals irregular flowers
Lesser Celandine 9 xviii xxvii-xviii	Heath Cudweed 181 xiv	Mountain Avens 81 xi	8 or more petals regular flowers
Daffodil 211 xviii	Navelwort 85 xiv	Bindweed 133 xi	tubular